BREAKING NEWS

BREAKING NEWS

SEX, LIES & THE MURDOCH SUCCESSION

PAUL BARRY

ALLEN&UNWIN
SYDNEY · MELBOURNE · AUCKLAND · LONDON

Allen & Unwin

83 Alexander Street
Crows Nest NSW 2065
Australia
Phone: (61 2) 8425 0100
Fax: (61 2) 9906 2218
Email: info@allenandunwin.com
Web: www.allenandunwin.com

Cataloguing-in-Publication details are available from the National Library of Australia
www.trove.nla.gov.au

ISBN 978 1 74175 978 5

Typeset in 12/17pt Adobe Caslon by Midland Typesetters, Australia
Printed and bound in Australia by McPherson's Printing Group

10 9 8 7 6 5 4 3 2 1

CONTENTS

PROLOGUE
EVER SO HUMBLE

'I'd just like to say one sentence. This is the most humble day of my life.'

Rupert Murdoch, 19 July 2011

Rupert's mouth is turned down at the sides and he is looking depressed. He has every right to be. He is almost totally bald, with spikes of grey hair on the back of his head, and a rash of liver spots up one side of his forehead. One observer will describe him unkindly as a walnut inside a condom.

His youngest son James has ushered him into the packed committee room in the House of Commons like the old man he is and shown him to his seat, helped by his young Chinese wife, Wendi Deng, in a pink tailored jacket, who has pulled back Rupert's chair, as if he can't find it himself.

The punters have been queuing around the block all morning to secure ringside seats and millions are watching live on TV around the world. In America, the stock market wants to know if Rupert, who is now entering his ninth decade, has still got his marbles. In his native Australia they'll be staying up past 2 a.m. to see how he goes.

1

It's not often you get a Murdoch grilled about his news-papers' abuse of power, let alone two of them at once. In fact it's absolutely unprecedented.

It has the air of an impeachment, a moment in history. And it certainly is for Rupert. He's worked for 58 years to build up News Corp, his US$40 billion media empire, and now it's all at risk. His greatest wish has been to pass it on to his children, so they can continue his work. And now that's all at risk too, with James facing imminent disgrace.

So what are his many enemies hoping for from his interroga-tion? For him to be humiliated, caught, cornered or brought to book? Perhaps even for him to say sorry? If so, they're not entirely disappointed. As James launches into a long-winded answer to the first of the MPs' questions, his father puts a hand on his arm to stop him. 'I'd just like to say one sentence,' he says earnestly. 'This is the most humble day of my life.'

Is it rehearsed? Probably not: one of Rupert's great attractions is that he rarely thinks hard before opening his mouth. Is it sincere? Up to a point. But 'humiliated' would be more accurate. In his entire business career he has never been brought so low: politicians have always come to him, and he has asked the questions.

So why is the world's most powerful media baron grovelling to these nobodies? Why has he submitted to this public shame? The answer is simple. He's been ordered to attend: the MPs have served him with a summons, delivered in person by the Deputy Serjeant-at-Arms to his concrete bunker in Wapping. The might of Parliament has been brought to bear.

And days before this—which is why MPs want to interrogate him—he's been caught red-handed, up to his elbows in shame and scandal. His journalists on the *News of the World* have been found hacking illegally into thousands of intimate, private voicemails, of princes, politicians, soapie stars and murder victims, to steal their secrets and turn them into stories. His grubby tabloid paper has been destroying people's lives to entertain the masses.

Even worse, some of his top lieutenants have been lying about it to Parliament and the public for the last five years, even as News has paid out millions of dollars to hacking victims to buy their silence, claiming the crimes were confined to 'one rogue reporter', and swearing it had never, but never, been part of the paper's culture. It has been a cover-up of monstrous proportions.

And worst of all, they've now been caught in these lies as well.

So does Rupert's new-found humility mean he'll take the blame? Well, no. Even though he runs his empire like the family firm, he claims that he's been betrayed by the people closest to him, that he too is a victim.

'Do you accept that ultimately you're responsible for this whole fiasco?' he is asked.

'No,' he replies.

'You're not responsible? Who is responsible?'

'The people I trusted, that I trusted to run it, and then maybe the people they trusted.'

But it is not just that Rupert's hired help have lied. James Murdoch, who ran the British newspapers, has joined the chorus of denial and authorised pay-offs to keep the story quiet. And even now, in the halls of Britain's Parliament, he's telling an untruth, claiming he was never shown the documents that could have warned him hacking at the *News of the World* was happening on an industrial scale.

Rupert, too, has aggressively trumpeted his paper's innocence, telling the world that all the investigations, inquiries and published evidence were just his enemies out to get him. It was the elites, the toffs, the riff-raff and the failures who resented his success, trying to bring him down. He's at it again today, blaming jealous rivals for making this into a witch hunt. 'They caught us with dirty hands,' he tells MPs, 'and they built the hysteria around it.'

People are now asking whether this could be the end of the Murdoch dynasty. Some pundits are saying the old man will be gone within the year and there is now no chance of James taking the throne, or of Rupert passing the crown to his kids. Some are suggesting that James could be charged and that perhaps even Rupert will feel a hand on his collar.

But even if they escape this fate, the Murdochs face a painful future of inquiries, interrogations, revelations, arrests and charges against the people who ran their British newspapers. Then there will be high-profile trials, and the dirty laundry will be washed again. Some of the people that Rupert trusted, like his favourite, Rebekah Brooks, who is almost like his surrogate daughter, may well end up in jail. But one thing's for sure: the worst is yet to come.

The big question is, can the Murdoch dynasty survive? Rupert is famous for being at his best in a crisis, for rising to a challenge, for really coming alive. But has the old man still got the energy to fight the fight, or will this catastrophe mark the end of his power in Britain and perhaps of his own brilliant career?

PART I

THE RISE OF THE SUN KING

1
THE PAPER PRINCE

'She was an okay mother.'

Rupert Murdoch

Rupert Murdoch is half puritan, half gambler, and that's the way he has always behaved. His father was from a long line of Presbyterian preachers and moralists; his mother the daughter of a handsome rake who lost a fortune to the bookies.

But it's not quite as simple as that.

All his life he has railed against elites, yet his father Sir Keith was a newspaper baron, who rubbed shoulders with political leaders in Australia and Britain, and Rupert is now one of the world's richest and most powerful men.

All his life, he has railed against toffs and inherited wealth, yet he was born into privilege. His family had money and huge estates; he was educated at private school and Oxford; and he is now set to bequeath billions of dollars to his own children.

So how can this be? Does he care nothing for the truth? Or does he see no contradictions in the portrait he draws of himself as an ordinary man, an outsider, even a victim?

It is perhaps a part of the answer that his father was an outsider too, a shy man with a stammer, who had to elbow his way to the top. But it is also that Rupert has a remarkable capacity to believe what suits him. He's a man with a massive ego, an elephant hide and an extraordinary sense of entitlement. And despite an old-fashioned morality, he often behaves as if rules are for others but not for him.

Rupert's father Sir Keith Murdoch was a famous journalist who dominated Melbourne as an editor and proprietor, for almost 40 years. He is undoubtedly best known for his seminal 'Gallipoli Letter', which exposed the horror of the war in the Dardanelles in 1915. But his real claim to fame is that he brought modern journalism to Australia and created the first national newspaper chain, building the Herald and Weekly Times into a powerful media group, which controlled around 50 per cent of the national newspaper market, owned a dozen commercial radio stations, and would carve out a similar position in television after his death in 1952.

Sir Keith was a genius at packaging and selling news, like his famous son, but he also had a 'gift for financial wizardry, a talent for blunt and rough-hewn writing, an unjaded curiosity about the events of every day and an inexhaustible appetite for work.' According to one of his newspaper editors, he also showed 'boyish piratical tendencies' which 'failed to mask his desire to make the world a better place, especially for himself.'

That thumbnail sketch might just as easily have been penned about Rupert 50 years later, as might the warning that Sir Keith's charm concealed a man who was not to be trusted, a man who was 'no more than a paper mask, lifelike and ingenious but still a mask, hiding a calculating, undeviating, insatiable seeker after worldly riches and temporal power.'

But there are many ways in which father and son are alike, despite their different upbringings. The Scottish, Calvinist streak runs deep in Rupert, as it did with his father, and so does a profound distrust of all things British, which perhaps stems from a colonial resentment of a mother country that looked down on them. Both men believe in their right to make and break politicians and to bully them into changing their policies; both are workaholics who lack a sense of humour; both carry a large chip on their shoulders; and both are determined to perpetuate a dynasty by handing it on to the next generation, which the modern Murdoch believes in despite his repeated attacks on inherited privilege.

Rupert's father was born in Melbourne in 1885, almost 130 years ago, long before the 19th century drew to a close, and grew up 'in the stringent economy of a clergyman's family' as one of seven children. So, it's no wonder that his son has old-fashioned attitudes to women and is careful with money. Nor is it a surprise that Rupert is a prude at heart, with so little sympathy for the sexual antics of his tabloid victims, because the Murdochs come from a long line of churchmen with an abiding sense of sin.

Rupert's grandfather Patrick sailed from Aberdeenshire on the far north coast of Scotland to take up a living in East Melbourne in 1884, and went on to become head of the Presbyterian Church in Australia. Though far more liberal than his own fire-and-brimstone-breathing father, who believed in terrifying his flock with visions of hell and damnation, Patrick Murdoch was worried that his children might succumb to sexual temptation, and admonished them thus:

Never do anything with your hands or look at anything with your eyes that you'd be ashamed to tell your mother about. Turn away at once from any picture that you feel to be filthy or indecent...You should get out of bed in the morning and as soon as you are awake, if possible, have a bath.

Taking heed of such warnings, Rupert's father Keith wrote home from England in his early twenties to express dismay at the moral depravity of London's streets, where prostitution was rife.

Unlike Rupert, who was born with a veritable mouthful of silverware, Keith had to make his own way in life, and was held back by a humiliating stammer which made school and work a torture. According to one biographer, 'his speech would collapse under stress; he sometimes could not even buy a railway ticket without scribbling a note.' As a result, he was shy, had great difficulty making friends and was doubly determined to succeed in his chosen profession.

Rupert's mother, Elisabeth, came from the opposite end of the social spectrum, with ancestors who included a governor of Hong Kong and an ambassador to the court of Versailles. Her father, Rupert Greene, was the official starter for the Melbourne Cup and a member of the Melbourne Club. An all-round sportsman, dashing man about town and Olympian charmer, he was a chronic and hopeless gambler, who lost whatever money he made on the horses or at cards.

From time to time, when their creditors drew near, the Greenes rented out their house and moved into digs in a poorer part of town. But, with the help of friends, they still managed to equip their daughter for a good marriage, sending her to Clyde, a top private school at the foot of the Dandenongs, where she made all the right social connections. In 1927, at the age of eighteen, Elisabeth made her debut in Melbourne society at a party attended by the Duchess of York, and it was soon after this that Keith Murdoch spotted a picture of her in one of his magazines, *Table Talk*, and fell in love.

Having engineered an introduction to her at a charity ball, he was too shy or too worried about his stutter to ask her to dance, but he phoned her the next day and whisked her off in his Sunbeam sports car for a trip to Portsea. Her mother was horrified: he was 24 years her senior and old enough to be her father. But Elisabeth was swept off her feet, and the family found Keith's money and power hard to resist.

The newly wedded couple bought one of the best mansions in Toorak, Heathfield, which was grand enough to go with the knighthood Keith soon received for helping to make Joe Lyons Australia's Prime Minister. Built in 1884 in the Italianate style, it had 30 rooms, a ballroom, balconies and a tower, and came complete with coach-house, stables, tennis court and a wonderful kitchen garden on four acres of land. Inside were chandeliers, carved antique mirrors and silk and satin wall hangings. Previously, it had belonged to one of the richest men in Australia, WL Baillieu, the chairman of BHP, and, before that, to the father of another prime minister, Stanley Bruce. It was the grandest in a district full of stately homes, on the crown of the hill, with a fine panorama of the city of Melbourne.

During Rupert's formative years, this swell abode would form the backdrop to a parade of charity balls, bridge tournaments, tennis matches and fabulous parties, like the one reported in Sir Keith's rival paper the *Argus*, in July 1934, shortly after the couple moved in with their three-year-old son:

Like a scene from an opera pageant, with the throngs of guests passing and re-passing from one reception-room to another, was the late

> afternoon party given after the races on Saturday by Lady Murdoch, at
> her home, Heathfield, Toorak. Sir Keith and Lady Murdoch received
> in the drawing-room, where pale gold lamps shone above the crystal
> chandeliers…In the dining-room, deep rose red blossoms and hothouse
> ferns adorned the polished table, while candles—like starry sentinels—
> twinkled on the sideboards, the flickering beams dancing over the
> antique silver sconces and quaint glass shades.

Australia was still struggling to escape the grip of the Depression, with one in four of the workforce unemployed, but Rupert's Mama, Lady Murdoch, was resplendent in 'a frock of the new georgette-surfaced crepe, its deep ebon black relieved by a belt of glimmering silver tissue braiding, matching the ebon and silver medallions on the bodice'.

Back from the brink of financial ruin, Rupert's grandfather Rupert Greene was also there with his wife, sporting a black velvet coat with deep fur collar, amid a crowd of lords, ladies, knights, hons, admirals, generals, judges and the merely rich. Among the guests of honour was the Victorian Governor's sister, Mrs Helme Pott, her daughter, the Hon. Sara Vanneck, and Melbourne's Lord Mayor, Sir Harold Gengoult Smith.

One can almost imagine young Rupert on the stairs, with his nanny, peering through the bannisters at the glittering throng. But perhaps he had already tired of doing so, for such gatherings were a regular feature of his childhood.

Rupert grew up at Heathfield surrounded by staff—at least ten and some say more—who served, cooked, cleaned, dressed, drove and gardened for the family. And if the future scourge of toffs and elites ever tired of exploring the house's long corridors and ample grounds, there were other homes to go to, including two large cattle properties near Gundagai in New South Wales. Best of all was the family's country retreat, Cruden Farm, with its 35 hectares and lovely gardens, 50 kilometres south of Melbourne, which Sir Keith had given to Elisabeth as a wedding present. Rupert's parents added Palladian porticos and fluted columns to the facade, and built new stables, transforming it into something like Tara, from *Gone with the Wind*. Here, his mother had another four staff on retainer.

Those were formal days, especially in the Murdochs' social milieu, and most of the family photographs of Rupert show the young boy in a suit and tie—at five, at twelve, and in his teens—looking dutifully at his mother or father. But when his parents weren't there, it must have been a glorious life for a child, riding in the fields, hiding in the gardens, fishing in the lake, or playing tennis and cricket on the lawns. And an even better one for the only boy, the chosen one, whose three sisters all adored him.

Rupert was 'naughty, daring, a terrific tease', according to his sister Janet, and forever playing pranks, like putting snakes in Nanny's bed, or pulling his sisters' pigtails, for which he would be spanked. Naturally, he is said to have showed early signs of entrepreneurial skill, buying rabbits for a penny off his siblings, who would skin them for him, so he could sell them for sixpence.

On Sundays at Cruden, the entire family would ride out en masse, to the delight and awe of their neighbours, who found it 'an unforgettable spectacle—a sort of medieval cavalcade of children, servants, outriders, horses and dogs'. Sir Keith would lead the way on a massive charger, 'immaculate in English tweed and riding boots', and the rest would follow on behind.

But it was not entirely an idyll. By many accounts, Rupert's father was distant, remote and reluctant to praise, while his son was desperate to please, yet never quite succeeded. Sir Keith complained to a family friend that he was a 'disobedient wild, sullen boy', and worried that his son didn't have the right stuff to succeed. Lady Murdoch was also concerned that Rupert was unworthy of his famous dad. She recalled that her husband had proclaimed joyfully, only hours before his death, 'Well, thank God; I think the boy's got it', suggesting that for 22 years he was not convinced he had.

Many years later, when camera crews and authors made the pilgrimage to Cruden to film her garden, celebrate her birthday, or ask her about her famous son, Dame Elisabeth (who was given a damehood for her charitable work) would scoff at the idea that Rupert had endured a difficult relationship with his father, whom she insisted he 'adored'. And she would dismiss as 'absolute nonsense' the suggestion that he had lacked a loving, happy family life. But she also avowed that her own parents had been 'very fond of each other', even though her drunken father had once threatened to cut her mother into pieces, as she lay sobbing, listening to them fight. Her attitude to hardship, she explained, was 'to pull yourself together and just get on with it'.

If anyone was tough on Rupert, said Dame Elisabeth, it was her. 'I was looked on as rather a disciplinarian. I had to be because his father wasn't,' she told the ABC. 'If Rupert wants to tease me, he says, "Of course, my mother used to beat me." I think there were two occasions when I used the slipper.'

Rupert's response to this was anything but teasing. 'She was an okay mother,' he let slip to his biographer, Michael Wolff, before acknowledging, 'that's a terrible thing for a son to say...but my father came first.'

What is certainly clear is that Mama did not believe in spoiling him, as one can gather from Rupert's tale of learning to swim. With the family on the high seas, sailing back from a trip to England, the young Lady Murdoch tossed her five-year-old son into the deep end of the ship's swimming pool and forbade anyone to rescue him. A screaming, frightened Rupert gamely doggie-paddled to the side and safety as she watched.

On several occasions, she made him sleep in the garden shed at Cruden to 'toughen him up'. And in one version of this story, which has been told and retold down the years, she exiled him to the outhouse every summer holiday until he reached the age of sixteen. Worst of all, perhaps, in terms of leaving a mark on the child, Lady Murdoch sent Rupert away to boarding school at the tender age of nine, with the same toughening-up in mind. Rupert's grandparents were shocked at this decision, and his father was 'not so very keen'. But Elisabeth was not to be thwarted. 'I was very young, rather determined, and perhaps I wasn't always very wise,' she later admitted.

Geelong Grammar was one of the top private schools in Australia, but Rupert hated his eight years there, on the wind-swept Corio Peninsular, 100 kilometres from home. He was teased and not much liked. Or, as his cousin put it, 'He was unhappy and rebellious and he made few friends.' He was also angry to have been banished. 'I think perhaps his home was such a happy one. And he did of course adore being with his father,' his mother later confessed. 'I think perhaps there was a slight feeling of resentment that he'd been sent away.' Or, perhaps, more than slight.

James Darling, Geelong's famous headmaster, was not much happier to have the boy as his pupil: he regarded young Rupert as the nastiest of the rich boys he taught, worse even than Kerry and Clyde Packer, whose father was also a powerful media mogul and a notorious bully to boot. As the headmaster recalled, Rupert was a rude, arrogant boy who was not interested in working; he resented authority and hated sport (two traits that were guaranteed to make him stand out), and he was famous for cutting games to duck off to the races.

Darling's opinion may well have been seasoned by his later view of Rupert's newspapers, which he loathed, telling another of Murdoch's biographers, William Shawcross, 'What is vile they offer to gloating eyes, what is vindictive they applaud.' But he was by no means alone in disliking the boy, who was variously known by his mates as 'Bullo', for being a bullshit artist, or 'Commo', for being a Communist. 'He wasn't very subtle or gentle,' another schoolmate recalled, dubbing him 'rough as guts'.

Young Rupert was also unpopular with some executives at his father's office. Towards the end of his time at Geelong, he would be chauffeured home for weekends in the family Rolls-Royce, and would stop by at the paper's neoclassical headquarters in Melbourne's Flinders Street to wait for his father. According to one veteran, he 'spent Friday afternoons in the boardroom supposedly doing his homework, but more often arrogantly marching around the building giving orders to the staff. He was called "the brat".'

After leaving Geelong, he did a short spell in the family business, as a cub reporter on the *Herald*, learning police and court rounds, and then spent another three months in England, subbing on the *Birmingham Gazette*, before starting at Oxford University in October 1950. Once again, he was delivered to his digs by a chauffeur-driven Rolls, after a brief visit to Rome with his parents for a private audience with the Pope. And at the end of his spell on the newspaper, he wrote to its owner, who was a friend of his father's, to advise him the editor should be sacked. Even at nineteen, the boy had a colossal cheek.

At Worcester College, family money and connections, or just plain luck, secured him one of the best rooms in college, the oak-panelled De Quincey Room, and he was one of a handful of undergraduates to have his own car. Though only an Austin A40, 'it was like having a private plane or a Rolls-Royce in terms of being noticed by your contemporaries', one of his friends observed.

The rich young heir didn't much care for study, according to his tutors, but threw himself into politics and journalism. He helped to run the student newspaper, *Cherwell*, and even talked of buying it; he also joined the Labour Club, which took him door-knocking in small towns in the run-up to the 1951 election. It was probably the first time he'd met anyone from the lower classes, apart from the servants back home, and he said it made him sympathetic to people less fortunate than himself.

Confronted with this new revelation of inequality, Rupert was serious enough about changing the world to spend some of his summer holiday at the Labour Party conference in Blackpool, which was a trip reserved for die-hards. He also kept a bust of Lenin on his mantelpiece, and referred to him regularly as 'The Great Thinker' in letters home. But this was probably more designed to annoy his father. And in this it certainly succeeded, prompting Sir Keith to complain to a famous, fellow press baron, Hugh Cudlipp, that his son was developing alarming left-wing views.

Some of Murdoch's fellow students found him loud, opinion-ated and direct: the Englishman's view of a typical Australian. One university friend, George Masterman QC, remembered him as, 'self-confident, arrogant, cocky, rich and, seemingly to the English, a communist'. And there's no doubt that he made himself unpopular. During his time at Oxford, Rupert was blackballed from the cricket team, and thrown into the lake for holding a party on the day of King George VI's state funeral.

But if being liked was not a priority (and would never become one), having a good time certainly was. He and his friends spent hours drinking beer in the cellars, and formed the grandly-named 'Voltaire Club', with Bertrand Russell as its patron, as an excuse for more eating and drinking. However, in October 1952, all this undergraduate fun was interrupted, just as he was about to start his final year, by the death of his father at the age of 67. Sir Keith had been in poor health for some time, had just undergone a second operation for bowel cancer, and had suffered from heart problems for years.

Back in Australia, the good knight's passing was met with gushing tributes from the Prime Minister, Bob Menzies, the Leader of the Opposition, Dr Evatt, the American ambassador, and a gaggle of politicians, press barons, editors, journalists and printers who said it was 'a great shock' and 'a tragic loss' that he was gone, and that he would be remembered as 'a good friend', 'a great employer' and 'one of the greatest newspapermen that ever lived'.

Sir Keith's will, written five years earlier, instructed his executors that the estate was to be left in trust for his wife and four children, but made it quite clear who was to inherit his mantle. 'I desire that my said son Rupert Murdoch should have a great opportunity of spending a useful, altruistic and full life in newspapers and broadcasting activities and of ultimately occupying a position of high responsibility in that field,' it said. His sisters' role was merely to support him in his endeavour, there being no thought of them doing this job themselves. 'We only had one possibility, Rupert,' his mother later explained.

But despite all this fuss about who should inherit the Murdoch empire, there was remarkably little to hand down to his son. Even though Sir Keith had run the Herald and Weekly Times for more than 30 years, and built it up into the most powerful media group in Australia, he owned hardly any shares. And his attempts to build a rival newspaper group had left him up to his neck in debt. In the early 1930s, he had borrowed money to buy into two Brisbane newspapers, the *Courier* and *Mail,* which he had then merged into one. Fifteen years later, he had borrowed yet more to buy 50 per cent of the Adelaide *News* and *Mail,* which he had persuaded his fellow directors at the Herald to sell to him on the cheap. And, most recently, he had been trying without success to combine all three papers with Melbourne's *Argus* to create a rival newspaper chain that would take on his own employers. This was an extraordinary thing for him to be doing while running the Herald and Weekly Times, and remarkable that his fellow directors had tolerated it, but it was a measure of his power and cheek that he thought he could succeed. It's not hard to see where Rupert gets his nerve from.

With Sir Keith gone, Dame Elisabeth was worried she couldn't carry these huge debts and pay death duties without putting their homes at risk. So when a senior Herald and Weekly Times director and family friend, Lloyd Dumas, drove out to Cruden Farm two days after Sir Keith's death and advised her to sell the shares in Queensland Newspapers (which owned the *Courier-Mail*), she reluctantly agreed. She had grown up with a father who had lost the family fortune at the races and didn't want to lose another. Thus, Sir Keith's colleagues, who had only recently discovered his plans to create a rival empire, were able to take revenge on their former boss by dashing his dream.

Rupert didn't get back in time for the funeral. The journey from Britain to Australia took three days, by slow, old Sunderland flying boats, landing at Rose Bay in Sydney, and Lady Murdoch insisted her husband be buried two days after his death. So, by the time the young man arrived in Melbourne, the decision to sell half his inheritance had already been taken. Years later, it would still rankle within the family. Not long before her death, his mother confessed, 'It was very hard to know what to do, because he wanted to keep certain properties [the Brisbane papers] and we knew that it was not possible…I insisted that we were not going into enormous debt and I'm sure that that was the right thing to do. But I think he will always regret it very much…because, you know, we couldn't just go on owing a lot of money at that stage. Rupert was too young.'

Rupert was certainly furious and told people angrily, 'They stole my inheritance. I could have raised the money in London.' And for the next 60 years, this deep sense of outrage was what would drive him: a desire to avenge his father, a desire to regain his birthright and a desire to right a wrong. Perhaps it was also this that allowed him to cast himself in the role of victim.

Almost a year later, in September 1953, Rupert turned up for work at News Ltd's offices in Adelaide, a newspaper proprietor at the age of 22, and was mistaken for the delivery boy. 'I was so young and so new to the business,' he later recounted, 'that when I pulled my car into the lot on my first day, the garage attendant admonished me, "Hey sonny, you can't park here."' And it was little better when he ventured inside. 'There were lots of old blokes in braces with bald heads and glasses, who had been in the business for 30 years. There was a lot of reluctance of course by the people there to give me any authority. I was just a kid out of college.'

Plump and cherubic 'with curly hair that had still only receded as far as Julius Caesar's', Rupert's own idea of 1950s style was 'drip-dry white shirts with rolled up sleeves, and red-and-blue paisley ties.'

Young though he was, he had not come straight into the job. He had gone back to England to finish his degree at Oxford (where he got a third in Philosophy, Politics and Economics) and had then spent a few months subbing on the *Daily Express* in London, where he lived in the Savoy, one of the city's swankiest hotels, despite earning just £10 a week. But eventually his mother had insisted he come home to claim his inheritance, and he had reluctantly agreed. He was still not convinced he wanted to go into the family business, but destiny called.

He arrived in Adelaide to find that his father's old colleagues at the Herald and Weekly Times were trying to drive him out of town. A month after Rupert took over, they set up a new *Sunday Advertiser* to take on the Murdochs' *Mail*, which had previously enjoyed a monopoly of the market. Then they wrote to Lady Murdoch offering to buy the family out for £150 000, threatening to bankrupt her if they refused to sell. Rupert's response was to splash the letter on the front page of the *News* with a banner headline BID FOR PRESS MONOPOLY.

The young man's chutzpah now served him well, as did the lessons learnt at his father's knee. But he was also lucky to have a talented, campaigning editor in Rohan Rivett, whom Sir Keith had appointed just before his death, and together they made a perfect team. Rivett ran the editorial side, while Rupert expanded the paper to 72 pages, slashed rates to attract advertisers and threw himself into winning readers and making it pay. 'All boundless energy, sleeves rolled up, wreathed in cigarette smoke, he would oversee every state of the paper's daily production, regularly subbing major stories and writing the sledgehammer headlines himself,' one writer observed. 'He cut costs, whittling staff to a minimum; senior reporters were asked to write up to twenty stories a day. The money poured in.'

The headlines were snappy and eye-catching, while the pages were full of crime, competitions, human interest and sport, which would all become part of Rupert's successful formula. Soon circulation was rising and catching the *Advertiser*, which sold twice as many copies. Better still, the *Sunday Mail*, run by Ron Boland, was holding off its upstart Sunday rival. And best of all, after two years of costly warfare, Sir Keith's old colleagues gave up the fight and agreed to merge their new weekend paper with the *Mail*. So peace was declared and profits soared.

Even before this battle was won, Rupert was busy expanding the frontiers of his empire and taking on more debt, just as his buccaneering father had done before him. In 1956 he picked up Perth's *Sunday Times* in a fire sale for £200 000 and began taking the six-hour flight every Friday to supervise production. The paper had been losing money, but Rupert's regime soon brought it back to health. He sacked staff, hired new people, jazzed up the copy, rewrote the headlines, and watched sales take off.

The same year, he bought the popular women's magazine, *New Idea*, published in Melbourne by Southdown Press, and by 1957 he was using its machines to launch a new title, *TV Week*, which sold for a shilling and went like hot cakes. It was only three colours at the start, and 'pretty shoddy', according to Rodney Lever, its founding editor, but everyone wanted to know about TV, which was the new, new thing. *TV Week* was soon pumping out Sydney and Adelaide editions and coining the money, boosting Southdown's profits from £200 000 to almost £2 million a year, and generating cash to fund yet more acquisitions. So, naturally, Rupert kept on buying.

As the 1950s drew to a close, he spent a few weeks flying and driving around Australia, buying any provincial newspaper he could get his hands on. According to Lever, his technique was simple: he would bully the existing owners into selling by threatening to start a competing paper in their town. This ploy succeeded in Darwin with the *NT News* and in Mt Isa with the *Mail*. He also bid successfully for one of Adelaide's two new TV licences, and went off overseas to buy a package of 400 Westerns to fill the schedule. His promotions director at the new Channel 9, Graham King, reckoned they were all made in one studio, because the cowboys all galloped past the same bit of cactus. But at £7 a pop they were so cheap that every night was ranch night.

In 1956, at the tender age of 25, Rupert married his first wife, a former air hostess, Patricia Booker. But he was too busy to spend much time with her. Rodney Lever remembers an evening alone with her in Adelaide in 1958 when she was pregnant with their only child, Prudence, and finding her down in the dumps. 'She was a very unhappy girl,' he says. 'She had no friends there. It was a very insular boring city. And Rupert was working all the time.'

Lever used to pick up his boss at the airport on his visits to Melbourne and drive him around town, often taking him to the races, where he loved to bet. One day, he collected £4000 in cash that the budding tycoon had won, which was enough to buy a good-sized house. Parking tickets were never a problem on these trips because Rupert would just rip them off the windscreen and tear them up. 'He didn't care,' says Lever. 'He had this idea that he was better than anybody else. If he wanted anything he just did it.'

Come 1960, Murdoch was barging his way into Sydney, the toughest market in the country, where years of circulation wars and public brawling had left the city's newspapers in the grip of two powerful families, the Packers and Fairfaxes. Undeterred by the knowledge that richer men than him had perished in the struggle, he picked up a local newspaper group, Cumberland Newspapers, for £1 million, by getting a Sydney businessman to buy it for him incognito. His next trick was to persuade the Fairfaxes to let him take the loss-making *Daily Mirror* and *Sunday Mirror* off their hands for a generous £2 million. To them it seemed like a safe bet, because no one else had been able to make a go of it, so they happily said yes, reasoning that he was only 29, knew nothing about Sydney, and would almost certainly go out of business trying to make them pay.

But of course he didn't. The young tycoon was soon feeding the papers a rich diet of sex and crime and pulling in readers by the score from the *Mirror*'s afternoon rival, the Fairfax-owned *Sun*, with headlines like DAWN RAIDERS FIND DOGS GAGGED; BODY IN SAND, DROWNED, BURIED SON, POLICE SAY; and the enticing GIRL 14 AND HER LOVER IN VILE CRIME. He put girls in swimsuits on Page Three, and splashed pictures of them on the front cover whenever he could, then kicked it all along with big TV advertising campaigns. As ever, he led the charge himself, arriving at the office at 5 a.m. to make sure the front page was right, to the editor's annoyance. Not yet 30, he was already inspiring great loyalty among his staff. 'He stood apart from the stiff-necked and conservative end of town,' one of his reporters observed, 'and his brash editorial approach was supported by a posse of hard-nosed editors and eager journalists who would do anything and go anywhere for Rupert.'

Murdoch was soon making a nuisance of himself to the Packers and Fairfaxes in another way. To counter his threat to their suburban papers, the two powerful rivals had combined forces and resolved to increase their local paper print run. But they had counted on downtime at the *Daily Mirror* to do so. And Rupert predictably slammed the door on this. Sir Frank's sons, Kerry and Clyde, promptly reacted by seizing the Anglican Press in inner-city Chippendale, which was in the hands of the receivers, to print the papers there instead. Murdoch's instant reaction was to round up a gang of friends to storm the printery and throw the Packers out, taking pictures for next day's *Daily Mirror* front page, which screamed, KNIGHT'S SONS IN CITY BRAWL. A year later, when the Packers and Fairfaxes were finally forced to sue for peace, Rupert was given the contract to print all their suburban papers at attractive rates, and scored a couple of extra titles as part of the settlement. He was already learning, if he didn't know already, that aggression pays, and never mind the rules.

Rupert was soon doing battle with them on a third front. Since Sydney's newly licensed TV stations had begun broadcasting in 1956, the Packers and Fairfaxes had been minting money in television, and Rupert wanted his share. Having failed to secure the city's third licence in 1962, he jumped on a plane to the US and splashed out $3 million on 2500 hours of racy programs from ABC Paramount, which was being attacked in the US Senate for showing too much sex and violence. He then returned to Sydney to announce he would beam this tasty fare to the city's 2 million viewers from a little TV station in Wollongong, 80 kilometres to the south, which he had just picked up for £160 000.

There was nothing in the law to stop him doing this, even though people would have to turn their aerials south to receive the signal. And it was a good enough threat to make Sir Frank Packer blink. Thus, another victory came his way, in which Rupert was allowed to buy a 25 per cent stake in Packer's Sydney and Melbourne Channel 9 stations and given two seats on the board. In return, Sir Frank bought shares in Rupert's Wollongong and Adelaide stations, and together they took control of Newcastle's TV licence to create a mini network.

Sir Frank—who was a rogue himself—couldn't help but admire the nerve of the young man, whom he regarded as far more likely to succeed than Kerry, his so-called 'idiot son'. Rupert was cheeky, charming, aggressive and smart. He took big bets with other people's money, and generally won. He would soon be setting up the country's first national newspaper, *The Australian*, and pouring millions of dollars into it to make it work. It was hard not to fall for him, even if you suspected he wasn't to be trusted.

2
RULE BRITANNIA

'I am constantly amazed at the ease with which I entered British newspapers.'

Rupert Murdoch

Roll forward a few years to December 1968 and the start of a hot Sydney summer, where we find Rupert in the back of his Rolls-Royce, reading the *Daily Mirror,* as he crosses the Harbour Bridge on his way to work. The camera follows him into his Surry Hills office, where three black Bakelite telephones dominate his desk, while the BBC's dulcet tones assure us he's 'chubby-cheeked and open-faced' but 'ruthless and iron-willed'. When asked, 'Do you like the feeling of power you have as newspaper proprietor?' he looks away, fiddles with his fingertips, shifts in his seat and then replies, 'The only honest answer to that is, yes of course one enjoys a feeling of power.'

Rupert has been filmed by Britain's public broadcaster because he's expanding his empire into London for the first time with a bid for the *News of the World*, the newspaper that will eventually get him into so much trouble, and no one yet knows what to make of him. But one thing is obvious: the Brits don't take him seriously. He's an Australian, after all, 'a wild colonial boy', so what could they possibly have to fear?

For more than 100 years the *News of the World* has been the biggest-selling newspaper in the English-speaking world. With weekly sales that have topped 8 million in the 1950s, it has been read by half Britain's adult population. Its readers claim to buy it for the news, much like those who say they get Playboy for its articles, but what they really love is the scandal that fills its pages with spanking colonels, lustful vicars and dirty scoutmasters. It is known as the *News of the Screws* for precisely this reason, and it's just the sort of paper that Rupert understands: back in Australia, he publishes an antipodean version, albeit with more politics and more bite, called the *Truth*.

By the time Rupert lands in Fleet Street, the paper's sales are wilting, profits are sagging and the share price is shrinking fast. The family that owns it is divided, and some of its members are keen to sell. Rupert has been looking to buy a British newspaper for more than a year and has engaged a merchant bank, Morgan Grenfell, to find him one. And then the notorious Robert Maxwell makes a bid and puts the *News of the World* into play. The stage is set for a battle in which Rupert's nerve, ingenuity and cunning will be laid bare and his reputation will be set. From now on, thanks to the satirical magazine *Private Eye*, he'll always be known as the Dirty Digger.

But watching him in this BBC profile, it's hard not to like him. He's an attractive man with a persuasive charm. He's polite, intelligent and refreshingly blunt. And there's a diffidence about him. He's softly spoken and rarely aggressive, even if what he says is calculated to provoke. Twenty years on, he's not the arrogant brat he was in his teens. And if he's a pirate, as many suggest, there's a bit of the Johnny Depp about him. It's one of the reasons people let him through the door.

By the time Rupert flew into Heathrow, the *News of the World*'s owners had already dismissed Maxwell's takeover offer with a front-page editorial saying he shouldn't be allowed to have it, because the paper was 'as English as roast beef and Yorkshire pudding', while Maxwell was a foreigner. Even more to the point, perhaps, though this was never mentioned, was that Jan Robert Hoch, as Maxwell had been born, was also a Jew.

Three days after Rupert's arrival, the group's chairman and major shareholder, Sir William Carr, welcomed the Australian to breakfast at his palatial Chelsea apartment with a heartfelt, 'Thank God you've come.' But he soon discovered that his rescuer was not quite the white knight he had hoped for. With a rough anti-podean charm, Murdoch told Carr and his banker, Harry Sporborg of Hambros, that he would not discuss anything until they gave him full control of the paper and the company. 'Gentlemen,' said their guest, 'either you concede to my wishes or I catch the next plane home.' He then got up and headed for the door.

Sir William was too shell-shocked to answer, but Sporborg suggested he wait outside. And before long it was agreed that Rupert would become managing director, while Sir William would stay on as chairman. With a seven-year written contract, there seemed to be little risk that Murdoch could dismiss him. And besides, he seemed to be so charming.

When Maxwell warned Carr, 'You will be out before your feet touch the ground,' Carr replied confidently, 'Rupert is a gentleman.' But his wife was not so sure. After taking him to lunch in Mayfair, she reported that he had little small talk, no sense of humour and had lit up a cigar before the first course. Nevertheless, the oleaginous Mr Maxwell—who would eventually jump from his yacht into the Mediterranean after stealing millions from his companies' pension funds—was clearly even less desirable. And this bold, young man was the only one who could keep the marauder at bay.

Murdoch was quick to admit he had no money to match his rival's offer—which at £34 million was more than ten times what he'd paid for Sydney's *Daily Mirror* eight years earlier—but he and his bankers had devised a plan to swap some of his Australian assets for a 30 per cent stake in the *News of the World*, which would give him and Carr control of the group and make it too big for Maxwell to swallow. He agreed to buy a further 10 per cent to strengthen the paper's defences, and promised not to seek full control.

He then flew back to Australia to see Prime Minister John Gorton and ask him to relax the country's strict foreign exchange controls so he could transfer some cash. He got the *Mirror*'s bureau chief, Eric Walsh, to drive him to the PM's official residence in Canberra, whence he emerged 'beaming from ear to ear', assuring Walsh as they drove home, 'Well, that wasn't difficult.'

Shortly after Christmas he was in London again, with his new wife, Anna Torv, and baby Elisabeth, beaming with confidence. And, as 1969 got under way, he promised the *News of the World*'s shareholders gathered at the Connaught Rooms that he would bring their company back to profit. He also told them he was delighted that Sir William—who received a two-minute standing ovation— would be staying on as chairman.

Maxwell was furious, but he could do nothing about it. His main supporter, Professor Derek Jackson, who was Sir William's cousin, fumed that the board was 'raving mad' to have turned down the cash, but he soon offloaded his shares to Rupert, which gave the Australian 49 per cent of the company. And after that, Murdoch no longer needed to keep his promise to the Carrs.

With the takeover sealed, Rupert gave a party in his new apartment on the Embankment, to which Sir William popped in briefly to say hello. The next day the paper's erstwhile owner was rushed to hospital with an aneurism. Murdoch kicked him out as chairman six months later, breaking his solemn pledge not to take control. Carr was outraged and called him a liar, but he, too, was powerless to resist. On his deathbed eight years later, he would write to Maxwell to say he was wrong to have spurned his offer, even though the 'Bouncing Czech' had by then been revealed to be a liar and a fraud.

Having won this valuable prize, with surprising ease, Rupert's first instinct was to tackle the print unions and get his costs down. Choosing a Saturday night—which perhaps wasn't wise with the paper going to press—he 'swept in with a retinue, sat down and astonished delegates by opening up with the words, "I'm now going to fucking tell you," and laying down the law.' According to his biographer, George Munster, this threat was not well received. One of the union leaders, Bill Keys of the Society of Graphical and Allied Trades who ruled Fleet Street at the time, replied, 'If you want to take over this newspaper, wash your mouth out and come back to us.' Murdoch then stormed out of the room, only to return ten minutes later and invite everyone into his office for drinks. Pay, conditions and manning arrangements were thereupon settled in record time.

Carr had ruled his domain from a big office full of priceless antiques, but Murdoch worked from a secretary's desk, and was more often to be found down on the floor, with his sleeves rolled up, making up the paper. The *News of the World*'s editor, Stafford Somerfield—another of the bald-head-and-braces brigade—soon found him dropping the leader page, taking editorial decisions, and asking to be told when reporters went abroad. By February 1970, Somerfield had followed Carr out the door, with a parting shot from Rupert that he hadn't come all the way from Australia not to interfere.

Back home in Melbourne, his mother was horrified. 'When he bought the *News of the World* it nearly killed me,' Dame Elisabeth admitted. 'And I said, "Rupert, why?" And he said, "Mum, you don't understand, there are tens and hundreds of thousands of people living in conditions around London and in England who have nothing in their lives practically and they want this sort of thing."'

Her shock was doubtless magnified by what he did next, which was to revisit one of Britain's biggest scandals, the Profumo Affair of 1963, by paying £10 000 for the memoirs of Christine Keeler, the glamorous call girl at its centre. He launched the first instalment of her so-called 'book' (which never in fact materialised) with a big TV ad campaign, promising spies, intrigue and even death, and Keeler pouting into the camera to sell her wares. 'I was young and naïve then,' she purred. 'But now I've had time to think. This is the first time the public will be able to read the real truth.'

Predictably, there was outrage. In the six years since Sir John Profumo had been forced to resign, after lying to parliament about his affair with the prostitute (who had also been having sex with a Russian spy), the former War Minister had been working with charities in the East End, in an attempt to make amends. It was poor form, said Murdoch's critics, to have brought it all up again and subjected this good man to further disgrace. But, just as predictably, Murdoch welcomed the controversy, because it gave him a news angle he didn't already have. He duly led the front page with STORM OVER KEELER BOOK and a Page One editorial saying why the story had to be told, or, rather, retold, and claiming somewhat fatuously that it was right to forgive the individual but wrong to forget what had happened. Fortunately, the BBC's cameras were there to catch him with his guard down, telling Somerfield that they might be lucky enough to keep the story bubbling away for weeks if it caused enough fuss.

Next stop was the BBC studio, where he was challenged by *Panorama*'s David Dimbleby to say if he was ashamed of this muck-raking, whose sole purpose was clearly to sell papers. 'Certainly it's going to sell newspapers,' replied Rupert, 'we're not ashamed of that.' As to his critics, who now included the Archbishop of Westminster, Cardinal Heenan, and the head of the Press Council, Lord Devlin, Rupert retorted, 'People can sneer as much as they like but I will take the extra 150 000 copies we're going to sell.'

As it happened, the promise of sex and spies helped the *News of the World* add 200 000 extra readers, but Rupert had an even better idea to make his new purchase pay. With its expensive printing presses sitting idle all week, he could turn out a daily paper on the cheap and share the costs. And as the Keeler row came to a head he had already found a way to do just that.

Today, *The Sun* is Britain's top-selling tabloid and an absolute powerhouse for its owner. Cheeky, rebellious, naughty and blunt, it's also Rupert's favourite paper, and the one to read if you want to know what he thinks. But when it came on the market in April

1969 it looked like a candle that was about to go out. In the seven years since it had risen out of the old *Daily Herald*, a socialist paper tied to the trade unions, *The Sun*'s sales had halved and its losses had mounted into the millions. Worse still, it had no flair, no market and no idea who it was writing for. Not surprisingly, its owners, IPC, who also published the *Mirror*, were desperate to get shot of it. Once again, they would live to regret giving it to Murdoch, because he would make it such a success.

And once again, it was Maxwell who made the first move, telling the *Mirror*'s Hugh Cudlipp he would take it off them for nothing. But the *Sun*'s print unions wouldn't agree to the redundancies he wanted, and threatened to stop the presses if the deal went ahead. So, for the second time in a year, Murdoch was invited to save the day. There being no other bidders, he was able to buy the paper for a paltry £200 000 in cash and the promise of three future instalments of £200 000, or roughly one-fortieth of the value that had been placed on the *News of the World* a few months earlier. The Board of Trade approved the deal in October, and the paper was relaunched in early November in double-quick time, with a new tabloid size, a new look, a new editor and new staff.

His fellow Fleet Street proprietors and other assorted experts were quick to write it off. But Lord Thomson of *The Times* was wise enough to temper his prediction that Rupert would fail with a warning that he could only hope to succeed by targeting lower income groups who were of little interest to advertisers, and that this in turn could only work if the *Sun* had a massive circulation. Murdoch, he predicted, would be forced to take the paper down-market and drag others with him. 'When a newspaper resorts to sex and sensationalism it's a surefire circulation builder,' the press lord explained, 'but it tends to lower the whole tone of the press. Other competing newspapers have to lower their standards as well...to hold their own.'

As it turned out, Lord Thomson was right on the money. Within two years, the *Daily Mirror*'s editor Michael Christiansen was calling the new *Sun* 'the worst thing that could have happened' to British journalism, and accusing Murdoch of setting back standards by ten or fifteen years. 'What has happened on my paper,' he lamented, 'is that one's major consideration each week is whether you should have a picture that shows off pubic hair.' Or, as his proprietor, Cecil King, observed, 'What his papers are about is going further, being louder and more vulgar.'

The first front page of Murdoch's new daily promised an EXCLUSIVE on BEAUTIFUL WOMEN and another on THE LOVE MACHINE. The fashion slot was UNDIES FOR UNDRESSING, while a series on adultery was promoted for the following day. Readers lasting longer were rewarded with PUSSY WEEK, and treated to artists' impressions of female tennis stars in the nude or crime reports that led with the sex lives of the villain or victim. *The Sun*'s first Page Three Girl was a pretty SWEDISH CHARMER, studying to be a systems analyst. By day two, she was showing a flash of nipple. A year later she was baring her breasts.

Naked girls apart, *The Sun* was a shameless copy of Britain's (then) best-selling tabloid, the *Mirror*, with the same red top, the same old slogan, FORWARD WITH THE PEOPLE, and the same old columns and cartoons, with slightly different names. But it was cheekier, naughtier and more lively. Murdoch and his new editor, Larry Lamb, reckoned the *Mirror* had become a paper written for its journalists. *The Sun* would make sure it served its readers and gave them what they wanted, which was sex, sport, crime, competitions and fun.

And give it did, with an avalanche of special offers and promotions to pull in the punters. 'Goody after goody after goody. Giveaways, competitions, special features, supplements, you name it, we threw it at them,' said Graham King, Murdoch's Australian promotions director, who had been with him since Adelaide days. 'The key to the success of *The Sun* was the realisation that a newspaper isn't or need not be all about news.' The promotions were backed by massive TV advertising, 'full of bright young readers and semi-naked girls…spattered with key words like LOVE! MONEY! and above all WIN!' In the first 100 days, sales leapt from 650 000 to 1.5 million. Two years later they were up to 2.5 million, and two years after that they were topping 3 million.

By comparison with what was to follow in the 1980s, when Kelvin MacKenzie took over and the paper became a bovver boy for Thatcherism, there was nothing much wrong with *The Sun* in that first decade, despite all the fuss that it caused. It was partisan but rarely bullying, never vile or vicious, and did not destroy people's lives as Murdoch's British tabloids would later do. It also produced some great popular journalism, explaining difficult topics in simple terms, and devoting several pages to in-depth coverage of major news events.

There was a sense that you could experiment and break all the rules, says Bill Repard, who joined *The Sun* in those early days and stayed with Murdoch for the next 30 years: 'We were doing things with newspapers that hadn't been done before; we were turning the world on its head.'

On his arrival in London, Murdoch had driven a Fiat to show he was a man of the people. But now he went back to his chauffeur-driven Rolls and settled in to a nine-bedroom, seven-bathroom house in Sussex Square, where Anna welcomed the BBC's David

Dimbleby and assured him, in a crisp, cut-glass voice, that her husband was kind and sensitive and no tycoon. He had newspapers in his blood, she said, and liked to take the Tube to work to see what people were reading. When they went into newsagents, he always rearranged the displays so his own papers were on top. All in all, she said, he was simply a good, hard-working Australian businessman who planned to show the British how to do it.

Sadly, however, they didn't want lessons from Murdoch, whatever he hoped to teach them. 'Just as we were being invited round to places we'd catch Lord Lambton in bed or something, and then we'd be barred from everything,' Rupert explained. Or, as Anna put it, 'Great Britain will accept you if you're willing to join and play by the rules. Rupert wasn't willing.'

So in 1973, they upped sticks and moved to New York. In an effort to explain their departure, Rupert told the *Village Voice*, 'Maybe I just have an inferiority complex about being an Australian.' But if that had been true before he arrived, it was surely even more so now he was leaving.

But Murdoch wasn't just running away: he also had new conquests in sight. 'Part of the Australian character is wanting to take on the world,' he explained to the *New York Times*. 'It's a hard, huge continent inhabited by a few European descendants with a sense of distance from their roots. They have a great need to prove themselves.'

As in Australia and Britain, Rupert now bought whatever he could, wherever it was, and applied the formula his father had learnt from Lord Northcliffe: that papers can be made to pay by giving the public what they want. Thus it was in December 1973 that the globetrotting media mogul flew into the airport in San Antonio and bought himself two local dailies, the *Express* and the *News* for a few cents shy of US$20 million. Meeting the owner at the Continental ticket counter, he signed the deal and flew straight out again, without bothering to go into town, and changed the local media landscape forever.

The city's number one paper at the time was the Hearst-owned *San Antonio Light*, which had the reputation of being the most sensational rag in Texas. But it was soon coming second to Rupert's revamped *San Antonio News*, which introduced the locals to huge headlines like ARMIES OF INSECTS MARCHING ON SAN ANTONIO, UNCLE TORTURES TOT WITH HOT FORK, SCREAMING MUM SLAIN, or MASS ALIEN SEIZURE BARED. Most famous of all was the hilarious KILLER BEES SWARM NORTH, which was followed by a warning that 'Ferocious swarms of man-killing bees are buzzing their way towards North America'. But even better, in terms of the sheer madness of content, was this ripping yarn: 'A divorced epileptic, who told police she was buried in a bathtub full of wet cement and later hanged upside down in the nude, left San Antonio for good this weekend. The tiny, half-blind woman suffering from diabetes recounted for the *News* a bizarre story of rape, torture and starvation.'

Some of these stories were clearly fabricated. Others were placed by advertisers and were nothing but puff pieces. But most came straight out of Ripley's reject bin. Rarely was there any room for news. Instead, as a local critic observed, there was a 'treasure trove of trivia, violence, shaggy-dog stories and the absurd: a man who converts abandoned refrigerators into doghouses, a Japanese appeal for 100 000 four-leaf clovers, an 88-year-old woman married for the sixth time...or the escape of two pet snakes aboard a German airplane.'

San Antonio's citizens were outraged that their newspaper had been hijacked by an alien invader. 'It makes you mad many, many, many times,' one of the town's leading business owners told the *Texas Monthly*; 'It's an insult to our community,' chimed another. The local police chief, Emil Peters, also complained, 'They make the city appear to be a crime capital.' One group of local worthies even tried to buy the paper, only to find Murdoch was now demanding twice as much as he'd paid, reflecting the fact that sales were booming—as usual.

On a rare visit to the city, Rupert defended himself by saying: 'We're not here to pass ourselves off as intellectuals, we're here to give the public what they want.' Years earlier, he had brushed off similar criticisms from Australia's ABC by saying: 'I'm not ashamed of any of my newspapers at all, and I'm rather sick of snobs who tell us they're bad papers, snobs who only read papers that no one else wants...[who] think they ought to be imposing their taste on anybody else in the community.'

With few other opportunities on offer, Murdoch decided to start his own weekly magazine, the *National Star*, to take on the hugely successful *National Enquirer*. Staffing it with Australians and Brits, he started by offering the same grubby fare as the *News of the World* in London and the *Truth* back home, but when the *Enquirer* switched its focus to Hollywood personalities, diets and columns by psychics and astrologers, the *Star* did the same. By the early 1980s it was selling four million copies a week—level pegging with its rival—and was coining an annual profit of $12 million, which was more than he had spent to set it up. Murdoch eventually sold it in 1990 to the *Enquirer*'s owners for $400 million, or almost 50 times what it had cost, and made a similar killing on his San Antonio papers, selling out to Hearst in 1993 for US$185 million, or almost ten times what he had paid. Love him or hate him, he clearly had the knack.

Back in 1921, his father had written to the British press baron, Lord Northcliffe, for tips on boosting sales at the Melbourne *Herald*, having just become editor. Northcliffe cabled him back: 'Find a good murder.' And soon they had. One New Year's Eve morning, the naked body of a twelve-year-old girl was found in a passageway known as Gun Alley in the centre of the city, and for the next two weeks, the *Herald*'s front pages pumped out raucous headlines such as BRUTAL MURDER IN CITY, GIRL OF 12 STRANGLED AND LEFT IN LANE and GUN ALLEY MURDER LATEST NEWS. Sir Keith also penned a front-page editorial to whip up the hysteria, warning, 'A monster exists in this city free to indulge bestial and brutal instincts, the monster who murdered little Alma Tirtschke.'

Finally, the *Herald* promised a reward for information, which prompted a city barmaid to accuse the innocent owner of the wine bar she'd just been sacked from. Police raided his home and found red hairs on a towel, which the prosecution's scientist claimed (after examining them under a microscope) matched those of the murdered girl. 'Such is life,' the convicted man observed as he stood with the noose around his neck, waiting for the trapdoor to open. Years later, DNA evidence would show they hanged an innocent man.

After it was all over, Sir Keith wrote to thank his mentor: 'You remarked to me that when a sensation comes, you would get all the readers you want. Perfectly true. I had only put on 8000 when we got a murder mystery, an unprecedented one, leading to such scenes as mounted police having to be called out to check the crowds about the residence of the supposed murderer. That left us with a steady 125 000. Then came the trial when we were averaging

230 000 or thereabouts. We are left with a steady 140 000 now, and I hope for a bit more.'

Rupert was lucky enough to make a similar killing with New York's serial murderer, Son of Sam, in 1976, when his newly acquired *New York Post* outshouted its rival, the *Daily News*, with fear-mongering headlines, like NO ONE IS SAFE FROM SON OF SAM. The *Post*'s coverage was led by chief crime reporter, Steve Dunleavy, a refugee from Murdoch's Sydney *Daily Mirror*, where he was famous for hard drinking, wild living and typing stories with his penis. With Dunleavy to whip it all up, the atmosphere in New York reached fever pitch: 'The purchase of locks and guns just rocketed…The Son of Sam virtually gave New York City this massive nervous breakdown,' Dunleavy recalled.

Among his craziest contributions—and there were several to choose from—was the classic LYRIC MAY YIELD SON OF SAM CLUE, which claimed to reveal that the Jimi Hendrix hit, 'Purple Haze', had someone singing, 'Help me, help me, help me, Son of Sam' in the background.

So what did Mr Murdoch think of such nonsense? We can only conclude he loved it because, according to the *Post*'s then managing editor, Robert Spitzler, he was right in the thick of it all: 'Rupert wrote headlines, Rupert shaped stories, Rupert dictated the leads of stories. Rupert was everywhere.'

Spitzler had initially welcomed Murdoch's purchase of the paper, believing it offered the best chance of turning the loss-making title around. But he was not the only one to be disappointed. The *New York Times* branded its proprietor's new style 'Mean, ugly, violent journalism', while the *Columbia Journalism Review* marked Murdoch as 'a force for evil' and 'a social problem', because he was dragging journalism into the gutter.

But crime wasn't his only angle. Murdoch also followed the formula that had worked so well at the *Mirror* and the *Sun*, where daily competitions had been a reliable circulation booster. Bingo soon followed, or Wingo as it was known at the *Post*. However, there was one guaranteed winner that Rupert could not get into the paper. He was keen to put topless girls on Page Three as a further boost to sales, which had already risen by 40 per cent, but his wife Anna got wind of the plan and told him she would leave him if he did so, telling his biographer, Thomas Kiernan, 'I will not have our children walking down on their way to school, walking past newsstands and looking at the *New York Post* with naked women on page three.'

The following year, when Murdoch made a successful bid for *New York* magazine, he was lampooned on the cover of *Time*, portrayed as King Kong astride the World Trade Center's twin towers, terrifying the city. By the time he made it into his newly acquired magazine to address the staff, 40 of them had already quit in horror at the prospect of him taking over. His purchase of the *Chicago Sun-Times* in 1983 would provoke a similar exodus, with the departure of 60 journalists and executives, led by the paper's Pulitzer Prize-winning columnist, Mike Royko, who quipped as he left, 'From what I've seen of Murdoch's papers in this country I don't know any self-respecting fish who would want to be wrapped in one.'

But Rupert didn't care: it was just those elites again, showing how little they knew or cared about what the public really wanted to read.

3
PLAYING POLITICS

'He has, on the whole, a pleasing character and has luck on his side.
He is, on the face of it, totally sincere.'

Sir Denis Hamilton

In October 1977, another 50 or 60 American journalists were up in arms at the way Murdoch ran his newspapers. But this time they came from his own *New York Post* and they were angry about the paper's blatant political bias in the city's race for mayor.

As the election campaign kicked off, Murdoch personally interviewed all the candidates and asked them what they would do about the unions. The Bronx-born Ed Koch said he'd smash them, which was no doubt music to Murdoch's ears, and two days later, he received a call at home, before breakfast.

'He said, "Congressman, this is Rupert",' Koch recounted. 'And I guess I was still a little sleepy maybe. I said to myself, "Rupert? Rupert? Rupert's not a Jewish name. Who could be calling me at 7 o'clock in the morning named Rupert?" And then suddenly, because he was speaking, I realised it was Rupert, the Australian. I mean, the voice came through. And I said, "Yes, Rupert?"

He said, "Congressman, we're going to endorse you today on the front page of the *New York Post* and I hope it helps." I said, "Rupert, you've elected me.'"

In the twenty-day-long Democratic primary campaign, which essentially decided who became mayor, the *Post* gave Koch four favourable front-page stories, four favourable headlines up the front of the paper, and nine mentions in 'Page Six', the paper's popular gossip column. His rival, Mario Cuomo, received no positive mentions at all on these pages, but did score some 'prominent snide comments'.

On the eve of the ballot, the *Post* led its front page with the headline: KOCH—A MAN WHO WON'T BE PUSHED AROUND. The next day it told its readers, VOTE TODAY, VOTE FOR KOCH. At times, its enthusiasm was so pervasive that it was hard to tell news reports from editorials.

By the end of it all, a significant number of *New York Post* journalists were so angry at the bias that they signed a petition to protest against the paper's 'slanted' coverage. Their union rep was promptly summoned to see Rupert and told it was up to the proprietor what went in the paper, and that anyone who had a problem could leave.

So why did Murdoch want to behave like a cartoon King Kong? An obvious answer is that he wanted to change the world—as he had in his idealistic days at Oxford—and the conservative Mr Koch was his kind of guy. Another is that he simply liked playing in the big league. 'I think he loves the idea that presidents and prime ministers pick up the phone and call him and say, you know, "Rupert, you'd be a big help to me if so and so",' said James Brady, who was then running the paper's 'Page Six'. Or, as the *Post*'s soon-to-be-sacked managing editor, Robert Spitzler, put it:

'Rupert is a power junkie, in the sense that he enjoys the company of people with power. When Rupert first came to New York, he was an Australian of no particular reputation. He bought the *New York Post*, suddenly he becomes an intimate, so to speak, with mayors, with governors and the president. You can't ignore a guy who runs a New York newspaper.'

But there were other more practical reasons for Rupert to be picking winners, which was a pastime he would always enjoy. Winners in politics could give him the business breaks he needed, and he was a master at suggesting they owed him their success. As one of his many biographers put it, 'Politicians live by fragile reputations; they believe that words can propel their careers forward or destroy them. On his visits to their locker rooms, Murdoch does not discourage these beliefs. On the contrary, he fosters the impression that he is able to deliver a kick beyond the professionals' reach.'

Ed Koch often said he would never have become mayor without Murdoch's help. Yet he claimed the media mogul made no demands once he was elected. However, the same cannot be said of the next mayor that Rupert propelled to power. In 1989 and 1993, his *New York Post* fired up the boosters for Rudy Giuliani, whose campaign manager, Roger Ailes, was subsequently hired to run Fox News. Three years later, when Time Warner refused to carry the new Fox News channel to 1.5 million viewers on its monopoly New York cable network, the tycoon called in the favour he felt he was possibly owed.

According to Time Warner's Richard Aurelio, 'Murdoch was furious' when told he'd have to wait at least a year for access, and hit back at the company with a 'ferocious display of political power'.

Following a face-to-face meeting between Rupert and Rudy to get the ball rolling, Murdoch's executives had 25 conversations and two private meetings with the Mayor's senior aides. Threats to revoke Time Warner's licence soon followed, and, when these failed to work, the city gave up one of its own cable channels for Fox's exclusive use. This arrangement was promptly struck down by the Federal Court, which ruled that the city had 'improper motives…to reward a friend', but renewed pressure from City Hall then persuaded Time Warner to give way. 'I thought it was pretty awful,' Aurelio said later. 'Giuliani was doing Murdoch's work.'

By using his papers to build his empire and trumpet his views, Murdoch was following in the great tradition of those famous British press lords, Beaverbrook and Northcliffe. But he was also copying his father, Sir Keith, who had helped 'Honest Joe' Lyons become Prime Minister of Australia in 1931 and then turned against him, boasting to friends, 'I put him there and I'll put him out.'

Rupert felt he had the right to use his power in this way, and rarely left anyone in doubt about whose side he was on. In the Australian election in 1972, his *Daily Mirror* and newly acquired *Telegraph* went hard in support of Labor's new champion of change, Gough Whitlam, and his 'It's Time' campaign. Murdoch flew to Sydney to supervise the operation and threw himself into the fray, writing press releases, drafting speeches, giving PR advice, running free ads in his papers and turning up daily at the party's campaign headquarters. He prefaced it all with a private cruise on Sydney harbour for Gough and his wife, Margaret, before wrapping it up at a dinner for the couple just before polling day. By the end, he was almost one of the family.

Murdoch doubtless figured Whitlam would win—and he did at a canter—but he also felt Australia needed radical change after 23 years of conservative government, which had left it, in his words, 'a second-hand society, a reflection of another hemisphere'.

Yet three years later, his papers fought even harder to get rid of Whitlam's government. Rupert had expected to be welcomed at the Lodge and to become intimate with the new prime minister, says his old colleague, Rod Lever, but Whitlam 'wouldn't take phone calls...or accept his offers of lunch or a weekend at Cavan [his farm near Yass in New South Wales].'

However, it was not just that he felt left out. Whitlam brought Australia's troops home from Vietnam, opened diplomatic relations with the People's Republic of China and criticised the US bombing of Hanoi, to the fury of President Richard Nixon, all at a time when Murdoch was trying to win favour in the US. As much to the point, perhaps, his government screwed up the economy and became comically incompetent towards the end.

Murdoch was certainly not the only one to be disillusioned with the Labor government by 1975, nor was he the first to attack. But his papers undoubtedly hit much harder than his rivals. *The Australian*'s assault in particular was 'ferocious', 'unfair' and 'undoubtedly in breach of journalistic ethics', according to one leading commentator, Max Suich, or 'brutal and single minded', in the view of another. Soon 76 members of the Australian Journalists' Association (AJA) who worked on the paper were handing Murdoch a letter of protest, complaining that its coverage was 'blind, biased, tunnel-visioned, ad hoc, logically confused and relentless'. The letter also objected to 'the deliberate or careless slanting of headlines, seemingly blatant imbalance in news presentation [and] political censorship'. Rupert did not bother to reply.

Two weeks later, when Whitlam was sensationally sacked by the Governor-General, Sir John Kerr, in Australia's biggest modern political crisis, Murdoch's national daily was alone in failing to question whether his dismissal was legal. In the ensuing election,

The Australian's coverage was overwhelmingly favourable to Gough's rival, Malcolm Fraser, with 56 per cent of its editorials supporting the Coalition and none supporting Labor. Its news stories and columns also scored two-to-one in favour of the Coalition, with copy often rewritten by subs and bylines removed.

'Journalists…were given specific instructions on what they could write and what they couldn't write,' claimed Mungo MacCallum, a political reporter who had just left *The Australian*. 'And where the instructions weren't specific, they learnt pretty bloody quickly because nothing appeared in the paper if it didn't follow the line. It was the most extraordinarily ruthless and one-sided political coverage I think any of us can remember.'

One of the nation's most-respected political commentators agreed with him. 'The news pages of the paper were…turned over almost to propaganda organs of the paper's editorial line,' said Paul Kelly, who quit *The Australian* shortly afterwards, only to rejoin the paper in later years.

The AJA duly sent the proprietor a second letter, asking for a meeting and threatening to publicise its grievances, to which Murdoch replied, 'If you insist on providing ammunition for our competitors and enemies who are intent on destroying us and all our livelihoods, then go ahead.' Shortly afterwards, News Ltd journalists and printers went on strike for 36 hours, and hundreds of protesters gathered outside the *Daily Mirror* in Sydney and burned copies of his papers.

Rupert later told the BBC's *Panorama* program that the journalists who complained were just left-wing troublemakers: 'You saw the people on the street, all carrying their red flags, rent-a-picket stuff.' And perhaps he believed this line. But some of *The Australian*'s most talented reporters were sacked or left in disgust, and it took years for the paper to recover its reputation. Clearly, Rupert believed in Sir Frank Packer's dictum about freedom of the press, that *he* should be free to have his newspapers say whatever he wanted them to.

Over in England, Murdoch kept out of the political melee for most of the 1970s, but eventually found a leader who both satisfied him ideologically and backed him in his business ventures. Margaret Thatcher shared his desire to break the unions, was passionate about private enterprise and despised Britain's toffee-nosed elites as much as he did. She was also an outsider, like him. Better still, from Rupert's point of view, she knew how important was *The Sun*'s support, and was prepared to bend the rules to get it.

By the 1970s it was becoming clear that elections were decided by a large group of floating voters who went for the party they disliked least. Typically young, Labour-leaning and skilled working class, they worried about housing, coloured immigration and the cost of living, and cared little about the welfare state or the rest of the world. Classified as C2s by advertisers, they were exactly the sort of people who read *The Sun*. And because they were concentrated in marginal seats, they were exactly the people that Thatcher needed to get onside.

The Sun had started its life under Murdoch tethered to Labour, as a radical newspaper whose instincts were all 'Left rather than Right'. It had backed Harold Wilson at the 1970 election, and cheered for the miners against Ted Heath in 1972 even with Rupert in charge. But by the end of the 1970s, Murdoch had lurched to the right, and Britain's Labour Party was way off to the left, with the unions in command.

In the run-up to the May 1979 election, Maggie knew how important *The Sun*'s support could be and went out of her way to flatter the editor, Larry Lamb, who had written the WINTER OF DISCONTENT headline to describe the wave of strikes sweeping Britain. She invited him to strategy meetings at her home, let him sit in on private chats with her PR guru, Tim Bell, and asked for his help in drafting speeches, as a result of which he became convinced that she was the answer.

But Rupert was less easily persuaded that his paper should back the Tory leader because he feared it would upset the paper's working-class readers. And he was not convinced she could do the job. An old-fashioned chauvinist, with no women on his board or senior executive team, he would ask his editor until 1978, 'Are you still pushing that bloody woman?' But it was even harder for him to stomach the Labour alternative, with its power cuts and rotting garbage on the streets. So, in the end, there was really not much choice. On polling day, *The Sun* duly carried a huge front-page editorial urging its readers to 'Vote Tory, Stop the Rot. There may not be another chance'.

After her victory, Maggie was convinced that Murdoch's paper had put her into Downing Street, not least because its C2 readers had swung over to her at twice the national average. And when the next election came round and a Tory media owner started bitching about *The Sun*'s parvenu proprietor, she rounded on him, asking, 'Why are you so opposed to Rupert? He is going to get us in.' On another occasion she cooed, 'We depend on him to fight for us. *The Sun* is marvellous.'

Over the next thirteen years, the partnership strengthened, with *The Sun* acting as cheerleader for the Falklands War, and Thatcher's government making a series of decisions that helped Murdoch expand his empire and increase his power. The first of these, which allowed him to storm the citadel of the British establishment, was what delivered his dominance of the British newspaper market.

By 1980, when *The Times* came up for sale, the nation's oldest and poshest paper had been losing money for years. Its Canadian owner, Lord Thomson, had kept it alive with cash transfusions from the *Sunday Times* and then from his North Sea oilfields. But his son Ken—who inherited the papers in 1976—soon tired of the haemorrhaging. In 1978, he shut both titles for almost a year in an attempt to force the unions to scrap the paper's primitive hot-metal typesetting. Then, when the journalists (whom he had kept on at full pay) struck for more money, he decided he had had enough. In October, he announced the papers would be sold, or close in March 1981 if no buyer could be found.

Murdoch made a bid, as did several others, and was quickly deemed to be the winner. On 16 January 1981, Times Newspapers' chairman and editor-in-chief, Sir Denis Hamilton, sent a memo to Thomson's board saying that he and the paper's two editors were unanimous in choosing Rupert as their preferred candidate. Praising him as 'ruthless', 'a newspaper professional' and 'a tough operator', who was just the man to tackle the unions, Hamilton enthused:

> He has, on the whole, a pleasing character and has luck on his side.
>
> He has had British University education (Oxford) and fully understands the British way of life and political system.
>
> He is neither greatly to the Left or greatly to the Right in politics.
>
> He has started a quality newspaper (The Australian).
>
> He is on the face of it, totally sincere in discussions so far about the independence of editors and the preservation of quality.

This displayed a touching faith in Rupert's good character, which Hamilton would soon realise to be misplaced, and was a powerful testament to the Australian's charm. But in the meantime there was a problem to be overcome. Rupert already owned *The Sun* and *News of the World* and had recently assured the American magazine *More* that he 'would not be allowed to buy another successful daily newspaper' because 'the Monopolies Commission would say "No"'. This, said Rupert, was 'quite correct and proper'.

Winning *The Times* and *Sunday Times* would give him 30 per cent of Britain's daily newspapers and 36 per cent of its Sundays—which, on past performance, he was likely to increase—so it was absolutely right for Murdoch to fear the commission would reject the takeover, especially since the 'Dirty Digger' was the last person most wanted to run this venerable British institution.

The law was also quite clear that the commission must be consulted. The *Fair Trading Act 1973* stipulated that the Secretary of State for Trade, John Biffen, could not approve a newspaper takeover of this size without first referring it, unless he was satisfied that the matter was urgent and that the paper would cease to exist if the bid was delayed.

Clearly, there was no such risk of extinction in the case of the *Sunday Times*, which was still profitable despite the unions. And there was no clause in the law that allowed him to lump the two papers together. Nor, to be frank, was there much chance of *The Times* going belly up because there were several serious bidders who wanted to keep it alive, including Lord Rothermere at the *Daily Mail*, who had made a higher bid.

But despite the lack of legal justification, John Biffen decided to tell Parliament he would approve the Murdoch takeover forthwith.

In the emergency debate that followed, one Labour MP told the House of Commons, 'I detect the opinions of the Prime Minister. I think that it is the Prime Minister who has dictated that Rupert is owed a favour and that the proposal should not go to the commission.' Another suggested that Biffen had been railroaded by his boss: 'That is the reality…This is a straightforward pay-off for services rendered by *The Sun*.'

Thirty years later, when Mrs Thatcher's private papers were released, it became clear how true this may have been. On 4 January 1981, three weeks before the bid was approved, Murdoch requested a Sunday lunch with the Prime Minister at her official country residence, Chequers. The purpose of this meeting, as a minute from her press secretary, Bernard Ingham, admitted, was for Rupert to brief her on his bid for Times Newspapers. Ingham's note recorded pointedly that Mrs Thatcher listened with interest, but 'did no more than wish him well'.

If the press secretary was to be believed, neither Rupert nor Maggie managed to utter the two crucial words 'Monopolies Commission' in the entire one-hour, or even two-hour, chat about the takeover. But all three people at the lunch clearly understood the need for discretion. As a result, the very existence of this private chat was kept secret for the next three decades, despite suggestions that something of the sort had clearly taken place. Mrs Thatcher decreed that Ingham's minute should not be circulated outside 10 Downing Street, while the official history of *The Times* asserted baldly that Rupert and Maggie 'had no communication whatsoever' during the bid. The source of this claim, which was clearly false, was Rupert Murdoch himself.

The Times's official history suggested that all lobbying of the government by News had been left to Woodrow Wyatt, a plump, bow-tied Tory MP, oft-known as 'Toad of Toad Hall', who was Rupert's friend, political gopher and a columnist on the *News of the World*. And after the takeover was approved, he would be quite sure that he had fixed it. After a dinner with Murdoch in June 1987, he wrote in his diary: 'I reminded Rupert during the evening how at his request and at my instigation she [Mrs Thatcher] had stopped the *Times* acquisition being referred to the Monopolies Commission, though the *Sunday Times* was not really losing money and the pair together were not.'

In 1995, he boasted in another entry, 'I had all the rules bent for him over the *Times* and *Sunday Times* when he bought them... Through Margaret I got it arranged that the deal didn't go to the Monopolies Commission, which almost certainly would have blocked it.'

However, these explosive claims only came to light seventeen years after the event, when the first volume of Wyatt's diaries was published in 1998, by which time it was far too late to do anything about it.

Since then, it has become possible to learn much more about how the decision was made, because the government's papers relating to the takeover have been publicly released under the 30-year rule. These reveal that Biffen was initially minded to refer the bid to the commission, as the law required. They also show that the pressure on him to wave it through came mainly from the Thomson Organisation, which wanted to meet a deadline it had given to the unions. And it was Thomson, too, who warned the sale to Murdoch would fall through if the Monopolies Commission got involved.

But at the end of it all, it's hard to avoid the conclusion reached by one of Thatcher's Cabinet ministers, James Prior, that it was a politically motivated decision to give Murdoch what he wanted, and a *quid pro quo* for *The Sun*'s continued support. And the Cabinet minutes tend to confirm this verdict, because Mrs Thatcher opened the discussion by drawing everyone's attention to the loophole in the law, which she said empowered Biffen to approve Murdoch's bid without consulting the commission or his colleagues. This would clearly have been a powerful signal to her ministers, who were renowned for doing what Maggie told them to.

Murdoch had promised all sorts of guarantees to assuage his critics, and Biffen agreed these should be given the force of law, since he was keen to avoid the accusation of going soft on the 'Dirty Digger'. Six 'national directors' of Times Newspapers Holdings were therefore required to 'agree' to the future hiring and firing of *The Times* and *Sunday Times* editors, who would then have full control over what news and opinions they printed and what staff they employed. Or that was the theory. And Rupert was happy to string them along.

Asked by the BBC, 'Would you play any part in determining the views they put forward at election times?' Murdoch replied, 'No, certainly not. They won't ask me.'

'Even if they were entirely opposed to what you felt was right?' the interviewer pressed.

'Absolutely,' Rupert replied. 'It will hurt like hell but I will just have to content myself elsewhere.'

But Britain soon discovered that Murdoch was not to be trusted. And they were warned of this by Lord Beaverbrook's nephew, Jonathan Aitken MP, who told the House of Commons that it was 'a sad day for Fleet Street and a sad day for the Conservative Party', of which he was a member. 'The plain fact,' said Aitken, 'is that Mr. Murdoch has strewn assurances and safeguards on newspaper and television ownership like confetti, all round the world, and the more one examines those assurances the more one has to say that in far too many instances they have proved to be worthless.'

The Tory backbencher, himself a journalist, then recited a litany of broken promises, beginning with Rupert's shabby treatment of Sir William Carr at the *News of the World* in 1969 and moving rapidly to his immediate record in Australia, where Murdoch had assured the Australian Broadcasting Tribunal in 1979 that he would make no changes to Sydney's Channel 10 TV station, and had then sacked the chairman, general manager and finance director within weeks of his promise.

Murdoch had made a similar pledge to the tribunal not to bid for Channel 10 in Melbourne, and had broken that promise too. He had also been found guilty of four contraventions of the *Australian Broadcasting and Television Act* and of misleading the Australian Stock Exchange over his purchase of Channel 10 shares. Furthermore, the Australian Press Council had found him guilty of misleading and unfair reporting. And finally, the tribunal had ruled against him acquiring the Melbourne TV station on the grounds that it was 'not in the public interest' for him to have more power than he already did.

'I have some understanding of the way in which Mr. Murdoch has exercised his stewardship of newspapers,' Aitken concluded. 'It makes me profoundly unhappy.'

Many people will know what happened next, and the rest will not be surprised. A year later, after interfering constantly with the tone and content of the papers—as he did with all his publications—Murdoch summoned *The Times*'s home editor, Fred Emery, to his office and told him bluntly: 'I give instructions to my editors all round the world. Why shouldn't I in London?' When he was reminded of his promises to parliament and the public that he would do no such thing at *The Times*, he hit back, 'Those guarantees are not worth the paper they're written on.'

Weeks earlier, he had been caught trying to shift the two titles into a subsidiary company that had no legal obligation to respect the guarantees he had given, but he had been forced by the national directors to rescind the move.

Murdoch also fought fiercely with *The Times*'s editor, Harold Evans, who had made the *Sunday Times* such a success. Eventually, Evans could take no more and walked out, saying as he left, 'The differences between me and Mr. Murdoch should not be prolonged. I am therefore resigning tonight as the editor of *The Times*.' He was soon adding, 'He is a good businessman and a lousy journalist, a lousy journalist in the sense he doesn't believe in public interest journalism and he doesn't keep his promises. He's a liar. He's incontinent in breach of promise and also he's a very treacherous person.'

By this time, poor Sir Denis Hamilton was gone as well, two years before retirement age. Murdoch had given him the job of chairman, as he had promised, only to sack him a few months later. 'This great distinguished man was denied a lunch tray at his desk, he was humiliated,' said Evans, claiming Hamilton was reduced to tears on his departure.

But *The Times* takeover wasn't the only occasion Murdoch got vital help from Mrs Thatcher. Without her support he would never have been able to move production of his papers from Fleet Street in the mid-1980s and bring in new technology to break the power of the British print unions. Nor would he have been able to build his pay-TV company Sky in the 1990s into the massively profitable enterprise it is today. Indeed, it's arguable that without Thatcher's backing, News Corp would have collapsed.

Murdoch started building his new plant at Wapping in the late 1970s on a huge empty site in London's docklands, and tried for years to persuade his printers to move. But they refused point blank to accept the massive job cuts involved and advised him that his best move would be to blow it all up.

However, he had watched his fellow proprietors give into blackmail for years and was determined to take them on. 'We employed 300 people to print the paper; we only needed 80,' his editor at the *Sunday Times*, Andrew Neil, explained. 'We employed Donald Duck. Ronald Reagan worked for me. They were all fictitious names that we had to pay. It was anarchy.'

Murdoch brought in American computers to control his new printing presses and tested them in secret in a South London warehouse, before shipping them to Wapping in the dead of night in unmarked crates. He made the plant riot proof by surrounding it with a four-metre-high spiked fence, topped with three rolls of razor wire, which was lit up with floodlights and watched by CCTV. He also hired uniformed guards and a Rhodesian anti-terrorist policeman to run security. And then he lined up the Australian trucking firm, TNT, owned by his mate Sir Peter Abeles, to ship his papers around the country, because he knew the unions would try to stop them going by rail.

Finally, he called on Mrs Thatcher, lunching with her again at Chequers, to tell her his plans and request her support. As Andrew Neil recently recalled:

> He made it clear to me one night in late 1985 in my office that he had gone to Mrs Thatcher to get her assurance—to 'square Thatcher' in his words—that enough police would be made available to get his papers out past the massed pickets at Wapping once the dispute got underway. She was fully 'squared', he reported: she had given him assurances on the grounds that she was doing no more than upholding the right of his company to go about its lawful business. I remember this because he

added that he could never have got the same assurances from the Mayor of New York or the NYPD, which was why, he told me, he could not 'do a Wapping' on his US newspapers, despite the grip of the print unions there too.

There was a precedent for Thatcher's action. Three years before, in Warrington, another newspaper proprietor and Thatcher supporter, Eddie Shah, had defied the print unions' demand for a closed shop, and violent battles between police and massed pickets had ensued. But in the clashes at Wapping even more would be at stake.

Using non-union labour, Murdoch pressed the button on his new presses in mid-January 1986, giving journalists at *The Times*, *Sunday Times*, *The Sun* and *News of the World* only hours to decide whether they wanted to make the move. In last-minute meetings with the print unions, who were now ready to give way, he took such a hard line that they voted to strike. As their members left work, all 5500 of them were handed dismissal notices. Thatcher's new laws meant they would not be eligible for redundancy pay, saving Murdoch millions of dollars.

And so the inevitable battle began, with staff ferried in and out of the plant each day in buses with blacked-out windows and protective wire mesh. As they drove through the picket lines, they were greeted with cries of 'Scab, Scab, Scab', and loud banging on the side. On Saturday nights, angry crowds of up to 5000 protesters gathered to stop Murdoch's TNT trucks getting his Sunday papers out of the plant, but without success. A hail of smoke bombs, stones and golf balls from two-man slingshots would be met by at least 1000 police on horseback or on foot with plastic shields and batons. It was like a replay of the miners' strike of 1984, in which *The Sun* had stood behind Thatcher.

The biggest battle of them all came on the first anniversary of the move, with 13 000 pickets ranged against 1000 riot police and 168 people injured in the fray. But that was the last hurrah for his enemies. One month later the war was over and Murdoch had won.

Police protection, at British taxpayers' expense, was essential to his victory, as were Thatcher's new union laws that outlawed secondary picketing and ensured the unions could not touch the papers once they got clear of the plant. Another vital ingredient was the support of the electricians' union, the EETPU, whose members breached the violent picket lines to man the Wapping machines. Murdoch promised to recognise the union once the dispute was over, but went back on his word, and showed 'not one spark of gratitude', according to the EETPU's leader Eric Hammond, proving yet again that he was not a man to be trusted.

Victory at Wapping transformed the economics of his British newspaper business, tripling its profit to £3 million a week, tripling News Corporation's share price, and tripling the value of his four titles, *The Times*, *Sunday Times*, *The Sun* and *News of the World*, to £1 billion, or more than twenty times what he had paid for them. For Murdoch and his executives, it was the sweetest of victories. 'In 20 years time, they'll look back at what Rupert did and realizse there wouldn't be any newspapers in the UK if this guy hadn't done what he did at Wapping,' says Bill Repard today. And he's probably right, however painful and ugly it was at the time. But none of it would have been possible had the Iron Lady not backed him up.

Thatcher's support for Murdoch was also critical in the success of Sky TV, where Murdoch again took a huge risk, bet the company, and finally pulled it off. Having lost his bid for Britain's new satellite-TV licence in 1986, he leased a Luxembourg-based satellite and started beaming the signal back into the country. This is what they had done with pirate radio in the 1960s, when Radio Caroline and Radio London broadcast from ships in the North Sea. Only now it was pirate TV, with Rupert as the pirate, operating from west London.

When Murdoch got Sky up and running in February 1989, the network HQ was still a construction site, with Nissen huts for offices, amid a field of mud, and the service could not offer movies to its customers because no one had figured out how to encrypt the signal. Viewers could tune in to news, sports and a general TV channel, but hardly anyone bothered to watch, even though it was free, because you needed a satellite dish to receive it. The critics also damned it as downmarket trash. Rupert, naturally, said he was defying the elites again and giving the punters choice.

By hurrying it into service, Murdoch's executives had given Sky a one-year lead on the competition at British Satellite Broadcasting, which had paid millions of pounds for the licence and was building its head office just down the road in Imperial Roman style. But even with this head start it was a huge and hugely expensive gamble, which lost more than £1 billion in the first three years. At its nadir, the new pay-TV experiment was sucking up £2 million a day from News. And even with the cash that *The Sun* was now producing, it was threatening to bankrupt the entire group.

But once again, Thatcher's government came to his aid, or sheltered him from attack. The new *Broadcasting Act* of 1990 introduced a ban on foreign ownership of TV stations, but exempted Rupert Murdoch, because Sky was a satellite service. The same law introduced new cross-media rules, which did apply to satellite TV, but Rupert miraculously escaped because the rules were framed to exclude *non-British* operators like him. And a year later, when Sky merged with its rival, BSB, to avoid going broke, and Murdoch had to admit he was now a *British* operator, he managed to squeeze through yet another loophole in the law with Maggie's blessing. It was comical but also scandalous. The rules were being bent every which way so Rupert could get his way.

Thatcher's media minister, David Mellor, told the Leveson Inquiry in 2012 that he saw Sky as a brave commercial venture, and was happy to exempt Murdoch from the foreign ownership restrictions because it would have driven 1000 jobs offshore. But he was less sure about cutting Rupert out of the cross-media laws, which would have forced him to sell a couple of his newspapers. 'You could say that was a mistake,' the former minister conceded.

Significantly, Mellor admitted that of all the important people who lobbied him, 'There was one person that I had to go and see, and there was no question of him padding round to our department, and that was Rupert Murdoch.' This chimes in nicely with how *The Sun*'s famous former editor, Kelvin MacKenzie, read the power relationship between his proprietor and politicians. 'The most incredible aspect I have seen in my lifetime,' he said recently, 'is the queue of politicians anxious to kiss Rupert's backside.'

And the same is true of Australia, where Murdoch was allowed to end up with 70 per cent of the nation's newspapers. Little more than a decade after Rupert helped bring down Gough Whitlam, the Australian Labor Party was again eating out of his hand, and giving him permission to buy the Herald and Weekly Times group, the newspaper chain his father had built up, which added the major papers in Melbourne, Brisbane and Perth to the ones he already owned in Sydney and Adelaide, as well as a string of provincial papers around the country.

It was a wonderful homecoming for him; his mother was thrilled; and it marked a huge milestone in his life. But why did the politicians allow it? It was the biggest newspaper deal the world had ever seen. It gave him a dominance that no one has had before or since. It was twice the share of the newspaper market that others already deemed too much in Britain, and it flew right in the face of what Murdoch himself had said back in 1969 when asked whether he already had enough. Back then he had replied, quite reasonably:

> I think the important thing is that there be plenty of newspapers with plenty of different people controlling them, so there's a variety of viewpoints, so there's a choice for the public. This is the freedom of the press that is needed. Freedom of the press mustn't just be one-sided for a proprietor to speak as he pleases, to bully the community.

Despite that, one could hardly blame him for asking. But why on earth did politicians always have to say yes?

4
THE SUN KING

'The Sun King is everywhere, even when he is nowhere. He rules over great distances through authority, loyalty, example and fear.'

Andrew Neil

So what made Rupert run? Why did he work so hard to create this global media empire? According to his mother, Dame Elisabeth, it was not for the love of power or money but for the challenge, the thrill of the game.

'I love them, I enjoy them,' was Rupert's own assessment of his papers. 'It's communicating with people, it's a challenge, it's competitive; there are many elements of it that I find stimulating.'

'He just likes running newspapers' was the prosaic, but possibly accurate verdict of Malcolm Colless, who worked for him for 40 years as a journalist and senior executive. 'It's not just about influencing governments; he just likes to go and sit down with his editors and be at the centre of what's going on.'

Or, as one of his former close aides suggested, 'He loves lighting fires, fanning fires, getting things stirred up to sell papers. He has a pure enthusiasm for what's going to excite people's passion and interest and he loves being a player in effecting change.'

Others who knew him well, like his nephew, Matt Handbury, concurred: 'His newspapers are his world; he's living it; he's really into it. He gets very excited by what's happening in the Middle East. It's all very real to him.'

'It was never just about money for Rupert,' said another Australian executive who had worked with the family for two decades. 'It was always about getting somewhere. Question is where. I'm fucked if I could ever work it out.'

And perhaps Rupert could not either. A regular refrain from people who had worked with him for years was that they never got to know him and suspected he didn't know himself. His second wife, Anna, was convinced he was gentle, idealistic and kind, but was shocked to discover his coldness in cutting her off in 1999, when he divorced her for Wendi Deng, and surprised that his ambition trumped everything else she thought he held dear. His third wife Wendi was perhaps almost as shocked when he decided to reinvent himself at the age of 82, become a single man again, and throw himself cheerfully into yet another phase of his life.

But let's leave this question of what makes Rupert so thrilled by the chase and jump to a moment in 2008 and the publication of Michael Wolff's biography, *The Man Who Owns the News*, because it says much about the man and the way he runs his empire. For some reason, which even the author failed to grasp, Rupert agreed to submit to 50 hours of interviews with the *Vanity Fair* writer, and instructed his wife, mother, children and top executives to tell Wolff anything they wanted. Perhaps he thought it would seal his legacy.

Two months before the book hit the shelves, Rupert got hold of a copy from a British newspaper bidding on the serial rights, and as he read it he became increasingly upset at the portrait it painted.

That day he left the author a dozen increasingly agitated voice-mails, disputing minor details and complaining about the tone. Then he went ominously quiet.

For the next three months the book scored not a single mention in any of Murdoch's newspapers, magazines or TV programs. Not one. Until, finally, the *New York Post* broke the silence on its gossip pages, by trumpeting news of the 50-something 'bald, trout-lipped' writer's extramarital affair with a 28-year-old 'hot blond'.

For the next few weeks, the *Post* kept to its task, chronicling Wolff's crumbling marriage, accusing him of trying to evict his 85-year-old mother-in-law, and making fun of him in cartoons. The barrage only stopped when Wolff threatened to post the recordings of his unedited interviews with Murdoch on the internet to settle the argument.

One can glean a couple of things from this tale, and indeed from Wolff's book. The first is that Rupert is constantly surprised at how he comes across: he has no talent for introspection and has no idea why people hate him.

The second is that his editors and executives, and even his family, do exactly what Rupert wants them to do, whether that be attacking his enemies, boosting his friends or keeping radio silence when necessary. Call it fear, charm, charisma, personality or respect, it's clear he has something that makes people want to do what he asks. Even though almost 90 per cent of the shares in News Corp are held outside the Murdoch family, none of the group's 51 000 employees or fifteen board directors is in doubt that they work for Rupert, that he's the boss, and that pleasing him is the way to get on. It's something that's worth bearing in mind as a background to the phone hacking scandal, where one of the most tantalising questions is what the Murdochs really knew.

You can get an idea of how Rupert runs his empire from any of a dozen books written about him over the years, or from talking to any of a hundred current or former executives. But it's rarely been better put than by the ex-*Sunday Times* editor, Andrew Neil, who was one of Murdoch's most-trusted executives before he morphed into his most trenchant critic. In his memoir, *Full Disclosure*, Neil famously likened working for Murdoch to being a courtier of the Sun King, whose light shines to all corners of his kingdom:

> All life revolves around the Sun King; all authority comes from him. He is the only one to whom allegiance must be owed and he expects his remit to run everywhere, his word to be final...Normal management structures do not matter...the Sun King is all that matters...The Sun King is everywhere, even when he is nowhere. He rules over great distances through authority, loyalty, example and fear.

According to Neil and other Murdoch editors and executives, like David Yelland who ran *The Sun*, Rupert's courtiers hang on his every word. They wake up wondering what he's thinking, and how he will react to what they plan to do. Even Rupert reckons they go too far in this. But it's hardly surprising that it should be so, because he knows his business better than anyone, and he knows their business better than them. Hierarchies and management structures mean nothing to him. Everyone in his empire is just a phone call away, and he rings day or night, wherever he is.

Rodney Lever, who managed a number of papers for News Ltd in Australia from the 1950s to the 1970s, described it thus:

> Rupert seemed to be everywhere and nowhere...It was all Rupert, Rupert, Rupert. Rupert said this, Rupert said that...At the first ring, people said: 'It's Rupert' and their face went white. He would ring people from anywhere in the world and never mind the time. Breakfast time, lunchtime,

dinnertime. What time is it in London? What was the time in New York, Singapore, Berlin, Moscow, Reykjavik? It didn't matter if Rupert wanted to call you.

And when he called you in the middle of the night or while you were busy in your office or entertaining friends at home, he would fire a question. You answered as best as you could. There would be a long silence while your nerves wondered whether you had given the right answer. Was he still there?

'Rupert?'

'Yes.'

'Are you still there?'

Silence …

Sir Larry Lamb, who edited *The Sun* in the 1970s and early 1980s, had the same experience:

He would bark down the phone, then break the connection when he had to dash off again. Then, anything from minutes to hours later, the phone in Bouverie Street would ring again and KRM would restart the conversation from the point he had left it as if there had not been a break.

Lamb's successor at *The Sun*, Kelvin MacKenzie, suffered a similar trial by telephone through the 1980s and early 1990s, although he took more long-distance bollockings than Lamb ever did. And Bruce Dover, who worked for Murdoch in Hong Kong, China and Australia until 2000, had a similar tale to tell:

Murdoch without a telephone was like an alcoholic without a drink. He would grow agitated, fidgety, desperately looking for a fix. Murdoch ran his empire by phone and at almost any time of his day—every day, 6 a.m. in the gym or midnight in his hotel room—there was someone he could call somewhere in the world who was in the middle of their day and able to take a call from the boss.

Rebekah Brooks, who became editor of the *News of the World* in May 2000, editor of *The Sun* in 2003, and ran News's British newspapers from 2009, was also in constant phone contact, speaking to Rupert 'every day' unless something important was happening elsewhere in the world, even though she technically reported to his son James.

By several accounts, Murdoch expected his every word to be listened to, but rarely paid the same attention to others. He would ask questions and not wait for the reply, talk over answers, and walk out of meetings in mid-sentence. Executives sharing lunch with him rarely spoke up and got squashed if they did. British MPs who visited him on the Avenue of the Americas in 2009 were struck by the way he banged his hand on the table while making a point. He never shouted; he didn't need to. His editors and executives knew that the easiest way to advance was to do what he wished.

There's a wonderful moment in the BBC's excellent 1981 *Panorama* profile when the nonplussed editor of Sydney's *Daily Mirror*, Peter Wiley, is asked whether he follows a line that he knows will please Rupert. He looks left, right, left, right, up, down and up again, then sucks in his breath, purses his lips and eventually agrees that, 'Yes', he wouldn't run anything he thought Rupert might disagree with.

Murdoch admitted in the program that he interfered too much with his newspapers when he was around. But it was clear he hardly needed to, because his editors already knew where he stood. He was anti-Communist, anti-abortion, anti-long hair and beards, anti-suede shoes and anti-gay rights. He was pro family and private enterprise, against high taxes, and had no time for poofters.

Yet he still interfered with energy and enthusiasm because it's what he loved to do. Adrian Deamer, one of *The Australian*'s most respected editors, recalled that Rupert would fly into town, come into his office and get all the back copies of the paper, then go through them and rip them apart. 'He knew what he was looking for,' said Deamer. 'They [the articles] were mostly political.' Deamer was sacked in 1971 for writing an editorial condemning the Springbok tour of Australia, but seven other editors of *The Australian* were shown the door in the paper's first sixteen years for a variety of reasons. 'He sacked more journalists than I've ever seen sacked before in my whole career,' said the paper's first editor, Max Newton. 'Oh, he's a tremendous sacker.'

Yet many people loved working for him, and many still do. 'It was fantastic, exciting, thrilling,' says Bill Repard, who joined *The Sun* in 1969 and worked for Murdoch for the next 30 years. 'You'd never get rich but it was fun. He always showed an interest in people. You'd be running a small newspaper in Perth and he'd come on the phone from the other side of the world to say, "You had a great week, well done." You wouldn't get that in other big companies.'

'You'd walk round the office in Sydney with him,' says another top Australian executive who moved on in the 1990s, 'and he'd stop to chat to someone from the press room he'd known years ago, and he'd remember their first name, and it was like a family business. He had the common touch; he could talk to anyone.'

Malcolm Colless, another Australian, who worked for Murdoch as a journalist and executive for four decades, says the same. 'It was like being part of a big family. You loved working for him. It was a way of life. Lots of people stayed forever. He'd give you a smack one minute, buy you a drink the next. He never bore grudges, knew how to motivate people, and knew how to relate to them. Anyone could go and talk to him.'

If you worked for Murdoch you could be sent all over the world at a moment's notice: Colless started his executive career running the *Northern Daily Leader* in Tamworth. Four years later he was in Beijing, building a media centre with China's CCTV. Two years after that, he was in Sydney running News Ltd's suburban news-papers; then he was moved to Melbourne to run the Herald and Weekly Times; then he was setting up pay-TV in Australia; then he was scouring the world for opportunities in new technology; and finally he was back home lobbying the Australian government on Murdoch's behalf.

People also loved working for Rupert because he was so smart, and knew so much about the business. 'I can't remember a meeting with him when I didn't learn something I didn't know,' says one long-serving executive who left the group in the early 2000s.

Wherever Murdoch went, he carried his blue book, with weekly print-outs of the financial status of every News Corp operation around the world. From this he could spot a rise in the price of newsprint in Cairns and ring his local manager to ask what he was doing about it. And he had a knack of asking the one question one didn't know the answer to.

He was always pressing to do things quicker, better, cheaper. 'If you spent a dollar he wanted to know how much you would get back,' another veteran Australian executive recalls. 'If you said 27 cents, he'd say, "Make that 33 cents," and then walk out. And you'd be left wondering, "How am I going to do that?"'

At heart, he was also a decent bloke, or at least a part of him was: 'He was well-raised by Dame Elisabeth, who was a class act,' says one close aide who worked with him for a decade, but adds that the other half of Rupert was 'deeply cynical'. Others found him well-mannered and polite, down-to-earth and 'remarkably ordinary'. Americans in particular were impressed at his very Australian habit of jumping in the front of a taxicab, alongside the driver, and not insisting on a limo.

Rupert's Calvinist upbringing and Scottish heritage had made him careful with money, despite his massive wealth. As time went on he acquired corporate jets, a luxury yacht and houses all over the world. But there was no greater personal triumph for him than to find a $1 haircut in Shanghai or save $10 by getting the trousers on his new cheap suit turned up for free in his Hong Kong hotel. He confessed his favourite wine was Grange, but never drank it if he was paying. He took the same approach in business, for all his billion-dollar deals, telling executives to ask themselves: 'If this were my money, would I be spending it?'

And despite all his wealth and fame, he was the same as he'd always been. He had no airs and graces. He'd stop and talk to journalists sent to stake him out, and stand around and chat to reporters at Gretel Packer's country wedding, while his rival Australian media mogul, Kerry Packer, snarled at the media. He was 'very normal, very informal, very Australian', says one of his executives. And so was News Corporation, even as the top levels of the organisation became increasingly American, and the centre of gravity moved more and more to the US.

Rupert relied on Australians to run the business because he understood them and trusted them to cut the crap. So he had John Cowley running Wapping; Col Allan in charge at the *New York Post*; Les Hinton running the British newspapers and then Dow Jones; David Hill in charge of Fox Sports in Los Angeles; Sam Chisholm running BSkyB; Gary Davey in Hong

Kong and then at Sky Deutschland; Bruce Dover in China; Tom Mockridge and Jim Rudder at Sky Italia; and Robert Thomson editing *The Times*, before taking over at the *Wall Street Journal* and finally ending up in charge of News Corp's entire publishing division.

The members of this expat network could call each other up at any time to have a chat, and tap into a shared mythology. 'If you were in the loop, it was like a brotherhood. It was loyalty, loyalty, loyalty,' one of these globetrotting Australians recalls.

But over the years, scores of editors and executives also became bitter and burned and felt they had been shafted. 'Rupert would sack anyone after 35 years with the company, even if it was a family friend or a relation,' says one of the discards. 'You don't get to where Rupert has got without dehumanising yourself. One day you're on the nose, you're on the nose, and when your desk gets moved closer to the fire exit you know you're in trouble.'

'Rupert is an unusual man, very intelligent, very smart, and it's a privilege to have worked for him,' says John Cowley, who was crucial to winning Murdoch's war with the British print unions at Wapping in the mid-1980s. 'But he uses people. When he's finished with you he drops you and doesn't bother to talk to you again. It's sad that he does that.'

Malcolm Noad was also frozen out after years of loyal service. Starting as a copy boy in the advertising department at News Ltd in Sydney, he rose to be advertising manager, sales manager and then general manager, which was effectively number two in the company. But he quit in 2004 after three decades with the Murdochs, when he fell out of favour with Lachlan, and Rupert never even bothered to ring and wish him good luck.

Yet even those who felt betrayed by Rupert and lost their love for the man often conceded his brilliance as a businessman. He was always ready to back his judgement, took risks that others would not, and invariably beat his rivals to the punch by acting quickly and decisively and following his instinct. Sure, he made mistakes along the way—like the half-billion dollar losses on MySpace, Delphi, WebMD and One.Tel, and the massive $6 billion loss on Gemstar—but he had had plenty more winners, some of which were far, far bigger.

In the US, in particular, he bet the company repeatedly from the mid-1980s, pulling off bigger and bigger gambles on Sky TV, 20th Century Fox, Fox TV, Fox News and the Fox Cable Network, revitalising a loss-making film studio, creating a fourth free-to-air television network, and then building the country's most successful and profitable cable service. With Fox News he took the extraordinary step of paying cable networks to take his service, thus risking hundreds of millions of dollars to build an audience that might never pay for the product. By mid-2012, these TV and movie businesses made up around three-quarters of News Corp's now US$60 billion market capitalisation and produced 90 per cent of its profits. So it was little wonder that those who worked for Murdoch were prepared to defer to his wisdom.

But as he neared his ninth decade, the doubts were beginning to grow. Was he past it already? How much longer could he last? Who could replace him? More and more the company was relying on one man who had gone well past the age at which most people give up. Within four months of buying the *Wall Street Journal* for US$5.6 billion in 2007, News Corp was forced to write off half the purchase price. 'All his top executives knew that Rupert was paying too much, that it was a vanity deal,' says one of his close advisers. 'Yet no one had the nerve to call him on it. Nor did the board.'

Murdoch's directors may well have assumed that he must be right because he so often was. But whatever the psychology of that particular moment, the fact remained that no one inside News Corp had the power to stop him doing what he wanted, and no one on the board had the balls.

'Most boards meet to make decisions,' the company's former chairman, Richard Searby, famously told a News Corp seminar in Aspen, Colorado, during the 1980s, with his boss in the front row of the audience. 'Ours meets to ratify yours.' And there was no doubt Searby knew what he was talking about, since he spent 21 years at the top of Rupert's corporate empire, from 1971 to 1992, and had shared a study with him in their schooldays at Geelong.

As to why no one inside the company dared take Rupert on, this, too, was easily explained: it was rarely a good career move. There was no room in the Sun King's court for people with too much power, as Sam Chisholm discovered in 1997 after making BSkyB a huge success. And there was no chance of succeeding to the throne if your name did not begin with 'M'. Whilst the family only had 12 per cent of the share capital, it controlled around 40 per cent of the voting shares, which gave the Murdochs an almost unshake-able grip on the succession. As a consequence, several of News Corp's best executives—like Gus Fischer, Andrew Neil, Barry Diller and Richard Searby—eventually departed, either because they were pushed out or because they knew they could rise no further. As late as 2009, News Corp's chief operating officer, Peter Chernin, would also choose to move on because he would never wear the crown.

Rupert was happy to let them depart: there was only room for one emperor, and he was determined his children would inherit the kingdom when he eventually stepped down from the throne. In the 1990s, he spent $800 million to buy his three sisters and their families out of News Corp, so that his own kids would have it all to themselves. But would he ever accept it was time to go? In 1996, he reached the age at which most people retire. Ten years later, and only half in jest, he was talking about sticking around for another twenty years, or until he was 95. And how would he choose his successor? Which one of his children would come out on top?

PART II

HEIRS TO THE THRONE

5
LACHLAN

'Lachlan will take over. He will be the first among equals.'

Rupert Murdoch

Unlike most tycoons, Rupert Murdoch is no philanderer. He is a puritan, a prude and a serial monogamist. In almost six decades since getting hitched in Adelaide in 1956 he has married three wives, sired six children and enjoyed just a couple of months as a single man.

His eldest daughter, Prue, now in her mid-fifties, is ten years older than his third wife, Wendi Deng, whom he is currently divorcing. His youngest daughter, Chloe, is ten. But it will be the ones in the middle, all now in their forties, who will end up running the Murdoch empire, if any of them ever gets to take over. Unless, of course, he surprises us all again.

Rupert married his first wife, Patricia Booker, a flight attendant and former model, in Adelaide, ten days shy of his 25th birthday. But they were not well-matched, and the marriage did not last. Pat was beautiful, gregarious and a party lover, who liked to get out and about and have fun. Rupert hated parties and had no interest in meeting people unless they could help him in business or tell him some gossip. He worked hard, travelled constantly, and preferred the company of men, as he has continued to do. He was married to his work. And Pat understandably felt abandoned.

Prue has never wanted to follow in her father's footsteps and is one of the few people who is happy to tell Rupert what she thinks, which is not always complimentary. She branded him a dirty old man when he married Wendi Deng, who was 37 years younger than him, and attacked him in the media after he famously forgot her existence and declared he had three children, who all wanted to take over. Nor has she ever worked for the family business, apart from a brief spell as a researcher on one of her father's magazines. And she has never been in the race to succeed him, not least because she's a girl.

Prue is plump and short, while her younger siblings are tall, slim and glamorous. But she enjoys the easiest relationship with Rupert because there is less at stake and she is more of an observer than a player in the great family game. She is also delightful, dry, self-deprecating and direct, and tells hilarious tales about her family, like going to a concert with Bill Clinton and upsetting her father by forgetting to shake his hand; or being given a private tour of the Vatican with Rupert and Wendi, and seeing treasures few have seen before, only for her 'stepmother' to cut it short by asking the Monsignor, 'What time do shops shut?'

Prue lives in Vaucluse with fabulous views of Sydney Harbour, but is an Anglophile at heart, missing England so much that she spent six months with the curtains drawn when she first returned to Australia. She is married to a tall, posh Scot, Alasdair MacLeod, who has worked for News Ltd without conspicuous success, and they live in faded grandeur with furniture that needs recovering. She worries that she can't afford to get the chairs reupholstered; she also worries about inviting her richer, smarter siblings, like Lachlan and his model wife Sarah, to visit, in case they find the house not clean enough and want to brush the seats before they sit down.

Prue has inherited some of her grandmother's frugality but also gives generously to the arts and charity, as Dame Elisabeth did. She knows that she will inherit billions of dollars when Rupert dies, but calls it 'Dad's money' and pretends it's not hers, so that she can live a normal life. And she has no desire to run the News Corp empire but will certainly have a say in who does, because she is one of the four children to have a vote in the Murdoch Family Trust, which controls 306.6 million Class B News Corp voting shares, or 38.4 per cent of the total.

Prue's three younger siblings who share this power are Elisabeth, Lachlan and James, the children of Rupert's second wife, Anna Torv, whom he met in 1966, when, as a young cadet on his *Daily Mirror*, she came to interview him. Slim, smart and gorgeous, and thirteen years younger than him, she was just the sort to dazzle her workaholic employer. 'I thought she was a very pretty girl,' Rupert said later. 'Her writing skills were not going through my mind.' She moved to Canberra to be close to him, and they married in April 1967 after Rupert secured his divorce.

At first sight Anna could easily be mistaken for a scion of the British upper class. Poised, charming, gracious and assured, she has the air of a woman born to rule. But she came up the hard way and acquired a few survival skills en route. Born in Glasgow, where her Estonian father and Scottish mother ran a dry-cleaning business, she emigrated to Sydney as a child and grew up in a Blacktown high-rise at the arse end of the western suburbs. In those early years, life was hard and luck was against her. The picnic park that her parents owned went bust, then her mother walked out on the family, leaving Anna to bring up her three younger siblings. She worked in a shop at weekends to supplement the family income, slit open toothpaste tubes to make the money go round, and left school at sixteen to take a job at the local crematorium. Finally, she landed a clerk's position in the finance department of Murdoch's *Daily Mirror*, after which, talent, determination and good looks did the rest. Five years later she was honeymooning in New York with the boss. This new high-flying life was dramatically different from her old one, but she brought to it a streak of steel that would prove invaluable in dealing with Rupert.

Over the next six years, she and her husband commuted between Sydney and London and produced three children. Then, in 1974, they moved to Manhattan and a huge, ritzy apartment on Fifth Avenue, with butlers, staff and nannies, just like Rupert had enjoyed in his childhood. Despite all these trappings, the children were 'delightful, well-bred kids' who were unspoiled by wealth, according to one of Murdoch's Australian executives who saw them regularly at Rupert's farm at Cavan. They had impeccable manners, too, which were a tribute to their mother and grandmother, but also to Rupert, who was still a puritan at heart. 'Personal modesty is becoming,' he explained, 'and you look for that in your children.' They caught buses, lived ordinary lives and never thought themselves special, until their father appeared on the cover of *Time* in 1977 as a monster King Kong, which was not something that happened to everybody's dad.

It was around then, according to Lachlan, the eldest boy, that Rupert started training them for their mission in life. 'Liz, James and I would come up for breakfast before we had to get the bus to school and all the papers would come out and we'd have the *New York Post*, the *New York Times*, the *Daily News* and the *Wall Street Journal*, and as we read the papers my dad would be handing out the stories and saying "Read that", or he'd say "Look at the headline—that's a shocking headline"... so from a very early age—I'm talking now seven or eight years old—we began to understand that we were part of the media business.' This, as it happens, was almost exactly how Rupert had been brought up.

Before long, the kids were also being told over the breakfast table that it would be their duty 'to challenge the old world order on behalf of the people', and that they would be obliged to be 'permanent outsiders and constant nomads'. It was that same old outcast theme playing again, even as Rupert and Anna entertained the political and business elites of New York and lived in luxury at one of the city's best addresses. But if this was exile, it was hardly a trial.

Dinner at the Murdochs' Manhattan residence was a formal affair with smart clothes and servants, which was often shared with an important political or media figure, like the mayor of New York. But before it began, the three kids would be granted a brief audience with Rupert. 'My father would come home; we'd have to get dressed up to see him,' said Lachlan. 'We would have half an hour alone with him before the guests came over.' It was all very old fashioned.

The family's life revolved around their famous dad: Anna would haul the children out of bed at 5.30 in the morning and get them ready to meet him if he was flying into town, because they never knew how long he would stay. It was usually not for long. On the rare occasions he was home, he was usually behind a newspaper, and it was often hard to get his attention. 'Is Daddy going deaf?' James once asked his mother. 'No,' she replied, 'he's just not listening.'

Busy and preoccupied, Rupert was not a very patient parent, and he was certainly no New Age dad. He didn't get down on the floor to wrestle with his kids, in case he rumpled his tie, and when he did find time to play, he always wanted to win, whether he was racing Elisabeth in the pool at Cavan or cheating at Monopoly. Competition among the children was encouraged and praise was rare, which perhaps explains why all three were (and still are) so desperate to prove themselves. He could also be 'insensitive verging on dangerous' in the way he took risks, Anna complained, like when he was giving the kids thrills by towing them at speed behind a snowmobile.

Naturally, neither Elisabeth, Lachlan nor James had any doubt that they would end up in the family firm. They went with their father on business trips to China, tagged along behind him as he tore strips off his editors, posed for pictures with piles of papers in the loading dock of the *New York Post*, and accompanied him to News Corp's annual get-togethers. 'It was always part of my universe that I lived and breathed in,' said Elisabeth. 'We were all completely dedicated to that…It felt completely who we are and what we did and what we all talked about.' It was a desperately serious life.

Nor did any of them have much doubt about who was the chosen one. By the early 1980s, Rupert was assuming that Lachlan would succeed him, telling one of his editors, 'I don't know of any son of any prominent media family who hasn't wanted to follow in the footsteps of his forebears. It's just too good a life.' In later years, he would say that both his sons were interested in taking over. But Elisabeth never figured in his calculations. Nor, of course, did Prue.

The rest of the world began playing 'Who will succeed Rupert?' when the kids started working in the family business in the early 1990s, with a sense that the handover could happen any day, because the media mogul was about to turn 60, 65 or 70. And even though Elisabeth insisted her dad would only retire when he retired from life, this guessing game continued, with Rupert happily playing along, even though it stoked the rivalry between the three children. In 1997, he announced that they had decided: 'Lachlan will take over. He will be the first among equals, but they will all have to prove themselves.'

Five years later, he was anticipating a closer contest, telling an interviewer, 'Lachlan, he has great leadership abilities…James has got great business abilities…He has not had the same experience yet. But there is plenty of time.' Once again, Elisabeth did not rate a mention.

Throughout all this, the children took turns to stress that they were 'a very close family' without 'backstabbing and rivalry', and to tell journalists 'we'd never let it come between us', but Elisabeth tempered this by publicly admitting that they were deeply competitive: 'We're not losers at all. We all want to win.' And James was privately going even further, perhaps. According to one unnamed executive inside News Corporation, he seized on one of the regular articles about Lachlan's destiny and 'Tore it up, crushed it into a ball, and stomped it on the ground'. James denied this story with a blunt 'It's not fucking true'. But another senior News executive recalled the two boys having chin-up competitions at the family's ski lodge in Aspen in their youth, which would only stop when one of them ended up with bloodied hands.

Rupert certainly encouraged his children to argue, come out fighting and disagree, and he was forever telling the media that

Elisabeth, Lachlan and James needed to prove themselves. As a result, Anna was long concerned the race would end in tears. In her novel *Family Business*, written in the 1980s, she imagined a media tycoon who died at the peak of his powers without naming a successor, after which his daughter took over, expanded the empire, and then sold out to a rival to thwart her warring children. In 2001, two years after the break-up of her marriage, she was even more explicit in voicing her concerns, telling the *Australian Women's Weekly*, 'I'd like none of them to [succeed]...I think there's going to be a lot of heartbreak and hardship with this.'

And so there would be, starting with Lachlan, if only because the weight of expectation was always such a great burden for him. As Rupert's oldest son, he was automatically the heir. He was also his father's favourite. Yet he was neither the smartest nor the toughest of the trio and almost certainly the least driven of them all. 'He was a decent, honest boy and a helluva nice guy,' says one man who worked with him for several years, 'but he was never going to be his father'. Yet that's exactly what Rupert wanted him to be.

Educated at an expensive private school in Manhattan, and Princeton University, where he majored in Philosophy and Ancient History, Lachlan was catapulted into a senior role in the family business at the age of twenty-three, straight out of college. In 1994, he was sent to Brisbane to be second-in-charge of Queensland Newspapers, publisher of the *Courier-Mail* and *Sunday Mail* and an assortment of regional titles which made it the most profitable part of the Australian group. There he was naturally measured against the young Rupert, who had taken charge of the *News* and *Sunday Mail* in Adelaide at a similar age, and was just as naturally found wanting. The unanimous verdict, which would be repeated every time he met new people or got promoted, was that he was not a patch on his old man. Unlike Rupert, who had rolled up his sleeves and grabbed his papers by the scruff of the neck, Lachlan was rarely seen on the editorial floor or the subs' desk at the *Courier-Mail*, and made no great name for himself as a journalist or a leader.

And if he did get noticed it was more often for his image than for his talent. At a time when most of Murdoch's managers were still wearing suits and ties, Lachlan sported jeans and boots, rode a powerful Kawasaki motorbike to work and liked to keep his sleeves rolled up to show off his tattoos. He rented a grand mansion in Hamilton, overlooking the river, with a swimming pool, billiard room and views across Brisbane, and liked to invite the younger reporters on the *Mail* up for a swim and a pizza. Occasionally, he would shout journalists a drink in the pub and offer his black Amex in payment, only to find to his puzzlement that Australian bars only took cash. Women constantly threw themselves at him, but he didn't hook up with any of them, which naturally started rumours that he was gay.

All agreed he was nice, pleasant and extraordinarily polite. And most thought he was a decent, genuine guy. He prided himself on his ability to talk to anyone, and was good at putting people at their ease. But some could see that he was swamped. 'Everyone wanted a part of him because he was Rupert's son,' says one executive who knew him well, 'and he just wanted to be treated like a normal human being.' One journalist, who was around his age, remembers him as a 'nice guy but probably not that tough'. Another, who has climbed high up the News Ltd ladder, swears he was 'whip smart...nobody's fool...in love with newspapers', and insists he 'kept people on their toes'. But it has to be said that's a minority view.

Lachlan's boss in Brisbane, the hard-drinking, tough-talking John Cowley, reckoned his young charge was 'a bit out of his depth', but this was hardly surprising, given his age and lack of experience. He had spent three months of his gap year working in the press room in Sydney, where the *Telegraph Mirror* was printed, and a college vacation subbing at *The Sun* in London. But that was just about it. He had not been a journalist, never done an MBA and certainly not run his own business or learnt how to manage people. Now, straight out of a university arts course, he was dealing with hardened newsmen twice his age, and supposedly telling them how to run the company.

The 23-year-old heir was soon to be seen in weekly production meetings, sitting quietly with his notebook, writing stuff down. He'd take the notebook to lunch as well, prompting one journalist to observe that if he were a billionaire's son he would not be working so hard. Keen as he was, the young man still struck some of Rupert's senior executives as terribly naïve. 'He was never going to get an easy ride, being the boss's son', one remembers. 'But he was embarrassing to be around…he kept asking the most basic questions.'

To some, Lachlan seemed to be there on sufferance. He talked to his father on the phone every day, hugged him whenever he came to town and signed off conversations by saying 'I love you'. But he couldn't hide the fact that he was in awe of him and desperate to impress. 'We'd all have dinner with Rupert when he came to Brisbane and there was always a lot of tension in the air,' one journalist remembers. 'Everyone would breathe a sigh of relief when he went to bed, and Lachlan was no different. It seemed Rupert was his boss too. But it must have been a difficult family to grow up in, because he was so dominant and scary.'

'I felt a bit sorry for him really,' recalls Greg Chamberlin, former editor of the *Courier-Mail*. 'He'd been thrust into the operation and everyone expected so much of him.'

It was even harder when he was sent down to Sydney eighteen months later to become deputy managing director of News Ltd, the Murdochs' Australian master company, because expectations were even higher and the job more difficult. One seasoned executive who worked closely with him recalls the young man wanting to show off his new motorbike and thinking that what he really needed was a mother to look after him.

But, as the first-born son, Lachlan could not escape the duties of the dynasty. In 2001, no doubt on Rupert's orders, he was interviewed for an ABC TV documentary on the Murdoch family. Dressed in a suit and tie, but with his hair sticking up like a young pop star, he said gravely, in the American accent he so wanted to shed, 'News Corporation business is my life, as it is my father's and brother's and the whole family—you'll wake up in the middle of the night and you'll be working...every lunch, dinner and even your friends that you make are somehow connected to your work...I hope it's healthy because it's the only thing I've ever known.'

Some felt that it wasn't at all healthy, and that he would have been far better off as a forester or working with his hands. He was more feminine than Rupert, with an interest in interior design and friends in the arts, like the film director Baz Luhrmann and actress Nicole Kidman. But he was also a puzzle. On the one hand he had visions of himself as a gym-going, beer-drinking macho male, with a yellow BMW M5, a race-tuned Ducatti, and a rock-climbing wall in his garage; the sort of man who could survive in the desert with a Bowie knife, or conquer the Sydney-to-Hobart yacht race the year that five boats sank. On the other, he was sensitive and soft. He called his first yacht *Karakoram* after a Pakistani mountain range, and a later boat *Ipixuna*, after a settlement in the Amazon. And on his first foray into the Sydney-to-Hobart, he, Baz Luhrmann and the crew all wore Hawaiian shirts and shorts as their uniform.

But there was nothing especially sensitive about his rise to the top at News Ltd. When he arrived in Sydney in December 1995, the role of second-in-command was already occupied by Bob Muscat, a popular bloke in his mid-fifties who had been in the business, doing a good job, for longer than Lachlan had been alive. But, after a year of conflict, Muscat decided he was never going to win a war with Rupert's son and left the company. His boss, Ken Cowley, brother of John, was soon minded to jump ship too because he didn't want to be stuck between Lachlan and his dad. As a favour to Rupert, Ken agreed to stay on as executive chairman of News Ltd to help steer the operation, but by September 1996, after less than three years in the newspaper business, Lachlan was in charge of the entire Australian business, at the age of 25.

Seeing what had become of Muscat and Cowley, most of News Ltd's senior officers decided to defer to their inexperienced new captain. But this suited Lachlan just fine, because he didn't seem to value advice from his elders, whom he regarded as being out of date and out of touch. 'He thought he had most of the answers,' one senior executive recalls. 'He thought he knew a bit more than he actually did. I don't think he could be taught.'

Other old stagers agreed that he was full of himself and not very smart. And even those with good things to say tended to sprinkle their praise with criticism. 'He was a fascinating mix,' says one News Ltd insider who worked alongside him. 'He was very savvy in lots of ways: he understood tabloids, and he had the respect of the newspapermen at News Ltd including some of the old hands, but he could also be petulant, immature and a spoilt brat, demanding that things be done yesterday without thought of the consequences.'

It was not hard to understand why Lachlan had such a high opinion of himself, given that politicians, fellow businessmen and his employees all competed to flatter him, but there was little in his record to justify his belief. On the credit side of the ledger, he had a better understanding than most of his executives at News Ltd that the company's newspapers needed to engage with the internet. And it was his decision to start the auction site GoFish (which failed), the job site CareerOne (which has been a great success), and to buy realestate.com.au, which would eventually make hundreds of millions of dollars for the group. But on the debit side, he was already responsible for some far more famous disasters.

In the mid-1990s, the Murdochs spent a fortune on a new Super League competition on the east coast of Australia in an attempt to steal the valuable TV rights for rugby league away from Channel Nine, and Lachlan was put in charge of the negotiations to sign up clubs and players for huge amounts of money. It was certainly not all his fault that it ended in tears, but News Ltd lost $500 million and was forced to surrender 50 per cent of Fox Sports plus 25 per cent of Foxtel to its rivals, which ultimately cost the group a great deal more. A couple of years later, Lachlan persuaded his father to put $400 million into One.Tel, a fast-talking, fast-growing but ultimately bankrupt mobile phone company, where News eventually lost its entire investment, and once again he did not cover himself with glory. He played no great part in the business, and in the inquiries and court cases that followed, he was an unimpressive and unhelpful witness, who appeared to remember little and care less about what had gone wrong.

Yet, in spite of these two landmark failures, Rupert rewarded him with a further promotion, bringing him to New York in October 2000, when he was still not 30, to help run News Corporation and be third-in-command of the Murdochs' entire global empire. This was just seven years after he had entered the business as a trainee in Brisbane, which even Lachlan recognised was too fast, too soon. It was probably unfair to expect him to cope with his new role, as one of his older colleagues kindly observed, but his father had asked him to go a year earlier, and a twelve-month stay of execution was all he had managed to win. Indeed, he had hesitated to tell Rupert that he didn't feel ready because he was scared of disappointing him, and had only spoken up at all after being persuaded by friends.

It was not just a fear of not being up to the task that made Lachlan reluctant to go. He was also in love with Australia and felt it was where he belonged. Two months after being sent to the US, he came back to host the annual News Ltd Christmas party at Sydney's Finger Wharf, where 250 of the group's senior journalists and executives gathered to bid him farewell. He was perhaps suffering from jet lag and a few sleepless nights with his new one-year-old son, but as he began talking about how he'd miss his home when he moved, he burst into tears. 'He was really crying. He was terribly upset,' says one person who was there. 'Everyone started clapping him, out of embarrassment, and to give him a chance to compose himself, but it was extraordinary. It seemed like he must have been having a really hard time.' And indeed he was.

In Australia, Lachlan was akin to a rock star: a famous billionaire's son with a beautiful model wife, doted on by the tabloids, which mostly belonged to his family. But in New York, billionaires were a dime a dozen and no one took much notice of him. Nor was it any better at the office, where he was in charge of the ailing *New York Post*, which continued to make heavy losses, and Fox TV, which was a poor cousin to the hugely profitable cable network. Rupert was also constantly going over his head, behind his back, and around him, while the company's two most powerful executives, who ran 20th Century Fox and Fox News respectively, consistently blocked his way. 'Peter Chernin would not let him get involved in Hollywood, and Roger Ailes would not let him get involved in anything,' one fellow executive claimed.

Worse still, many simply felt Lachlan wasn't up to the job. 'Everyone who came across him shook their heads,' says a senior executive who worked in the inner sanctum of the company. 'Charitably, you could say he walked to his own drumbeat. Uncharitably, you would say he was a mediocrity; actually that may not be uncharitable. I'm sitting in meetings with him and I'm thinking I'm smarter than this guy, yet he's holding forth about how we're going to change the way we've always done things.'

Lachlan surrounded himself with a small cadre of loyal follow-ers, and was soon known as 'The Prince' for what was perceived as his petulant and demanding behaviour. 'No one took any notice of him, and everyone tried to avoid contact,' says the former executive, 'because they knew it would be painful, because he didn't listen to adults.'

The tensions came to a head in mid-2005 when Ailes and Chernin decided to take him on. Both extremely talented and smart, they had been toughened by years of high-level corporate combat, and Lachlan simply wasn't in their league. By now, he had also fallen out with his father, who had dressed him down in front of his fellow executives and gone over his head once too often. And he was longing to go back to Australia, which he still regarded as home: he ate Vegemite on toast every morning, followed rugby league, despite almost five years in New York, and had a wife who was keen to return.

The endgame began when Ailes complained to Rupert about a new TV series, *Crime Line*, which he had suggested would be a winner for the 35 Fox TV stations Lachlan ran, but which the young man had refused to commission. Ailes wanted to produce the series himself, and Rupert gave him the go-ahead to do this while his son was away in Australia, telling him, 'Do the show. Don't listen to Lachlan.'

It was a petty thing but it rankled, and as he flew back from Sydney, Lachlan began brooding about his position within the company. According to *New York* magazine's Steve Fishman, who appears to have got the inside running from Lachlan, 'He loved his father, but he felt undercut, maybe humiliated...Where was the respect due a successor, a deputy...a son?'

As soon as he landed in New York, Lachlan jumped on another plane to Los Angeles to have it out with Rupert, knowing his father would never change. 'As their talk progressed,' wrote Fishman, 'both became emotional. "I have to do my own thing," Lachlan told his dad. "I have to be my own man." Then the heir apparent walked away.' It was a huge step to take, because News Corporation had been his entire life since he was seven or eight years old, and he was challenging his father for perhaps the first time ever. Yet the main thing he felt after doing it was relief. 'Not like an anger, not like a disappointment,' Lachlan confided. 'It's more cathartic.'

His elder sister Elisabeth had advised him it might be easier to be a Murdoch from outside the family business, so he made a promise to Rupert in parting that they would get on better in the future. And so it soon proved. Within weeks, he was telling friends, 'My relationship with my dad is better than ever.'

According to Fishman, Lachlan felt he had earned some respect. 'He felt that his dad was secretly proud that he'd walked. "Proud that you are doing your own thing," Lachlan thought, "and you got the balls to do it, the guts to leave, the courage to leave."' But it was perhaps significant, and a touch sad, that as he made this grande geste, Lachlan was still so focused on what his father thought of him.

From the company's point of view it had not been a difficult decision to make. If Rupert was being asked to choose between Chernin and Ailes on the one hand and Lachlan on the other, it was really no contest, because Chernin ran the entire Fox Group, while Ailes had built the hugely profitable Fox News. So, even though Lachlan was his favourite son and had been eternally loyal, Rupert didn't try especially hard to keep him. He did tell him, however, that the door would always be open, and that he would be welcome back in four or five years' time. Lachlan seemed comforted by the thought that this might be possible, although he would have known deep down that things would have to change dramatically for that to occur. 'If I come back, I want to come back on my own terms,' Fishman reported him saying to friends. 'I don't want to be in the same position I was in before.'

A couple of days later, as if to show how unlikely it was that things could ever change that much, Ailes moved into Lachlan's New York office on the Avenue of Americas, thereby underlining the significance and permanence of his defeat.

Lachlan's decision to walk away from his inheritance in August 2005 was a huge shock to his siblings Elisabeth and James, who had grown up with the idea that they would one day share in the running of the business their father had created. For the first time it made them realise that their Murdoch birthright could not be taken for granted, and, quite possibly, that none of them would ever succeed. But it also offered a huge opportunity for one of them to step up and take Lachlan's place. So, which of them was it likely to be?

6
ELISABETH

'She was quiet, sober, almost austere, and very, very straight.'

Howard Gipps

If Elisabeth had been born a boy, back in Sydney in 1968, it would be her birthright, not Lachlan's, to inherit the family's billion-dollar media empire, with its newspapers, movie studios, satellites and TV networks around the world. And she would probably be much better suited to the task.

By common consent she is the toughest, savviest and most ambitious of Rupert's three children with Anna, and the most like her father. She is also the one with the best people skills, as well as being tall, blonde and striking, which is certainly no handicap. Yet she has never been taken seriously as Rupert's successor because her father is an old-fashioned chauvinist, who is far more comfortable with men and saw no need to appoint a female director to News Ltd until he'd been running the business for almost 30 years.

Reading between the lines, Elisabeth had a less-than-wonderful childhood. After being shuttled between England and Australia for the first six years of her life, she grew up in New York as an immigrant and an outsider: a runny-nosed kid with knee socks and a pom-pom, who was 'completely uncool', or so she maintains. Like her two brothers, she was sent to an exclusive day school in Manhattan, where most of the families were as rich and famous as her own. But at the age of thirteen, she was packed off to boarding school in Australia for a lonely year at Geelong Grammar, which she hated almost as much as her father had done. And after that, she was dispatched to another posh establishment in Connecticut, where she lasted six months before being suspended for smuggling rum into school and getting her classmates smashed. Her mother refused to talk to her for four days afterwards, while Rupert, ever the indulgent father, told her not to worry. Having been a rebel himself, he was pleased to see that some of it was rubbing off onto his children.

These constant changes of school and country meant she continually had to make new friends, and this perhaps affected her self-confidence, as did the fact that her brothers were so much more important in the Murdoch clan. In her teens, she was awkward and overweight, until, mid-way through university at New York's exclusive Vassar College, she went on a diet, started studying hard and, according to a schoolmate, 'completely turned herself around'. Yet even then there remained something slightly bruised about her.

Despite not being seen as her brothers' equal, Elisabeth never questioned the fact that she would go into the family business. But she was not to be parachuted into a top job at News Ltd for the start of her brilliant career. Fresh from her studies, she was sent to Channel Nine in Sydney, where she served an apprenticeship as a programming and promotions assistant before ending up as a researcher on *A Current Affair*, chasing

TV repairmen and neighbours from hell. Had she not already realised she wasn't the chosen one to succeed her father, this would surely have been enough to convince her. But if she felt this was unfair—and you can bet she did—she just buckled down and tried twice as hard.

Those who worked with the 21-year-old Elisabeth remember a diligent, modest young woman with an American accent and a serious outlook on life. 'She was quiet, sober, almost austere, and very, very straight, a bit like a convent girl,' says Howard Gipps, who was a reporter on the program. Others judged her to be 'sweet', 'chaotic', 'hard working' and 'fun to be with', and none would have guessed she was a billionaire's daughter, had they not already known. 'She had no airs and graces and no expectation she'd be treated specially,' says David Hurley, who was then *A Current Affair*'s chief of staff. 'We had instructions from on high to be nice to her but to do her no favours. I think Rupert fixed that with Kerry.'

Unlike her younger brother Lachlan, who would have a huge house in Elizabeth Bay, an expensive ocean racer and fashionable film-star friends, Elisabeth lived a remarkably ordinary life. She worked hard and did all the shit jobs, including the hated 5 a.m. and weekend shifts, without complaint. She rented a modest house in Cammeray, drew most of her friends from Channel Nine, and had yet to cut her filial ties to home. She called her father once a week, but was much closer to her mother, Anna, who flew out to Australia to help clean her house before she moved in. 'I remember thinking if I had their money I'd pay someone else to do it,' says Sharon O'Neill, then an ACA producer.

Though in her twenties and away from home, Elisabeth still took orders from her mum about what to wear. When she flew over to London in 1993 for Gretel Packer's wedding, armed with an outfit bought in Sydney, Anna immediately deemed the choice unsuitable and marched her off to the shops to find another. She even put up with her mother's hand-me-down computer, despite the family's enormous wealth. 'It was a crappy laptop with a whole lot of her mother's files still on it,' says Gipps, who was asked to fix it when it went wrong. 'I couldn't understand why, with all their money, they wouldn't fit her out with the best bit of technology available.' But that was how the Murdochs ensured their children didn't end up like other rich brats.

As a producer, young Liz didn't shoot the lights out, but was 'a good kid, and quick on the uptake' according to Hurley, and she was popular, too. 'I really liked her,' says David 'Tangles' Ballment, a sound recordist, who remembers her as 'incredibly capable for someone that young...She was only 21 or 22 but she was able to take charge.' And despite her youth, this hard-working Cinderella already had a talent for making people feel special. The ABC's Eric Campbell, then a reporter on *Getaway*, met her at a party and will never forget the impression she made. 'Even as a young intern she had the networker's gift of making you the most interesting person in the room. For ten minutes, a crappy Australian travel program I worked on was the most fascinating thing she'd ever heard of.'

After two years in Sydney learning the trade (which would be enough for Lachlan to become deputy managing director of the Murdochs' Australian business), Elisabeth moved to the back-blocks of the US to be program director at News Corp's Fox13 TV station in Salt Lake City, where she became lasting friends with the news director, Lisa Grigorisch, who is now one of America's top TV news producers. 'I have a million fond memories of Liz,' she says. 'We went to lunch every day, just her and I. The local sushi place even named a roll after us. It was like a California roll but with eel on top.'

But once again, the biggest impression she made was in how diligent she was. 'She was a harder worker than anybody I've ever seen,' Lisa recalls. 'I think she had something to prove to herself and to her family about independence. I'd get in at 7.30 a.m. and she'd already be there, and she was still there when I left at 6.00 p.m. that night.'

Fox13's station manager, Steve Carlston, was also impressed, finding her bright, humble and teachable, and a good team player, and adding, 'She never made you feel like her last name was Murdoch.' An hour after he sat her down for her annual performance review, she was back in his office to tell him how she planned to improve. She was also brave: a fearless skier, who rode her mountain bike to work along the freeway, much to Carlston's amazement, and wasn't afraid to stand up for what she believed in, like defending gay rights in this fiercely Mormon city. On one occasion, says Carlston, Fox13 ran a story on date rape, which caused a business associate to tell her at lunch that 'No doesn't always mean No, because sometimes women really do want it, and they just play games', or something like that. 'And Liz tore shreds off his argument. She said very calmly, "You are wrong and this is why." The guy kept pushing though, and she told him she wouldn't be budged on her opinion. He was being really nasty, but she didn't lose her cool. She just ended the luncheon and left.'

Elisabeth was soon leaving Salt Lake City, too, taking another small step on the News Corp ladder to work on Fox's new FX channel in Los Angeles, where she was a junior programmer, selling 'daytime TV from a loft in Manhattan to cable operators who all wore cowboy hats'. But in late 1994, with Lachlan already nearing the top at News Ltd in Australia, she decided she might climb faster and gain more respect from her father if she struck out on her own. So, just 26, with almost no experience in management, she persuaded Rupert to guarantee a US$35 million bank loan to fund the purchase of two tiny TV stations in California, midway between San Francisco and Los Angeles. This was a brave move, even for a Murdoch, especially since her father was sceptical, but at least he was standing behind her. Making it braver still was the fact that she was seven months' pregnant with her first child. The previous year she had married Elkin Pianim, the son of a well-known Ghanaian dissident who had spent ten years in jail. Her new husband, whom she had met at college, was funny, smart and good-looking, but since he was black and had studied Marxist economics at university, he was perhaps not what her father had wished for.

With Pianim and a baby daughter in tow, Elisabeth threw herself into making the two TV stations a success, even riding in the local rodeo to clinch a car dealer's sponsorship. Naturally, she also relied on the Murdoch family recipe of introducing a bit more crime and sex, and cutting costs by sacking staff. And this caused instant outrage with the locals. 'People who had been there for many years suddenly found themselves out of work,' says San Luis Obispo talk-show host, Dave Congalton, who led the campaign against her. 'I understand why she did what she did, but it was callous and paid no respect to the place she'd just rocketed into. She was a Murdoch and that's how she did things—but we're a small town and it's not how we are here.'

Liz also fired the popular news anchor, Rick Martel, who had been there for years and was a local favourite. 'I'm a tired old man,' he says today, 'and I don't want to dredge up bad memories. But it was terribly distressing for me and a lot of my co-workers. She was an ass, and she wouldn't listen to any advice.'

'The backlash was incredible,' Martel's replacement as newsreader, John Summer, recalls, 'and there's still some bad feeling in the community. Other media were cruel to her, very harsh.' But she was tough enough to confront her critics, manning the phones at the TV station to take a flood of angry calls. And this earned her grudging respect. 'She was prepared to take the heat,' admits Congalton. 'Instead of slinking off, she sat at the desk and took every complaint call herself, for hours and hours.'

Liz was also smart enough to win over the local chamber of commerce, whose president, David Garth, was an opinion leader in the town. 'She was blunt and straightforward,' he recalls, 'but she was also powerful, and all that made her attractive.' Summer, too, was won over by her looks and her apparent sincerity. 'She was young and beautiful and seemed driven to prove herself,' he says. 'You got a sense that she actually cared.'

The San Luis Obispo station, in a rundown 1920s radio building, was a crumbling little facility with outdated equipment and everyone crammed into one tiny office, but 'the people were wonderful', according to Summer, and they gave their best for their popular young boss, who often brought her daughter along to meetings. And together they made it all work. After sixteen months, ratings had risen, profits were up 30 per cent and Elisabeth was selling out for a $12 million profit. George Lily, who bought the station, was hugely impressed: 'I'm a fan from beginning to end,' he says. 'She was gracious, helpful, and hands on with everything. She had natural leadership skills, was good at delegating, knew everybody's name and got the best out of them. If I'd had the chance, I would have hired her on the spot.'

Asked by a local reporter what she planned to do next, Elisabeth said she might buy another TV station or do an MBA at Stanford, but her real ambition was to run something at News Corp. And for once, her father was listening, because he was soon on the phone telling her scornfully, 'You don't need a fucking MBA. Go to Sky and learn about digital television.'

So, in 1996, after her brief flurry of independence, she found herself back in the family firm, at BSkyB in London, which was then being run for Rupert by the legendary Australian TV executive, Sam Chisholm, who was not in the least delighted to see her. At first, she found herself banished to the call centre in Livingston, Scotland, 700 kilometres from headquarters. Then, after her father had elevated her to chief programmer and brought her back to London, she was belittled as the 'management trainee' by Chisholm, who told his colleagues she knew 'fuck all' about television. Finally, she went off on maternity leave with her second child and discovered that he had changed her program schedules, whereupon she complained to her father, and Chisholm quit in a huff, clutching a large pay-off. The two alpha males had been clashing repeatedly, with Sam fielding abusive calls from Rupert in Los Angeles and feeling he deserved more thanks for making BSkyB such a success, so his exit was probably inevitable. But he had discovered how dangerous it could be to stand between Murdoch and his children.

Not wanting to suffer a similar squeeze, BSkyB's managing director, David Chance, also packed his bags and left. Yet, even with these two departures, Elisabeth still missed out on the top job at the network. To make things worse, her father then told her via the newspapers that she wasn't yet ready for the responsibility, and needed to work out how many children she was having. Not surprisingly, she did not take this criticism well, and would have walked out there and then, had she been more confident. But she stayed lest her father think her a failure, and bristled as her brothers continued to rise. She hadn't yet worked out that it might be Rupert's fault they were doing so much better than she was.

By this time, her personal life was also in disarray. Playing superwoman in California, where she had managed a family and two TV stations, had stretched her to the limit. But she now had a second daughter and was exhausted by her battles with Chisholm. Her short-lived marriage to Pianim had also broken apart; her own parents were splitting up after more than 30 years; and to cap it all, she was having an affair with the married Matthew Freud, who was handling BSkyB's PR. She was thin, stressed and overworked, and her colleagues were worried about her.

Despite all these pressures, she buckled down to a new job as head of Sky Networks—running everything but sport—and won the respect of her team. 'She was fantastic, very savvy, hugely enthusiastic, and a great person to work for,' says one Australian executive who worked closely with her. 'But she could also be pretty fucking hard if you got on the wrong side of her. She absolutely had that steel.' Others who had been in the Chisholm camp were not so convinced of her talents, suggesting she was 'hard as nails', 'remarkably cocky for someone who knew so little about television', and had only got the job because of her father. There was also gossip about how hard she was partying with Freud, whom most of her colleagues and her father clearly disliked.

It was perhaps not surprising, then, that she again missed out on the top job at BSkyB when the CEO's role fell vacant for a second time, in 1999. For almost a year she managed to swallow her disappointment, but then decided she had to leave. She was angry at being undervalued, and desperate to have something her father couldn't take away from her, but she also wanted to be more creative and make TV. And above all she needed to prove she was worthy, that common ache of the Murdoch children. She broke the news to her father in May 2000 by faxing him a copy of the press release announcing her resignation. In the row that followed, she told him, 'Dad, you are so pissed at me now you might as well know I'm pregnant with Matthew's child.'

Matthew Freud was seriously well-connected long before he bedded a Murdoch. A great grandson of Sigmund Freud, who introduced the world to psychoanalysis, he was also the son of Sir Clement Freud, a well-known MP and author, the nephew of Lucian Freud, one of Britain's leading modern painters, and the brother of Emma Freud, the TV host married to Richard Curtis, who wrote *Four Weddings and a Funeral*. But he was rich and successful in his own right, too. In the 1980s and 1990s he had made millions in PR, with celebrity clients like the Spice Girls and Uri Geller, and international brands like Pepsi, Mars and Nike. And he had also become close to Tony Blair and New Labour, whom he had latched onto as an unofficial adviser.

Freud had also picked up plenty of enemies along the way, earning himself unflattering nicknames like 'Matthew Fraud' and 'Roland Rat', and had enjoyed what one might describe as a colourful career. In his youth, he had been expelled from Westminster, one of the most expensive schools in England, where he had sold *Playboy* centrefolds stolen from his father. Shortly afterwards, he had been busted for possession of cocaine and marijuana, which his girlfriend claimed he was selling to rock stars and royalty. Then, having escaped with a £500 fine, he had landed a public relations job for a record company, where having such stuff on your CV can be an advantage. And before long he had become almost a rock star himself.

By the time *Vanity Fair* called at his country house in early 2001 to write about his impending marriage to Elisabeth, with whom he had just had a daughter (her third), he was getting about in a chauffeur-driven Bentley, a Ferrari 360 or a huge Lincoln Navigator, favoured by drug lords in *The Wire*, and riding a big Harley-Davidson. He was also greeting the interviewer in 'skin-tight Agnes B leather pants' displaying a bulge the size of a codpiece. No doubt all this was hugely exciting for someone as straight-laced as Liz, with her Presbyterian heritage and convent-girl past.

She told the magazine that they were soul-mates and perfect for each other. But before the article was even published, they had split for the second time in a year. A brief nervous breakdown later— on Matthew Freud's part—they married in the private chapel at Blenheim Palace in Oxfordshire, home to the Dukes of Marlborough. Her two younger brothers both made speeches, while her father read a toast to the bride. This was written by the new editor of the *News of the World*, Rebekah Brooks, who had just become the youngest editor on Fleet Street. Already a favourite of Rupert's, the formidable Ms Brooks (or Wade as she was then) was close enough to Elisabeth to have rented a cottage nearby and to be one of the half-dozen women invited to her hen party in Paris.

Five months earlier, in March 2001, Elisabeth had launched her new TV production company, Shine, despite a warning from her father that she was 'completely insane', and had found herself staring at the wall of a small, empty office at the scruffy end of Ladbroke Grove, wondering whether it had been such a good idea. But she had not entirely cast herself adrift, because BSkyB had stumped up money for a shareholding and agreed to buy a proportion of her output for the first two years, while her business partner, Lord Alli, the former head of one of Britain's biggest TV companies, Carlton, had already made a killing with a similar venture. She was also not cutting her ties from the Murdoch clan for good. 'I'll never leave the family business,' she assured one interviewer. 'I don't see this as something that means I would never go back.'

Elisabeth claimed to be inspired by great BBC programs, like *Walking with Dinosaurs*, *Spooks* and *The Office*, but she was soon turning out stuff that was much more tuned to a mass-market audience, of the sort that might read *The Sun*, with programs like *The Biggest Loser*, *Gladiators*, *MasterChef*, *100 Greatest Sexy Moments* and *The Unofficial World Records of Sex*, which took a light-hearted look at 'feats of a biological nature', such as how many tiddly-winks can be stuffed inside a man's foreskin. Almost all were enormously successful.

Elisabeth's grandmother, Dame Elisabeth, probably never caught the foreskin show back home at Cruden Farm, but she was none-theless shocked that Elisabeth was daring to compete for her brothers' birthright. 'She is very ambitious, very ambitious,' she told the *Australian Women's Weekly* somewhat disparagingly in 2003, adding that she had never been close to her namesake, and that her grand-daughter was the only Murdoch child who had never written to thank her for presents. 'She's running her own company now,' she observed. 'Apparently, she is much happier.'

And so she was. Having already demonstrated a talent for managing and motivating people, Elisabeth now found she had the knack of picking the public taste. She was soon boasting that she had alerted her father to *Pop Idol* before it was transformed into one of the world's most popular shows. She was in Britain on a Saturday evening, she later recounted, while the entire country was watching the show. 'I called Dad because I was so excited about it. "Dad, I don't know if anyone at Fox knows about this show, but I'm telling you that you have to buy this show."' The people at Fox were sceptical of its merit, but Rupert ordered them to buy the rights, nevertheless, and his daughter's instinct was dramatically vindicated. For the next ten years, *American Idol* was the top-ranked TV show in the US.

Even better than this, perhaps, Elisabeth soon showed she had inherited her father's eye for a deal. Before long, Shine was buying up other production companies and cornering the market. And while it was Murdoch family money that made this all possible, she spent wisely and well, so the business prospered. This was better than Lachlan was managing to do in Australia, where, after quitting the company in 2005, he spent hundreds of millions of dollars without success, in an attempt to show he could also go it alone.

Almost as soon as Elisabeth left the fold, Rupert was admitting he would love to have her back, telling one journalist, 'She is a very, very hard-working and intelligent person, and she just loves the business.' But he was aware that this was unlikely to happen soon. 'I don't think she wants to, at least for a few years,' he said. 'She wants to be sure she has been successful in her own right. She will probably sell it [Shine] for a bloody fortune to someone. And then she will come knocking on the door, and she will be very welcome.'

Not only was Elisabeth well on the way to proving her father right, by turning Shine into one of Britain's leading production companies, she and Matthew were also rapidly becoming one of the country's most powerful couples, with top-level connections in politics, the media and show business. Widely renowned for their A-list dinners in London, with guests like Bono, Mick Jagger,

Michael Bloomberg and Hollywood movie mogul Harvey Weinstein, they soon joined the ranks of the landed gentry by acquiring
a magnificent 22-bedroom mansion in Oxfordshire, called Burford
Priory. Complete with private chapel, library, loggia and seven
reception rooms, Matthew and Elisabeth bought it off the Bene-
dictine nuns in 2008 for £4.5 million, and then spent another
couple of million pounds on renovations, adding a swimming pool
and private cinema. Not content with a two-to–three-metre-high
wall around the property, they also added closed-circuit TV and a
lodge, to house a full-time security guard.

Originally an Elizabethan house, which had been remodelled in
the mid-1640s by the Speaker of the House of Commons, William
Lenthall, Elisabeth and Matthew's new weekender had seen kings
and queens gracing its halls down the years, and the new owners
did their best to prolong that tradition with a series of spectacular
parties. Shortly after moving in, they held a big bash for Elisabeth's
40th birthday, at which the former prime minister, Tony Blair, and
future prime minister, David Cameron, were among the guests,
along with the then Foreign Secretary, David Miliband, the future
Treasurer, George Osborne, and the well-known Labour fixer,
Peter Mandelson. Also present were the editors of Rupert's notorious tabloids, Rebekah Brooks and Andy Coulson.

In recognition of this networking power, Britain's society
magazine, the *Tatler*, was soon anointing Elisabeth and Matthew
as the nation's second most powerful couple and identifying
Elisabeth, somewhat absurdly, as 'the world's most powerful
blonde', while London's *Standard* was cooing, 'If the media is the
new royalty, then these two are on the throne.'

But come August 2005, when Lachlan quit News Corp and
threw the race for the Murdoch succession wide open, much

of this fame and fortune still lay ahead of her, and Elisabeth was showing absolutely no signs of wanting to rejoin the family business that her brother was so keen to abandon. And this appeared to leave James as the only one of Rupert's children who was still in the running.

7
JAMES

'I saw someone thrown in the deep end, wondering what the hell to do.'

Warren Fahey

Given that they were born only eighteen months apart, it was almost inevitable that Lachlan and James would be rivals, especially since the younger boy was reckoned to be smarter than his brother. And, because James knew he would never be first choice to take over the empire, he tried doubly hard to prove his worth, which in the Murdoch family was quite an achievement.

At the exclusive Horace Mann School in Manhattan, he was 'a smart, sweet, interesting kid' who worked 'really, really hard', according to one of his teachers, because he was desperate to excel.

He was also 'creative', 'gifted' and 'a talented artist', according to his old classmate Greg Corbin, who remembers him doing huge charcoal sketches and tacking them up on the walls around the school. 'You knew he was a Murdoch because of the name,' says Corbin, 'but he never talked about it, never, ever, ever. James was a very humble guy.'

At Harvard University, where he studied visual arts and entertainment, he was forever busying himself with artistic projects, or drawing cartoons for the *Harvard Lampoon*, for which he created a character called Albrecht the Hun, a gentle warrior who preferred reading to rape and pillage, and rarely did what was expected of him. That was much like James, according to his friends.

Back then, the youngest Murdoch was the rebel of the family, who claimed to have no desire to join the family business. He grew a beard, dyed his hair blond, and had a tattoo of a light bulb on his arm. He also dropped out of college before the end of his course, drove his Harley-Davidson around America, spent a year on an archaeology dig in Italy and was mad about German punk music. But best of all, he famously fell asleep at a press conference in Sydney, where he was sent by Rupert as a fifteen-year-old to spend his school holidays working on the *Daily Mirror*. What better symbol could there be of disdain for the dynasty than for the son of the world's most powerful newspaper proprietor to be caught snoozing on the job and end up with his picture in the *Sydney Morning Herald*, owned by the Murdochs' biggest rivals?

But these pointers aside, it's hard to believe James's rebellion ever ran too deep. At Harvard, he was a member of the superexclusive Porcellian Club, which counts the celebrated Winkelvoss twins among its recent members and a former US president among its famous luminaries. And, despite his constant attempts to appear cool, he is generally remembered as earnest, serious and hard working, despite his radical garb.

'He had red or blonde hair, torn jeans and piercings,' says Dan Bruns, the former chief executive of Delphi, the internet company where James was sent for work experience in 1994. 'But he was smart and engaged and respectful, and it was obvious he wanted to learn.' The 21-year-old made no fuss about his father forcing him to work during his college vacation and he was certainly no rabble-rouser. Indeed, he came across as humbler than his elder brother, Lachlan, who wore shiny suits, 'thought he knew a lot' and struck Bruns as 'a bit of a twat'.

But in 1995, at the end of his third year, James did indeed drop out of Harvard and move back to New York to help a couple of college friends set up a hip-hop record label. 'I wanted to break out on my own,' he explained in that familiar Murdoch refrain. 'This is something I can prove myself with.'

Soon afterwards, he was hanging out at Rawkus's office in Manhattan, 'a funky Tribeca loft situated between a porn shop and a falafel joint', among half-eaten takeaway meals and empty Marlboro cartons. Doing his best to escape his Murdoch heritage, he had stuck a Chairman Mao poster on the wall and was wearing 'a moth-eaten sweater and thrift-shop corduroys', according to the *New Yorker*, while exuding 'a guileless, I'll-wash-my-hair-one-of-these-days charm'.

But, again, the radical image masked a less confident side to James. One person who worked alongside him at Rawkus remembers a shy, distant, buttoned-up young man, who was awkward around artists and 'a stiff kind of character'. And some were not clear why he was there, because he didn't seem to understand hip hop or the music business. However, from the company's point of view, his role was vital, because Rawkus was burning cash by the bucket load and he was signing the cheques. Indeed, James seems to have been spending his own funds on the project, which might explain why his rebellion did not last too long.

When tackled by a journalist about nepotism—always a touchy subject in Murdoch circles—he snapped back that his father had nothing to do with the business, and Rawkus intended to remain independent. But, two months later, Rupert made him and his partners an offer they couldn't refuse. There is no public record of the price News Corp paid, or of the state of the company's finances, but estimates start around US$20 million for a half-share in the business, which was losing money and had only been around for eighteen months. No doubt, this was small change for the Murdoch empire, but the deal was of highly questionable value to other News Corp shareholders, who found, not for the first or last time, that family matters outweighed strict business interest.

So, in December 1996, James's year of glorious revolution came to an end, and he was catapulted onto the corporate ladder, as Lachlan had been, far nearer to the top then he deserved. Barely 24, and with no business experience, he was put in charge of News Corp's music and internet division. Days later, when he was wheeled out for his first news conference in Los Angeles, he had bought himself a Brooks Brothers suit, cut and washed his hair, and become the Ivy League boy he was so keen to escape.

Perhaps shocked at what he had done, or in a vain attempt to burnish his fading rebel image, he was soon telling News Corp's annual get-together that the job his father had given him was 'bullshit', because he had no money and nothing to manage. But this wasn't entirely true.

For a start, it was James's job to sort out the future of Festival Records in Sydney, which had once been a great Australian company. With its roll call of famous stars, like Johnny O'Keefe, the Bee Gees, Kylie Minogue and Olivia Newton-John, Festival had made News a fortune since 1960, when Rupert had snapped it up for £80 000, but it had fallen on hard times, was losing money, and was stuck in a time warp. Housed in the beautiful art-deco Castrol building in Pyrmont, it still employed tea ladies and offered a tuck shop; its contracts with artists were written on paper napkins and piled into shoeboxes; and there was no email or internet. Worst of all, its warehouse still contained 60 000 different recordings, most of which were lucky to sell a couple of copies a year.

James was supposed to be mentored in his new role by one of Rupert's most experienced managers, Alan Hely, who had run the company for years. But there were some sharp disagreements, and Hely quickly decided he had had enough. He later described James as 'a nice-enough young man' but 'naïve and full of himself'. Nor was Rupert around to assist. He had visited Festival only a couple of times in three-and-a-half decades, and had never been interested in the company unless it had spare cash to offer. And he had even less time to be bothered with it now News Corp had become so big. Besides, he seemed more than happy to give James his head and let him learn the trade in a business where it wouldn't cost too much if he made mistakes.

So, with the help of Roger Grierson, an ex-punk musician hired from Polygram, the new young boss set about making the much-needed changes himself, dumping the smaller labels, culling the stock and sacking staff, amid much pain. He and Grierson then began jetting round the world to conferences and holding strategy meetings to plot a way forward. But it was becoming harder and harder for independents to compete against the big multinationals, and, according to Warren Fahey, who ran the company's Larrikin Records division, it was an impossible task. 'We knew LPs were finished, CDs were on the way out, digital downloads were taking over and piracy was a huge problem. But we didn't know what to do about it. We were all scratching around.'

Fahey remembers sharing a train journey with James from Cannes to Rome and finding him great company. 'He liked to smoke and drink the odd bourbon and coke, or four, and he had good ideas,' he says. 'But I saw someone thrown in the deep end, wondering what the hell to do. We all were.'

Grierson travelled with James a lot and liked him enormously. They drank together in a succession of bars in London, Los Angeles and New York, where he would happily chat away to strangers. 'No one had any idea who he was. I'd tell them he was James Murdoch, and they'd say, "No kidding, he's a really nice guy."' According to Grierson, the young man also had principles. 'He wasn't just interested in profit. He wanted to make Festival into the best record company, to restore it to its former glory.'

But even though they signed one of the best Australian bands of the time, Powderfinger, and notched up more local #1 albums than any of their rivals, there was nothing much they could do to stem the tide. And one of James's deals was a conspicuous failure. Shortly after taking the job, he agreed to buy out News's partner, Michael Gudinski, from Mushroom Records for some $40 million, to stop him shifting the company's business to Sony. Grierson maintains this had to be done if Festival were to have a chance of survival. But James paid well over the odds, and his expensive bet did not come off. The purchase was eventually reversed at a fraction of the price, and Festival was sold for a pittance in 2005, long after James had moved on.

However, if the trainee tycoon couldn't save the business, he gave it a good shot. He was 'smart and focused', according to Grierson, and 'good at getting to the core of the problem'. So was he up to the job? 'Let's say it was great experience for him, and if you're a Murdoch you can afford to have experiences like that,' says Jeremy

Fabrinyi, another key executive. 'But Festival never really delivered what News wanted in terms of profit, so on that basis maybe he wasn't a great success.'

James also left a good impression with his colleagues. Fabrinyi found him 'charming, friendly, and great to work with', while Grierson remembers him as 'self-deprecating, funny and respectful', and recalls he insisted on calling everybody, including the barman, 'Sir'. They couldn't help noticing that he talked to Rupert every day, mostly about family stuff, and that he clearly adored his father. 'He worshipped him,' says Grierson. 'He couldn't get enough of him.'

Like all the Murdoch children, James had been brought up to be courteous and polite. And in these days he never behaved as though he was born to rule. Nor was he a typical alpha male. Still a bohemian at heart, he preferred books and music to survival tests, and displays of wealth left him cold. When Lachlan bought a waterfront house in Sydney's Point Piper, with a big pool and glass elevators, James laughingly referred to it as his 'James Bond super-villain pad' and shook his head, saying, 'Sometimes I really wonder about my family.' His own taste was more artistic: he owned a 1976 Cadillac Eldorado convertible and a 1960 Alfa Romeo, which he kept in Los Angeles, where he spent much of his time.

Back in the US, the youngest Murdoch was responsible for much larger amounts of money being risked in News Corp's new media division, where it mattered far more if he was a failure. But there was no one at News Corp who appeared to have the magic touch in this area. Since the early 1990s, Rupert and his advisers had been trying to make their fortune on the internet by finding great new ideas or great new entrepreneurs, like Yahoo's Jerry Yang, who was then on track to his first $1 billion. But their bets on online gaming companies like Kesmai, or internet providers like Delphi, had racked up close to $1 billion in losses. And James proved equally inept at picking winners, which was hardly surprising, given that he had no experience in computer technology, venture capital, high finance, management or the media, any of which might have come in handy.

His first triumph, in January 1997, a month into the job, was to persuade Rupert to pay US$450 million for Pointcast, which James believed was 'a change-the-world kind of product'. Based in Silicon Valley, along with its chief rival, Yahoo, it promised to guide people through the bewildering new world of the internet, by getting its 'push technology' to deliver news, sport and stock prices to people's screensavers without the need to go surfing. By late 1996, the company had output deals with the *Los Angeles Times*, *Boston Globe* and CNN; marketing agreements with Netscape and Microsoft; and funding from the likes of General Electric, Compaq and Knight Ridder Newspapers. It was also adding 250 000 new customers a month, which had plenty of people, apart from the Murdochs, tipping it as the 'next big thing'.

'They were planning to go public that summer,' James explained. 'We approached them and talked about working together.'

Fortunately, by a great stroke of luck, News Corp's near half-billion-dollar offer was rejected, because the sellers held out for more money, and James was able to dodge the bullet. Within a year, Pointcast had been run out of town by Yahoo; within two years it had disappeared into the sunset and been sold for a paltry US$7 million. A decade later, the *Wall Street Journal* and Fox News would brand it one of the ten worst ideas the net had ever seen, because it had demanded so much bandwidth that companies banned it from their networks and users grew old waiting for it to load.

Another of James's picks, in December 1999, was a US$1 billion punt on Healtheon-WebMD, to link patients, doctors and insurers over the net, but this fared even worse than Pointcast, losing almost half the money that News committed. Most of this disappeared within the first six months, as the share price tanked and the company racked up losses of US$4 billion. But worst by a long chalk was the disastrous US$9 billion merger between TV Guide and Gemstar International, championed by James, which eventually cost News Corp a mind-boggling US$6 billion, making Lachlan's mishap at One.Tel look like chump change.

Just in case any further insult were needed, James fared almost as badly in Asia, where he caused News to spend US$150 million at the height of boom on some twenty dot.coms, including NetEase, renren and Indya. 'Within a year none of these investments would be worth a fraction of the value paid for them,' says Bruce Dover, then one of the Murdochs' top people in China. 'Within two years all but a couple had disappeared altogether.'

Yet, amazingly, none of these mishaps slowed the young maestro's progress up the ladder, because Rupert continued to believe in him.

On his 28th birthday, in December 2000, after four not very successful years in the business, James was promoted to the board of News Corporation, the Murdochs' master company. Seven months before that, he had been given the job of running STAR TV, the US$2.5 billion pay-TV network, based in Hong Kong. Explaining to *Time Asia* how his promotion had come about, James confessed he had been sitting in a London restaurant when he got a call from his father, telling him to 'Think about China'. Days later, in New York, Rupert had followed this up by asking him, 'Do you like Chinese food?'

'And that was kind of it,' James recalled. 'It had been decided.'

Whether it had really been so cavalier, only he or Rupert could say. But as the magazine wryly observed, no other college drop-out with his track record could have snagged a job running a network that beamed its signal across Asia in eight different languages. However, James was ready for these cries of nepotism. 'People say, "He's a Murdoch. He doesn't know what he's doing,"' he told the magazine, 'but we deal with it. My brother deals with it, my sister deals with it. My family deals with it.' And in some ways, the appointment was perfect, because the Chinese respected dynasties and were flattered to have a direct line to the boss, who was only a phone call away. 'I talk to him as much as I can,' James explained. 'He's great at all this.' There was even a picture of Rupert on James's office wall—instead of Chairman Mao—towering over Manhattan in his King Kong garb on *Time*'s famous front cover.

When James took over at STAR, News Corp's investment was looking decidedly sick. Over the previous seven years, it had sunk almost US$2 billion into the network in the hope of getting access to the lucrative Chinese market, where a potential audience of 1 billion people awaited, but it had been blocked all the way by the Chinese government. Back in 1993, Rupert had sealed his own fate by predicting that the internet and satellite TV would cause huge problems for totalitarian governments, because they would connect their citizens to the world. Coming just four years after China's brutal crackdown on democracy protesters in Tiananmen Square, this boast had incensed the Communist leaders, who had instantly squashed any chance of STAR broadcasting to their citizens, first by banning the distribution, sale and use of satellite dishes, then by getting the Public Security Bureau to confiscate those already in use.

Since then, Rupert had been grovelling furiously to China's rulers to repair the damage. First, he had dropped the BBC from STAR's Hong Kong satellite service. Then he had paid Deng Xiaoping's daughter a reputed US$1 million for English rights to her biography of 'China's Paramount Leader'. Next, he had canned former Hong Kong governor Chris Patten's critical memoirs in 1998. Then he had laid into the Dalai Lama as 'a political old monk in Gucci shoes'. And finally he had apologised to Premier Jiang Zemin, pretending his original remarks had not been about China at all.

So James's first priority was to have another shot at getting the satellite ban removed, and within months he was proving at least as good as his father at putting profit before principle. Glossing over the fact that at least 100 members of Falun Gong had died in Chinese prisons of torture or neglect, and that many thousands were still incarcerated, he publicly defended the Chinese government's persecution of the sect, which he characterised as 'dangerous' and 'an apocalyptic cult'. In the same speech to a conference in Beverly Hills in March 2001, he also took aim at Hong Kong's democracy movement, by advising them to 'accept the reality of life under a strong-willed absolutist government'. And finally, he wrapped it all up by attacking the western media for 'painting a falsely negative portrait of China' by focusing on human rights.

Even for Rupert, who was in the audience to watch his son deliver this message, it was vintage stuff. And China's leaders were clearly delighted. Within months, STAR was launching a new Chinese-language channel called Xing Kong Wei Shi, or Starry Sky, investing heavily in local programming and asking the government's propaganda bosses, whom Rupert had cultivated, for permission to deliver the new channel via China's local cable services. And at last the answer was yes.

However, despite James's boast that it was a 'historic' agreement and 'a milestone' for STAR, it was really no great leap forward. The network was only getting access to 600 000 cable customers in Guangdong, near the border with Hong Kong, who were already well-served by Chinese services. And almost all of these customers spoke Cantonese, while Starry Sky's programs were in Mandarin. There was also a quid pro quo that James had omitted to mention, which was that the Murdochs' cable TV stations around the world would all take China's propaganda channel, CCTV9, in exchange.

Nevertheless, STAR at last had a foot in the door, and James was convinced it would soon be flung open if they didn't offend the censors. Indeed, he was sure that if STAR's service was popular enough, the Chinese public would demand access, and the barriers would be broken down. Thus, STAR was soon spending a fortune on local versions of hit shows like *Judge Judy*, leasing glitzy offices in Shanghai and Beijing, taking on hundreds of employees and waiting for the bonanza to begin.

But the long and short of it is that it never did. In 2005, the door was slammed shut by a new generation of Chinese leaders who took a much harder line than Jiang Zemin on opening their TV market to foreigners, and, in September that year, Rupert was forced to admit they had 'hit a brick wall'. Soon afterwards, the shiny new offices shut down. The Murdochs' former China man, Bruce Dover, believes it had never occurred to Rupert that the Chinese might ultimately say no: he was just so used to getting his way.

And in India, an almost identical strategy did work. When James took over in 2000, Rupert was commissioning a Hindi version of *Who Wants to be a Millionaire* with 10 million rupees in prize money. After the show rocketed to number one, James invested heavily in more local programming, and STAR was soon hauling in advertisers and boasting fifteen of the top twenty Hindi shows in India.

He also managed to boost subscription revenue by cracking down on piracy. Millions of people were watching STAR's satellite service, but hardly anyone bothered to buy a dish. Instead, they paid money to a cable wallah and watched on a communal screen or had the service piped illegally to their home. The first step to combat this was to encrypt STAR's signal; the next was to charge a fee to the wallahs based on the size of their audience. When most refused to sign new contracts, James threatened to cut off their service on the eve of an England–India test match. 'You can't do that,' they told him, 'we'll all be killed.' 'That's your choice,' he replied. And sign they did. The net result was that STAR turned around from a $100-million-a-year loss to a $10-million-a-year profit in the three years that James ran the network, even without the expected China bonanza.

It was therefore no great surprise when Rupert decided in 2003 that James should be promoted again, this time to run BSkyB in London. Nor was it a surprise that there were again loud cries of nepotism and suggestions he was not up to the job. Not yet 31, he was to be the youngest chief executive in the history of the FTSE 100, had only three years experience in TV and knew practically nothing about Britain. But, since News owned around one-third of BSkyB's shares, it had the power to put him there, despite objections from some of the company's directors and vigorous opposition in the media. And Rupert insisted James had been given the job on merit in any case. 'He just had the misfortune of having my name,' he protested. 'I know everybody in this business, and who could do better? They put him through psychometric tests and pretty exhaustive interviews by members of the committee. He aced it.'

At that point, not much was known about James, because he had always kept out of the spotlight and hated being interviewed. His American wife Kathryn Hufschmid, who was blonde and a former model, with more than a passing resemblance to his mother, insisted he was a romantic, who loved seersucker suits, panama hats and mint juleps. And, as if to confirm that, he had read her a poem by Pablo Neruda at their wedding in Connecticut in 2000. But it was hard to get a handle on him, apart from the fact that he was undoubtedly clever, serious and sure of himself, and arguably a bit of a prig. He never went to parties, hated the high life and was rarely seen out on the town. You might run into him browsing for CDs in a record shop on Hong Kong island, or out to dinner with young fogeys like himself. But most of all, he liked going home to his wife and two young kids, where he could be the father that Rupert had never been. And it would be the same in London, where he again shut himself off from the media as he set about making BSkyB a success.

Here, too, he was constantly on the phone to Rupert, who happened to be BSkyB's chairman, and together they adopted a strategy to build the network's audience by spending on programs and promotion, as James had done at STAR. On his first day at the office, he called his chiefs together to impart this message and was soon struck by the fact that the program makers glanced nervously at the bean counters every time they put forward a new idea. BSkyB's chief financial officer, Martin Stewart, happily explained why this was so: 'It's because we run a tight ship here, we keep costs down, we have to think of our shareholders.'

'Well, I have an idea,' James replied. 'Why don't we make programs for our viewers for a change and not for the shareholders?'

'No, no, we can't do that,' the CFO responded, 'We don't do it like that round here.'

'Well, maybe we should,' suggested James.

'No, no, that can't happen,' Stewart insisted.

'Well, it looks like one of us will have to go, doesn't it?' said James. 'And I've only just got here.'

'So are you firing me?' Stewart inquired.

'I guess I am,' replied James.

That story may well be embellished, but it's a fair approximation of what happened. Stewart, who had been the City's pick for the top job, announced he was leaving almost immediately James walked through the door, whereupon BSkyB set an ambitious new target of 10 million subscribers, or one-third more than they had, which caused James's critics to doubt him even more.

But, just as he had spent a fortune at STAR, James now opened the corporate wallet at BSkyB to make this happen. He also took a strategic decision to spend £211 million on a broadband internet provider, Easynet, which made it possible to switch customers to cable and, even more importantly, to bundle phone, internet and TV in one package. Over the next few years, this so-called Triple Play, 'took BSkyB to a new level', according to one top Australian executive, who says, 'It cost a frigging fortune, but it was worth it. He understood the business, and he understood the technology.'

With James in charge, there were other advances: TV for mobiles; movies for Xbox and PlayStation; wireless hubs at home; the ability to watch several channels at once; and the opportunity to catch up on last week's TV (including the BBC). What had once been a Holden Commodore company became a Mercedes.

And the results showed in the bottom line. By 2010, BSkyB had topped James's 10 million subscriber target, doubled its revenues and more than quadrupled profits, which were on their way to topping £1 billion a year.

On this performance, the Murdoch family at least had one candidate who was capable of taking over from Rupert. The youngest son was aggressive in business, had good gut instincts and was prepared to take huge risks, just like his father. He was also more than happy to get stuck into his competitors.

In 2009, as BSkyB's coffers began to overflow, James delivered a scathing attack on the BBC at the annual Edinburgh TV Festival, branding it 'state-sponsored journalism', as if the popular public broadcaster were some sort of Soviet news agency, and accusing it of throttling press freedom by driving its rivals out of business. 'The scope of its current activities and future ambitions is chilling,' James claimed, before invoking George Orwell's *1984* as a reason why the BBC's licence fee should be dramatically reduced, and then telling his shocked audience that profit was the 'only reliable guarantor of independence'.

Once again, it was a message his father would have been proud of, even if it went down like a lead balloon with the majority of Britons, who still trusted the BBC a great deal more than *The Sun* or BSkyB. But if James was a chip off the old block in this respect, he was also very different from his dad, especially in his lack of guile. While Rupert was relaxed, informal and charming, a constant surprise to those who were determined to dislike him, James appeared to be preppy, uptight and pleased with himself, and was far more likely to confirm people's prejudices. He seemed to like provoking confrontation and had lost his old humility. 'The old James has gone missing,' his friends and family complained.

'Success at BSkyB went to his head,' says one executive who has been with the Murdochs for many years. 'He became overconfident, arrogant, and less likely to listen.' He also gained a reputation for having a fierce temper, and not suffering fools. 'I went to one dinner with him,' the executive recalls, 'and he was effing and blinding and being very outspoken. He had strident views on a whole lot of subjects. I was quite taken aback by how forthright he was.'

Nor did James have his father's elephant hide, which had allowed Rupert to cope with the perpetual unpopularity of being a Murdoch. During the May 2010 UK election campaign, *The Independent* newspaper ran a series of ads to assure its readers that they would elect the next government, while union money and City financiers would not. One of these ads featured James's father, with the mildly provocative caption, 'Rupert Murdoch won't decide this election. You will.' James's response was to storm into the paper's offices late at night, march onto the editorial floor and abuse the editor, Simon Kelner. Waving a copy of the offending article, and raging that he was 'a fucking fuckwit', James accused the startled journalist of 'impugning' the reputation of the Murdoch family. As he paced up and down, accusing Kelner of having 'enjoyed' the Murdochs' hospitality many times, Rebekah Brooks chimed in, 'We thought you were our friend.'

'Their use of language and the threatening nature of their approach came straight from the "Mafioso for Beginners" handbook,' Kelner observed, claiming that it laid the Murdoch mindset bare: 'If you come to our parties, if you join us on our yachts, if you are at our cozily arranged dinner table, we might expect something in return, but we certainly don't expect you to act in a way contrary to our interests.'

Not only was it remarkably thin-skinned for James to complain so violently, since the Murdoch papers bashed up their enemies on a regular basis, it was also staggeringly immature. So perhaps he wasn't yet ready to take over the empire. But by this stage it was clear the job was his for the taking. Having been promoted to run the British newspapers and the entire European operation in December 2007, James was elevated again by Rupert in early 2011 to be deputy chief operating officer of News Corp, perhaps with a view to taking over from Chase Carey as chief executive in 2014, when the latter's contract expired.

However, before he departed for New York where his new job was based, there was one important task he wanted to complete, which was to buy up the rest of BSkyB (in which News Corp now owned 39 per cent) so that the pay-TV group's future profits would flow through to the family. 'Project Rubicon', as the £8 billion takeover plan was called, had been on the drawing board since 2009, but it now had the help of a Conservative-led government to push it through.

By June 2011, after much frantic lobbying, this bid had been approved in principle by Britain's Culture Secretary, Jeremy Hunt, and James was all set to consolidate his claim on the Murdoch empire. But with the deal awaiting its final all-clear, the *News of the World* phone-hacking scandal suddenly exploded onto the front pages of every newspaper in Britain. And in the holocaust that followed, James's plans disappeared up in smoke.

On 4 July 2011, *The Guardian* newspaper revealed that in 2002 the *News of the World* had hacked into the phone of a missing thirteen-year-old, Milly Dowler, and apparently deleted some of her voice messages, giving her parents hope that the murdered girl was still alive. James, Rupert and Rebekah Brooks were immediately forced to accept that their journalists had committed this disgraceful act. And, after five years of vehement denials, they were also forced to admit that their paper had hacked into the private voicemails of politicians, sports stars, celebrities and ordinary members of the public, as *The Guardian*, the BBC and the *New York Times* had been claiming since 2009.

The greater significance of the Milly Dowler story was that it made the public angry for the first time about what the Murdoch press had been up to, even though its intrusions had long been public knowledge. Hacking into David Beckham's or Hugh Grant's or Prince Harry's voicemails had never fired the public's anger, because celebrities and the Royals were deemed to be fair game, but prying into the private grief of a family whose daughter had been brutally murdered was about as low as anyone could go. And the outrage was overwhelming.

It was 'inhuman' and 'evil', thundered Tom Watson MP, who had fought for two years to expose the extent of phone hacking by the Murdochs' Sunday scandal sheet. It was 'cruel and immoral' and 'a stain on British journalism', agreed the leader of Britain's Labour opposition, Ed Miliband. It was 'a truly dreadful act and a truly dreadful situation', Britain's Prime Minister, David Cameron, pronounced.

In the two weeks that followed, the Murdochs' British empire was shaken to its foundations. The *News of the World* was shut down after 168 years of production; a judicial inquiry was set up to investigate the press; and two of London's most senior policemen were forced to resign for failing to reopen the police investigation in July 2009, when *The Guardian* had first alleged that there were up to 3000 hacking victims.

Two of Rupert's closest and most-trusted executives were also forced to walk the plank. Les Hinton, who had been by his boss's side for 52 years, since the early days in Adelaide, and had been the first to publicly deny that the *News of the World* was hacking people's phones, clearly had to go. So, too, did Rupert's court favourite, Rebekah Brooks, who had been the *News of the World*'s editor in 2002 when Milly Dowler's voicemails were violated, and who had run the Murdochs' British papers since 2009, while vital evidence was destroyed, victims were paid to keep quiet and the denials became ever more strident.

Forty-eight hours after Brooks was dumped, with a massive pay-off, she was arrested by detectives from the Metropolitan Police's Operation Weeting on suspicion of phone hacking, and questioned for nine hours. Her erstwhile deputy at the *News of the World*, Andy Coulson, who had succeeded her as editor in 2003 and gone on to run the Prime Minister's press office at 10 Downing Street, had already endured a similar arrest and interrogation, along with four other senior journalists on the paper. And although none had yet been charged, it was likely they soon would be.

But as all this was happening, a deeper and more permanent change was taking place: the aura of power and invincibility that had surrounded the Murdochs for so many years was dissolving. Politicians and the press suddenly felt free to speak up without fear of being targeted. And years of pent-up anger and resentment were being released.

As part of this new-found confidence, the House of Commons Culture, Media and Sport Committee now ordered Rupert and James to explain what they knew about their minions' misdeeds. And, for once, its MPs refused to take no for an answer. When James indicated he was busy and Rupert declined to appear because he was an American citizen, they despatched the Deputy Serjeant-at-Arms to deliver a legal summons, threatening imprisonment if the Murdochs failed to comply. The official made his way across London on the Underground, without his ceremonial robes, and turned up unannounced at News International's Wapping headquarters, where he handed the writ to one of the company's lawyers. Father and son then agreed to come quietly.

Less than eighteen months earlier, in February 2010, the committee had been forced to abandon an investigation into phone hacking because it could go no further in its search for the truth. In doing so it had accused the Murdochs' executives who had given evidence of 'deliberate obfuscation', 'collective amnesia' and attempting 'to conceal the truth about what really occurred'. Now those MPs wanted to find out if they had actually been lied to, which is why on 19 July 2011, Rupert and James were being interrogated under the TV lights with the eyes of the world upon them. It was a historic occasion, especially for the Murdochs, whose British empire would never be the same again.

Looking at James in his light grey suit, Bob Haldeman buzz-cut hair, and wire-framed glasses, it was clear that he had no clue how to handle this test. It didn't help that he spoke with an American accent and appeared to have swallowed a business dictionary. It didn't help that he had no idea when to keep quiet or how to be brief. And it didn't help that he was keen to show it could not have been his fault. But most of all, it didn't help that he couldn't utter three simple words, 'I am sorry', and leave it at that. What was really needed was a display of contrition and remorse, and James just didn't have it in him.

'He looked like a young smartarse,' says one of Murdoch's former lieutenants, who watched it from home in Australia. 'He's not as clever as he thinks he is. You can't get away with that sort of swagger in Britain. But he just doesn't get it.'

Watching him perform, it was clear he would never be a match for his famous father. But even if he had been the best actor in the world with the best possible lines, James would still have been trapped by his situation. He had run the British newspapers from 2007 to 2009, and had then been executive chairman, and Brooks's boss, as the cover-up went on around him. He had approved at least one massive pay-out to silence a hacking victim, and he had joined the chorus of denials as News had savaged its critics for even daring to investigate. So, however vigorously he denied responsibility, he was sure to be damned. If he had no idea about the goings-on at the *News of the World*, nor any inkling of the five-year cover-up, he was obviously a fool. And if he did know about it all, as many suspected, then he was clearly a liar. Neither made him a suitable choice to succeed his father as the head of an international media empire.

Over the next eighteen months, one of the key questions would be, how much did James and Rupert know? And how far up did the cover-up go? Many would guess that it was all the way. But in one sense the answer was irrelevant, at least for James, because nothing could exonerate him from the charge that, if he didn't know, he certainly should have done.

And against this background, it would be hard to believe that either he or Rupert had been completely in the dark about what their British tabloids were up to. Because, hacking or no hacking, one only had to read newspapers like the *News of the World* and *The Sun* to see the grubby way in which they made their living.

PART III

A STAIN ON THE EMPIRE

8
TABLOID TALES

'This is what we do. We go out and destroy other people's lives.'
Greg Miskiw, *News of the World* news editor

Kelvin MacKenzie, the long-serving editor of Rupert Murdoch's best-selling *Sun,* was once asked what he thought about tabloid ethics. In a favourite quip he would recycle many times, he famously replied: 'Ethics? As far as I'm concerned, that's a place to the east of London where people wear white socks.'

Another lesser-known Murdoch journalist, Greg Miskiw, who was once news editor of the *News of the World*, and now faces charges of phone hacking, summed up his paper's culture even more eloquently. 'This is what we do,' he explained to a stressed-out reporter. 'We go out and destroy other people's lives.'

Had Miskiw's candid confession not been taped, in vintage *News of the World* style, no one would ever have believed it. But the recording was proof that he said it. And if you thumbed through copies of the Murdochs' Sunday scandal sheet, published between 2000 and 2006, when Rebekah Brooks and Andy Coulson were editing the paper, you could see why he believed it, and why the paper was often known as the *News of the Screws*.

Almost all its big stories involved humiliating the famous for the joy of the masses, by exposing celebrities, sports stars and politicians for their illicit affairs, drunkenness or homosexuality. But it was the style of these exposés as much as the content that made them so brutal because Murdoch's weekly tabloid never showed any mercy to its hapless victims, whom it gleefully kicked, slapped and ridiculed for the pleasure of its readers.

Over the years, the *News of the World* won a number of newspaper awards for some remarkable scoops, like catching the Duchess of York selling access to the Royal Family, nailing three Pakistani cricketers for match fixing, or, more controversially, revealing David Beckham's affair with Rebecca Loos. But most of its investigations had no public interest or importance, even though they undoubtedly packed a punch. And the paper's front-page EXCLUSIVE from July 2006 on gay pop star, George Michael, was a prime example.

Headed, GEORGE IN NEW SEX SHAME, and written by the paper's chief reporter, Neville Thurlbeck, it began: 'Mega Rich pop superstar George Michael this week sank to new levels of depravity—trawling for illegal gay sex thrills in a London park. *News of the World* investigators caught the singer red-handed and red-faced as he emerged from the bushes after cavorting with a pot-bellied 58-year-old jobless van driver.'

Thurlbeck told the paper's readers in shocked tones that it 'was all in a public place and totally illegal'. But a more honest description might have been that the unspecified acts had taken place in pitch dark, in thick undergrowth, at three o'clock in the morning, when everyone apart from the paper's fearless investigative team was fast asleep. And Michael's 'depraved' behaviour had in fact been so private that even the paper's snappers with their powerful telephoto lenses had been unable to see what he was doing. If public decency had been offended, it was only because Thurlbeck and Miskiw, and their editor, Andy Coulson, had chosen to put it all on the front page of the paper.

Typically, the *News of the World* also failed to mention that it had only got this story because its crack reporters had sat outside the singer's house for several hours, or perhaps days, before following his car at 1 a.m. to Hampstead Heath, where they had shadowed him for two hours until he finally scored. But this was how the paper's fearless sleuths habitually spent their time.

Not content with exposing Michael's midnight meanderings, the reporting team had also followed the man they described as 'a pot-bellied 58-year-old jobless van driver' 100 kilometres back to Brighton, so they could push their way into his flat, bully him into a quote about the star and report that his 'Dingy place was littered with rubbish, dirty crockery and filthy laundry', and that his only companion was 'a twenty-year-old cat'.

Two weeks earlier, the *News of the World* had featured another Neville Thurlbeck story, titled, RANDY ANDY'S TEENY WEENY TARTAN HANKY SPANKY, which revealed that the former Scottish soccer star, Andy Gray, might be 'A giant among TV pundits' but was 'a midget in the bedroom'. The EXCLUSIVE kiss-and-tell interview with his Italian ex-lover, Deanna Franco, highlighted his pot belly and small penis. 'The sex was always awful,' she told the paper, no doubt for a suitable fee, adding that, 'lovemaking would only last a couple of minutes, then he would roll over and go to sleep.'

A previous issue had boasted a similar EXCLUSIVE on the star of *The Trip* and *I'm Alan Partridge,* which began, 'The secret lover of comic Steve Coogan last night dumped him and branded him a sick PERVERT addicted to warped sex, hookers, cocaine and Viagra.' Pretty Victoria Vanegas sobbed: 'He's one of the most depraved men I've ever met. I'll be ashamed of the disgusting things he made me do for the rest of my life.' The long-suffering Ms Vanegas, whose hard time with the actor was perhaps now being compensated for by a substantial payment from the *News of the World*, sobbed that she had whipped him, slapped him and performed 'a bizarre sex act too disgusting to mention in a family newspaper'. But she did not explain why she had stuck around for two years if she found it all so abhorrent.

Yet another story that July took aim at comedian Russell Brand, with an EXCLUSIVE headed RUSSELL B-RANDY: 3AM HE BEDS KIMBERLEY, 12PM HE SMOOCHES SADIE. And, naturally, the *Screws* also brought its readers up to date on the Royal Family with another EXCLUSIVE titled FLIRTY HARRY TRIED TO DO DIRTY WITH ME, which announced that, 'A pretty masseuse has told how Prince Harry couldn't keep his hands off her after she gave him a sexy rub down.'

Most of these stories, and there were three or four in every issue, read like a *Private Eye* parody of the genre, and would have been funny had real people not been involved. But the targets of these tawdry tales were clearly of no concern to the paper's journalists, who obviously believed they deserved to have their reputations ruined, if only because they were richer and more famous than their readers. And the *News of the World*'s proprietor, Rupert Murdoch, made it clear that he also had no problems with this collateral damage. Back in the 1980s, when *The Sun* was running a series of scandalous and unsubstantiated stories on Elton John, he was famously confronted by one of Britain's popular breakfast TV presenters, Anne Diamond, who asked him, 'How do you sleep at night, knowing that your papers ruin people's lives?'

'It was just water off a duck's back,' Diamond later recalled. 'He looked at me and said, "I don't ruin people's lives. They ruin their lives." And those were his values...if you somehow get into his newspapers it's your fault.' This was doubtless a legacy of Rupert's puritan upbringing: these people were sinners, so they deserved their fate.

Three weeks after the encounter with Rupert, Diamond discovered that Murdoch's tabloids were after her, too, when *The Sun* splashed news that she was having an affair with her producer (whom she later married). Not long after that, the paper ran a front-page story, ANNE DIAMOND KILLED MY FATHER, dredging up a seven-year-old road accident in which a man had died. Diamond, who was driving one of the cars involved in the collision, had been exonerated at the inquest. 'I was utterly terrified,' she said of her reaction to the headline. 'I thought the world would believe I was a murderer.'

It was of little comfort to the personable TV host that Britain's Press Council later ruled *The Sun*'s article to be 'an irresponsible and grievous intrusion into privacy', and found the headline, 'wholly misleading'. Because, having run the original story across Page One, the paper buried its apology to Diamond down near the bottom of an inside page.

It's an interesting question whether Rupert Murdoch was aware of this campaign of vilification, or, indeed, responsible for it. His ex-butler, Philip Townsend, told Channel 4 in 2011 that it was the mogul who set his paper onto the TV host by ringing to complain that she had been rude to him. Diamond says she can't be sure Rupert's journalists were acting at his behest, but observes, 'Having asked that one question of Murdoch, I was hounded and vilified on newspaper front pages for many years. The effect upon me and my family truly cannot be overstated…the coverage was persistent, cruel, grossly intrusive and enormously damaging and hurtful. At the time, it did indeed feel as though I was being targeted.'

In 1990, after a series of far more vicious attacks on the openly-gay TV host, Russell Harty, who *The Sun* insisted had died of AIDS, despite vehement denials by his doctors, Murdoch told the BBC's Terry Wogan that he read every issue of the *News of the World* and *The Sun* and was extremely proud of both papers.

'Even when you see someone's life has been stomped on, their prospects ruined and their family's life dragged through the mire?' Wogan inquired.

'You very rarely see that in *The Sun*,' Rupert replied, before adding, 'We believe that people who set themselves up in positions of privilege, or as public figures or as public role models, and either make money from that or get power from that, we believe they should be looked at.'

Fair enough, Wogan agreed, but did that really justify the way they had persecuted Russell Harty for his sexuality?

'I wouldn't deny there have been excesses,' Murdoch responded.

'Will you stamp on that?' Wogan asked.

'I do stamp on that, and we do look at it and think very hard about things.'

But if Rupert ever did take such matters seriously, and rein in these excesses, it was never for long. And there's no reason to think he had a problem with the genre. His office in Los Angeles was plastered with front pages of *The Sun* and *News of the World*, and he loved his tabloids. But he also delighted in telling people about the dirt they had collected on politicians and public figures.

'We have pictures of him,' he often boasted to his biographer, Michael Wolff, who found him 'most entertaining and caustic on the subject of other people's losses, lapses and screw-ups'. And he loved to trade titbits. 'There are two currencies in the Murdoch organisation,' the ex-editor of the *Sunday Times*, Andrew Neil, once observed. 'One is money, the second is gossip. He loves gossip.' And, as we know, Rupert didn't worry too much about who got hurt.

Another to suffer at the hands of Murdoch's British tabloids was the famous young singing star, Charlotte Church, even though she had performed for Rupert at his wedding to Wendi Deng in 1999. Then just thirteen years old, the child prodigy had already sung for the Pope at the Vatican's Christmas service and for President Clinton at the White House, so the fee she was offered to perform 'Pie Jesu' on Rupert's yacht *Morning Glory*, where the marriage took place, was a handsome £100 000. But she was persuaded to forgo the cash in exchange for favourable treatment from the Murdoch papers in a deal brokered by Elisabeth's consort, Matthew Freud. Call it advertising, PR or protection money, she soon found that it spectacularly failed to deliver.

Church, whose debut album was titled 'Voice of an Angel', was pursued from the age of fourteen by most of Britain's tabloids, who liked to portray her as the devil in disguise, because she wasn't quite as chaste or pure as her image suggested. But it was *The Sun* and *News of the World* who led the pack, with the former featuring a tasteless clock that counted down the days to her sixteenth birthday when she could legally lose her virginity, and the latter running stories about her mother's suicide attempt. In between, they got stuck into the singer about her weight, her drinking, her smoking and her private life. 'It was utterly horrifying at times, and devastating to my family,' Church said recently.

In December 2005, the *News of the World* ran a picture of the then–nineteen-year-old in a huge front-page splash, CHURCH'S 3-IN-A-BED COCAINE SHOCK, which told its readers: 'Voice of an Angel star Charlotte Church flew into a furious rage at stepdad James after discovering he's a cocaine-snorting love cheat.' Inside, in an even bigger, double-page spread, it boasted, 'Superstar Charlotte Church's mum tried to kill herself because her husband is a love rat hooked on cocaine and three-in-a-bed orgies the *News of the World* can reveal.' It then quoted the step-father's 'mistress' as saying, 'He goes off fucking anything that moves, leaving Maria [his wife] to drink herself into a stupor. It was hell for her. She was in turmoil and thought she was going to lose the man she loves.'

Having run this story, which was almost guaranteed to make Church's mother try again to take her own life, the paper's reporters blackmailed Maria into talking to them. 'The *News of the World* wanted an exclusive story of her breakdown, self-harming and attempted suicide, in exchange for not printing a follow-up story about my father's infidelity,' Church recently revealed. 'She felt she had no choice other than to play by their rules.'

Thus, the paper (then being edited by Andy Coulson) was able to run another front-page EXCLUSIVE in which 'Singer Charlotte Church's distraught mum' could tell the *News of the World* how the young singer had found her unconscious after an overdose, and how she had 'repeatedly slashed herself with knives to cope with the agony of her husband's cocaine-fuelled three-in-a-bed fling'.

According to Church, 'This sequence of events drove my mother to additional self-harming and had a dramatic impact on her mental health.' Meanwhile, Charlotte's TV jobs dried up, sponsors abandoned her, and she dumped several close friends because she became convinced they were leaking personal stories about her.

Another famous singer, Elton John, had an even worse time at the hands of *The Sun*, way back in the 1980s when Kelvin MacKenzie was running the paper. MacKenzie, who was then Murdoch's favourite editor, claimed to understand his readers, and believed, like Rupert, that his journalists should write with their prejudices in mind. 'He's the bloke you see in the pub, a right old fascist, wants to send the wogs back, buy his poxy council house,' MacKenzie once famously opined. 'He's afraid of the unions, afraid of the Russians, hates the queers and the weirdoes and drug dealers.'

And Elton John, of course, was a queer, or a 'pooftah' as Rupert would have described him. Thus, almost twenty years before George Michael graced the cover of the *News of the World*, he was all over the front page of *The Sun* in a story headed ELTON IN VICE BOYS SCANDAL. Inside the paper, in the mandatory double-page spread, the tale unfolded with ELTON'S LUST FOR BONDAGE.

This extraordinarily defamatory article, which alleged that John had indulged in drug-fuelled S&M sessions, was based on the uncorroborated evidence of a homosexual prostitute, who had not even mentioned Elton's name at his first meeting with *The Sun*. He was also being paid handsomely for his revelations, which gave him an obvious incentive to invent or embellish. The paper's lawyers strongly advised MacKenzie not to run the story, as did several senior journalists, and told him there was no chance of proving it to be true. Yet MacKenzie went ahead and ran it anyway, on the basis that it 'sounded right' to him.

John, who was in Australia recovering from a cancer scare, immediately denied the allegations and announced he would sue the paper. *The Sun* then raised the stakes with another story, headlined ELTON'S KINKY KINKS and ELTON'S DRUG CAPERS, whereupon John sued again. And when they hit him with another, YOU'RE A LIAR ELTON, he issued a third writ. Before long, *The Sun*'s rivals were investigating the story and ripping it to shreds, not least by proving that the singer had been in New York on one of the dates on which he had supposedly been tied up in a London orgy.

Assuming that John would never dare have his private life picked over in court, *The Sun* whisked the rent boy out of the country to Marbella and put him up for a month in a five-star hotel, all expenses paid. But their prize witness soon tired of this and flew home to London, where he was arrested by the Vice Squad. The newspaper then hired another homosexual ex-prostitute to find new witnesses to the singer's sex life, paying £1750 for each affidavit he secured and a further £500 to any rent boys he persuaded to come to the party. 'We used to bring people to hotel rooms and they would tell us that they had an affair with Elton and you know—it was pure crap,' the prostitute later told Thames TV, admitting that he had nine convictions for fraud and one for attempted murder.

The Sun's chances of proving its case took another huge hit when their original and only source for the story recanted and admitted he had made it all up, crowing to the *Daily Mirror*, 'It's all a pack of lies, I only did it for the money,' and adding, '*The Sun* was easy to con. I've never met Elton John…I've never been to one of his concerts or bought one of his records.' By this time, the singer had issued a total of seventeen writs against the paper.

Yet still *The Sun* continued its crusade, paying £10 000 for ten-year-old pictures of a naked Elton with his male lover, which they splashed as ELTON'S PORNO PHOTO SHAME, before they finally alleged that he had debarked his 'vicious Rottweiler dogs' and turned them into 'silent assassins'. This created an additional problem because, as *The Sun*'s photographer soon discovered, the dogs were actually Alsatians. And they barked.

Eventually, on the first day of what promised to be the defamation trial of the decade, *The Sun* decided it was time to give in and admit it was wrong. It duly published a huge front-page apology, headed, SORRY ELTON, which made it clear that the paper had no basis for making any of its allegations and had paid him a record £1 million in damages. But despite the fact that *The Sun* had made a string of factual errors and published a deeply damaging story with no public-interest justification, and without a shred of reliable evidence, Rupert still allowed Kelvin MacKenzie to keep his job as editor, even though he had driven the coverage. It was no wonder the poor man couldn't tell Essex from ethics.

A dozen years later, Murdoch's biographer, William Shawcross, challenged Murdoch about this sort of journalism in an interview for *Vanity Fair*, suggesting that *The Sun* was a vicious paper, which savaged its victims. 'I don't think that's any longer true,' Murdoch replied. 'But it depends what you mean by savaging. There's nothing wrong with hitting your adversaries hard. I mean, if you get into a political fight and you believe in your cause, you should be tough.'

Shawcross pointed out that it savaged 'love rats' as well, and that it led the way in this.

'I wouldn't say that. I wouldn't say that at all,' Rupert replied. 'When it thinks people are bad, it says so. Life isn't easy.'

Shawcross then suggested that the tabloid culture was a cruel culture and *The Sun* was perceived to have created it.

'I don't think it's fair to call it a tabloid culture,' Murdoch protested.

'Well, some people call it the Murdoch culture,' Shawcross returned.

'Well, good luck to them,' replied Rupert. 'Some people used to call it the Northcliffe culture or the Hearst culture…It's the old business about shooting the messenger.'

At the time this interview took place, Rupert had just walked out on Anna, his wife of 32 years, and was about to get hitched to Wendi Deng, who was ten years younger than his daughter Prudence. But when Shawcross pointed out that *The Sun* and *News of the World* were particularly savage on people whose marriages had fallen apart, he replied contemptuously: 'Yeah. Well, like whose marriages? I mean, football stars, film stars, celebrities.' It was another example of his belief that the victims of his tabloids had only themselves to blame for the treatment they received, and that celebrities in particular had no rights to decent treatment or dignity.

Murdoch undoubtedly had a similar view of the savaging given to Max Mosley by the *News of the World* in 2008, when the newspaper devoted two weeks, ten pages and an online video to proving that the F1 motor racing boss was a 'secret, sadistic, sex pervert'. The tale of Mosley's NAZI DEATH CAMP ORGIES shocked readers all around the world and was gleefully repeated in countless newspapers and blogs, which meant it could not have done a better job of ruining his reputation and wrecking his life.

Written by the paper's recidivist chief reporter, Neville Thurlbeck, and headed, F1 BOSS HAS SICK NAZI ORGY WITH FIVE HOOKERS and EXCLUSIVE: SON OF HITLER-LOVING FASCIST IN SEX SHAME, the story did its best to give Mosley a right royal kicking and, in particular, to suggest he was a closet Nazi. 'The son of infamous wartime fascist leader Oswald Mosley is filmed romping with five hookers at a depraved NAZI-STYLE orgy in a torture dungeon,' the front page trumpeted. 'Mosley barks ORDERS in GERMAN as he lashes girls wearing DEATH CAMP uniforms and enjoys being whipped until he BLEEDS.'

Inside, the *News of the World* told its readers: 'In public he rejects evil past, but secretly he plays Nazi sex games in dungeon orgy.' Naturally, there was a picture of Hitler to go with this, and another of Max's father, Sir Oswald, performing the Blackshirt salute, along with a helpful caption: 'Evil father was a Hitler wannabe.'

It was like 'coming home and finding your front door open and everything in your house removed by thieves,' Mosley said afterwards. 'It is the most terrible thing you can imagine…It is like taking all your goods, taking all your money; in fact it is worse because if someone took your goods and your money you have some chance of replacing it…but if somebody takes away your dignity… you can never replace it. No matter how long I live, no matter what part of the world I go to, people will know about it…If there was a huge genuine public interest in subjecting a family or individuals to that sort of thing, of course one should do it, but it has to be a very big public interest because the suffering you impose not just on the victim but on his family is really, really serious.'

In parts, the *News of the World*'s coverage was more like a Beano comic than a newspaper, as the following extract makes clear. But the effect was far from funny.

FASTEST SLAP Racing boss Mosley wallops one of the squealing hookers with leather paddle.

SO SICK In the midst of one beating, a panting Mosley watches one hooker take off her Nazi uniform.

IN CHAINS Mosley lies face down on a bed trussed up before his punishment.

TAKE ZAT! Formula One supremo Mosley is bent naked and chained over the torture bench in the S&M dungeon as one of the hookers lays into his bare buttocks so hard with a cane he needed a dressing to cover the wounds.

Rarely can a man have been so humiliated. But rarely has there been such a world-class beat up. Mosley had indeed hired three girls to give him a spanking and had then spanked them in return, before having sex with one of them, but the orgies weren't Nazi at all and the 'death camp' story was a total fabrication.

The fact that Mosley's antics had been recorded on video, with a hidden camera provided by the *News of the World*, doubtless made the paper and its lawyers feel secure. And they would also have been confident that Mosley would be too ashamed to sue. But they were wrong on both counts, because Mosley was a tough old bird—and a lawyer to boot—who felt he had been grievously wronged, and was determined to get redress. He first considered suing for defamation, then opted to take action for breach of privacy, because he knew he could get the case into court far quicker. And, thus, within three months, the *News of the World*'s methods were being pulled apart by Mosley's legal team in London's High Court.

The central issue in the case was whether the breach of Mosley's privacy could be justified by a public interest in revealing that he liked a bit of S&M. This in turn came down to the question of whether the Nazi allegations against him were true, not least because the Holocaust Centre condemned that part of his behaviour as an 'insult to millions of victims, survivors and their families', and because the Nazi charges were easily the most damaging to Mosley's reputation and career.

The *News of the World*'s claim that he was a Nazi sympathiser had been repeated in a second series of articles a week after the first, which had accused him of being a liar as well as a sadistic pervert. Under the headlines, MAX DEATH CAMP LUST, SECRET TAPES REVEAL VILE MOSLEY'S TRUE DEPRAVITY, MOSLEY'S TWISTED NAZI-STYLE RANT AT HOOKERS, and 'Sick games WERE like death camps', the paper had offered ten rather feeble reasons why Mosley was indeed a Nazi, despite his denials:

1. Two hookers wore German military jackets with eagle and tunic collars.
2. Three of the vice girls wore striped prison uniforms.
3. Mosley played a death camp inmate – guards checked him for lice and took measurements with a clipboard.
4. He is told to face the floor as girl signs for him on clipboard.
5. One 'guard' uses the term 'facility' – the sort of clinical language associated with Nazis.
6. Mosley gives out brutal beatings – like concentration camps.
7. He is shaved – just like the Jews.
8. Other camp 'victims' are forced to watch their friends being abused.
9. Mosley speaks in German.
10. He uses fake German accent to speak English.

But as the videotape revealed, the Nazi theme was the *News of the World*'s invention. The S&M session had kicked off with one of the women telling Mosley 'Welcome to Chelsea', rather than Dachau or Belsen, and introducing herself as 'Officer Smith', rather than 'Schmidt', 'Kommandant' or 'Gruppenfuhrer'. Mosley himself had adopted the name of 'Tim Barnes', which, again, was neither Jewish nor Germanic.

Nor were the uniforms of Nazi origin, although two bore some resemblance to those worn by the modern Luftwaffe. And as for

Mosley being shaved like a Jew, this was also nonsense. As Justice Eady pointed out, it was only his bottom that was shaved by the guard, while Mosley shook with laughter.

Meanwhile, the hookers' evil 'Death Camp uniforms' were in fact striped pyjamas that had been bought for £11.90 from a local joke shop. And the 'SS-style clipboard', which the *News of the World* cited as proof he was a death camp inmate, was an ordinary spiral-bound notebook. As for Mosley's SS commandant's uniform, this was a plain white shirt and suit trousers.

Summing it all up, Justice Eady concluded: 'There was no evidence that the gathering on 28 March 2008 was intended to be an enactment of Nazi behaviour or adoption of any of its attitudes. Nor was it in fact.' He went on to say, 'I see no genuine basis at all for the suggestion that the participants mocked the victims of the Holocaust.'

Awarding Mosley £60 000 in damages, plus costs of £425 000, the judge commented, 'No amount of damages can fully compensate the Claimant for the damage done. He is hardly exaggerating when he says that his life was ruined.'

But there was more punishment in store for the *News of the World* and its chief reporter, Neville Thurlbeck, whose evidence Justice Eady found to be 'unconvincing', 'disingenuous' and full of 'inconsistencies', and whose 'best recollection' was 'so erratic and changeable' that it was unsafe to rely on.

In particular, the judge suggested Thurlbeck had tried to blackmail the hookers into giving false evidence against Mosley to back up the Nazi allegations, by offering the girls £8000 for an exclusive interview, and telling them that if they refused to do it, their names and unpixillated photographs would be published in the paper.

'This was a naked threat, wasn't it, Mr Myler?' the *News of the World*'s editor was asked by Mosley's counsel.

'I think it could be interpreted as a threat. I'm not so sure,' the editor replied.

'Come on, Mr Myler, please.'

'Well, clearly it could be interpreted as a threat, but I think by this time the girls who took part would have known that the *News of the World* had the photographs anyway.'

'What's it called when you threaten to reveal publicly the identity of somebody who has done something embarrassing...unless they cooperate with you?' Mosley's counsel inquired.

'I think you know what it's called,' Myler replied. 'You're talking about the potential use of blackmail.'

Quoting this exchange in his judgement, Justice Eady noted that when one of the women finally succumbed to the threat of exposure, she found that Thurlbeck had already written her lines, and all she had to do was sign her statement. This included the important claim that, 'It wasn't a one off. Max has been hiring us to do this for years. He is addicted to sado-masochistic sex involving Nazis and beatings.' However, this was 'plainly false', according to His Honour, and Thurlbeck 'must have known it was false when it was put it into the article'.

Rarely can a newspaper or its journalists have received such a public thrashing from a court. But in spite of the judge's depiction of Thurlbeck as a liar and blackmailer, and in spite of the fact that the false claims in the article had cost the *News of the World* £1 million in costs and damages, the paper's chief reporter was neither sacked, disciplined, nor reprimanded. In fact, his editor, Colin Myler, did not even bother to talk to him about it. Nor, indeed, did Rupert sack, reprimand or have words with Myler, who promptly chose the Mosley story as the paper's entry in the British Press Awards' Scoop of the Year.

Rupert Murdoch was asked by Lord Leveson in April 2012 whether he had studied any of Justice Eady's damning comments, but he claimed to know nothing about the judgement, despite the fact that he read every issue of the *News of the World* and was in constant touch with the people who ran it. Yet the original story had generated worldwide publicity, and the High Court decision led to loud protests about the dangers to press freedom. What was more, Rupert was always fully alert to his journalists' successes. 'On one memorable occasion, he stormed into our editorial conference after we won a raft of industry awards,' says the paper's ex-head of publicity, Hayley Barlow, who remembers him 'fawning all over *News of the World* executives', and saying 'Bloody great paper, bloody great journalists, keep it going…it's just bloody great.'

Of course, not all the *News of the World*'s stories were as vicious, unprincipled and mendacious as its evisceration of Mosley. Nor were all *The Sun*'s exposes as bad as the attack on Elton John. But they illustrated the culture that prevailed at Murdoch's British tabloids in the years before the hacking scandal exploded: the absence of doubt, mercy or sympathy for victims, and the lack of moderation or apology when stories were found to be wrong.

Rupert characterised this boots'n'all style as giving the public what they wanted, or democracy in action and freedom of the press, but it was more akin to journalism of the lynch mob, with the Murdoch papers finding the victims and whipping up a frenzy for the public to hunt them down. Sure, it was usually only reputations or livelihoods—and not lives—that were lost, but the principle was much the same, as was the enthusiasm with which his tabloids went about the task of seeking out homosexuality, adultery, infidelity, drug use, alcoholism, depression, a gambling habit, or whatever else befell the rich and mildly famous.

This approach was not just tolerated by the boss. It undoubtedly came from Rupert himself, who, to his credit, did not sue if journalists did the same to him. And it was manifest in other parts of News Corporation, right around the world. You could see the same arrogance and aggression in *The Australian* or on Fox News or in the *New York Post*, even though the targets were more political in nature. It was a culture where they hit their enemies hard, played the man and left no room for doubt; where it was them and us, we're right, don't get in our way. Murdoch's powerful tabloid editors tended to be particularly contemptuous of their critics and convinced they could do as they liked.

And few showed this better than Rupert's redtop queen, Rebekah Brooks, or Rebekah Wade as she was known when she first rose to fame.

9
RUPERT'S REDTOP QUEEN

'She was like the Queen Bee and we were the workers.'

Paul McMullan

When Rebekah Brooks took the helm at the *News of the World* in May 2000 at the age of 32, to become the youngest editor of a British national newspaper, she was already a Fleet Street legend. She was also a Rupert favourite, and not just because of her editing skills.

People who were close to the ageing media mogul could see that he was besotted with her. She organised dinners for him when he came to London, and made sure he remembered his children's birthdays. She was by his side when he arrived at business meetings or social functions. She ensured his glass was full at parties and reminded him to take his pills. She had even learnt to sail, because that was how the Murdochs all relaxed. Rupert was like a father to her, and she his dutiful daughter. Typically, she managed to get close to his children too, and especially to Elisabeth and James, even though she was arguably competing with them for his affections.

Only twelve years earlier, at the age of 20, Rebekah had marched into the office of an ailing tabloid in the north of England and announced she was joining as a secretary. With a posh accent that occasionally slipped, some guessed she might be a vicar's daughter, but no one really knew where she came from, and Rebekah was in no hurry to enlighten them about her origins.

The truth was her father had worked as a tugboat deckhand on the Manchester Ship Canal, and her mother had been a secretary in a small accounting firm. Dig out a copy of the *Warrington Guardian* from 15 April 1965, and you can see what a handsome couple they were on their wedding day. John Wade, at nineteen, was a dead ringer for the film star James Dean; Deborah, at 22, was the spitting image of her daughter: tall and striking with an amazing mass of curly red hair. Old stagers in the village of Hatton, a little hamlet on the road to nowhere, still remember her for it.

Rebekah was born there in 1968, three months before Elisabeth Murdoch came into the world in Sydney, and grew up in a tiny worker's cottage owned by her grandfather, a labourer on nearby New House Farm. Luckily, she was an only child, because the four of them had to squeeze in together for the first fifteen years of her life, her parents being unable to afford a house of their own.

By the early 1980s, her father had started a gardening business, which did well enough for the family to take foreign holidays, but towards the end of the decade her parents split up. It may have been John's drinking that ended the marriage—he died aged 50 of cirrhosis of the liver—or there may have been other things in play. Either way, Rebekah did not see much of him in the years before his death, and when the local paper announced her engagement in 1996 to a TV soapie star, Ross Kemp, he admitted he'd never even met his daughter's beau.

School for Rebekah was three kilometres from home in the village of Daresbury, where she was captain of the netball team and clearly the centre of attention. You can see her in class photographs, at the age of eleven, in the middle of the front row. It's evident that her mother had high standards because she's always dressed smartly, in uniform and tie, while most of her classmates are not. One of them, Christian Matheson, remembers her as 'a lovely girl'. But others saw she was already a champion at getting her way.

'It was obvious she was going to get places in life,' her best friend, Louise Weir, recalled. 'There'd be fall-outs with friends... but if she needed something from that person she'd be able to sweet talk them round. She has always been very charming, she has always been able to get what she wants out of people, even if they don't really like her.'

Rebekah had set her heart on being a journalist, and by the age of fourteen she was hanging around the offices of the *Warrington Guardian* at weekends, helping out and making tea. But her rise really began six years later, in 1988, when she breezed into the office of a local tabloid called *The Post* and announced she was coming to work there. 'It was late on a Friday, and I was just packing up,' features editor Graham Ball recalls, 'and she walked up to say, "I'm going to be your assistant." I was nonplussed, and told her that wouldn't be possible because I was moving down to London that weekend to open a new office. Well, I got to Lambeth on Monday morning, and she was waiting for me. It was a *fait accompli*.'

No one knew how she'd landed the job or who had told her to report for duty. 'She was very deceptive, very hard to pin down. We couldn't quite work her out,' says Ball. And no one was quite sure if her tales were true. 'She told me she'd studied a lot, and been to the Sorbonne in Paris,' says *The Post*'s chief reporter Charles Rae, who was later *The Sun*'s royal correspondent. 'But I'm not sure it meant as much as it implied. It may only have been a one-and-a-half week course.'

But what all could see was she meant to succeed. 'I've never met anyone so burningly ambitious,' says another ex-*Post* reporter, Tim Minogue.

'She would go and sit next to people and ask, "What are you doing, who are you ringing, what are you going to ask, why are you doing that?"' Graham Ball recalls. 'It was a bit exhausting really.'

In the male-dominated world of tabloid newspapers, Rebekah was noticed for her Alice-in-Wonderland looks as much as for her journalistic skills. Rae was smitten by her 'great, wide green eyes', while Minogue was struck by her 'Titian hair'. But sex wasn't her calling card, except perhaps in the promise of preferment. 'I don't think she slept her way to the top, if that's what you mean,' says Ball. 'But she would lean in close to you, play naïve, flatter you and ask for help.' And even at this stage she was a tireless networker: 'Any name that came in, she'd note it down. She was really good at befriending people,' says Ball. 'She could charm the legs off a donkey,' Rae agrees.

The Post shut its doors a few weeks after Rebekah's move to London, but this didn't slow her progress. With Rae's help she landed a job as an assistant on the *News of the World*'s colour magazine, where she soon graduated to writing stories, and came to the attention of the paper's young editor, Piers Morgan, who was impressed by her willingness to do anything to get ahead. On one occasion, she bugged a hotel room for reporters who were about to offer Princess Di's lover, James Hewitt, £500 000 to spill the beans on their affair. On another, she dressed as a cleaner and hid in a toilet for two hours to steal an advance copy of the rival *Sunday Times*, also a Murdoch paper, so they could pinch exclusive extracts from a new tell-all book on Prince Charles.

Before long, her reputation had spread, and she was getting noticed by people who mattered even more than Morgan, like Murdoch's loyal deputy, Les Hinton, who had just been brought back from the US to run the British papers. Hinton was so impressed that he picked her to be deputy editor of *News of the World* in 1995 at the age of 27 and then deputy editor of *The Sun* in 1998.

Rebekah's fellow journalists struggled to explain how she had come so far so fast, since few regarded her as particularly talented. But most believed it was a mixture of charm, guile, hard work and ambition. And all agreed she had something special. 'She was like the Queen Bee,' says one of the *News of the World*'s gun reporters, Paul McMullan, 'and we were like the workers, all scrabbling around, trying to impress her.'

For the men in her orbit, Brooks's flirtatiousness was certainly a part of the cocktail. 'She was very tactile, touching you on the arm, looking straight into your eyes as though there was no one more important in the room,' a male colleague confessed. 'From the way she acted, you would think she wanted to sleep with you… but she didn't want to sleep with the help; she was way too up the scale for that.'

In 1998, Hinton threw a 30th birthday for her at the swanky Belvedere Restaurant in London's Holland Park, by which time she was also on Rupert's radar, and lighting up his screen. Two years later, she was promoted again to be editor of the *News of the World* and crowned Queen of the Redtops, as Britain's tabloids are known in the trade.

Brooks's first big splash as *News of the World* editor came only two months into her reign, following the murder of eight-year-old Sarah Payne, who was abducted near her grandparents' Sussex home. With the little girl's mother and father claiming she was the victim of a convicted sex offender, Brooks decided to reveal the names of paedophiles living in the community. Under the headline NAMED, SHAMED, the *News of the World* told its readers, 'There are 110 000 child sex offenders in Britain...one for every square mile. The murder of Sarah Payne has proved that police monitoring of those perverts is not enough. So we are revealing WHO they are and WHERE they are, starting today.'

The paper carried names and head shots of 49 child-sex offenders, with details of their offence and the town in which they were living, making it a relatively simple task for locals to track them down. The article warned readers not to take the law into their own hands, yet gave them the tools to do exactly that.

Immediately, there were violent incidents all round the country. In the coastal town of Portsmouth, vigilantes marched through the street waving placards that said 'Kill Paedophiles'. Four families in the town were also forced to flee their homes, and a policeman took a brick in his face when a 150-strong mob set two cars on fire and ransacked the home of a local taxi driver named by the newspaper. In Manchester, a smaller crowd surrounded the house of another suspected sex offender, chanting 'Paedophile, paedophile', and lobbed a brick though his window because he had a neck brace similar to someone in the *News of the World*'s rogues' gallery. In south London, another man sought police protection after 500 letters outing him as a paedophile were pushed through neighbours' letterboxes. This, too, was a case of mistaken identity. And in Wales, a 30-year-old woman fled her home after her house was daubed with graffiti accusing her of being a 'paedo'. The mob apparently didn't understand that 'paediatrician' was a type of doctor.

Even before these attacks, government ministers, senior policemen, probation officers and several children's charities had been warning that the campaign would be dangerous and counterproductive, because it would discourage sex offenders from reporting their whereabouts to the police or seeking treatment. Consequently, when violence flared again, after a further 34 names were published, Brooks agreed to end the witch hunt, vowing instead to fight for a new public register that would allow people to know if paedophiles were living in their area. Modelled on Megan's Law in the US, introduced after a seven-year-old girl was raped and murdered in 1994, it would be called 'Sarah's Law'.

'As a result of our "naming and shaming" campaign I believe the introduction of Sarah's Law is now inevitable,' Brooks said in a statement, explaining the paper's rapid back-down, then in the same breath threatening, 'Our job now is to force the government to act—and we'll name and shame every politician who stands in our way.' Sure enough, the *News of the World* soon carried out this threat by printing unflattering pictures of MPs who spoke out against the proposal, with the obvious implication that they supported paedophilia.

Four days after the name-and-shame campaign was called off, a 55-year-old grandfather in Manchester, facing trial for child-sex offences, committed suicide. His house had been surrounded by a 70-strong mob, who had thrown bricks and threatened to set it alight. 'He was literally scared to death,' said his solicitor. 'That is what drove him to this.'

With the *News of the World*'s rivals labelling Brooks 'a crude newspaper thug' and 'a nasty piece of work', and suggesting that it was all just a stunt to boost the paper's sales, she finally put her head up in the media for the first time to defend the crusade and attack the 'pathetic male' editors who had criticised her.

Rupert loved her for it. He had always liked a good campaign, and this one had given the paper huge publicity and added 95 000 new readers. What's more, it had clearly been a matter of public interest, even if one disagreed with the paper's actions. But, as so often with the *News of the World*, there was a downside to it all, which was that the reporter who did the leg work, Paul McMullan, had got the story by lying to the Boy Scouts and stealing their database of sex offenders. 'I asked to see how they screened Boy Scout leaders to ensure there were no paedos,' he admitted. 'They opened up their database for me and when they weren't looking I copied down fifty names and addresses.' This no doubt explained why the 49 people the paper identified appeared to fit no obvious pattern in terms of where they lived and what they had done.

In the three years that Rebekah Brooks was editor of the *News of the World*, paedophile stories remained a regular staple of the newspaper's diet, but she switched its focus more and more towards hard-hitting celebrity scandal, pushing out general news and consumer stories and filling the paper's pages with stories of the rich and famous being unfaithful, drunk, on drugs, fat or just plain nasty. Some of these scoops were phoned in by readers, who were told, 'We pay big money for sizzling shots of showbiz love-cheats doing what they shouldn't ought to. A-listers looking the worse for wear or Premiership idols on the lash the night before a crucial game.' But large amounts of cash were also available to persuade housekeepers, au pairs, bodyguards, PAs and lovers to inform on their celebrity employers or partners.

It helped that the *News of the World* had a whopping £3-million-a-year features budget to pay for this, which Brooks herself had supervised in the early 1990s, when she was features editor, and had splashed around to great effect.

'We bought up Princess Di's security team. We paid thousands of pounds to one of her protection officers,' says Paul McMullan, who was her deputy at the time.

'And did Rebekah sanction those payments?' he was asked.

'Yeah, for sure,' he replied.

'I gave another guy connected with the Spice Girls £30 000 in cash in two carrier bags to tell us about the arguments they had in the back of the van,' McMullan added.

'And did Rebekah authorise that?' he was asked again.

'Yes,' he replied.

To help the *Screws* get more stories about stars behaving badly, Brooks brought in Andy Coulson, editor of *The Sun*'s 'Bizarre' gossip column, to act as her deputy, and together they transformed the character of the paper so that it became more of a scandal sheet than it had ever been. With his neat, mousey hair, grey suits, dull ties and wire-rimmed glasses, Coulson looked more like a bank clerk than a tabloid tyrant, but he was perfect for this job. Born in a council house in Essex to working-class parents, he had joined the *Basildon Echo*, at the age of eighteen, fresh out of school, and had started a gossip column in this local paper before moving onto *The Sun*. His first editor, Peter Owen, remembered him as a 'nice guy' who could charm his way across the doorstep, while a London PR agent paid him the greatest compliment you could bestow on a tabloid journalist, which was: 'You could get completely turned over by Andy and still end up liking and respecting him.' Quiet and thoughtful, attributes not expected from an editor at the *News of the*

World, he was also tough, ambitious and close to Rupert Murdoch, who admired his ability to get the story, no matter what—which was what tabloid journalism was all about.

But despite all the money the paper's editors had at their disposal, there was still huge pressure on reporters to come up with stories, because the *Screws* needed a constant supply of victims to keep the presses rolling. Failure was not an option. The consequence of this, in the words of one ex-*News of the World* reporter, Graham Johnson, was that the culture in the newsroom was 'driven by fear'.

This pressure on reporters to find scoops increased considerably when Brooks and Coulson took control. 'The culture did change when I first joined,' says Sharon Marshall, who worked at the *News of the World* from 2002 to 2004 in the relatively relaxed role of TV editor. 'I'd say it was a different paper. Yeah, it certainly got to be a very tough working environment.'

Some years after leaving the paper, Marshall described the atmosphere in the newsroom in the foreword of her novel *Tabloid Girl: A True Story*: 'Hacks are pushed by deadlines, pushed to fill the paper, pressured as they face a relentless daily push to deliver, whilst all the time being challenged by younger, cheaper shifters coming up through the ranks,' she wrote. 'Add to that the constant threat of redundancy as circulations fall and staffing levels decrease each year so newspapers can survive.'

'There was massive pressure from the top to break stories,' an ex-*News of the World* sports reporter, Matt Driscoll, agreed. 'It was largely accepted that this pressure came from the proprietors and editors, on the basis that big, sensational stories sell papers and therefore make more money.'

Driscoll ended up suing the paper for unfair dismissal in 2008, alleging he was bullied by Coulson, and winning £800 000 in damages. An ex-news editor, Ian Edmondson, now facing phone-hacking charges, lodged a similar action, claiming that there was a culture of bullying at the *News of the World*, which was far worse than on any other Fleet Street tabloid.

'Where did it emanate from?' he was asked.

'Everything emanates from the editor…Every part of the paper is dictated and controlled by the editor,' Edmondson replied.

Brooks certainly wasn't the biggest bully in the history of the Murdoch press; she faced fierce competition for that title. *The Sun*'s famous former editor, Kelvin MacKenzie, 'would rage and rant, the veins standing out on his forehead…sometimes pressing his face so close to the victim's they would have to go and wash the spittle off afterwards'. Peter Chippindale and Chris Horrie reported in their seminal book, *Stick it up Your Punter!*, 'People were bollocked in private in his office, bollocked publicly at their desks, bollocked when they were walking across the editorial floor, bollocked even when they were trapped with him in the lift.'

'The language he used was always crude in the extreme,' Chippindale and Horrie observed: 'This stuff's all fucking crap. You useless c***s. It's crap. Absolute fucking crap.' And sometimes it went further than verbal abuse. Peter Court, a graphic designer, claimed MacKenzie had offered a knife to one journalist, with the advice: 'Do us all a favour you useless cunt—cut your throat.'

But few dared say no to Rebekah Brooks either. Charles Begley, the reporter on stress leave who was told by Greg Miskiw that it was the *News of the World*'s job to 'go out and destroy other people's lives', had walked out of the office because the editor had ordered him to attend news conferences in his Harry Potter outfit. On the afternoon of 11 September 2001, the day that almost 3000 people died in the World Trade Center, he had been called into Brooks's office and rebuked for not being in character. Amazed, angry and incredulous, he had phoned Neville Thurlbeck the next day to see whether she was serious:

> Begley: Hi, Neville. I just wanted to check, given the enormity of events in America—will the editor still need me dressed up as Harry Potter for conference?
>
> Thurlbeck: Well, she knew exactly what was going on yesterday afternoon and she still wanted you to dress up then. I think you should just assume she wants you to do it now.

Begley was soon being told by Miskiw that working at the *News of the World* was not 'a business for prima donnas'. But nothing could lure him back. His story was then told in a rival newspaper, where it was flatly denied by Brooks, who said, 'That is just ridiculous...I have no idea what his problem is but this is absolutely not true.' His account was also derided by the paper's managing editor, Stuart Kuttner, now facing phone-hacking and corruption charges, who called it 'complete drivel'. But unfortunately for both of them, Begley had recorded all his conversations, as *News of the World* reporters were trained to do.

Andy Coulson, who took over from Brooks as editor in January 2003, drove journalists just as hard and was possibly even more demanding. On one famous occasion, the *News of the World* and its rivals whipped themselves into a frenzy when a whale got stranded in the Thames in the middle of winter. Hearing that the *Sunday Mirror*'s reporter had already donned a wetsuit and jumped into the freezing water so a colleague could take snaps of him frolicking with the mammal, Coulson ordered staff to tell the *News of the World*'s reporter: 'If he doesn't get into that river and get a picture of us saving the whale by pushing it out to sea, he doesn't need to bother coming back.'

With Coulson and Brooks in charge, the paper's reporters did whatever it took to win the prize, donning lingerie to infiltrate suburban swinger parties or spending 24 hours inside a plastic box, hanging above the newsroom, to replicate a stunt by the American 'endurance artist', David Blaine. They also went through rubbish bins, put people under surveillance and bribed journalists on rival papers to sell their news lists. Paul McMullan readily admits he stole pictures from people, ripped off his sources and impersonated a rent boy in the course of his work. Lying, too, was an essential part of the job. 'You can't get through the day on a tabloid newspaper if you don't lie, if you don't deceive, if you're not prepared to use forms of blackmail or extortion or lean on people, you know, make people's lives a misery,' said Graham Johnson, who was a reporter on the *News of the World* in the late 1990s when Brooks was deputy editor.

And, like all the other Fleet Street tabloids, the newspaper paid a fortune to private investigators to buy or con personal information from banks, hospitals, phone companies, hotels, the Department of Social Security, the Police National Computer and the DVLA, or Drivers and Vehicle Licensing Agency. 'Almost all stories that you worked on involved the use of private detectives and accessing various records, which were either illegal or confidential,' said Johnson. 'So for instance, medical records, bank accounts, telephone records—this kind of data. It was all a phone call away. Within a few days of working at the *News of the World* I was given several numbers for private detectives.'

Fleet Street's roaring trade in confidential information was first exposed in March 2003 when the Information Commissioner's Operation Motorman raided the offices of a Hampshire private detective, Steve Whittamore, and found a treasure trove of documents, which revealed that Britain's tabloids were using his services on a massive scale. Over the previous three years, 305 different journalists from 21 newspapers and eleven magazines had bought more than 13 000 different items of information from him at an average cost of about £50 a time.

The vast majority of these purchases—of addresses, ex-directory phone numbers, call records, credit card statements, intimate health records, criminal records and the like—involved clear or probable breaches of the *Data Protection Act 1998*. In other words, the papers were buying information that was being illegally obtained. And in most cases they were fully aware that they were breaking the law.

Whittamore's network of suppliers included a civilian at a South London police station who tapped into the Police National Computer; a public servant in Devon with access to the Department of Social Security database; and a couple of people at the DVLA who dug out driver's licence and car registration details; as well as a Hells Angel bikie who blagged (that is, conned) ex-directory numbers out of British Telecom.

To the delight of investigators, the private detective kept ledgers, workbooks and invoices for each transaction, naming the newspaper and journalist, the information supplied and the price that was paid, which showed that the stories he chased were typical tabloid fare, such as 'Bonking headmaster', 'Dirty vicar', 'Judge affair', 'Royal maid', 'Orgy boss' and 'Hurley and Grant'. Not surprisingly, the people whose numbers, addresses and health records he sold included footballers, broadcasters, *Big Brother* contestants and politicians. But others just happened to be connected to someone famous, like the 'mother whose show-business daughter had featured in a number of lurid press stories about her private life'. This was a reference to Charlotte Church, who observed, when shown the volumes of information gathered on friends and family, 'It was about literally everybody I had ever known. Anybody I had ever come into contact with…Lots of my parents' friends…some of my mum's old work colleagues… a phenomenal amount of information.'

Whittamore's biggest customer was the *Daily Mail*, followed by the *Sunday People*, *Daily Mirror* and *Mail on Sunday*, with the *News of the World* trailing in fifth. But the paper's modest demands were almost certainly explained by the fact that it had its own sleuths, doing the work in-house. One of these was a notorious private investigator called Jonathan Rees, who was paid £150 000 a year by the newspaper for supplying illegal information from the Police National Computer and other confidential databases. Rees's work for the *Screws* was interrupted in December 2000 by a seven-year jail sentence for perverting the course of justice, after he planted cocaine on a woman involved in a custody dispute. But when he came out of prison in 2005, Andy Coulson was happy to resume normal service and put him back on the payroll (he was later tried and acquitted for murder). Another private eye who supplied the paper with criminal records, ex-directory phone numbers—and a great deal more—was Glenn Mulcaire, who was on contract to the *News of the World* from 1998 to 2006 at the rate of £104 500 a year.

Even so, the paper's news editor, Greg Miskiw, still managed to be one of Whittamore's best customers, with 35 requests to obtain information illegally, and another 200 requests that the Information Commissioner judged to be 'probably illicit'. And while Miskiw was never prosecuted for this potential lawbreaking, he and the *News of the World* certainly knew that Whittamore had been busted and that their own activities were illegal. Rupert Murdoch's old friend Les Hinton, who ran the British newspapers, would also have known this, because he was a leading member of the Press Complaints Commission, which was instructed to clamp down on the illicit trade.

In fact, no journalists were prosecuted as a result of Operation Motorman, despite the extraordinary volume of criminal activity that it revealed. One possible explanation for this is that the Information Commissioner was too scared to take on the tabloids. Another is that the penalties were derisory: unless one could bring a charge of corruption, the maximum penalty under the *Data Protection Act* was a fine of £5000. Amazingly, Whittamore and his three main accomplices escaped even that. In April 2005 at London's Blackfriars Court, they all pleaded guilty to offences under Section 55 of the act and received a conditional discharge.

In her three years as editor of *News of the World*, from 2000 to 2003, Rebekah Brooks not only knew that the Sunday tabloid was buying information from Whittamore, she was also one of his customers, making two requests for ex-directory phone numbers. What's more, she inadvertently admitted to the House of Commons Culture, Media and Sport Committee in March 2003 that the newspaper she ran for Murdoch had broken the law.

Asked by Chris Bryant MP whether the *News of the World* had ever paid private detectives, used listening devices, entrapped people or employed subterfuge, she replied that they did all of these things, but only if they were justified in the public interest.

'And on the element of whether you ever pay the police for information?' Bryant inquired.

'We have paid the police for information in the past,' she replied, tailing off.

'And will you do it in the future?'

'It depends,' said Brooks, whereupon Andy Coulson interjected hurriedly, 'We operate within the code and within the law and if there is a clear public interest then we will. The same holds for private detectives, subterfuge, a video bag, whatever you want to talk about.'

But, as Chris Bryant pointed out, paying the police for confidential information was always illegal. Full stop. And as he might also have added, very few of the *News of the Screws* stories had a public interest justification.

Not long after this revealing exchange, the Labour MP found that he, too, became a tabloid target, just as Anne Diamond had done after challenging Rupert Murdoch about his newspapers' behaviour. Later that year, the *News of the World* and *The Sun* both published prominent pictures of Bryant in his underpants, with the latter running a headline across the top of the page, 'Message from Chris Bryant MP (Labour, Rhondda Valley): I'D LOVE A GOOD LONG ****.' Bryant, who was an ex-vicar and campaigner for gay rights, had used these words in an anonymous profile on Gaydar, a gay dating site, and had then sent the picture to a prospective date. It was a fabulous tabloid story, and one could hardly blame *The Sun* for wanting to run it. But the paper's most popular columnist, Richard Littlejohn, ensured readers did not forget the politician's embarrassment by returning to it several times in the next few weeks. And even *The Sun*'s former editor, Kelvin MacKenzie, eventually joined in the fray by urging voters to give Bryant a 'Rhondda rogering'.

The MP also got payback from Brooks herself. Eighteen months after their parliamentary spat, he was invited by a journalist on *The Times* to tag along to a News International reception at the Labour Party conference in Brighton, where they were met at the door by Rebekah, who greeted him with a caustic, 'Ah, Mr Bryant. It's dark, isn't it? Shouldn't you be out on Clapham Common by now?' To which her then husband, the actor Ross Kemp, responded angrily, 'Oh shut up, you homophobic cow.'

But even that wasn't quite the end of it. Bryant claims he was also banned from a literary weekend at Hay-on-Wye, after being told by Sky Arts that James Murdoch personally objected to his presence. And on another occasion, he was asked to leave a BSkyB reception at the House of Commons and told by the group's head of public affairs, 'Rupert wouldn't like it. He doesn't forget, you know.'

That's what happened if you took on the Murdochs. It made you a marked man.

10
GOTCHA!

'They are confident they have Clive and GM bang to rights on the palace intercepts.'

Tom Crone

But even Chris Bryant still hadn't got to the heart of the matter, in terms of how the *News of the World* was getting its scoops. That joy was yet to come.

In November 2005, the Sunday tabloid published a short story in its 'Blackadder' column about the heir to the British throne, Prince William, injuring his leg in a kids' soccer game. Hidden away on page 32, and lasting barely 200 words, it claimed the prince was having physio on his knee and his pals were worried the injury wouldn't heal by January when he was due to start at Sandhurst.

It was hardly a great scoop, even for addicts of Royal Family gossip, and it certainly did not send people rushing out to buy the paper. But it soon proved to be the most damaging story the paper's royal correspondent, Clive Goodman, had ever written, because it inadvertently revealed how the *News of the World* was getting its leads. As Prince William read this silly little snippet over his Sunday breakfast, with his leg now better after a remarkable recovery, he could not comprehend how the reporter could have got the story, unless someone at the newspaper had been listening to his private voicemail messages.

A few months later, the *News of the World* gave itself away again in another royal exclusive, headed CHELSY TEARS A STRIP OFF HARRY. Written by Goodman and Neville Thurlbeck, it recounted how Prince William had left a joke message on his brother's mobile phone, in which he impersonated Prince Harry's girlfriend Chelsy Davy. This time, the newspaper was rash enough to quote William/Chelsy verbatim as he berated the party-loving prince for having too much fun at a lap-dancing club, saying, 'How could you? I see you had a lovely time without me. But I miss you so much you big Ginger and I want you to know how much I love you.'

The Royal Family did not need to wait for this second warning that someone at the *News of the World* was hacking into their phones. By the time the story was published, the princes' staff had long since complained to the Royal Protection squad, and the Met's anti-terrorist branch, SO13, had begun a secret investigation. The main concern of Operation Caryatid was that members of the Royal Family might be at risk, because terrorists and criminals, and not just journalists, could also be breaching their security, but naturally the police were also concerned about the invasion of the princes' privacy.

The Met's first move was to approach Vodafone and O2, the mobile phone companies used by William and Harry's personal secretaries, Jamie Lowther-Pinkerton and Helen Asprey, to find out who had been dialling into their voicemails. And they soon discovered that one number kept coming up, which turned out to be Clive Goodman's home phone. When they pulled up his call records, they realised he was also hacking into the voicemails of other Royal Family members and staff, and thereby snooping on Prince Charles and Camilla, the Duchess of Cornwall, as well.

Since the phone companies could not actually prove from their records that any of the messages had been intercepted, the anti-terror squad set out to catch Goodman red-handed. In mid-May 2006, its detectives began monitoring calls to Lowther-Pinkerton's and Asprey's direct voicemail numbers (which were separate from their mobile numbers and supposed to be known only to them) and set up a camera outside Goodman's house in south London to make sure he was using his phone when the voicemails were accessed.

It immediately became clear that Goodman wasn't the only person doing the hacking. Regular calls were coming from a phone registered to 'Paul Williams', who was calling from an office in south London. The rent there was being paid by a 36-year-old private investigator and ex-professional footballer, Glenn Mulcaire, who had a reputation on Fleet Street for being able to procure top-class confidential information. And analysis of his bank records revealed that he was receiving regular payments from the *News of the World*.

By now, O2 had also unearthed tape recordings of 'Paul Williams' ringing the phone company's customer service to reset the PIN code on Asprey's voicemails, so he could collect her messages. And on further investigation, they found he had done this with scores of their customers, by impersonating an employee from credit control. Finally, it became clear that he was hacking into their voicemails on a regular basis. It wasn't long before the police were able to confirm that he was also doing the same thing with scores of customers at Vodafone, and that 'Paul Williams' was just an alias for Glenn Mulcaire.

By the end of May 2006, the Crown Prosecution Service was noting that 'a vast number of unique voicemail numbers belonging to high-profile individuals…have been identified as being accessed without authority'. Britain's Secretary of State for Culture, Tessa Jowell, who ran Britain's media policy, was among them, as was the PA to Britain's Deputy Prime Minister, John Prescott, whose affair with his secretary had been front-page news in all the tabloids, including the *News of the World*. There was now an even greater security risk and a need, in the eyes of the police, to end the hacking as fast as possible.

On the morning of Tuesday, 8 August 2006, a team of 60 police officers carried out raids on thirteen houses, offices and cars, and arrested Goodman and Mulcaire at their London homes. The royal reporter was dragged out of bed at 6 a.m. and taken to the *News of the World*'s offices in Wapping, where four policemen managed to get past security and onto the newsroom floor. Armed with a warrant that allowed them to search Goodman's desk and the *News of the World*'s finance area, they were hoping to find voicemail transcripts, tape recordings and evidence of any payments the newspaper had made to Mulcaire. They were also after a map of the newsroom to show where journalists sat and which telephones they used, because hundreds of voicemails had been hacked from a hub number at the *News of the World*'s offices. But they were soon stopped in their tracks. Before they could access Goodman's computer or open his safe, the police were surrounded by journalists and the night editor telling them their raid was illegal, then by photographers taking pictures, and this soon developed into an ugly stand-off, which the officer leading the raid feared could get violent.

As reporters began carting away rubbish bags full of documents, the search team agreed to back off and wait in a conference room for the *News of the World*'s lawyers to arrive. Meanwhile, the forensic unit was stranded downstairs, having been refused entry. Then the legal arguments began, with *News* threatening to seek a court order unless the search was abandoned, and finally, after two hours, the police were forced to beat a retreat, without the safe, without getting to the finance area and without their phone map. They never came back to finish the search, and never got what they were after. 'I think the moment had been lost with regard to the information we sought,' the investigating officer, Detective Superintendent Keith Surtees said later. 'It, I think, had gone, quite frankly.' Asked whether this meant he believed that the *News of the World* would have destroyed the evidence by the time they returned, Surtees replied, 'Yes'.

Luckily, the other police team was having much more success at Mulcaire's house in south London, where they seized white boards, a computer and 11 000 A4 pages of handwritten notes, with names, addresses, phone numbers, direct voicemail numbers and PIN codes, plus 30 CDs containing transcripts and recordings of voicemails that the private investigator had intercepted.

Among the documents was a contract in which the *News of the World* agreed to pay the private investigator £104 500 a year for providing the paper with an exclusive 'research and information service'. There were also three or four smaller contracts for individual stories, including one promising Mulcaire £7000 for information on a former professional footballer, Gordon Taylor. In addition, there were records of cash payments from the newspaper, typically at £250 a time, for celebrities, sportsmen and politicians the investigator had targeted, none of whom had any connection with the Royal Household. On one account, these payments totted up to an extraordinary £200 000 for the five or six years Mulcaire had kept records of working for the paper, which indicated that he had chased an awful lot of targets in this time.

Significantly, the private investigator was not receiving money for his work from any other newspaper. As the *News of the World* already knew, he was weaving his magic only for them. He was their dirty little secret.

Following the raids, Mulcaire and Goodman were taken to separate London police stations, where both refused to answer questions. The next day they were charged with conspiracy to intercept communications under the *Regulation of Investigatory Powers Act 2000*, which carried a maximum two-year jail sentence.

For the next few days, a dozen officers from Special Branch worked around the clock to transfer Mulcaire's voluminous notes into a master spreadsheet. The Blue Book, as it would come to be known, listed hundreds of potential victims, with their mobile numbers, direct voicemail numbers, PIN codes, bank details and other personal information. Reviewing its contents, Superintendent Surtees concluded that the *News of the World*'s pet private investigator had been running an 'extremely wide, illegal operation with the intention of unlawfully intercepting a vast number of voicemail accounts'. And, as he wrote in Operation Caryatid's decision log, it was apparent that the private eye had been doing this for many years because of the vast number of cash payments he had received from the Murdoch tabloid.

Almost exclusively, it was people's sex lives, infidelities and marital break-ups that the *News of the World* was spying on. The Liberal Democrat MP, Simon Hughes, was a target because *The Sun* had run a story about him phoning a gay chat line; the

Australian supermodel, Elle Macpherson, was of interest because she was breaking up with her long-time lover Arki Busson and fighting over the children; John Prescott had been caught having an affair with his secretary; Gordon Taylor was in their sights because they suspected (wrongly) he was doing the same; while David Beckham had been publicly accused of bonking his personal assistant, Rebecca Loos. And so it went on. None of it involved matters of public interest or national importance.

Before the raids, the police had reckoned that the Murdochs' paper had at least 180 potential hacking victims. The Blue Book jacked this figure up to 418. Later counts (which drew on an analysis of records supplied by the phone companies) boosted the tally nearly tenfold, to 4332 names or partial names and 2978 complete or partial mobile numbers. But even on the lowest figures, it was clear that Mulcaire was illegally hacking voicemails for the *Screws* on a massive scale. Analysis of his own phone records showed he was in the habit of targeting lists of people, one after the other, and that he spent his days doing little else. Significantly, Clive Goodman was only involved in one very limited area, hacking into voicemails of the Royal Household. And this meant that other journalists at the *News of the World* must also be breaking the law.

There were several leads as to who they might be. The private investigator generally wrote a name in the top left-hand corner of his notes, which was invariably 'Clive' when he did jobs for Goodman. It was more than likely that the 28 other first names he had recorded could be matched to *News of the World* journalists by searching for the published stories he had worked on. Better still, there was an email containing transcripts of 35 of Gordon Taylor's voicemails that Mulcaire had intercepted, which were marked 'For Neville'. This clearly referred to the paper's chief reporter, Neville Thurlbeck, and had been sent by another named journalist on the paper, Ross Hindley. And finally, two named, senior editorial executives at the *News of the World* had signed contracts to employ Mulcaire or reward him for his work on individual stories.

Some of these editors and reporters featured several times in Mulcaire's meticulous records, and the case officer on Operation Caryatid, Detective Sergeant Mark Maberly, identified three he particularly wanted to interview. But on the assumption that they would all follow Goodman's example and stay silent, the police decided they needed more evidence. So Maberly duly asked News International for a range of information and backed up the request with a threat to seek a production (PACE) order under the *Police & Criminal Evidence Act* if it was not forthcoming.

The draft order that police delivered to the *News of the World* asked the paper to hand over Mulcaire's employment records, the details of all payments made to him by the paper, the details of stories he had worked on, and the names of journalists and editors he had worked with. But possibly its most potent request was for a list of all the phones in the newsroom, a map of where they were located, the names of the people who used them, and a record of calls that had been made and received. The implications of this would have been blindingly obvious to the *News of the World*, but in case there was any doubt, the police made it clear that they had 'cogent evidence' Mulcaire had committed 'further offences' and that they were seeking to identify his 'fellow conspirators'.

Unfortunately, the police request met the same brick wall that had greeted the search team at the *News of the World* in August. Within days of that raid, News had hired a firm of criminal lawyers, Burton Copeland, to 'help' the police with their inquiries, but had clearly told them to do exactly the opposite. As a result, none of the information sought was ever supplied, with the lawyers writing back to say there were no records of any work that Mulcaire had done, no records of any information he had handed over and no records of the journalists or editors he had dealt with. There was also no phone map, no floor plan and no call data.

The one file that Burton Copeland did manage to find was a sheaf of Goodman's expenses, which conveniently showed he had paid for Mulcaire's phone-hacking activities with £12 300 in cash that he had handed over to 'a new confidential source' named 'Alexander'. According to the Murdoch group, this had allowed the reporter to keep his and Mulcaire's illegal activities hidden from the editors on the paper. Quite how the private eye had been paid for his other 410 or 4332 victims remained a mystery.

In an attempt to justify the absence of any other evidence, the law firm asserted (almost certainly incorrectly) that a PACE order could only be used to obtain information held by an *individual*, and that the *News of the World* did not keep documents belonging to Goodman or Mulcaire. Amazingly the police weren't game to challenge this fanciful claim, so the threat to ask the High Court for a production order was never carried out.

As this stand-off reached its height, someone at the Met took the extraordinary step of giving Rebekah Brooks (now editing *The Sun*) a full briefing on the police investigation. The supposed rationale for this was that her voicemails had also been hacked and that she might agree to make a complaint (she did not). But, even so, she was given a huge amount of information that was not offered to other victims, and certainly not to five *Mail on Sunday* journalists whose phones had also been targeted.

Brooks was told that Mulcaire had illegally hacked into the voicemails of 100 to 110 people in all walks of life; that he had kept tapes and transcripts of some of the hacked messages; and that Goodman was not the only *News of the World* journalist they were after. She immediately passed on this information to News International's in-house lawyer, Tom Crone, who promptly emailed the *News of the World*'s editor, Andy Coulson. Headed 'Strictly private and confidential', it warned:

Andy, here's what Rebekah told me about info relayed to her by cops:

1. They are confident they have Clive and GM bang to rights on the palace intercepts.
2. In relation to Glenn Mulcaire, the raids on his properties produced numerous voice recordings and verbatim notes of his accesses to voicemails. From these they have a list of 100–110 victims.
3. The only payment records they found were from News International, that is the *News of the World* retainer and other invoices. They said that over the period they looked at (going way back) there seemed to be over £1 million of payments.
4. The recordings and notes demonstrate a pattern of victims being focused on for a given period and then being replaced by the next one who becomes flavour of the week/month.
5. They are visiting the bigger victims, ie where there are lots of intercepts.
6. Their purpose is to ensure that when Glenn Mulcaire comes up in court, the full case against him is there for the court to see (rather than just the present palace charges).
7. All they are asking victims is: 'Did you give anyone permission to access your voicemail, and if not, do you wish to make a formal complaint?'
8. They are confident that they will get, say, five to ten people who will give them the green light and that they can then charge Glenn Mulcaire in relation to those victims.
9. They are keen that the charges should demonstrate the scale of Glenn Mulcaire's activities so they would feature victims from different areas of public life, politics, showbiz, et cetera.

But the most interesting bit came next, in the context of whether the police investigators would now pursue the other journalists on the Murdoch tabloid. Here, Crone reported:

In terms of *News of the World*:

(a) They suggested that they are not widening the case to include other *News of the World* people but would do so if they got direct evidence, say *News of the World* journos directly accessing the voicemails (this is what did for Clive).

(b) But they have got hold of *News of the World* back numbers to 2004 and are trying to marry Clive Goodman accesses to specific stories.

(c) In one case, they seemed to have a phrase from a *News of the World* story which is identical to the tape or note of Glenn Mulcaire's access.

(d) They have no recordings of *News of the World* people speaking to Glenn Mulcaire or accessing voicemails.

(e) They do have Glenn Mulcaire's phone records, which show sequences of contacts with *News of the World* before and after accesses. Obviously they don't have the content of the calls so this is, at best, circumstantial.

If Coulson and Brooks had not already known that their journalists were hacking into people's voicemails on an industrial scale, they certainly did now. And so did News International's most senior lawyer, Tom Crone, who had looked after the *News of the World* and *The Sun* for the previous twenty years. Yet neither they nor their bosses at News made any attempt to find out who was responsible for this wholesale law breaking or, of course, to hand over information to the police, so that the offenders could be brought to justice. Perhaps this was because they already knew who they were.

No one on the paper was disciplined or sacked. And nothing, of course, was printed in *The Sun* or the *News of the World*, despite the fact that this story would have been front-page news anywhere else on Fleet Street. Nor, we are asked to believe, did Brooks, Coulson or Crone pass on what they had learnt to News International's chief executive, Les Hinton, who had been with Rupert Murdoch for almost 50 years, since the early days in Adelaide, and had run the British papers since 1995. This was despite the fact that the two editors talked to him on a daily basis and sat down with him every week for detailed budget discussions. Finally, no whisper of the alleged crimes reached Rupert—or so he claims—even though he was on the phone to Brooks, Coulson or Hinton every day, was famous for knowing what went on at his tabloid papers and, according to Hinton, was 'extremely concerned' about the Goodman case.

Instead of investigating and rooting out criminal activity, News set about trying to cover it up. It rapidly agreed to write out a large cheque for Goodman's defence to Britain's most expensive trial lawyer, John Kelsey-Fry QC, even though the royal reporter had committed a crime and heaped scandal on the paper. Fortunately, Goodman and Mulcaire then decided to plead guilty, which ensured that none of the prosecution evidence would come out in court. In November 2006, both men put up their hands to one charge of conspiring unlawfully to intercept communications, while Mulcaire admitted he was guilty of another five charges of hacking into the voicemails of Gordon Taylor, Simon Hughes and Elle Macpherson, plus the PR guru, Max Clifford, and a well-known footballers' agent, Sky Andrew.

Two months later, on 26 January 2007, the two men appeared at the Old Bailey for sentencing and were given four months and six months in jail, respectively, for what the judge described as a 'grave, inexcusable and illegal invasion of privacy'. Details of the offences they committed were kept to a minimum. But the fact that Goodman had not been charged with intercepting voicemails of the five non-Royals was highlighted by Mulcaire's own defence counsel, who emphasised that transcripts of Taylor's and Andrew's voicemails had been supplied, '*Not to Mr Goodman*—I stress the point—*but to the same organisation*', or, more bluntly, to other journalists on the paper. In his sentencing remarks, Justice Gross also flagged this point by noting that Mulcaire '*had not dealt with Goodman but with others at News International*'.

Tom Crone was in court to hear these remarks, but again we are asked to believe that he failed to report them to Les Hinton, and that this clear warning of other journalists' involvement never made it up the line to Rupert Murdoch. Crone later admitted that he believed the police must have had a strong case against three or four more *News of the World* journalists, because their investigation had been immaculate and everything they had alleged stood up. Indeed, Goodman's lawyer had told him it was the best-prepared criminal case he'd ever seen.

So why had the police failed to go after any of the other 28 people on the Murdoch paper who had been named by Mulcaire, especially since two senior Cabinet ministers had been among the victims? And why had they not been more concerned that the private eye's records contained the mobile numbers of people in the top-secret witness protection program, which suggested that Mulcaire had paid corrupt police for information?

The simplest answer, and the best, is that the Anti-Terrorist Branch was too busy protecting the public, and far more interested in its day job. Back in July 2005, a series of Al-Qaeda bombs on the London Underground had killed 52 people, put Britain on red alert, and placed unprecedented pressure on the nation's anti-terrorist police. By the time it arrested Goodman and Mulcaire a year later, SO13 was running 70 separate investigations, some of which it was unable to staff. And this squeeze on resources then got even worse. On the day the two men were charged, a plot to blow up ten commercial airliners over the Atlantic was exposed and two dozen suspected terrorists were arrested in night-time raids across London.

The anti-terror squad did consider asking another division of the Met to take over the investigation and chase others involved in the hacking, but they were reluctant to compromise the Royal Family's privacy and delay the arrests, and they were not sure anyone would accept the job. They also felt they had achieved their goal, which was to shut down the security risk to politicians and the Royal Family and put the hackers out of business. Finally, they reasoned that the mobile phone companies had tightened security to make hacking more difficult, and that a successful prosecution of Goodman and Mulcaire would send a message to other journalists that they, too, could end up in jail.

All of this added up to a compelling case for not going after the *News of the World* as an organisation, especially since no one was going to die if they failed to do so. But these weren't the only reasons to stop. The police also faced a massive amount of work to investigate all the victims, difficulties in proving that voicemails had actually been intercepted, and the prospect that journalists they charged might escape with modest penalties, as had happened with Operation Motorman.

And to cap it all, they faced a complete lack of co-operation from News International, and the likelihood that they would get into a nasty public battle if they chose to take them on. So it's perhaps not surprising that they took the easy way out. As SO13's commander, Assistant Commissioner Peter Clarke, explained, 'Given...a criminal course of conduct that involved gross breaches of privacy but no apparent threat of physical harm to the public, I could not justify the huge expenditure of resources this would entail over an inevitably protracted period,' adding that it was 'not anywhere near...the top of our concerns'.

Unfortunately, this decision allowed the *News of the World* to get away scot-free. At least for a time. This was undoubtedly a mighty relief for the Murdochs and News, who would have faced multiple claims from hacking victims, severe reputational damage and the prospect of several more journalists going to jail. But in the long term, the reprieve actually served to make matters worse, because it permitted News to compound the original crimes by continuing a cover-up that would become more and more desperate and involve bigger and bigger lies as time went on.

And it did not take long for Murdoch's managers to begin weaving their tangled web.

11
ONE ROGUE REPORTER

'Other members of staff were carrying out the same illegal procedures.'

Clive Goodman

In the immediate aftermath of the guilty verdicts, a line of sorts was drawn. Andy Coulson resigned as editor of the *News of the World* after almost twenty years with the Murdochs and quit the company. He insisted he had no idea that hacking was taking place on his watch, but accepted responsibility, nonetheless. He claimed the decision to quit was his alone.

A month later, Clive Goodman was sacked. He had remained on the payroll after pleading guilty, helping with book serialisations and reviews, and had continued receiving his salary while he was in jail. But on the day he was sentenced he was dismissed by Les Hinton. The blow was softened by a pay-off of £90502, one year's salary, even though he could have been sent on his way without a cent.

Unfortunately for News, however, this generous handout was not enough to make him go quietly, because the royal reporter was furious that he had been dismissed at all. In a letter to the head of human resources at News International, Daniel Cloke, on 2 March 2007, he explained why, with the startling revelation that, 'Tom Crone and the editor promised on many occasions that I could come back to a job at the newspaper if I did not implicate the paper or any of its staff in my mitigation plea.' He then added menacingly, 'I did not, and I expect the paper to honour its promise.'

Thus came the first serious test of News's strategy to bury the scandal, because Goodman also alleged in his letter that hacking had been rife at the *News of the World*, and that several senior journalists and editors—whom he named—had either known about it or been doing it themselves. In particular, he claimed (with names removed):

> The actions leading to this criminal charge were carried out with the full knowledge and support of xxxx.
>
> Payment for Glenn Mulcaire's services was arranged by xxxx.
>
> Xxxx and other members of staff were carrying out the same illegal procedures.
>
> This practice was widely discussed in the daily editorial conference, until explicit reference to it was banned by the Editor.

Goodman's letter was copied to the *News of the World*'s managing editor, Stuart Kuttner, and to Les Hinton himself. So now the warning had undoubtedly gone right to the top of the Murdochs' British operation.

In all, the royal reporter named five people who had allegedly ordered him to hack voicemails, or conspired in Mulcaire's illegal activity. This Famous Five featured most of the top editorial executives at the *News of the World*, including Andy Coulson, the editor, Stuart Kuttner, the managing editor, and Ian Edmondson, the news editor, who are all now facing hacking charges, plus Neil Wallis, the deputy editor, and Jules Stenson, the features editor, who are not. In a follow-up letter, Goodman demanded to be given copies of recent emails he had exchanged with these five people, so he could use them as evidence in an unfair dismissal case. This request was denied by Hinton, who nevertheless asked Cloke and Jonathan Chapman, News International's commercial lawyer, to see what the material contained. The two executives duly reviewed 2500 emails and reported that there was nothing of concern.

A firm of external solicitors, Harbottle & Lewis, was then hired to review their findings, with a clear brief not to go looking for illegal activity or investigate the paper's dealings with Mulcaire, but merely to say if the emails backed up Goodman's allegations. It was made clear to the lawyers that bad publicity was what News was worried about, with the main concern being what might come out in court if Goodman pursued an employment claim.

The lawyers were surprised to find that some of the emails supplied to them were cut off at the bottom or missing part of their content, which they assumed had been caused by a glitch in the IT system. They were also surprised to find that no emails from Mulcaire were included, because Goodman had not thought to ask for them. But one batch from 2003 did back up Goodman's claims, nevertheless. Luckily for News, the solicitor at Harbottles, Lawrence Abramson, never got to read them, because they were only discovered by his paralegal after he had gone away on holiday.

Even so, Abramson still had some concerns. A number of the emails suggested that *News of the World* journalists had been breaking the law by making corrupt payments to police officers for information, just as Rebekah Brooks had admitted to Parliament in

2003. Others suggested that there had been concerted attempts to interfere in Goodman's defence (perhaps in pressing him to plead guilty). But when Abramson raised these two issues with News's lawyer, Jonathan Chapman, he was told it was not covered by his brief. So he duly delivered an opinion which said that the emails contained 'no reasonable evidence' to back Goodman's claims.

Despite getting the assurance they had been hoping for from their lawyers, News still agreed to pay the disgraced royal reporter a further £153 000 to stop him going to court, which topped up his total pay-off to £243 502, or roughly four times the amount he could have won from a tribunal, in the unlikely event of his claim succeeding. As Chapman later admitted, the pay-off was made purely for 'reputational' reasons, or, more bluntly, to stop Goodman going public with allegations of wholesale illegal activity. By this time, the top brass at News International had got hold of a copy of Justice Gross's sentencing remarks, which also made it clear that other journalists and editors at the *News of the World* were involved in criminal activity.

But it wasn't enough to just pay Goodman. Naturally, Glenn Mulcaire also had to be silenced, which took a cheque for £80 000 and a contribution to his legal fees. And, naturally, both settlements came complete with confidentiality agreements to ensure that the two men kept their mouths shut.

According to Chapman, this hush money was Les Hinton's decision. But, again, we are asked to accept that Rupert was never told about it. This is hard to believe, given how close the two men were and that Murdoch had just stuck his neck out by assuring *The Guardian* that none of his journalists had broken the law, telling the paper in February that 'Illegal tapping by a private investigator …is not part of our culture anywhere in the world.' Clearly, fresh allegations of endemic hacking at the *News of the World* were something he would have needed to be told about. And, once again, there seemed to be absolutely no reason why Rupert's old friend, who, as a copy boy in Adelaide had brought him his sandwiches, would want to hide it from him.

However, Hinton certainly did keep it secret from the rest of the world. On 6 March 2007, four days after receiving Goodman's letter, but before the pay-off had been agreed, the urbane, silver-haired chief executive appeared before the House of Commons Culture, Media and Sport Committee for a public interrogation, and took another crucial step in the cover-up. Asked whether News had conducted a proper investigation into hacking at the paper, he dodged the question twice, while assuring the MPs smoothly that Goodman was just a one-off. All payments to Mulcaire for hacking had been in cash and hidden from the editor, said Murdoch's man, so no one at the *News of the World* could possibly have had any idea what the two men were up to.

The Conservative chairman, John Whittingdale MP, then asked him directly, 'You carried out a full, rigorous internal inquiry, and you are absolutely convinced that Clive Goodman was the only person who knew what was going on?'

'Yes, we have,' Rupert's loyal lieutenant replied. 'And I believe he was the only person, but that investigation, under the new editor, continues.'

There had in fact been no proper investigation. Nor was one in prospect. And there was considerable evidence—in Mulcaire's guilty plea, in the judge's sentencing remarks, in the police requests for information, and in Goodman's letter—to suggest that journalists at the *News of the World* had been using the private investigator to break the law on a daily basis.

As to any 'investigation' being conducted by the new editor, Colin Myler, who was an old friend of Hinton's from their days on *The Sun*, the latter was far more interested in the future than in delving into the past. He would later admit that he believed there might be 'bombs under the newsroom floor', but he was in no hurry to detonate them. And it was not his job to find out 'what the hell had gone on', as Rupert Murdoch later claimed. Nor was he obviously suited for such a cleansing task.

An old tabloid warrior from the north of England, Myler had started his career on the *Catholic Pictorial* in Liverpool before ending up as second-in-command at the Murdochs' *New York Post*. But he was certainly no altar boy. Back in 2001, he had been forced to resign as editor of the *Sunday Mirror*, after publishing a story that aborted a big criminal trial. And nine years earlier he had provoked a huge row by publishing peephole pictures of Princess Di in a London gym. These had been taken with a spy-camera concealed in the wall, and showed her working out in a leotard, legs akimbo. Splashed on the front page as WORLD EXCLU-SIVE, DI SPY SENSATION, and given six full pages inside, they were billed as 'The Princess of Wales as you have never seen her before...stunning pictures...secretly taken, of the world's most coveted cover girl'. The snaps had already been turned down by a rival Fleet Street paper because they were clearly in breach of the Press Complaints Commission's code of conduct. But Myler and his bosses at the Mirror Group had pressed on regardless, paying £100 000 to the gym owner, and had provoked a storm of public outrage that brought new calls to curb the tabloid press.

With this colourful background, Myler was hardly a champion of journalistic ethics. Nor was he a prime choice to put the *News of the World* back on the straight and narrow. But Hinton and

Murdoch clearly liked his style. And he was soon serving his masters well.

At the time of Goodman and Mulcaire's arrest, the Press Complaints Commission had warned the *News of the World* it would want to quiz its editor about phone hacking once the court cases were over. But, with Coulson gone, they questioned Myler instead, and he duly trotted out the party line that there had been a thorough independent investigation, that Goodman had hidden his illegal activity from everyone except Mulcaire, and that they were absolutely sure no other journalists on the paper had been involved. Describing it as 'an exceptional and unhappy event in the 163 year history of the *News of the World*', Myler assured the PCC that all of his journalists adhered to the code of ethics and that Goodman was just a 'rogue exception'.

Given that Myler had not been involved in hacking at the *News of the World*, because he had not arrived at the paper until February 2007, he had nothing to hide and no personal motive to lie, so the only possible reason for him to be part of a cover-up was to protect his bosses and the reputation of the paper. But wittingly or otherwise, he now added his strong voice to the chorus of denials.

So impressed was the PCC by the new editor's performance, which included an account of how he was getting everyone to obey the commission's code of conduct and cutting down cash payments at the paper, that it went out of its way to congratulate the Murdoch group on its magnificent response to the crisis.

Thus, nine months after Goodman's arrest, the first big danger had passed, and it seemed the hacking affair was truly dead and buried. But, unfortunately for News, one of Mulcaire's hacking victims was determined to bring it all back to life.

12
BUYING SILENCE

'Our position is very perilous. The damning email is genuine and proves we actively made use of a large number of extremely private voicemails.'

Tom Crone, News International lawyer

As all these dramas unfolded at the *News of the World*, with the Metropolitan Police raiding its offices, the paper's royal correspondent going to jail and Les Hinton being interrogated in Parliament, James Murdoch was busy running BSkyB, 20 kilometres away from Fortress Wapping, on the other side of London.

But even from this distance he had a grandstand view of what was going on, and would have been taking more than a passing interest. And it was not long before he was dragged right into the middle of the mess. In December 2007, Hinton went off to New York to run the *Wall Street Journal*, which Rupert had just caused News Corporation to buy for a whopping US$5.6 billion, and James took over responsibility for the family's British newspapers.

There's no doubt the youngest Murdoch was less interested in the papers than his father because he had never been a journalist and had not spent 50 years falling in love with them. But even if he referred to *The Sun* and *The Times* as 'products' and their readers as 'customers', and cared little about what they put on the front page, it was now his job to make the papers pay and to lead the executive team that ran them.

He also moved across town to Wapping, where all four of News International's British titles were based, and soon set about making his mark there. One of his first acts was to refurbish Hinton's top-floor office in ultra-modern style, chucking out the wood panelling and newspaper front pages and replacing them with bare white walls and huge sheets of glass. Everyone on the management level could now see their boss at work, standing in front of a large lectern-style desk, with a huge screen on the wall in front of him. And he could also see his senior employees. One press of the button would bring up a list of all the people on the network; another would bring them up on the video link for a live chat. Rebekah Brooks, Colin Myler and Tom Crone were all just a fingertip away.

And doubtless James knew what questions to ask when he called them up on his screen. 'He is very single-minded and a very clear thinker,' one of his close friends told *Intelligent Life* magazine at around this time, adding that he was 'very driven on detail'. This insider's view is worth keeping in mind when one considers how the heir to the Murdoch empire dealt with new threats to expose the hacking scandal, which, despite all the hush money and lies, had still not gone away.

Gordon Taylor, head of the Professional Footballers' Association, was one of five people outside the Royal Household whose voicemails Mulcaire had pleaded guilty to hacking for the *News of the World*, in an attempt to dig up dirt on his private life. Back in June 2005, the Murdoch tabloid had been set to splash a story about an affair they (wrongly) believed the 63-year-old was having with his PA, Joanne Armstrong. But stringent denials and legal threats had forced them to back down.

Taylor's solicitor, Mark Lewis, was reminded of this incident in January 2007 as he watched a BBC TV report of the hacking trial and saw his client's picture pop up. And he immediately wrote to Taylor and the four other non-Royal victims to ask if they wanted to take action for invasion of privacy. Taylor said yes, and duly issued a claim against Mulcaire and News Group Newspapers (NGN).

Lewis wasn't expecting much in damages. The biggest settlement ever in a privacy case was £15 000, which had been awarded to Michael Douglas and Catherine Zeta-Jones in 2000, after *Hello* magazine published their wedding pictures without permission. But he knew he'd struck lucky when the *News of the World*'s lawyer Tom Crone came all the way up to Manchester to see him. Previously, in all the seventeen years Lewis had dealt with News, Crone had refused to set foot outside Wapping, let alone take a two-hour train ride to the grey and drizzly north of England. So he cheekily upped the damages figure to £250 000 and waited to see what would happen. The only problem, as he soon found out, was that Taylor had no real evidence that his phone had been hacked, and NGN was not prepared to hand over anything in discovery. Indeed News's solicitors, Farrer & Co, who also acted for the Queen, advised that the case was 'so weak it ought to be struck out'. And in due course, News tried to do exactly that.

But Lewis was not to be fobbed off so easily. A cunning and clever opponent, he had suffered from multiple sclerosis for twenty years, which had left him with a withered arm and a limp, and perhaps a chip on his shoulder. So when NGN failed to surrender any evidence, he sought a third-party disclosure order against the

Metropolitan Police, who had prosecuted Mulcaire, and against the Information Commissioner, whose Operation Motorman had exposed the tabloids' trade in illegal information.

It took Lewis until December 2007 to win the High Court order, and it was not till April 2008 that the material actually arrived. But as soon as it did, he knew he had hit the jackpot. First out of the box was the *News of the World* contract agreeing to pay Mulcaire £7000 if a story on Taylor was published; next was a tape of the private investigator teaching an unidentified reporter how to hack Taylor's phone; and finally there was the email containing transcripts of 35 voicemail messages that Mulcaire had intercepted, roughly half of which were on Taylor's phone and half on Armstrong's. Sent by a *News of the World* reporter to shadowmen.co.uk on 29 June 2005, it famously began, 'This is the transcript for Neville.'

It did not take a genius to work out that Neville was the *News of the World*'s chief reporter, Neville Thurlbeck, and not just because he was the only one at the paper with this old-fashioned name. Three days after the email was sent, on Saturday, 2 July 2005, Thurlbeck had knocked on Armstrong's door in the north of England and confronted her about the supposed affair. By this time his story had already been written and he was merely looking for a quote to drop into next day's paper. Instead, he was met with such vehement denials that the *News of the World*'s editor, Andy Coulson, held the story back, before taking Tom Crone's legal advice and killing it.

As Lewis read the transcripts, he realised that Thurlbeck's tale had relied on a misreading of one of the voicemails, in which Armstrong told Taylor, 'You were wonderful yesterday.' According to the lawyer, she had merely been thanking him for the speech he had made at her father's funeral the previous day.

This so-called 'For Neville' email had been sent to Mulcaire by a second *News of the World* reporter, Ross Hindley, who had transcribed the original tapes. But the documents also revealed the involvement of a third journalist at the paper because the £7000 contract had been signed on the *News of the World*'s behalf by the news editor, Greg Miskiw, author of the famous dictum that 'we go out and destroy people's lives'. This made a nonsense of the claims by Hinton and Myler that Goodman was the only *News of the World* journalist who had dealt with Mulcaire, and that the royal reporter was just a 'rogue exception'.

Lewis had also struck gold with the Information Commissioner, who provided a list of 27 named journalists at the *News of the World* who had paid Steve Whittamore for information, along with details of what they had bought, most of which was illegally obtained. Miskiw was at the top of this list (which has still not been published), while Rupert's favourite, Rebekah Brooks, who was still editing *The Sun*, also stood out.

News received all this material in late April 2008, and, by 24 May, Crone and Myler had decided it was time to tell James Murdoch that News had no choice but to settle the case. Since Crone was going off on holiday, the lawyer agreed to write a memo for the editor to use with the chief executive the following Tuesday, 27 May, and he duly supplied two pages setting out the story. Having explained where the documents came from and how they had come to light, Crone highlighted the importance of what had been handed over. First of all, from the police:

> Amongst the prosecution paperwork…was a contract dated 4th February, 2005, between Mulcaire and the *News of the World* to pay him £7000 for information on an affair being conducted by Gordon Taylor. Another was

an email from a *News of the World* reporter to Mulcaire, enclosing a large number of transcripts of voicemails from Taylor's telephone.

And then from Operation Motorman:

> Amongst the documents from the Information Commissioner is a list of named *News of the World* journalists and a detailed table of Data Protection infringements between 2001 and 2003 (this is based on evidence seized in a raid on another private investigator who was subsequently prosecuted). A number of those names are still with us, and some of them have moved to prominent positions on *News of the World* and *The Sun*. Typical infringements are 'turning round' car reg and mobile phone numbers (illegal).

And finally, he explained what it all meant for News and the Taylor court action:

> This evidence, particularly the email from the *News of the World*, is fatal to our case…
>
> Our position is very perilous. The damning email is genuine and proves we actively made use of a large number of extremely private voicemails from Taylor's telephone in June/July 2005 and that this was pursuant to a February 2005 contract, ie a 5/6 month operation.

Crone's memo went on to explain that he had commissioned a QC's opinion to help them decide what to do next, but that Taylor was claiming 'both ordinary damages and exemplary [punitive] damages' and would win on both counts. Finally, he warned, 'This case will be expensive.'

There's no record of James Murdoch and Colin Myler having their meeting on 27 May, and both would later claim to have no memory of discussing the case. But there's absolutely no doubt that they did, because Myler phoned Julian Pike at Farrers that day to tell him what James had said, and Pike helpfully scribbled it down in a file note, whose first line stated: 'Spoke to James Murdoch. Not any options. Wait for silk's view.'

A week later, on 3 June 2008, the legal opinion from Michael Silverleaf QC brought even more devastating news. According to counsel, the documents revealed a whole series of activities at the *News of the World* that would severely damage the paper if they were to be made public. So it would be disastrous for News to defend the action, even if it ultimately won, which was extremely unlikely.

The QC's verdict was that 'at least three NGN journalists' had been involved in hacking Taylor's phone, and that the chances of News avoiding legal liability were 'slim to the extent of being non-existent'. He went on to say, 'In the light of these facts, there is a powerful case that there is (or was) a culture of illegal information access used at NGN in order to produce stories for publication. Not only does this mean that NGN is virtually certain to be held liable to Mr Taylor, to have this paraded at a public trial would, I imagine, be extremely damaging to NGN's public reputation.'

Worse still, Silverleaf warned, 'There would seem to be little doubt that Mr Taylor's case will be advanced on the basis that Mr Mulcaire was specifically employed by NGN to engage in illegal information gathering to provide the basis for stories to appear in NGN's newspapers.'

As to damages, the QC predicted that Taylor could win as little as £25 000 or as much as £250 000, and 'possibly even more, although I think this extremely unlikely'.

News promptly offered Taylor the maximum, £250 000, and was immediately knocked back. The same day, Pike was told to increase the offer to £350 000. Since this was already way beyond what Crone and Myler were normally authorised to settle for, it suggests they had already been given the green light by James Murdoch, and that he understood the importance of what was at stake.

Three days later, Lewis rang Pike at Farrers to turn down the £350 000 offer and tell News what his client was seeking. It was far worse than they could have imagined. Taylor now wanted 'seven figures not to open his mouth' and to be 'vindicated or made rich'. Lewis explained that his client was determined to push on with the action, even if he ended up bearing some of News's costs, because he wanted to punish the newspaper and its executives for what they had done and for lying about it thereafter. He wanted 'to show that the *News of the World* stories had been illegally obtained' and that hacking into people's voicemails had been 'rife in the organisation'.

Pike again took notes as Lewis laid out his demands, and then emailed Tom Crone, late on Friday afternoon to tell him the bad news, which he summed up in three sharp bullet points:

From: PIKE, Julian
Sent: 06 June 2008, 17.18
To: Crone, Tom
Subject: Strictly Private and Confidential
Tom,

Just [to] confirm my without prejudice conversation with Taylor's lawyer, Mark Lewis.

Taylor's attitude is that he wishes to be vindicated or made rich

He wishes to see NGN suffer. One way or another he wants this to hurt NGN.

He wants to demonstrate that what happened to him is/was rife throughout the organisation. He wants to correct the paper telling Parliamentary enquiries this wasn't happening when it was.

Pike's email also warned that Taylor wanted to see the *News of the World* and its owners, the Murdochs, 'publicly hung out to dry'.

The next day, Tom Crone passed on this email from Julian Pike to Colin Myler with an accompanying memo, which warned of 'a further nightmare scenario' that Joanne Armstrong might also sue once Taylor had been dealt with. Two hours later, Myler forwarded it all to James Murdoch, on the end of his own short email, which warned Rupert's son:

> Update on the Gordon Taylor (Professional Football Association) case. Unfortunately, it is as bad as we feared. The note from Julian Pike of Farrers is extremely telling regarding Taylor's vindictiveness. It would be helpful if we could have five minutes with you on Tuesday.

It being a Saturday afternoon, James was at home with his kids in Holland Park, where he received the message on his Blackberry. Three minutes later, he fired back a reply: 'No worries. I'm in during the afternoon. If you want to talk before, I'll be home tonight after seven and most of the day tomorrow.'

James would later claim that he did not scroll down the email to see Pike's damaging bullet points, although these would have been hard to miss. But it's difficult to believe that he didn't already know what they were facing, given that he had met with Myler to discuss the case two weeks earlier. It is also clear from the language on both sides of this brief conversation that he appreciated the urgency and was familiar with the Taylor problem.

Three days later, on Tuesday, 10 June 2008, Tom Crone and Colin Myler met James Murdoch in his goldfish-bowl office at Wapping, as planned, and talked for half an hour. What they told their chief executive is a matter of dispute, but common sense would suggest that they must have discussed Pike's bullet points, the 'For Neville' email and the legal opinion from Michael Silverleaf QC. It is also certain that they would have talked about the danger of letting Taylor loose in court. This, after all, is why they had already offered him a fortune to keep his trap shut.

But whatever was discussed in that half hour, James ended up giving Crone and Myler authority to settle the case—perhaps at any price—and a deal was then done to pay Taylor £425 000 in damages and £220 000 in costs. This was 30 times as much as anyone had ever won before in a privacy action, and for an article where nothing at all had actually been made public. But the value was that it kept the case, and its revelations, under wraps. A condition of the settlement, imposed by News, was that the size and existence of the pay-off was kept a secret, and that the High Court files were sealed, so that no one would ever be able to get access to them.

By now, the PR people at News had been brought in on the act because the story was 'getting worse' and there was a danger that it would spin right out of control. One of the people in that department says adamantly that there is 'no doubt James knew about all this. There is no doubt in my mind that he was absolutely aware of it.' Yet even now, with clear and powerful evidence that at least three other journalists at the *News of the World* had been breaking the law and committing a crime that could send them to jail, News and the Murdochs did not order an investigation, either because they didn't want to know what had gone on, or more likely because they already knew. Nor did they apparently contemplate sacking Thurlbeck, Miskiw or Hindley, despite evidence to suggest that all three had been enmeshed in Mulcaire's lawbreaking. Crone asked the trio whether any of them had been involved in hacking; they all denied it, and that was the end of it.

Having bought Gordon Taylor's silence for a record pay-out of £700 000, James Murdoch and his fellow executives at News International now needed to hope that the victim and his lawyer stayed silent, and that none of Mulcaire's other targets got wind of the settlement. But the first signs were not encouraging. As Mark Lewis and Tom Crone enjoyed a post-coital lawyers' lunch in The Strand, and then repaired for a drink at Fleet Street's famous watering hole, El Vino, Lewis informed his companion that News would soon be receiving a claim from Taylor's PA, Joanne Armstrong, and that he would be acting for her. In the famous phrase made popular by *News of the World* reporters, Crone apparently 'made his excuses and left'.

13
LIES, LIES, LIES

'All of these irresponsible and unsubstantiated allegations against
News of the World *and its journalists are false.'*

News International, July 2009

Just over a year after the settlement with Taylor, and three years
after the arrests of Goodman and Mulcaire, *The Guardian* newspaper dropped a bomb that should have blown the hacking scandal
sky high.

On 9 July 2009, after an eighteen-month investigation by gun
reporter Nick Davies, the paper's front-page accused News of
paying Taylor, Armstrong and another unnamed victim £1 million
to cover up criminal activity at the *News of the World*. *The Guardian*'s
explosive allegations claimed that police were sitting on evidence
which showed 2000 to 3000 people, including MPs and Cabinet
ministers, had had their voicemails illegally hacked by Mulcaire,
and that at least three other *News of the World* journalists, apart
from Goodman, had been involved.

Accusing Hinton and Myler of misleading Parliament and the
Press Complaints Commission with the claim that hacking had

been confined to 'one rogue reporter', *The Guardian* boasted that its revelations could 'open the door to hundreds more legal actions by victims...as well as provoking police inquiries into reporters who were involved and the senior executives responsible for them.'

But in fact the exposé did nothing of the sort: partly because the public didn't care, since only politicians and celebrities were involved; partly because other Fleet Street papers ignored the story, since they were up to similar tricks; but mostly because the claims were swamped by a torrent of denials from News, the Metropolitan Police and the PCC, who all had something they wanted to cover up.

Predictably, it was the *News of the World* that led the attacks on its broadsheet rival, with a typically aggressive editorial that told its 4 million readers, '*The Guardian*'s reporting was inaccurate, selective and purposely misleading.' By then, News had also issued a statement declaring, 'All of these irresponsible and unsubstantiated allegations against *News of the World* and its journalists are false.' With a nerve that was simply amazing, it went on to proclaim:

> From our own investigation, but more importantly that of the police, we can state with confidence that...there is not and never has been evidence to support allegations that:
>
> *News of the World* journalists have accessed the voicemails of any individuals.
>
> *News of the World* or its journalists have instructed private investigators or other third parties to access the voicemails of any individuals.

This was followed by the even more confident assertion that:

> Had the police uncovered such evidence, charges would have been brought. Not only have there been no such charges, but the police have not considered it necessary to arrest or question any other member of the *News of the World* staff.

And, on the end of it, came five even more definite denials, which were either misleading or downright false.

Almost anyone reading these bold assertions would have concluded that *The Guardian* had got its facts wrong because, surely, no public company in the world would dare to lie about such serious matters. But *The Guardian* could find no way of countering the barrage because none of Davies's sources at the Metropolitan Police, the *News of the World*, or in the legal profession, would go on the record.

News's statement—written by Rebekah Brooks, who had just taken over from James Murdoch as chief executive of the British newspapers—failed to mention that the police had been denied vital evidence and had been met with hostility and silence. (Indeed, it falsely claimed the investigators had been given every assistance.) It also ignored Goodman's claim that hacking was rife at the paper, and Brooks's tip-off from the police that 100 to 110 hacking victims had been identified. Needless to say, it also glossed over Mulcaire's £7000 contract to dig the dirt on Gordon Taylor, and the damning 'For Neville' email with its 35 hacked voicemail messages, which had convinced Murdoch, Crone and Myler to pay Taylor £700 000. And last but not least, it completely failed to take account of the massive amount of evidence that was sitting in the *News of the World*'s database at Wapping, waiting to be discovered by the police if they ever resumed their investigation.

So what was James Murdoch doing while Rebekah bashed out these denials in the office next door, and the nation's best-selling Sunday paper denounced *The Guardian*'s investigation as a pack of lies? News International's chairman would ultimately admit that Davies's claims were 'drawn to his attention' and that he inquired whether Taylor had been paid to stay silent. He would then maintain that he was given the assurance, 'That it wasn't true, that there was no other evidence, that there, you know, this, you know, this has been investigated to death and this is, you know, a smear.'

It's hard to know where to start with this nonsense, except that the familiar Murdoch paranoia about smears and enemies rings true. For James not only knew all about Taylor's hush money, he had authorised it. And if he didn't realise that the £700 000 was being paid to shut him up, he was the only one on either side of the negotiations who failed to grasp this crucial point.

But even if he had heard no rumours about illegal hacking at the *News of the World* until *The Guardian*'s claims were published, he was now on public notice that hard evidence existed. Yet he still did nothing to act on the warning, beyond one casual question and answer. Given that he was the chief executive of a multi-billion dollar business whose parent company was quoted on stock exchanges around the world, it was an absolute disgrace for him to be so derelict in his duty.

And in reality, James was much more involved in rebutting *The Guardian*'s claims than he has ever admitted. One News International insider says that Rupert's son was in and out of the crucial meeting on 10 July 2009, which drafted the Brooks statement, and that he was not merely taking an interest, he was 'directing it all'. This is something he has certainly never owned up to.

James's father also saw *The Guardian* story, and he also dismissed the allegation that Taylor had been bought off, telling the media airily, 'If that had happened I would know about it.'

Later that day, as the story hit the headlines in the US, Rupert was asked about it on his own Fox News channel, while attending a media conference in Idaho. And his response was soon delighting and shocking his critics on YouTube:

Fox: Mr Chairman thanks very much for joining us. We appreciate it, Sir. The story that's really buzzing all round the country and certainly here in New York is that the *News of the World*, a News Corporation newspaper in Britain, used…

Murdoch: No I'm not talking about that issue at all today, sorry…

Fox: OK, no worries, Mr Chairman, that's fine with me.

Even though the story was all over New York, Rupert made no more effort than his son to look into *The Guardian*'s allegations, suggesting that he, too, didn't want to know what had gone on, or already knew well enough.

But once again, the Metropolitan Police made it easy for the Murdochs and News to get away with these high-handed dismissals because it rejected the claims almost as vigorously. Only a few hours after Davies's incendiary story was published, the Met's Assistant Commissioner for Special Operations, John Yates, stood up outside Scotland Yard and stamped out the fire by telling the media, 'No additional evidence has come to light. I therefore consider no further investigation is required.' For good measure, he added that police had found hundreds, not thousands, of potential hacking victims; that most had been the subject of legitimate journalistic inquiry; that a very small number had actually been hacked; and that anyone whose privacy had been invaded had been notified. These assertions were all either false or grossly misleading.

Yates's review of the 2006 investigation had taken him less than eight hours from start to finish, and had been pretty much sewn up by lunchtime. He had given Operation Caryatid's commander, Detective Chief Superintendent Philip Williams, a couple of hours to prepare a brief for an 11 a.m. meeting, which had galloped to the conclusion that no further action was required.

According to the minutes, Williams reported that, 'There was no evidence to expand the investigation…no evidence to support wider phones had been intercepted…no evidence at that time to implicate the involvement of any other journalists…and no evidence to justify…reopening the investigation.'

Quite how Williams managed to reach this conclusion is a mystery. But Yates had given the superintendent no time to get the files out of archives or consult Operation Caryatid's crucial decision log, which would have shown everyone the true picture. He had then failed to ask any of the obvious questions raised by *The Guardian* article, such as, who had asked Mulcaire to obtain hundreds of voicemail numbers and PIN codes; to whom had he supplied his information; was it right to suggest no other reporters were involved; and why had the police decided to limit the charges to only eight victims when, even on their own admission, 'hundreds' were involved?

It is hard to comprehend how two such senior police officers could make such an appalling mess of this task. But they clearly believed *The Guardian* had made an unwarranted attack on the integrity of the Metropolitan Police and were determined to defend its reputation at any cost. They were also desperate to rush out a response as quickly as possible. And it has to be said their speed paid dividends. The TV news that night and the papers next day all led with the claim that there was no new evidence, so the police would not reopen the case. Had they waited any longer to respond, *The Guardian*'s allegations would have got far more coverage.

The Met's rebuttal was quickly backed up by an ex-top cop writing in *The Times*, and not just any top cop at that. As head of Special Operations in 2006, Assistant Commissioner Andy Hayman had been in charge of the very investigation *The Guardian* was criticising. But having quit the force during an investigation into his expense claims, he had signed on as a Murdoch columnist on £10 000 a year. And he now earned his keep by defending his past and present employers. 'The list of those targeted...ran to several hundred names,' he helpfully recalled, before emphasising, 'there was *a small number, perhaps a handful*, where there was evidence that phones had actually been tampered with.' He then reassured his readers that Operation Caryatid had left no stone unturned, and there was no way his lads would have failed to follow up any leads. 'Had there been evidence of tampering in the other cases,' he wrote soothingly, 'that would have been investigated, as would the slightest hint that others were involved.'

Again, it is hard to see how Hayman could have come to this conclusion. But once he and Yates had done their bit, there was really no way back, because battle lines had been drawn. A week later, when DCS Williams and DS Surtees dug the files out of archives and wrote a summary of the investigation, which painted a much fairer account of the evidence gathered and the reasons for not going further, it was too late for the police to retreat.

But apart from the obvious desire to protect its reputation and avoid a fight, it's possible the Met had other reasons to claim the *News of the World* was in the clear, because the two organisations were the best of friends.

Murdoch's British papers were naturally on good terms with London's police because they always thumped the tub for law and order. But a special bond had developed in the mid-1980s when the Met's officers had kept Rupert's papers going through the violent disputes at Wapping. And this had been strengthened in the mid-1990s, when *The Sun* had created the Police Bravery Awards, which delivered an annual burst of much-needed good publicity for the force. A decade later, in 2005, News's tabloids had also defended the Met when the anti-terrorist squad had shot and killed an entirely innocent man on the London Underground. So there was an obvious temptation to keep the friendship going.

But there was also a revolving door between the two organisations. Reporters at News International often ended up as PR flacks at the Met, where ten of the 45 press officers were ex-Murdoch staffers. And several top policemen had landed comfortable billets at News on retirement. Lord Stevens, who served as the Met's Commissioner from 1998 to 2003, had his autobiography serialised in the *News of the World*, and was then hired by the paper to write a column called 'The Chief'. Soon afterwards, Hayman landed his part-time writing job on *The Times*.

The *News of the World*'s editors and executives had also made a point of cultivating the Met's most senior officers. And, in the case of Assistant Commissioner John Yates, this had blossomed into a personal friendship with Neil 'Wolfman' Wallis, who was a powerful figure at the Murdoch tabloid. The two men lived near each other in the west of London, shared a love of sport, and had children of similar ages. Yates had even helped Wallis's daughter get a job at the Met by passing her CV to the relevant department. They also went to soccer matches together several times a year and met up regularly in expensive restaurants. Indeed, they had dined at Scalini's in Knightsbridge just a month before Yates rubbished *The Guardian*'s story. They did so again at Scott's in Soho two months afterwards. And three weeks after that, they had dinner together at Cecconi's in Burlington Gardens. Another two months later, they were at it again.

This friendship should have been seen as a problem by the Assistant Commissioner because Wolfman had been Coulson's deputy editor back in 2005, when phone hacking was first uncovered, and was still in that role in 2006 when the Met arrested Goodman and Mulcaire. Indeed, he had been named by the royal reporter as one of the five people at the *News of the World* who allegedly knew about his illegal activities.

So Yates's mate was *potentially* involved in the very activities that the policeman was charged with re-examining. And, as a result, the Assistant Commissioner should clearly have stepped aside, especially if he intended to carry out his duties in such cavalier fashion. But he did not.

However, that wasn't the end of Yates's conflict of interest. In September 2009, two months after refusing to reopen the investigation into hacking at the *News of the World*, the Assistant Commissioner agreed to hire Wallis (who was leaving the paper) as a PR consultant to the police force on £1000 a day, with a guaranteed payment of £24 000 a year. And two months after that, he was being entertained to a slap-up dinner at The Ivy by the *News of the World*'s editor, Colin Myler, and crime editor, Lucy Panton. Almost a year later, when a terror bomb was discovered at West Midlands Airport, the paper's news editor decided that the paper's hospitality had left the policeman in their debt, so he sent Panton an email suggesting, 'John Yates could be crucial here. Have you spoken to him? Really need an exclusive splash line, so time to call in all those bottles of champagne.'

Now, whether Yates's contacts with Wallis and other senior editors at the paper really made a difference to the way he approached his review of Operation Caryatid one cannot be sure. But it's obvious that his refusal to reopen the investigation was 'pretty crap' and 'a poor decision', as Yates himself eventually admitted.

And the Assistant Commissioner wasn't the only senior policeman working hard to kill *The Guardian*'s story. On 10 December 2009, the Met's Commissioner, Sir Paul Stephenson, paid a visit to the newspaper's editor, Alan Rusbridger, in his full regalia, to tell him that the paper's coverage was 'exaggerated and incorrect' and that he should drop the investigation. A somewhat-shaken Rusbridger got the distinct impression that the head of London's police force was warning him off. Before this meeting, Stephenson was briefed by John Yates. Straight afterwards, the two men met for dinner with the Met's Director of Public Affairs, Dick Fedorcio, so it was clearly more than a spur-of-the-moment visit.

With the police almost as keen as the *News of the World* to make sure the hacking investigation was never reopened, it was left to Britain's elected representatives to give *The Guardian* some much-needed support. Disturbed by the idea that they had been lied to in 2007, the MPs on the House of Commons Culture, Media and Sport Committee decided to call Les Hinton back for a second round of questioning. And for good measure, they asked Andy Coulson, Tom Crone, Colin Myler and Stuart Kuttner to come along as well.

Armed with a copy of the Mulcaire/Miskiw contract and the 'For Neville' email, which Nick Davies had now managed to obtain from his sources, the MPs at last had some documents to show that News's one-rogue-reporter defence was a nonsense. But Coulson, Crone and Myler nevertheless repeated the Murdoch mantra that Clive Goodman had acted alone. They also insisted that News had conducted a thorough investigation, that the police had received full co-operation, and that Gordon Taylor had not been paid to keep quiet.

'I'm absolutely sure that Clive Goodman's case was a very unfortunate, rogue case,' MPs were assured by Andy Coulson, who was now working for the Tory leader, David Cameron, as head of communications. 'What we had…was a reporter who deceived the managing editor's office and, in turn, deceived me. I have thought long and hard about this,' he said with hand on heart. 'But if a rogue reporter decides to behave in that fashion, I am not sure that there is an awful lot more I could have done.'

Three years later, Tom Crone and Colin Myler would admit that they knew in 2007 or 2008 that the one-rogue-reporter defence was a lie. But on this day in 2009 they were more than happy to lead the chorus of denial. 'At no stage did any evidence arise that the problem of accessing by our reporters, or complicity of accessing by our reporters, went beyond the Goodman/Mulcaire situation,' Crone crowed, while Myler chirped up that News and its lawyers had gone through all the payment records and found 'no evidence of anything going beyond'.

The trio also sang in unison on the question of co-operating with the Met, with Crone assuring MPs that the police had 'seized every available document' during the raids and had 'searched all the computers, the files, the emails' at the *News of the World* before asking for anything else they thought might be relevant.

He implied—but didn't say—that they had got what they wanted.

Coulson added helpfully that he had 'brought in Burton Copeland, an independent firm of solicitors to carry out an investigation' and that News had 'opened up the files as much as we could. There was nothing that they asked for that they were not given.'

Crone then chimed in that the lawyers had been instructed 'to go over everything and find out what had gone on'. And Myler provided the finale, by proclaiming that their job had been: 'To give whatever facility the police required...Any enquiry, any question, that they wished to get; whether it was...emails, whether it was contracts, whether it was financial records...whatever the police asked for it was Burton Copeland that provided it.'

This, of course, was totally untrue, as Burton Copeland would eventually admit, because the police had been obstructed by News from start to finish, and Burton Copeland had handed over almost nothing that investigators had asked for.

The committee then came to the matter of the Taylor settlement, where MPs naturally wanted to know if he had been paid to keep quiet. This time it was Crone and Myler doing a duet:

Chairman: Was the size of that payment greater in order that the proceedings should be kept secret?

Myler: Absolutely not as far as I am aware.

Crone: No.

Chairman: Was it [the agreement to keep the settlement secret] at Gordon Taylor's request?

Crone: Actually I think he mentioned it first...It was raised by him before it was raised by us, but we fell in with it.

This, again, was absolutely at odds with what both men knew at the time and what they later admitted. More bluntly, it too was a lie.

The next big question was whether Goodman had been paid £200 000 to keep quiet, as had been rumoured in *Private Eye*. And, again, the MPs found Murdoch's men singing from the same songsheet:

Myler: I am not aware of any payment that has been made.

Crone: I had nothing to do with that area.

Philip Davies MP: If that did take place, who at News International would have been involved?

Crone: It did not take place, I do know that.

Davies: It did not take place?

Crone: No. I am not saying no payment, but that is an inaccurate report.

In fact, *Private Eye* had *underestimated* the amount by £43 502, but Crone was not about to tell MPs that this was the inaccuracy. He finally admitted under pressure that there might have been 'some payment'. And managing editor Stuart Kuttner agreed. But neither had any idea of the details. Subsequently, News International told MPs in a letter signed by Rebekah Brooks that Goodman and Mulcaire had both received settlements, but that these had been 'some way below the £60 600 statutory limit'. This was also grossly misleading, in that the total amount had been more than four times this figure.

Two months later, when Les Hinton was persuaded to appear by videolink from New York, he was unable to remember how much Goodman had been paid, even though he had ordered and approved the settlement. He also refused to say whether the reporter or private investigator had been made to sign confidentiality agreements and whether Mulcaire had been given an indemnity against future damages, telling MPs loftily, 'I am not going to discuss the terms of the agreement...I cannot remember the detail and, in any event, I have been told by News International not to discuss it.' Amazingly, MPs did not force the issue.

Calling MPs by their first names and giving a convincing impression of being a charming incompetent, Hinton gave a truly masterful performance. For the most part he claimed to know nothing, saying 'I don't know', 'I did not know', 'I just do not know', or 'I absolutely do not know' more than 30 times. Yet he was nonetheless sure that News was as clean as a whistle. He, too, assured MPs that there had been a rigorous internal investigation, and that 'Andy and Tom and then Colin' had 'worked very hard to see if there was any tangible evidence that they could act upon. There was none.'

And just in case there was any doubt, he added, 'There was never any evidence delivered to me that suggested that the conduct of Clive Goodman spread beyond him.' This was despite the fact that he had clearly read Goodman's letter and that he also knew of Justice Gross's sentencing remarks.

At one stage, Hinton was asked the simple question of whether News had paid Goodman and Mulcaire's legal fees. This is how he dealt with it.

> Philip Davies MP: First of all, did you in any way pay for any of the legal fees for Clive Goodman or Glenn Mulcaire?
>
> Mr Hinton: I absolutely do not know. I do not know whether we did or not. There were certainly some payments made...but on the matter of legal fees I honestly do not know.
>
> Philip Davies MP: The problem I have here is that whenever we have questioned anybody who was involved at the *News of the World* or News International, even including very senior people such as yourself, everybody has always said they do not know and they have also been able to further add that they have no idea who would know. This is all becoming rather incredible that some of the most senior people involved in News International either did not know or did not know who would know. Stuart Kuttner said that he did not know and he said that he did not know who would know. Now you are saying you do not know. Who on earth would know these things?
>
> Mr Hinton: That is a fine flourish of a question, Mr Davies, but I have answered your question: I do not know.

Philip Davies MP: Well, who would know in your organisation? You were a senior person in this organisation. Who in your organisation would know?

Mr Hinton: If we paid their legal fees the company would know; I do not.

Philip Davies MP: Who at the company would know? The company is not a person. What person would know?

Mr Hinton: Sorry?

Philip Davies MP: What person at the company would know if the legal fees had been paid or not?

Mr Hinton: Well, I would guess the Director of Human Resources but I do not know. When employees get into difficulty it is not unusual for them to be indemnified by the company that employs them and for their legal fees to be paid, but I am sorry, I just do not know. I am just surprised that of all the people you have had before you in the past two months you have not asked that question before. I just do not know, I am sorry.

Remarkably, the committee did not demand an answer on this either. Nor did it seek to question James Murdoch, even though he had been News International's chief executive in June 2008, when Gordon Taylor was paid off. And, while the MPs did ask Rebekah Brooks to appear, she simply refused. First, she told them she was too busy; then she told them she knew nothing; finally, she just said no. But she did have time to write a letter to the committee claiming that *The Guardian* had 'substantially and likely deliberately misled the British public', which News immediately leaked to the BBC.

James was certainly aware that Brooks was refusing this request from the people's representatives. Indeed, he was present in a meeting when she joked about the prospect of Black Rod coming after her with a summons. But just as the MPs hadn't pressed Hinton for answers on Goodman's pay-off, they now chose not to force her to appear, even though it was in their powers. According to Labour's Tom Watson MP, whom News had marked out as the committee's chief rabble-rouser, they were afraid the *News of the World* would dig dirt on their private lives. And they had good reason, because a concerted effort was already being made to shut them all up.

Neville Thurlbeck later confessed to Watson in a conversation that he believed to be off the record: 'All I know is that when the [Culture, Media and Sport Committee] got onto all the hacking stuff there was an edict come down from the editor, and it was find out every single thing about every single member: who was gay, who had affairs, anything we can use. Each reporter was given two members and there were six reporters that went on for around ten days [sic].'

Expanding on this in an article for the *New Statesman* magazine, Thurlbeck claimed, 'The objective was to find as much embarrassing sleaze on as many members as possible in order to blackmail them into backing off from its highly forensic inquiry into phone-hacking. It was a plan hatched not by the *News of the World* but by several executives at News International—up the corridor in "Deepcarpetland", as the area staffed by managers and pen-pushers was known. And it failed because the reporters [presumably including Thurlbeck] had grave reservations.'

Whether the reporters really did find themselves ethically challenged for once is unclear, but the man chasing Watson had no such qualms. Mazher Mahmood, who was better known as the *News of the World*'s Fake Sheikh for his habit of dressing up as a rich Arab to entrap his victims, tipped off the news desk that the MP was 'shagging' a female politician and would be at the Labour Party conference in Brighton with her, where he might be caught 'creeping into her hotel'.

Within minutes of receiving this email, the *News of the World*'s news editor, Ian Edmondson, replied that it was a 'great story' and advised Mahmood, 'You might want to check his recent cutts [cuttings], v interesting!' Immediately afterwards, the *News of the World*'s tame gumshoe, Derek Webb of Silent Shadow, was despatched to follow the Murdochs' critic round Brighton for five days and nights, which he did, without success, from 28 September to 2 October 2009, at a cost of £1125.

Webb was a former detective who had left the police force in 2003 and had been employed exclusively by the *News of the World* since then, to follow people they wanted to write about. Initially hired by Thurlbeck, he had subsequently been used by 27 named reporters on the paper to follow more than 150 people, including politicians, journalists, lawyers and policemen, as well as criminals, brothel owners and members of the public. Most of the time it was MPs and celebrities that he was set onto, and almost always it was to check out a tip that they were having an affair. He was commissioned over the phone, to ensure there was nothing in writing, and told by the paper's accounts department to keep his targets' names off the bills. But since his jobs had to be signed off by someone high up in the newsroom, and Webb was pounding the streets most of the time, it was pretty obvious that plenty of people in the *News of the World* knew about his activities. And this certainly included Tom Crone and Stuart Kuttner, who got him to sign a confidentiality agreement in 2007, when he was temporarily laid off by the paper after being charged with professional misconduct by Thames Valley Police. By the time he chased Watson in 2009, the investigator had changed his company name to Derek Webb Media and was pretending to be a freelance journalist, at the request of the *News of the World*. But he was still doing exactly what he had always done.

At the Labour Party conference that weekend, as Webb waited in vain to catch Watson dropping his daks, was the MP's most virulent opponent, Rebekah Brooks, who buttonholed the BBC's political correspondent, Nick Robinson, twice in one evening to ask, 'What am I going to do about this Tom Watson?' albeit in rather more colourful language.

The MP's sources at Downing Street had already told Watson that Brooks was furious about the inquiry, and demanding he be pulled off or sacked. She was also complaining bitterly about him to Prime Minister Gordon Brown's PR guru, Peter Mandelson, and insisting that the committee be reined in.

As Thurlbeck eventually confided to Watson in their frank and revealing chat, which Watson presumably recorded: 'She didn't like you at all. She took an absolute pathological dislike to you. She saw you as the person that was really threatening. She tried to smear you as mad. She was briefing. She was saying to Blair: "We've got to call this man off, he's mad."'

Watson had only joined the Culture committee in June 2009, after winning a defamation battle against *The Sun*, but he had arrived with a reason to dislike the Murdoch press. As a whipper-in for Labour's prime minister-to-be, Gordon Brown, he had earned the hatred of the Murdoch clan in 2006 by calling on Blair to quit Downing Street. Shortly afterwards, he was told by *The Sun*'s political editor, George Pascoe-Watson, 'Rebekah will never forgive you for what you did to her Tony.' This was followed by a further warning that 'Rupert never forgets', and that the Murdoch papers would pursue him for life.

By and large, Brooks and *The Sun* had lived up to this promise. In early 2009, the tabloid had branded him 'poisonous', a 'hatchet man' and a liar, and followed this with a column describing him as 'Treacherous Tom Watson', 'A tub of lard' and 'Two Dinners Tommy', with 'his bloated, bulging neck'. These attacks had left

Watson on the edge of a nervous breakdown and caused him to resign as a junior minister. He had then joined the Culture Committee, and found himself face to face with his tormenters again when *The Guardian* story broke a month later.

Given what *The Sun* was writing about him, it was obvious that he was no favourite of the people who ran News. But Brooks was remarkably open in telling Blair's press secretary, Alastair Campbell, that they were keen to get revenge. 'I recall Rebekah… telling me that so far as she was concerned with Tom Watson it's personal and we won't stop until we get him,' Campbell wrote in his diary.

Amazingly enough Blair's senior adviser also found himself under attack from the Murdoch clans for his own critical comments on hacking. As one of the few people who took the story seriously, Campbell did a number of television interviews in which he warned that 'evidence of systematic criminal activity on an industrial basis' was emerging at the *News of the World*. Shortly afterwards, he received 'what can only be termed threatening text and phone messages from both Rebekah and the office of James Murdoch'.

It was yet another warning that those who took Murdoch on did so at their peril. But, fortunately, there were still some who refused to be cowed.

14
KEEPING IT BURIED

'We have repeatedly encountered an unwillingness to provide the detailed information that we sought, claims of ignorance or lack of recall, and deliberate obfuscation.'

House of Commons Culture, Media and Sport Committee

Even if the MPs on the Culture Committee couldn't prove their suspicions, they clearly did not believe a word they had been told by Murdoch's executives. And in February 2010, they produced a report that bluntly accused News International of a cover-up.

Slamming the one-rogue-reporter story as just not credible, the MPs pointed out that it had been directly contradicted by Justice Gross at the original trial, and added: 'Evidence we have seen makes it inconceivable that no-one else at the *News of the World*, bar Clive Goodman, knew about the phone-hacking.'

The MPs also panned the newspaper's own investigation as 'far from rigorous', and commented tartly that they had been 'struck by the collective amnesia afflicting witnesses from the *News of the World*'. Finally, they fired a broadside at the Murdoch managers involved in the story by accusing them of 'deliberate obfuscation', 'claims of ignorance or lack of recall', and trying to 'conceal the truth about what really occurred'. Short of branding Crone, Coulson, Hinton and Myler as liars, or charging them with contempt of Parliament, this was about as tough as they could have been.

But once again, in true Murdoch style, News's response was to hit back harder, with Rebekah Brooks laying into the MPs to accuse them of bias, unfairness, irresponsibility and 'violating the public trust'. The following Sunday, the *News of the World* also put the boot in with a full-page editorial, which told its readers, 'The victims here are YOU, the public. If these MPs get their way, our media landscape will be changed forever.' Pumping itself up to its full self-importance, the paper then declared, 'Bear in mind the forces that are at work trying to silence us and keep you in ignorance. They are many and they are powerful. And right now they're doing their damndest to wreck the most precious of basic press freedoms—your right to know.'

Finally, the paper declared that it would continue to campaign for freedom and truth: 'We'll take no lessons in standards from MPs—nor from the self-serving pygmies who run the circulation-challenged *Guardian*. But we promise this: As long as we have the power to fight, you can rely on us to keep doing what we do best—revealing the misdeeds that influential people are desperate to hide. And we'll let YOU be our judge and jury.'

The arrogance of it was breathtaking, given that Murdoch's executives had done so much to hide their own misdeeds and lawbreaking. And even more so because of what happened next. Only a few days after berating Britain's parliamentarians, Brooks agreed to buy off another prominent hacking victim by promising the celebrity agent, Max Clifford, almost £1 million to drop his case. Back in 2005, the *News of the World* had got Mulcaire to hack the PR guru's phones because he had fallen out with Andy Coulson and stopped giving the paper scoops about his clients, such as *The Sun*'s famous FREDDIE STARR ATE MY HAMSTER story. Listening to his voicemails had been a way of getting these tip-offs again for free.

Clifford's pay-off was arranged with Brooks over an intimate lunch at the exclusive Mews of Mayfair restaurant, and did not involve any admission of wrongdoing or payment of damages. Instead, News International agreed to pay his legal fees and a retainer of £220 000 a year to feed stories to the *News of the World* for the next three years, which allowed them to claim no deal had been done. The cost of buying his silence was £300 000 more than the record pay-out to Taylor. But the price rise was understandable because it would have been Armageddon if the case had gone ahead. Glenn Mulcaire had admitted to the High Court in pretrial hearings that he had given transcripts of Clifford's voicemails to the news desk at the *News of the World* and not to Goodman. And he had immediately been ordered by Justice Vos to name the journalists and editors he had dealt with. The judge had also told News to reveal details of its £700 000 settlement with Taylor and to hand over the list of the 27 *News of the World* journalists (including Brooks) who had paid Steve Whittamore for information. It would have been a disaster if any of this had been allowed to happen.

The deal was done on a handshake between Brooks and Clifford, with an agreement to keep it quiet. But the agent almost immediately leaked the story to *The Guardian*. 'The so-called secret settlement wasn't secret for more than, I think, a day,' his lawyer, Charlotte Harris, later confessed. 'When I realised that the case was being settled, I had a furious argument with Max and I said, "What happens now? It might be the end." And he said, "Don't worry, poppet." And he was right.'

But one damning detail had still not been revealed. Three weeks before the Culture Committee accused Murdoch's managers of a cover-up, News International had agreed to pay Mulcaire's legal fees and indemnify him against damages, so he could fight the High Court disclosure order. So the company was now paying a convicted criminal to stop him from telling the truth about their crimes.

One would imagine this new step was something James Murdoch would have wanted to know about, along with the £1 million pay-off. He might also have wanted to know that Clifford and Mulcaire were about to blow the *News of the World*'s hacking defence to pieces. And he had plenty of chance to find out because he and Rebekah had adjacent offices at Wapping and talked to each other several times a day. But he could also have figured out what was happening from *The Guardian* story, after the settlement with Clifford, which made it clear that Mulcaire would no longer need to name names.

Rupert would also have been able to brief himself fully, given that he spoke to his favourite female executive on a near-daily basis.

But in case the three of them never managed to swap notes, they had a golden opportunity to chat about the case at Cheltenham races on 18 March 2010, when they all went to watch Rupert's daughter, Elisabeth, ride in the Ladies Charity Sweepstake. This was only nine days after Brooks's £1 million deal with Clifford had been exposed in *The Guardian* and less than a month after MPs had accused News executives of a concerted cover-up. It is hard to believe that Rupert didn't want to be briefed on these major developments. And it is clear from pictures of him, James and Rebekah together at the track that he had plenty of opportunity to discuss it with them.

James would later be forced to admit that he knew about the Clifford settlement 'in very general terms'. And one would have thought this might have prompted him to ask a few basic questions, such as, why was the PR man being paid nearly £1 million, what was News getting for its money, and what would happen if they declined to settle? But there's no paper trail to prove that he did any of this.

While Brooks and the two Murdochs were apparently avoiding these delicate subjects, News's lawyers were beginning to fret that Clifford's win might release a flood of new claims. Tom Crone and Julian Pike were also worried that the lawyers who had run the Taylor and Clifford cases, Mark Lewis and Charlotte Harris, might be sharing information obtained in the legal actions, which News had locked up with confidentiality agreements. They were also perhaps keen to shut them down, as Brooks had wanted to do with the Commons committee.

In any case, Derek Webb soon found himself tailing enemies of the paper again. On two separate occasions in April 2010, the *News of the World*'s silent shadow was commissioned to follow Lewis, Harris and another Manchester solicitor, with whom they believed her (wrongly) to be having an affair. When the paper's news editor, Ian Edmondson, complained this would not lead to a story, he was told by Tom Crone that, 'the main reason to investigate was that it could provide good leverage against the two individuals'. Webb therefore sat on their tails for a week, parking outside houses and following Lewis's wife and teenage daughter into a garden centre with a hidden camera, only to draw a blank, as he had with Tom Watson.

While Webb was digging for dirt on the victims' lawyers, *The Guardian* was also getting anxious because News's denials had virtually killed the story. None of Britain's other national papers had reported the Clifford settlement and, apart from *The Independent*, they had also ignored the House of Commons' report. The *Daily Mail* had run a 154-word story about Coulson being cleared; *The Sun* had run a piece on page two claiming that the MPs had tried to smear him but failed; and *The Times* had run an item on page 15 rehashing what *The Sun* had written. But no one in the print media had showed any real interest in taking up the baton, either because they were part of the News International stable, or because their own newspapers had been up to similar tricks.

With the police and the Press Complaints Commission also rubbishing their work, *The Guardian* sorely needed an ally. So Rusbridger called Bill Keller, the Executive Editor of the *New York Times*, and asked for help, in the hope that the US paper might force the world to listen. Within days, three of its gun reporters were in his London office listening to Nick Davies tell them what he had uncovered. For the next four months, the *New York Times* trio went backwards and forwards across England, talking to Davies's sources and finding more of their own. And in September 2010, they published the results in a 5000-word investigation that lined up a dozen former *News of the World* reporters and editors to say that phone hacking at the paper had been 'pervasive', and that the police had failed to follow vital leads. 'Everyone knew. The office cat knew,' one former staff member claimed.

Best of all, perhaps, the *New York Times* persuaded the *News of the World*'s former showbiz reporter, Sean Hoare, to go on the record, which no one had yet done. Hoare admitted that he had hacked into David and Victoria Beckham's voicemails and claimed he had played tapes of intercepted messages to Coulson when they were on the 'Bizarre' column at *The Sun* together. He also said the editor had 'actively encouraged' him to keep on hacking at the *News of the World*.

Several other former staffers backed him up, painting a picture of 'a frantic, sometimes degrading atmosphere' in the *News of the World*'s newsroom, with reporters going to almost any lengths to satisfy the paper's demands. One former editor claimed that Coulson had openly discussed hacking and the dark arts, and that he had attended 'dozens if not hundreds of meetings with Andy' when the subject had come up. Coulson would ask where a story came from, and his editors would tell him, 'We've pulled the phone records' or 'I've listened to the phone messages'.

A week later, one of the *News of the World*'s leading investigative reporters, Paul McMullan, also popped his head above the parapet to say that everybody at the paper had been hacking phones, often from their desks in the newsroom, and that Coulson must have known about it. Another veteran told *The Guardian* anonymously, 'Andy Coulson absolutely knew. They all knew. He sat in the newsroom, often on the backbench on Friday and Saturday. It was a regular daily joke in conference: "say no more."' Yet another was equally adamant:

> The paper was paying Glenn Mulcaire £2000 a week, and they wanted their money's worth. For just about every story, they rang Glenn. It wasn't just tapping. It was routine. Even if it was just a car crash or a house fire on a Saturday, they'd call Glenn, and he'd come back with ex-directory phone numbers, the BT list of friends and family and their addresses, lists of numbers called from their mobile phones. This was just commonplace. He was hacking masses of phones. We reckoned David Beckham had thirteen different sim cards, and Glenn could hack every one of them. How could senior editors not know that they are spending £2000 a week on this guy, and using him on just about every story that goes into the paper?

McMullan also opened up about the *News of the World*'s illegal trade with Steve Whittamore. 'I would speak to Steve nearly every day when I was deputy features editor,' he recalled. 'Getting information from confidential records, we did that regularly, time and time again. Some of what Steve did was legal, like using the electoral register, but if he went a step further, I would not have given a second thought to whether that was illegal, because that's part of your job.'

Once again, executives at News ridiculed these revelations, even though they came from their own journalists, and issued a statement to say, 'We reject absolutely any suggestion or assertion that the activities of Clive Goodman and Glenn Mulcaire…were part of a culture of wrongdoing at the *News of the World*.'

The Sun's former editor, Kelvin MacKenzie, also tipped a bucket of cold water on it all, telling Australia's ABC TV:

> They've had six years to look at it. They've had parliamentary inquiries. They have had police inquiries, Scotland Yard inquiries; they've had Crown Prosecution's inquiries. They've had Department of Public Prosecution inquiries. Everybody has trailed all over this and not one piece of evidence, outside the evidence that sent these two guys to gaol, has been discovered.

And this time, even Rupert joined the chorus of denial. Questioned about hacking at News Corporation's annual general meeting in the Darryl F Zanuck Theater at Fox Studios in Los Angeles, he replied scathingly that he had not read the *New York Times* and would not believe anything that it or *The Guardian* wrote. It was all a conspiracy of his enemies, he said, and there was not a shred of evidence to back them up.

Questioned by the Australian journalist and shareholder activist, Stephen Mayne, he said:

Murdoch: There was an incident more than five years ago. The person who bought a bugged phone conversation was immediately fired, and in fact he subsequently went to jail. There have been two parliamentary inquiries, which have found no further evidence or any other thing at all. If anything was to come to light, we challenge people to give us evidence, and no-one has been able to. If any evidence comes to light, we will take immediate action like we took before.

Mayne: Did you read the 5000-word piece in the *New York Times* claiming they had spoken to no less than twelve former editors and reporters for the *News of the World*, confirming that the practice was wide spread?

Murdoch: No.

Mayne: You haven't read that *New York Times* piece?

Murdoch: No.

Mayne: The actual committee said in its report, there was 'deliberate obfuscation' by your executives, there was 'collective amnesia' by the executives and you've just demonstrated this again, and this point...

Murdoch: I'm sorry. Journalists who have been fired, who are unhappy, or work for other organisations, I don't take them as an authority, and least of all I don't take the *New York Times* as authority which is the most motivated of all.

Obviously, the News Corp board had also ignored the *Times* article, as well as the regular revelations in *The Guardian* and the accusations of a cover-up that had been levelled by the House of Commons, because the directors sat there meekly and listened. Even though they were legally responsible for running the News group, and paid by shareholders to do so, they clearly weren't game to challenge Rupert's determination to ignore these serious allegations. Needless to say, they also declined to take action.

As before, the Metropolitan Police was only marginally more inclined to take notice, with Yates telling the Crown Prosecution

Service he had no plans to re-examine the files but would investigate whether there was any new evidence. In this connection, his team made a cursory attempt to interview Coulson, who chose to remain silent, and also Sean Hoare and Paul McMullan. But instead of treating the whistleblowers as potential witnesses, the Met's detectives attempted to put them both under caution and question them as suspects. And, not surprisingly, they too declined to say anything.

So, once again, the police and News managed to keep the lid from blowing off. But it was becoming harder and harder to resist the pressure that was building up. Brooks's old sparring partner, Chris Bryant, and former Deputy Prime Minister, John Prescott, were now petitioning the High Court for a judicial review of the Met's handling of the hacking investigation, which would inevitably reveal what the police had found. And they had been joined by a former Deputy Assistant Commissioner of the Metropolitan Police, Brian Paddick, who was also sure his phone had been hacked. Paddick had fallen foul of the Murdoch papers since coming out as Britain's first gay police chief in 2002, and was convinced the Met was refusing to reopen the hacking investigation to safeguard its relationship with News.

As their case trundled towards the High Court, news of Clifford's £1 million windfall was prompting other hacking victims (including several of his clients) to try their luck with legal action. Foremost among them was the actress, Sienna Miller, who had been the subject of a dozen articles in the *News of the World* in 2005 and 2006 that had revealed details of intimate private conversations and rows with her partner, Jude Law. As with several other victims, the paper's snooping had driven her crazy, causing her to fall out with friends and family and accuse them of betraying her.

Miller had also been chased, abused and spat upon by paparazzi, who had been a constant presence in her life since she was 21. 'I would often find myself at midnight running down a dark street on my own with ten big men chasing me,' she said. 'And the fact that they had cameras in their hands meant that that was legal, but if you take away the cameras, what have you got? You've got a pack of men chasing a woman and obviously that's a very intimidating situation to be in.'

Before going ahead with her damages action, Miller obtained a High Court order forcing the police to disclose documents they had seized in their raid on Mulcaire. Then, on 6 September 2010, she told the *News of the World* she was suing. And now the cover-up went a dramatic step further. Three days after receiving Miller's notice of action, a senior executive at News International ordered the urgent destruction of emails that might help her case. Back in November 2009, the company had taken a decision in principle to get rid of all incriminating documents, 'that could be unhelpful in the context of future litigation'. And over the next ten months, a senior News executive had tried to hurry this along. But Miller's action made it urgent. Late in the afternoon of 9 September, an employee in News's IT department sent an email (presumably to the company managing the archives) saying, 'If the deletion need to wait till tomorrow that is fine. There is a senior NI management requirement to delete this data as quickly as possible.'

Shortly after this, News International's entire email archive up to 30 September 2004 was erased. The following January, after a further instruction from a senior News executive, all emails up to 30 September 2007 were wiped, destroying some 300 million messages in total. News also destroyed the computer belonging to the journalist named in Miller's action, and seized the opportunity to take the hammer to all its other journalists' computers.

It was while this was going on that Rupert Murdoch told his shareholders at the Los Angeles AGM that he challenged anyone to give him evidence of his journalists being involved in hacking. It was also now that he gave the inaugural Margaret Thatcher Lecture in London and promised solemnly, 'We will vigorously pursue the truth, and we will not tolerate wrongdoing.'

However, even this wholesale destruction of evidence was not enough to keep Miller and her legal team at bay. In December, the police coughed up uncensored copies of Mulcaire's files, which showed he had collected nine mobile phone numbers, with PIN codes and passwords, belonging to Miller or her family and friends, along with reams of other personal, private data. The private investigator's notebooks also revealed the corner name of the journalist at the *News of the World*'. Even worse, as far as the Murdochs were concerned, was the material made it clear that Miller was a 'project' for the paper, and part of a much wider scheme to target celebrities.

In mid-December, this damning new evidence was presented to the public, when *The Guardian* published extracts from a court document written by Miller's lawyers, which revealed that the *News of the World* had asked Mulcaire in January 2005 to get information on celebrities, MPs and members of the Royal Household, to 'use electronic intelligence and eavesdropping' to do so, and to 'provide daily transcripts'.

On 5 January, the *News of the World*'s news editor, Ian Edmondson, was suspended from duty. Nine days later, the head of the Crown Prosecution Service, Keir Starmer QC, called a meeting with the Metropolitan Police and announced his intention to do a 'root and branch' review of the original hacking investigation, which would examine all the material seized from Mulcaire, including all the stuff that had never been properly processed. Somewhat reluctantly, the police were persuaded to fall into line.

'I was absolutely clear in my mind at the beginning of that meeting I was going to settle for nothing less than a full review of all this material unless somebody blocked my access to it,' Starmer explained. 'To be fair to Mr Yates, he did not seek to block that approach, and in the end agreed to it, but I have to say by then I had reached the stage where I really was not in the mood for being dissuaded.'

Twelve days after that, as the review led by Alison Levitt QC got under way, News International handed the police three emails that it had been forced to disclose to Miller's lawyers in the court action, which showed that Edmondson had indeed dealt with Mulcaire. And on that same day, 26 January 2011, the police launched a brand new investigation into hacking, led by Commander Sue Akers: Operation Weeting was born.

Now it all began to unravel fast. On 5 April, two former *News of the World* reporters, Edmondson and Thurlbeck, were arrested. Three days later, News agreed to pay Sienna Miller the £100 000 she was seeking in damages, and publicly admitted that the one-rogue-reporter defence was untrue. Acknowledging that their investigations had not been 'sufficiently robust', Rupert Murdoch himself apologised 'unreservedly' and promised to pay compensation. Six days later, another *News of the World* reporter, James Weatherup, was arrested at his home.

Finally, News also launched an investigation of sorts. On the evening of 19 May 2011, Rupert held a council of war over dinner at his luxury London apartment in Buckingham Gate, just a stone's throw from the palace where all the hacking fun had started. Rebekah Brooks and James Murdoch were among those invited, as were Will Lewis and Simon Greenberg from News International, who had been increasingly involved in battling the scandal. But three top executives had also flown in from the US parent company, News Corp: the chief executive Chase Carey, chief legal counsel Lon Jacobs and Rupert's senior adviser, Joel Klein. At their side was a hard-nosed Washington lawyer, Brendan Sullivan Jnr, who had made his name defending Lt. Col. Oliver North in the Iran–Contra scandal in the 1980s.

According to *Business Week*, who reconstructed the meeting in February 2012, Rebekah and Rupert took their places as hosts at each end of the table, while Murdoch laid out the ground rules, telling the assembled company, 'I will handle the board... Everyone else stay out of it.' Sullivan then opened the proceedings by assuring them that Rebekah Brooks was 'innocent' and that 'criminal charges would not be warranted'. Emphasising that the most important thing was to keep Rupert and James Murdoch 'at arm's length from the scandal', he averred that the investigation would be handled by News International's executives in London, and run by Brooks.

Lon Jacobs apparently sat listening to this with his head in his hands. Three weeks later he resigned. He had been arguing with Rupert and Klein for weeks, insisting they launch an investigation from New York and do it properly, while James and Rebekah had been pushing equally hard for her to keep control. Now Rupert had backed his son and favourite, and Brooks would be investigating herself, despite the fact that Mulcaire had worked for her at the *News of the World*, that Coulson had been her deputy and friend, and that she had led the company's denials for the last two years.

Perhaps Rupert still believed she was not involved. Perhaps he even clung to the idea that nothing much had happened, despite the three arrests and News's recent admissions. Or perhaps he didn't want anyone looking too hard at what Rebekah and James had done. But most of all, perhaps, he was hoping it could all be battened down for a few more weeks or months, so that News Corp's £8 billion bid for BSkyB could get through. Project Rubicon, as it was known inside the company, was facing fiercer and fiercer public opposition, not least because of the growing scandal surrounding the *News of the World* and its crimes. But James had been given assurances that the government was backing the bid and that it was only a matter of time before final approval came through.

And, so far, the hacking arrests and legal victories had not been enough to stop this from happening. In mid-June 2011, Prime Minister David Cameron signalled how little he cared about the revelations by giving the keynote speech at the Murdochs' invitation-only conference at Wapping. That same week, he joined Rupert and James at News International's summer party at the Orangery in Kensington Gardens, as lines of big black cars disgorged politicians and the powerful to pay their respects to Britain's biggest media tycoon.

The Opposition leader, Ed Miliband, was also among those who joined the throng, tucking into free oysters and Moët and Chandon. And so, of course, was Rebekah Brooks, working the crowd with Rupert on her arm.

That evening saw Murdoch's British empire at the peak of its power. Despite everything that had been revealed about what the *News of the World* had done; despite the arrest of (now) four of its journalists; despite the £100 000 pay out to Sienna Miller; despite Rupert's apology to the victims and his admission of wrongdoing, the nation's power elite was still lining up to pay homage to the king. Two weeks later, at the end of June, the BSkyB bid would get the nod from Cameron's coalition government, and the way would be opened for Murdoch to acquire yet more power.

But there were black clouds in the sky over London that night, with heavy rain and the threat of lightning, which caused the party to break up early and the guests to run for cover at 9 p.m. And it must have been an omen because a violent storm was just about to break.

15
FAMILY FEUDS

'Rebekah has fucked the company.'

Elisabeth Murdoch

It could have been just another hacking story. But the report by Nick Davies and Amelia Hill that went up on *The Guardian*'s website at 4.29 p.m. on Monday, 4 July 2011 created more havoc than anyone could ever have imagined.

Within a week, it had forced Britain's biggest-selling Sunday tabloid to close and prompted a government inquiry that would recommend tough new regulations for the press. Within a fortnight, it had torpedoed News's bid for BSkyB, caused London's two top policemen to resign and forced Rupert Murdoch's two most trusted executives to walk the plank; it had also wrecked James's immediate chance of succeeding his father at the head of News Corporation and sullied the Murdochs' reputation further. And that was just the start of it.

After years of no one caring what the *News of the World* had done, everyone suddenly rushed to condemn the paper. It was as if the floodgates had burst or the Berlin Wall had come tumbling down. There was an avalanche of publicity, a torrent of revelations and a mad scramble of people wanting to express their disgust.

The Guardian's revelations concerned a thirteen-year-old Surrey schoolgirl, Milly Dowler, who had gone missing on her way home from school in March 2002, wearing her blazer and grey skirt and carrying a backpack full of books. She had been missing for nearly six months until she was found murdered.

It had been a huge story for the tabloids at the time, and especially for the *News of the World*, then being edited by Rebekah Brooks, which had done everything it could to beat its rivals to the punch.

And, as *The Guardian* now sensationally reported, this 'everything' had included obtaining Milly's mobile phone number and hacking into her private voicemails. Worse still, the *News of the World*'s reporters had apparently deleted some of her messages to make space for more, and had given her distraught parents hope that their missing daughter was still alive.

As Milly's mother, Sally, explained, she had rung the teenager's mobile several times a day in the desperate hope that she might answer it, but had soon started getting a message that the voicemail box was full. Then she had phoned again and was amazed to hear the teenager's voice coming back at her. 'I had got through to her personal voice message. I jumped out of my seat and screamed,' she recalled. 'I was just so elated to think that there was a possibility that Milly had accessed her voicemail and was therefore still alive...It is impossible to put into words what it felt like.'

'She's picked up her voicemails, Bob. She's alive!' she screamed to her husband. And soon she was excitedly telling friends the same thing: 'She's picked up her voicemails; she's alive, she's alive.' But of course she wasn't.

The revelation that Milly Dowler's phone had been hacked by the *News of the World* carried an extraordinary emotional charge, almost as if its reporters had been in league with the poor girl's killer. Suddenly, the Murdochs and their tabloid journalists were seen as criminals, pariahs, the lowest of the low. And everyone wanted to condemn them.

Britain's Prime Minister, David Cameron, who was visiting the troops in Afghanistan, led the charge by telling the media he found it 'quite, quite shocking'. Hard on his heels, the nation's Home Secretary, Theresa May, declared, 'I think it's totally shocking; frankly, it's disgusting. The mindset of somebody who thinks it's appropriate to do that is totally sick.'

The Deputy Prime Minister, Nick Clegg, branded it as 'beneath contempt' and 'grotesque'. While Tom Watson, who had spent the last two years trying to get people to care about the *News of the World*'s hacking activities, tweeted, 'I feel physically sick. Some people are inhuman, simply evil.'

Britain's Opposition leader, Ed Miliband, also joined in the kicking, by describing it as 'truly immoral'. Braver than most, he blamed it on the culture of the Murdoch paper and called for Rebekah Brooks, who had been editing the *News of the World* at the time, to resign. This provoked a furious reaction from *The Sun*'s political editor, Tom Newton Dunn, who told the Labour Party's media chief, Bob Roberts, 'We're going to make it personal to you. We won't forget.'

Even the Metropolitan Police Commissioner, Sir Paul Stephenson, who had tried to stop *The Guardian* pursuing the story, added his voice to the chorus by saying, 'My heart goes out to the Dowler family. I'm not sure there is anyone who wouldn't be appalled and repulsed by such behaviour.'

It would in fact turn out that *The Guardian* was wrong in its key accusation, and that it was the phone company, rather than the *News of the World*, that had deleted Milly's messages, but by the time this was revealed, several months later, it was far too late for the damage to be undone.

And there was never any doubt about the rest of the story: the Murdoch paper had hacked into Milly's voicemails and caused the Dowlers pain. Some weeks after their daughter went missing, Bob and Sally had walked the route she would have taken home from school, deciding to do this on the spur of the moment, telling no one else, and checking to ensure there were no photographers around. Along the way they stopped to look at a poster of their daughter on a tree, and Sally became emotional. Three days later, a picture of this intensely private moment, taken with a telephoto lens, appeared in the *News of the World*. Furious, they now asked the police if their phone might have been bugged, and wondered if the newspaper had known their movements because Glenn Mulcaire had intercepted their messages too.

Yet, remarkably, anyone reading the *News of the World* at the time could have known what its journalists were up to. As would the lawyers and editors on the Sunday tabloid who had checked its stories for publication.

On 14 April 2002, early editions of the *News of the World* quoted verbatim from two voicemails left on the murdered teenager's phone on 27 March, six days after her disappearance. The first of these told her, 'Mortlake in Putney by Tangles,' and signed off, 'Piggo, baby.' The second, from an employment agency in the Midlands, said, 'Hello Mandy [Milly's real name was Amanda], we're ringing because we have some interviews starting. Can you call me back?' At the time no one thought to ask where they had got them from.

To get the agency to give them more information, the *News of the World*'s reporters had impersonated Milly's mother and pretended to be working hand-in-glove with the police, and had got the lead that she might be working at an Epson inkjet factory near Birmingham. Convinced that the missing girl was still alive and they could land the scoop, the paper's acting news editor, Neville Thurlbeck, had then scrambled eight reporters and photographers to stake out the factory, hoping to snap her as she came out the gates. When she didn't show for the next three days, the paper had settled for a story headed MESSAGES ON MOBILE PROBED, which focused on these voicemails and suggested that the police had missed a vital lead. By the second edition, this had morphed into MILLY HOAX RIDDLE and the claim that a hoaxer was deliberately trying to mislead investigators. Even more significantly, all quotes from Milly's voicemails had now been removed, and all but one reference to the messages had been erased. Furthermore, the entire story had been sourced to Surrey Police, which suggested that someone on high at the *News of the World* had realised how dangerous it would be to give their game away.

In ringing the police several times for comment on the day before publication, the *News of the World* had made no secret of the fact they had obtained Milly's mobile number and PIN code and listened to her voicemails. Indeed, a reporter had played the tape down the phone to an officer to convince him the story was true. Yet Surrey Police had not seen fit to mention this to anyone else, either at the time, or in the five years since Goodman and Mulcaire had been charged.

On the morning of Tuesday, 5 July 2011, as *The Guardian*'s revelations were picked up by the other papers and followed up on radio and TV, Rebekah Brooks let it be known that she was 'deeply shocked' by the allegations and that the company had been 'working through the night' to discover if there was any truth in them. She also made it clear she had 'spoken to Rupert Murdoch' and was 'under no pressure from him to stand down', because he was 'backing her 100 per cent'.

At lunchtime that day, she confirmed she was going nowhere and was entirely innocent of this awful crime. 'It is almost too horrific to believe that a professional journalist or even a freelance inquiry agent working on behalf of a member of the *News of the World* staff could behave in this way,' Brooks said in a statement to staff. 'If the allegations are proved to be true then I can promise the strongest possible action will be taken, as this company will not tolerate such disgraceful behaviour.' And just in case there was any doubt about her own position, she added, 'I hope that you all realise it is inconceivable that I knew or worse, sanctioned these appalling allegations.'

That same day, someone at News International tried to take the heat off their boss by suggesting that the company now knew who had sanctioned the hacking of Dowler's phone (which was supposedly not Brooks), and by leaking a tip that Andy Coulson had authorised corrupt payments to the police. But the fire was already burning out of control.

Other *News of the World* hacking victims were now queuing up to complain that their privacy had been violated. These included the parents of two murdered ten-year-old girls, Holly Wells and Jessica Chapman, whose death in 2002 had shocked Britain, and the mother of eight-year-old Sarah Payne, whose murder in 2001 had inspired Brooks's notorious paedophile name-and-shame campaign.

The families of people killed in London's terror attacks had also been targeted. Graham Foulkes, whose 22-year-old son David had been blown up on a Circle Line train on 7 July 2005, was horrified when he heard the news, telling the BBC, 'We were in a very dark place. You think it's about as dark as it can get and then you realise there's someone out there who can make it even darker...If it happens that they were indeed listening, these people really need to be subject to the law.'

Relatives of British soldiers who died in Iraq and Afghanistan had also been on the *News of the World*'s eavesdropping roster. Rose Gentle, whose son Gordon had been killed by a roadside bomb in Basra in 2004, told the BBC she was 'totally disgusted...I'd never buy that paper again, if this is true, they need to be brought to justice for this, they need to pay.'

On Wednesday 6 July, the House of Commons held an emergency debate, and Britain's MPs were able to swell the crescendo of outrage. Now back from Afghanistan, David Cameron promised there would be an official inquiry, although as yet he offered no details. A week later, he went the Full Monty: a comprehensive review of the 'culture, practices and ethics of the press' that would examine phone hacking at the *News of the World* and the conduct of the police investigation, but also inquire into relations between the press and police and the press and politicians. Chaired by a distinguished senior judge, Lord Justice Brian Leveson, with powers to compel witnesses to appear, it would also be asked to recommend a new regulatory framework to replace the system that had so clearly failed. It could not have packed a bigger punch.

In the meantime, advertisers were deserting the *News of the World* en masse. Within 48 hours of *The Guardian*'s story breaking, Ford, Vauxhall, Mitsubishi, Lloyds TSB and Virgin Holidays had all abandoned the Murdoch tabloid. So, too, had Sainsbury's, Asda, Dixons, Boots, Specsavers, Halifax and the Co-op. Newsagents were also saying they would refuse to handle the newspaper.

A day later—and still only 72 hours after *The Guardian*'s story—News decided it had no choice but to shut down the *News of the World*, 168 years after it had first promised readers, 'Our motto is truth'. The decision was hammered out in a conference call between Rebekah and James in London and Rupert in Colorado, amid whispers that the elder Murdoch opposed the move but that his son, and daughter Elisabeth, had pushed him into it.

That afternoon, Brooks called staff to the middle of the newsroom and broke the news. There were cries of disbelief, a few shouted, 'No!', but most were stunned to silence as she told them the paper had become 'toxic' and no one wanted to touch it. The editor, Colin Myler, who was speechless, appeared not to have known it was coming. No one said a word to Brooks, who spoke for only two minutes before calling for questions, and then leaving. Seconds later, the Murdoch-owned Sky News was running a breaking-news ticker—perhaps put out by her PR people—that Brooks had been in tears as she made the announcement and that there had been a lynch-mob mentality among the 200 staff whose jobs were now at risk. Neither of these claims was true.

James then sent a much lengthier email to employees, explaining why the decision was inevitable. With one eye on the public gallery, he declared that what had happened was 'inhuman' and had no place in the company. 'The *News of the World* is in the business of holding others to account,' he said. 'But it failed when it came to itself.' He was quick to add that he himself had known nothing about the hacking scandal or the cover-up, and that he had only approved Gordon Taylor's £700 000 settlement because he had not been 'in full possession of the facts'.

The next day, Brooks braved staff again in a town hall meeting. Flanked by two security guards, and with the internet and phones temporarily disabled, she told them, 'You may be angry with me, I understand, but I'm angry with the people who did this and feel bitterly betrayed.' The *News of the World* was closing, she said, because no one wanted to advertise. She blamed this on their enemies, *The Guardian* and BBC, who had led a 'witch hunt' and an 'onslaught of attacks', but she also warned there was worse to come and that in a year they would understand why closure was the only option. 'Eventually, it will come out why things went wrong and who was responsible,' she told them ominously, 'and that will be another very difficult moment in our company's history.'

For the first time, Brooks also admitted that News might be partly to blame for the paper's demise. 'One of the problems now is how we dealt with it at the time,' she said. 'In 2006, everybody drew the line in the sand in the wrong place. Everybody...The police said there was nothing else to see and we believed them... and we went absolutely there's nothing to see. I think that's definitely part of our problem.'

There were several calls from the floor for her to resign, and far more from outside the building. Not only had she been the editor in 2002 when the paper was hacking into Milly Dowler's phone, she had also led the fanfare of denials that had got them in this mess. But she had no intention of quitting while the Murdochs were still supporting her, and James made it clear that they were.

In an interview peppered with pauses, Murdoch Jnr told Channel 4 News, 'I am satisfied that Rebekah, her leadership of this business and her standard of ethics and her standard of conduct throughout her career are, are very good.' Or as one communications analyst transcribed it—suggesting that his hesitations signalled doubt—'I am satisfied [pause] that Rebekah [pause], her leadership of this business [pause] and her [pause] standard of ethics [pause] and her standard of conduct [pause] throughout her career [pause] are very good [pause].'

But now the spotlight swung onto Rupert, because he and Brooks were so close, and he was the one who was really protecting her. The old man was lying low in Sun Valley, Idaho, at the Allens media conference, but the media now caught up with him on his way to a morning session in his holiday garb of chinos, trainers and a cheap-looking sports cap. As the throng rushed towards him, seeking a comment, the media tycoon put his head down and hurried through the pack, saying he had no comment to make and nothing to add. The next day, as he ran the gauntlet again, he was persuaded to say somewhat tetchily, 'we've already apologised…we were let down by people we trusted', and to affirm that his support for Brooks was 'total'. But it seemed as if he believed it would soon be business as usual.

That weekend, he flew into London to shore up the BSkyB deal—which was looking shaky—and to mourn the last edition of the *News of the World*. He was driven to Wapping in the front seat of a red Range Rover, reading a copy of the paper whose cover declared THANK YOU AND GOODBYE. His dying tabloid had at least had the decency and common sense to print a full apology, with an editorial from Colin Myler that admitted: 'Quite simply we lost our way. Phones were hacked, and for that this newspaper is truly sorry. There is no justification for this appalling wrongdoing. No justification for the appalling pain caused to victims, nor for the deep stain it has left on a great history.'

That evening, Rupert braved the media pack to take a walk with Rebekah outside his Mayfair apartment, to show the world he was still supporting her. Asked by a reporter, 'What's your first priority?' he could easily have replied 'the Dowlers', or 'the 200 staff at the *News of the World* who have lost their jobs', or 'restoring the trust of the British people', or even 'helping my son, James'. But instead he looked fondly at Brooks and said, 'This one.'

It was a shocking misjudgment on all fronts, and 'up there with the most hurtful moments in this whole sordid ordeal', as the *News of the World*'s head of PR, Hayley Barlow, would later say. It was also a real slap in the face for James, who had received no such public display of support, and for Elisabeth, his real daughter, who was now blaming her old friend for the mess they were all in.

Not long afterwards, the *Telegraph* was reporting—although she straight-out denied it—that Elisabeth had told friends that Rebekah had 'fucked the company'. Others added that she had accused her brother of doing the same, which she denied as well. Only 36 hours before the Dowler story broke there had been another lavish party at Burford Priory, her magnificent 17th century mansion in Oxfordshire, with fabulous food and wine, an E-type Jaguar for guests to drive, and the usual array of high-powered politicians and media players. Several partygoers reported that Rebekah and James had been locked in conversation together for half the night, so it seemed that they had known what was coming.

Whether or not Elisabeth had actually uttered the F-word, she certainly believed Rebekah had to be sacked if they were to survive the crisis, and told her father so. Rupert was extremely reluctant to get rid of her, having backed her publicly on more than one occasion, but his hand was forced by Alwaleed bin Talal, the Saudi Prince who owned 7 per cent of News Corp's voting stock, who told the BBC from his luxury 86-metre yacht in Cannes that if there was any evidence of her involvement in hacking or the cover-up, there was no choice: 'For sure she has to go, you bet she has to go.' The next morning, 15 July 2011, Brooks duly resigned, explaining that her continued presence was interfering with the company's 'honest endeavours to fix the problems of the past'. The universal reaction was that it was the right decision, only several days too late. She would keep her chauffeur-driven car and a London office and get a multi-million-dollar pay-off, although the full magnificence of her golden handshake had yet to be revealed.

Rupert's old friend, Les Hinton, also fell on his sword and resigned as head of Dow Jones in New York, after more than five decades with the company. The man who had tried so hard to cover up the hacking scandal—either for or from his boss—had suddenly discovered that 'the pain caused to innocent people is unimaginable'.

The *News of the World*'s lawyer, Tom Crone, who had been in the vanguard of the cover-up since 2007, had already been sent on his way by Rebekah Brooks, but with no such golden goodbye. Andy Coulson, who had pushed the one-rogue-reporter defence as well, had gone long ago. Stuart Kuttner, the paper's managing editor, who had also toed the party line to Parliament, had been ditched in July 2009. And there was no longer a job for Colin Myler, now that the *News of the World* had closed.

Liz tried to persuade her father that James must also join the exodus, or at least stand down, because he had run News International while the cover-up was in full swing. Rupert had rung to tell him this, then next morning changed his mind, because his instinct was that they could still tough it out. With rumours raging that James was for the chop, Rupert also rang the *Wall Street Journal* to hose them down, insisting that his son had 'acted as fast as he could, the moment he could'. He added that they had handled the crisis 'extremely well in every way possible' and had made only 'minor mistakes'.

Few would have agreed with this assessment. Even now, Rupert hadn't apologised to the Dowlers or the British public. Even now, he was complaining that his enemies were telling lies. Even now, he hadn't realised that this time it was different. He told the *Wall Street Journal* he was tired and getting annoyed with the negative headlines, but that the damage was 'nothing that will not be recovered'. Yet, almost as he said this, he must have realised it was wrong, because it was clear that the crucial £8 billion BSkyB deal could no longer go ahead. With the government telling Parliament it would refer the takeover back to the independent regulator, Ofcom, Murdoch and his second-in-command at News Corp, Chase Carey, decided it would be politic to withdraw the bid altogether, to avoid it being blocked. At this stage, they probably hoped they could renew the offer when the fuss died down.

Just as this news was being digested, it was confirmed that the FBI had opened investigations in the US into whether the *News of the World*'s phone hacking and corrupt payments to public officials meant that News Corp had broken the law in America.

As the family circled the wagons, and argued about how to deal with the growing furore, Rupert's ex-wife Anna flew in from New York to be with her youngest son and make sure his father stood by him. Lachlan also left his job running the struggling Ten Network in Sydney and flew to London to tend to his father and give him support, making sure he ate properly, took his pills and had his acupuncture. Even Prue rallied to the cause and flew to London to help.

A year earlier, Rupert and his four grown-up children had resorted to family counselling to help them repair their increasingly fractious relationship, deal with their father's expectations and settle their own sibling rivalries over the succession. But having come to some sort of decision that the kids should band together and support James, and that Rupert should stop undermining his youngest son by trying to show him who was boss, the crisis had made the rifts wider again. Rupert was blaming James for the disaster; Elisabeth and James were no longer talking to each other (they would still be at daggers drawn more than a year later); and all the family were fighting about how to proceed.

In this climate, Rupert finally arranged to meet the Dowlers, as David Cameron had already done. He bowed his head and said how awful he felt. He told them about his father and Gallipoli and the great tradition of News's papers and said how humbled he was. But they refused to join him in a statement and left him to the media, who had been tipped off about the meeting by the Dowlers' lawyer, Mark Lewis. 'It was extremely tense and a little surreal,' Sally Dowler said later. 'There was little that he could say apart from acknowledge that what had taken place was unacceptable and apologise to us, which he did. Gemma asked Mr Murdoch how he would have felt if it had happened to someone in his family. He just sat with his head in his hands.'

That weekend, *The Times* headlined its front page DAY OF ATONEMENT, to mark the fact that News International was taking out full-page ads in all of Britain's national dailies. Headed WE ARE SORRY, and signed by Rupert himself, this personal apology told the public in nine short, sharp sentences:

> The *News of the World* was in the business of holding others to account.
> It failed when it came to itself.
> We are sorry for the serious wrongdoing that occurred.
> We are deeply sorry for the hurt suffered by the individuals affected.

We regret not acting faster to sort things out.

I realise that simply apologising is not enough.

Our business was founded on the idea that a free and open press should be a positive force in society. We need to live up to this.

In the coming days, as we take further concrete steps to resolve these issues and repair the damage we have caused, you will hear more from us.

Sincerely,
Rupert Murdoch

Five years earlier it would almost certainly have been enough to kill the scandal stone dead. Now, it hardly slowed it for a moment.

However, this was not the only thing the Murdochs had decided must be done. Five years after they should have set up a proper investigation, they finally established one. No doubt, this, too, was part of the atonement process and an attempt to get the crisis under control, but another major motive was that the group needed to show the FBI it was co-operating with investigators. If it failed to do that, there was a risk that officers or directors of News Corp— including Rupert and James—might end up in jail for breaching the *Foreign Corrupt Practices Act*.

The task of cleaning the stables was entrusted to a new Management and Standards Committee (MSC), chaired by Lord Grabiner QC, who was one of Britain's most illustrious commercial lawyers. Crucially, this new body would be independent of News International and its executives and would seek its own legal advice. It would report to Joel Klein, a former US Assistant Attorney General, in Rupert's New York office, and be answerable to a News Corp board committee led by Viet Dinh, a Professor of Law at Georgetown University.

The MSC would take charge of dealing with the Metropolitan Police, the FBI, the US Department of Justice, the House of

Commons, the growing number of civil actions, and all official inquiries, including Lord Leveson's. It would have the power to obtain and disclose documents and to direct co-operation from anyone at News. It would also be investigating the five-year cover-up of hacking and corruption, and the destruction of evidence, since that was what so many of these inquiries were concerned with.

Its establishment was potentially a landmark decision because if the MSC did its job properly, it would effectively set the company against itself and hand over a massive amount of evidence to the police, as journalists on *The Sun* and James Murdoch would soon discover.

16
BETRAYED

'People I trusted…have let me down…and it is for them to pay.'

Rupert Murdoch

Two days after walking the plank at News International, Rebekah Brooks was arrested by Operation Weeting and questioned for nine hours at a London police station on suspicion of phone hacking and corruption. Having declared that the most important thing was to get to the truth of the allegations, she was now swept up in them herself. Andy Coulson and Neil Wallis had already been questioned at similar length a few days earlier, as had Clive Goodman for the second time around, while Neville Thurlbeck, Ian Edmondson and James Weatherup had been collared back in April in the first wave of arrests. And although none of them had yet been charged, it was only a matter of time before this happened.

The day after Rebekah was arrested, a laptop, phone and papers were discovered in a rubbish bin at a car park near the Brookses' Chelsea Harbour home. Her husband Charlie tried to claim the bag but, by the time he did so, the security guards had called the police, who took it away to examine the contents. With closed-circuit television cameras covering the entire facility, it was likely to be a simple task for them to discover who had dumped it. Amid speculation that Brooks might have been trying to get rid of evidence, a spokesman told the media that the computer belonged to Charlie and had 'nothing to do with Rebekah or the case', and that he was 'expecting the stuff back forthwith'.

The following day, James, Rupert and Rebekah were all hauled before the House of Commons to answer questions from the Culture Committee, which wanted to know whether executives from News had lied to Parliament. After all this high drama, the Murdochs were finally going to be forced to say what they knew about the scandal that had gripped Britain for two weeks. Televised live, it would give millions of people around the world a ringside seat.

With some describing it as the most important committee in history, Tom Watson tried to hose down expectations. 'There is going to be no killer blow,' he said. 'We will get the symbolism of Parliament holding these people to account for the first time... [but] this story has been like slicing a cucumber, you just get a little bit closer to the truth each time.'

Outside Portcullis House, the modern annex where the hearings were to be held, lines started forming at 6.30 a.m. By lunchtime, there were around 100 people waiting to go through security and some 40 protesters wearing Murdoch masks, with T-shirts that proclaimed 'Murdoch Wanted for News Crimes'. The star turn was a man in a huge Murdoch puppet head, who pulled up in a black cab and stepped out onto the red carpet, to the delight of the TV crews and photographers, who shouted, 'This way, please, Mr Murdoch, this way please,' to attract his attention. Some even tried to ask him questions, but the man inside the giant head could barely hear and had no way of answering.

In this carnival atmosphere, amid rare British sunshine, with London's police looking on, an anonymous black car slipped in through the main gates of the ancient parliament building, from where its occupants could get to the committee rooms unmolested without wading through the crowd. Word spread that James had arrived. Unbeknownst to the crowd, his father had entered by the same route two hours earlier to avoid all the bother.

The two Murdochs had been preparing for the interrogation all week with their lawyers and PR people, first in their London offices, then in a small group down in the country. 'It was very, very, very, very intense,' according to one family adviser. And it had not gone well, perhaps because Rupert hated rehearsals. In the US papers, there were reports that News Corp's independent directors had a plan to replace the 80-year-old as chief executive, and were just waiting to see how he performed. This seemed unlikely, given the Murdoch family's iron grip on the share register, and the reports were quickly denied. But people who had watched the old man in rehearsals were said to be worried about his performance.

Out in the market, there were increasing concerns about News Corp's share price, which had plunged by almost 20 per cent since the crisis had broken, and wiped more than US$6 billion off the value of the group. Some stockbrokers' analysts were now openly suggesting that Rupert should step down. Others were running the numbers and concluding that the empire would be worth at least 50 per cent more without him, because the company would not keep acquiring overvalued newspapers.

Rupert was under huge pressure. And so it looked. The over-riding impression he gave once hearings got going, was that he was

old, doddery and confused, and had forgotten just about everything, except how useful it could be to lose one's memory. But, as
always, the media tycoon knew how to grab a headline, with his
opening gambit that this was the most humble day of his life.

Humiliating was possibly a better word because for most of the
time he wasn't remotely humble. And he was certainly not going
to accept any blame.

'Mr Murdoch, do you accept that ultimately you are responsible
for this whole fiasco?' he was asked at the outset by Labour's Jim
Sheridan. 'No,' he replied, without elaborating.

'You are not responsible. Who is responsible?' his interrogator
inquired.

'The people that I trusted to run it, and then maybe the people
they trusted.'

These guilty parties, whoever they were, did not include
his loyal lieutenant, Les Hinton, the media mogul made clear.
'I worked with Mr Hinton for 52 years and I would trust him
with my life,' he said.

'This terrible thing happened on your watch. Mr Murdoch,
have you considered resigning?' asked Tory MP, Louise Mensch,
following up.

'No,' he replied, once again without embroidery.

'Why not?' Mensch inquired.

'Because I feel that people I trusted—I am not saying who,
and I don't know what level—have let me down. I think that they
behaved disgracefully and betrayed the company and me, and it is
for them to pay. Frankly, I think that I am the best person to clean
this up.'

But apart from being sure that it wasn't his fault and he wasn't
stepping down, the charming old fox had little to offer. He had

never heard of Gordon Taylor and knew nothing about his £700 000 pay-off; nor had he heard of Neville Thurlbeck or the fact that the judge in the Mosley case had accused him of blackmail; and he certainly hadn't clocked that MPs on this same committee had accused his executives of collective amnesia and covering up the truth. Furthermore, he knew nothing about Clive Goodman being paid off with two year's salary, and it was news to him that his company had forked out cash for Goodman and Mulcaire's legal fees. He couldn't even recall saying eight days earlier that Rebekah Brooks was his top priority.

To cap it all, Rupert wasn't sure when he had discovered that he had got it all so wrong. For five years, he and his executives had sworn black and blue to the media, the public and his shareholders that News and its journalists had committed no crime. He had said this himself in 2007, 2009 and 2010, many, many times: that his journalists were innocent, that there was no evidence of wrongdoing, and that it was all a conspiracy of his enemies. His executives had repeated these protestations to Parliament and the Press Complaints Commission. So, had he not been horrified to discover after all this time that he had been lied to or misled? Was the moment he discovered these denials were false not etched in his memory? Well, no, it was not. The best he could do when asked if he first knew this in January 2011 was to reply, 'I forget the date.'

Rupert's explanation for his all-pervasive ignorance was that the *News of the World* was only 1 per cent of his business and that he 'very seldom' talked to its editor, probably only 'once a month' and only 'to keep in touch'. But as he had admitted at the beginning of his evidence—in making a different point—he normally spoke to James and Rebekah on the phone every day. So it seemed that they, too, must have been kept in the dark or had chosen to keep everything from him.

Those who had worked with the media tycoon over the years found it hard to recognise their boss in this I-know-nothing cameo. Rupert's editors and executives remembered him as a man who came on the phone at all times of the day and night, picking, probing and pointing to the one question you could not answer; he was the man who knew the price of newsprint in Cairns, even when he was 10 000 miles away, who knew your business better than you did. And none found the performance less convincing than his old enemy, Conrad Black, who scoffed at the spectacle of his former rival, 'Bumbling into a parliamentary hearing...supported on each arm like a centenarian semi-cadaver, mumbling about humility.'

This 'old possum routine' of Rupert's was nothing more than an act, claimed the former proprietor of Britain's *Telegraph* and Australia's *The Age* and *Sydney Morning Herald*.

Having suffered at the hands of the Murdoch papers when charged with fraud, Black now took gleeful revenge. 'For decades, Murdoch has smeared, lied, double-crossed,' he thundered. 'Now [his] company has been stripped naked as the lawless hypocritical organisation it has long been...He is, in my personal belief, a psychopath. I think behind his nondescript personality lurks a repressed, destructive malice. His is, and has been proved to be, in some measure, a criminal organisation.'

If Rupert had genuinely known so little about what was going on, how come no one had ever told him? Had he never asked? Or had they simply lied? We got a part of his answer when Tom Watson asked about Murdoch's October 2010 Thatcher lecture, in which he had again denied that there was evidence of widespread hacking, despite the *New York Times*'s detailed investigation.

'So if you were not lying then, somebody lied to you. Who was it?' Watson asked.

'I don't know,' Rupert replied. 'That is what the police are investigating, and we are helping them with.'

'But you acknowledge that you were misled?'

'Clearly.'

We got a little bit more when the subject of editors was raised, and Rupert claimed it had been Colin Myler's job to find out 'what the hell was going on'. James, too, was soon pointing the bone at the man who had arrived long after the crimes were committed. But both Murdochs also blamed the Metropolitan Police, the Press Complaints Commission and their own lawyers, Harbottle & Lewis, who had supposedly persuaded them that there was nothing to worry about.

One of the concerns in the Murdoch family was that James was too arrogant, and that he lacked Rupert's subtlety and charm. This now became obvious as we saw the two men side by side. But James clearly lacked his father's communication skills as well. Rupert's answers were generally far briefer than the interrogator's questions, often responding with just one word, yes or no. James's replies were ten times longer than the original inquiry, and he strangled the English language as he struggled to respond. Asked whether News had carried out a proper investigation, he came back with:

Again, I think the very fact that the provision of the new information to the police in the first place when there was no police investigation ongoing that then led to, in part, the re-opening, or this new investigation being established can, I hope, be testament to some proactive action and transparency with respect to getting to the right place to find out the facts of what happened, understanding all the allegations that are coming in and moving forward to aid the police in successful completion of the important and serious work that they are doing.

And to the next question of whether Crone, Brooks and Hinton had been sacked by News because they were part of a cover-up, he replied:

> I have no knowledge and there is no evidence that I am aware of that Mrs Brooks or Mr Hinton, or any of those executives, had knowledge of that. Certainly Mrs Brooks' assertions to me of her knowledge of those things has been clear. None the less, those resignations have been accepted, but there is no evidence today that I have seen or that I have any knowledge of that there was any impropriety by them.

It sounded like a man who had been programmed by lawyers to say as little as possible in as many words as he could. But for all the differences of approach, father and son had one thing in common: they had absolutely no knowledge of the terrible things that had gone on in their company. And, like a pair of butchers who had suddenly discovered what went into their sausages, they were shocked and horrified to be told.

However, at the end of his tortured performance, James did offer one very specific denial that would soon come back to haunt him. For the very last question of the session, Tom Watson was allowed to come back for a quick second shot, and at last he hit the target.

'James. Sorry, if I may call you James, to differentiate,' he asked, 'when you signed off the Taylor payment, did you see or were you made aware of the "For Neville" e-mail, the transcript of the hacked voicemail messages?'

'No,' replied the younger Murdoch. 'I was not aware of that at the time.'

It was only one answer. Just ten words. But it would soon cause him a multitude of problems, because the famous 'For Neville' email would undoubtedly have told him, if he had ever read it

272

back in 2008, that hacking at the *News of the World* had gone well beyond Clive Goodman and that the one-rogue-reporter defence to which the company clung was a bald-faced lie.

So was he now telling the truth in claiming that he knew nothing about it, or was he misleading Parliament, as so many of his fellow executives at News had already done? Almost immediately, his former employees, Crone and Myler, issued a public statement to say that the young Murdoch's evidence was 'mistaken' and to add, 'In fact, we did inform him of the "For Neville" email, which had been produced to us by Gordon Taylor's lawyers.'

This took the affair to a whole new level. A finding that James had misled Parliament or, worse still, had lied to the committee, would be devastating for his reputation and career. But even if the MPs were to clear him of any such charge, he would surely have to come back and face them again. And that was the one thing that Murdoch's lawyers and PR people had been desperate to avoid.

In the meantime, however, the headline writers had their eyes elsewhere. After more than two hours of questioning, the hearings had been interrupted by a comedian called Jonnie Marbles planting a foam pie in Rupert Murdoch's face, after somehow smuggling a plate and a can of shaving foam through House of Commons security. Almost as quickly, the tycoon's young wife, Wendi, who had been reminding the world of her importance in the tycoon's life by sitting directly behind him in the front row of the audience in a bright pink jacket, had leapt up from her front-row seat and landed a haymaker slap to send the attacker reeling. Her gallant defence was soon setting the Twittersphere alight, and by next day it was leading the morning TV bulletins in Rupert's home town of New York. NBC News gave it two-and-a-half minutes, while the network's top-rating *Today* program devoted almost seven, replaying the incident four times over in a breathless eulogy to the 'young, fit, former volleyball player' who had leapt to protect her ageing husband. Wendi Deng Murdoch was 'a huge asset to his businesses', 'a celebrity among celebrities', and 'a stand-out even among political and business elites', *Today* gushed to its 5 million viewers. A panel of experts, led by *Newsweek*'s Beijing bureau chief, Melinda Liu, *Vanity Fair*'s Murdoch specialist, Sarah Ellison, and *New York* magazine's Gabriel Sherman, then took turns to marvel at how tough she was.

As to whether the Murdochs had demonstrated that they knew nothing of hacking at the *News of the World* or of the five-year cover-up, the item merely reported that Wendi had been telling friends for weeks that Rupert's tabloids had done nothing that wasn't common practice on Fleet Street, which is what Rupert would tell journalists on *The Sun* in an unguarded moment almost two years later. They did not, of course, report the rumours that Wendi and her husband had been drifting apart, but perhaps they didn't yet know.

As Sherman pointed out, the pieman's misguided attack had been a Godsend. 'It's an amazing PR move. They couldn't have asked for better,' he enthused. 'It's changed the entire narrative of the hearing. I mean we're talking about this sympathetic moment of her standing up for Rupert Murdoch, where if that had never happened we'd be talking about the hacking allegations.'

And so they were, proving once again, perhaps, that we all get the media we deserve.

17
UNDER ATTACK

'You must be the first mafia boss in history who didn't know he was running a criminal enterprise.'

Tom Watson, MP

Watching Murdoch Senior's performance before the House of Commons committee from his home in Australia, one former top executive couldn't help but be struck by how old and frail his ex-boss looked. 'Rupert is an extraordinary character and he's built an amazing business,' he observed, 'but he's looking old and doddery and can barely hear. Retirement age is 65. You can keep going till you're 70 if you're Winston Churchill, with the help of a few bottles of brandy, but he's 80 for heaven's sake.'

The media pundits were equally dismissive, although for a different reason. Martin Bashir predicted that Rupert would be gone in eighteen months because one of three criminal investigations now running would inevitably catch up with him. And his biographer, Michael Wolff, was even quicker to write him off, predicting that he would be forced out of office by December.

Over the next few weeks, these prophecies began to look as though they might come true, as more details of the cover-up emerged, and as a series of lawyers who had been employed by the Murdochs cast doubt on the veracity of James and Rupert's evidence.

Just down the corridor from the House of Commons committee room where the Murdochs faced their interrogators, Lord Macdonald of River Glaven QC had also been giving evidence, and had revealed another occasion on which the *News of the World* executives had concealed criminal behaviour by its journalists. In May 2011, just after the first hacking arrests, the distinguished lawyer had been asked by News Corp to re-examine the batch of emails that had been shown to Harbottle & Lewis in 2007, when the law firm had been asked if the documents supported Clive Goodman's claim that hacking was rife at the *News of the World*. Now Macdonald told the Home Affairs Committee it had been 'blindingly obvious' to him, within three to five minutes of reading these messages, that they contained evidence of corrupt payments by *News of the World* journalists to police and public officials. He told MPs that he had immediately informed the News Corp board, face-to-face, and advised them to go to the police. The group's directors (which included James, Lachlan and Rupert Murdoch) had been 'stunned and shocked' at the news, but had agreed that he should do so. And on 20 June 2011, Macdonald had handed the file over to the Met, which had immediately set up Operation Elveden.

Four years earlier, the eminent QC had been Britain's Director of Public Prosecutions, and he now told MPs that the police investigation into corruption at the Murdoch paper would have started in 2007 had News or Harbottle & Lewis given him the file. Instead, of course, Harbottles had been persuaded by News to keep silent, on the basis that it was outside their brief to comment on this particular offence. So the file had been sent to the archives, and the crimes had escaped exposure.

As Lord Macdonald was recounting this story, James and Rupert were assuring the Culture Committee that Harbottle & Lewis had conducted a thorough investigation in 2007 and given the *News of the World* a clean bill of health, and that they had relied on this clearance to dismiss reports that hacking was widespread. But the law firm soon wrote to the MPs to deny this vehemently, saying they had never conducted any such investigation, had never given the company an all-clear, and had never been asked to find out 'what the hell was going on', as Rupert claimed.

Given limited exemption from professional privilege, the lawyers then proceeded to demolish a key part of their client's defence, characterising Rupert and James's evidence as, 'self-serving', 'hard to credit' and 'inaccurate and misleading'.

Worse still for the Murdochs, the law firm then served up details of Clive Goodman's 2007 pay-off, showing that the jailed reporter had received the extraordinary sum of £243 500. They also handed MPs a copy of Goodman's incendiary letter in which he revealed that hacking at the *News of the World* was endemic and that several senior journalists were aware of it.

This skewered Andy Coulson because he had allegedly told Goodman he could have his job back if he kept his mouth shut. But it also nailed Les Hinton, who had been sent the Goodman letter four days before assuring Parliament there was absolutely no evidence of anyone except the royal reporter being involved in hacking. And, finally, it nailed Rebekah Brooks and News International, because details of the Goodman pay-out showed he had received more than four times what she and the company had told MPs he had been paid. So there was another lie laid bare.

. Tom Watson described the letter as 'absolutely devastating' and 'the most significant piece of evidence that has been revealed so far', adding somewhat portentously, 'This is one of the largest cover-ups I have seen in my lifetime.'

But further challenges to the Murdochs' evidence soon followed. Having already told MPs that James was 'mistaken' in his claim that he knew nothing about the damning 'For Neville' email, Crone and Myler came back to the House of Commons in September to assure MPs that they *had* made him aware of it and had told him why it was so significant. As Crone put it several times in several different ways, 'I explained that this document meant there was wider *News of the World* involvement.'

'It was clear evidence that phone hacking was taking place beyond Clive Goodman,' the newspaper's lawyer continued. 'It was the reason that we had to settle the case. And in order to settle the case we had to explain the case to Mr Murdoch and get his authority to settle. So it would certainly have been discussed.'

However, anyone expecting the two ex-Murdoch employees to follow this up by turning Queen's Evidence and stitching up their ex-boss was to be disappointed. Crone had been News International's lawyer for more than 20 years and still had some residual loyalty, despite his threat in July to speak out 'if they really screw me over'. He was also hoping for a pay-out. Moreover, both men had spent four years swearing black was white, and were hardly going to tell the committee they had been lying from the start.

Nevertheless, News's outside lawyer, Julian Pike, soon added to James's troubles by telling the story of the Taylor pay-out far more bluntly. Pike told MPs he had advised News in 2008 that, 'three journalists other than Goodman were involved in phone hacking', that the company would 'have to admit liability', and that there was 'a powerful case' to suggest the *News of the World* had a culture of 'illegally accessing information in order to get stories'.

'Were you aware of which three journalists...were involved in phone hacking?' Tom Watson asked the lawyer.

'I had three names, yes,' Pike replied.

'Did you tell Tom Crone?'

'He did know that.'

'So he was aware at that point that the external lawyers had raised their view that others were involved in phone hacking?

'Correct.'

Given a limited waiver of professional privilege, Pike told MPs he also believed James had been briefed on the significance of the 'For Neville' email. And, punching yet more holes in the young Murdoch's story, he also said that money had been paid to Taylor to buy his silence (which James had denied) and that Myler and Murdoch had discussed the Taylor case at another meeting, on 27 May (which James had also denied).

Pike also told MPs it was the 'For Neville' email that had made News pay Taylor so much money, and that the company wouldn't have paid him a cent had it not existed. He also told them that it was 'quite clear' that the email showed News's 'one rogue reporter' to be untrue. So it was now even more important to know if James was telling the truth when he said he was not aware of the email, had never seen it, had never read it, and had no idea what it contained.

Unluckily for James, Pike also agreed to give the committee three documents that could throw light on what James might have known. First was a legal opinion from Michael Silverleaf QC on 3 June 2008, warning News Group Newspapers that a 'culture of illegal information access' existed at the *News of the World* and that it would be 'extremely damaging to NGN's public reputation' if the case went to trial. Second was a two-page briefing note of 24 May from Tom Crone, which had highlighted the 'damning' email that made their situation 'extremely perilous' and was 'fatal' to News's case. And third was the note of Pike's phone call with Colin Myler on 27 May, in which Myler had told him about discussing the case with James. None of these documents had yet been seen by MPs, who had not even been aware of their existence. And, significantly, it was not News that was providing them.

So in November 2011 James Murdoch was hauled back to the House of Commons for a second time to face the charge that he had misled MPs in his original evidence. His only possible defence could be that he hadn't read any of the documents that now confronted him. And this was indeed his story. But he actually went further than that.

'I want to be very clear,' he told the committee. 'No documents were shown to me at that meeting or given to me at that meeting, or prior.'

He then enlarged on this to swear that he was never told that the documents disclosed hacking by anyone except Clive Goodman. 'Mr Silverleaf's opinion was not shown to me or discussed in that context, nor was any evidence of wider-spread phone hacking, nor any reason to carry out any further investigations, shown to me or discussed with me at that time,' he said. 'And that is what I have testified to consistently to this Committee in person and in writing over the last number of months.'

And now Murdoch was forced to name the two people who he claimed had betrayed him and his family.

'Mr Murdoch, let me just ask you again: did you mislead this Committee in your original testimony?' Watson inquired.

'No, I did not,' Murdoch replied.

'So if you did not, who did?' asked Watson, 'Was it Mr Crone, a respected lawyer and in-house legal adviser for many years?'

'Who did what?'

'Who misled this Committee.'

'As I said to you, as I wrote to you, and I issued a public statement, certainly, in the evidence that they gave to you in 2011, with respect to my knowledge, I thought it was inconsistent and not right, and I dispute it, vigorously.'

'So you think Mr Crone misled us?'

'It follows that I do, yes.'

'And so do you think Mr Myler misled us as well?'

'I believe their testimony was misleading, and I dispute it.'

Try as they could, Tom Watson and his fellow MPs were unable to demolish James's version of events, but the disbelief on their faces soon said it all. Many smirked as they asked their questions. Several also chose to voice their incredulity. Tom Watson signed off his interrogation by likening the Murdochs' corporate behaviour to the Mafia, before quipping, 'You must be the first Mafia boss in history not to know he was running a criminal organisation.'

Labour MP Paul Farrelly was almost as scathing, telling James, 'The one thing from the outset of this that really showed us, and any ten-year old, that the *News of the World*'s line did not stack up was that Gordon Taylor was not a member of the Royal Family.'

But it was a Tory MP, Philip Davies, who best summed up Murdoch's apparent failure to ask even the most basic questions about the huge pay-out he had approved. 'I find it incredible, absolutely incredible, that you didn't say, "How much? Half-a-million pounds? Let me have a look at that." I cannot even begin to believe that course of action is one that any self-respecting chief executive, any self-respecting chief operating officer could possibly take with so much of the company's money and reputation at stake.'

The critics next day were only a little bit kinder. The BBC's Robert Peston wittily headlined his comments, 'James "knows nothing"'. The *New York Times* reckoned he had been 'unflappable'. And *The Guardian* agreed he had been 'cool', even though it believed he had also 'damaged his reputation'.

But as the dust was settling on this little skirmish, yet another bomb landed on James's head. A month after he had told MPs that he had neither seen nor been given *any* documents relating to the Taylor settlement, a new one popped out of the woodwork with his name on it. On 12 December 2011, the London law firm, Linklaters, which was acting for News Corp's Management and Standards Committee (MSC), gave MPs a copy of the email that Colin Myler had sent to James on 7 June 2008, in which the *News of the World*'s editor had warned Murdoch, 'Unfortunately it is as bad as we feared. The note from Julian Pike at Farrers is extremely telling regarding Taylor's vindictiveness.'

Further down the email, and obvious to anyone who took even a cursory look, was Pike's pungent three-point summary, which said:

- Taylor's attitude is that he wants to be 'vindicated or made rich'
- He wishes to see NGN [News Group Newspapers] suffer: one way or another he wants to hurt NGN
- He wants to demonstrate that what happened to him is/was rife throughout the organisation. He wants to correct the paper telling Parliamentary enquiries that this wasn't happening when it was.

It was the third of these points that was clearly the most damaging. But it wasn't just important for what it might have told Murdoch at the time; it also gave the lie to any suggestion from the Murdochs—which both of them would continue to make—that Myler had actively tried to conceal the facts from his boss. Here was an email telling James—if he could be bothered to read it—that hacking had been 'rife' at the *News of the World* and that the company he ran had misled Parliament. It really could not have been made any clearer than that.

Faced with this electronic record, James was now forced to back-track again, and admit that he had been sent the email and might even have been told about it. But again he relied on the trusty defence that he had neither read it nor been made aware of what it contained. It was a bit like that old Bill Clinton line about smoking dope and not inhaling.

James had received this email on a Saturday afternoon on his Blackberry and replied within three minutes. So it was quite possible he hadn't read it at the time. But the tone of his reply suggested he was already no stranger to the Taylor case and its problems, which was absolutely not what he had told MPs. And to believe he had remained ignorant of everything these documents contained, one had to accept that this frighteningly intelligent man had emerged from discussions with Crone and Myler without the one key piece of information that everyone else had seized upon, which was that Goodman had not acted alone.

Even more remarkable was the fact that this hugely damaging email hadn't emerged before. But there was soon an explanation. One month later, in January 2012, the MSC confirmed that the email had been deleted from James Murdoch's inbox 'by an IT worker' on 15 January 2011, just days before Operation Weeting began. Colin Myler's copy of the same email had also been deleted, but in his case, by a 'hardware failure'.

It brought to mind that famous recurring punchline from the popular Australian movie, *Muriel's Wedding*, 'What a coincidence. What a coincidence.'

Another key question that MPs wanted answered was why Julian Pike and his law firm, Farrer & Co, had taken so long to set the record straight, given that News's legal adviser had known since the middle of 2008 that his clients were misleading Parliament.

'At what stage did it become clear to you that the line that we were being given was not the truth?' he was asked by Paul Farrelly MP.

'It would have been at the point it was given to you,' the solicitor replied bluntly.

'Right, and what did you do, as a professional lawyer, about that?' Farrelly inquired.

'To be honest,' said Pike, 'I have not done very much.'

'Does that make you uncomfortable?' Farrelly continued.

'Not especially, no,' replied Pike.

'Do you have any scruples?' Farrelly asked.

'Yes, I do.' Pike came back.

'What are they?' Farrelly inquired.

'I do behave with integrity,' Pike suggested.

'Do you consider that you have behaved with integrity in this affair?' asked Farrelly.

'Yes,' said Pike.

Pike's failure was pursued further by Louise Mensch MP, who asked him tartly: 'You, as the representative of a very senior firm of solicitors with an impeccable reputation, were aware that phone hacking had gone wider than one rogue reporter, and that Parliament was being lied to. And yet, again, there were absolutely no consequences. No legal advice was given to News

International that it should make a clean breast of it or that it should stop giving false testimony to Parliament. How do you explain that to people watching, who will not understand why lawyers—both internally and externally—for News Group appeared to condone very serious breaking of the law?'

Pike said he couldn't answer that because it fell 'outside the Taylor case' and so it was still covered by professional privilege. He was then asked an even curlier one, which was why neither he nor News had reported a crime.

'Were you surprised that the company did not tell the police that criminal wrongdoing had taken place in the newsroom?' Tom Watson inquired.

'Probably not,' said Pike. 'I wasn't surprised.'

'Why was that?' Watson replied.

'I think at that stage I was being instructed that they wanted to settle this case on confidential terms, and, having done so, it would be quite surprising therefore if they were to go and do something which was going to open the can, as it were.'

'What stopped you as a solicitor reporting crime to the police?' asked Therese Coffey MP. 'There is no obligation on me to do so,' replied Pike, pointing out that News's other lawyers, Harbottle & Lewis, had also failed to tell the Met they had found evidence of corrupt payments to the police in the famous Goodman emails.

So two law firms had now joined Murdoch's executives and the *News of the World* in their attempts to keep all this illegal activity quiet.

But even this wasn't the last challenge to the Murdochs' story that they had done all they could to stamp out illegal behaviour by their journalists. Or as Rupert had so eloquently put it in his Thatcher lecture, that they had 'zero tolerance of wrongdoing'.

A week before Rupert and James gave evidence to the House of Commons in July, Assistant Commissioner Peter Clarke, who had led Operation Caryatid back in 2006, accused News International of trying to hinder the police investigation. His search team at the *News of the World*'s offices in August had met with 'hostility and obstruction', Clarke revealed to the Home Affairs Committee. And News had subsequently failed to help track down other journalists on the paper who the police believed were engaged in illegal hacking. Clarke told MPs he was 'not only suspicious' about News's motives for this, he was as certain as he could be 'that they had something to hide'. This of course was contrary to everything that James and Rupert Murdoch and their executives had always said, which was that they had fully co-operated with the police inquiry, given them anything they wanted, and that 'no stone had been left unturned'.

A week later, the Home Affairs Committee endorsed Clarke's version of events with an official verdict that declared, 'It is almost impossible to escape the conclusion...that they [News executives] were deliberately trying to thwart a criminal investigation,' adding that they were 'astounded' at the length of time it had taken for the group to cooperate with the police.

But other interesting revelations were soon to follow from the same committee, when it was revealed that Clarke's boss, Assistant Commissioner Andy Hayman, ex-head of Special Operations, had met senior *News of the World* journalists and executives several times while the Goodman/Mulcaire investigation was in full swing.

On 25 April 2006, Hayman and the Met's media chief, Dick Fedorcio, had been taken for an expensive dinner at Soho House, an exclusive London club, by the editor, Andy Coulson, and deputy editor, Neil Wallis. Four months later, on 26 August, Hayman had met the paper's crime reporter, Lucy Panton, and two months after that, he had spent a couple of hours with Wallis again. The last two meetings had come after the police had been thrown out of the *News of the World*'s offices and right in the middle of the tense stand-off about providing evidence, at which point the police were considering whether to take News to court. By this time the investigators had also made it clear that they believed several *News of the World* journalists were involved in phone hacking.

Hayman was still happily writing for *The Times* on 12 July 2011 when he was questioned about this by MPs and, not surprisingly, he was asked, 'Have you any idea how that looks to the public?'

'It could look bad if there was some...' Hayman began.

'It does look bad,' Nicola Blackwood MP assured him.

'Does it?' a bemused Hayman inquired.

'We all think it looks bad,' chairman Keith Vaz MP replied.

'All right,' said the ex-policeman. 'I will take that on the chin...'

By the end of his performance, several of the committee's members were shaking their heads in disbelief. 'I have to say some of your comments so far have been quite incredible,' one MP ventured. 'I feel a little bit like I have fallen through the rabbit hole,' another agreed. Finally, the chairman, Keith Vaz MP, sent him on his way by telling him: 'I normally sum up people's evidence, but on this occasion I think your evidence speaks for itself.'

Hayman had assured MPs he had had no detailed knowledge of the hacking investigation and had never discussed it with his hosts. But their report didn't let him off the hook. 'Even if all his social contacts with News International personnel were entirely above board, no information was exchanged and no obligations considered to have been incurred,' the MPs concluded, 'it seems to us extraordinary that he did not realise what the public perception of such contacts would be—or, if he did realise, he did not care that confidence in the impartiality of the police could be seriously undermined.'

Hayman had claimed that the Met's PR chief had been with him at all three meetings with the Murdoch executives. But Fedorcio roundly denied this, leading MPs to comment:

> We do not expressly accuse Mr Hayman of lying to us in his evidence, but it is difficult to escape the suspicion that he deliberately prevaricated in order to mislead us. This is very serious.

Which they followed up with another rebuke:

> Mr Hayman's conduct during the investigation and during our evidence session was both unprofessional and inappropriate. The fact that even in hindsight Mr Hayman did not acknowledge this points to, at the very least, an attitude of complacency.

This attitude of complacency seemed to have infected several other police officers involved in the phone-hacking saga, who had failed to notify more than a handful of the *News of the World*'s victims that their privacy had been invaded.

It had also infected those officers in the Metropolitan Police who had failed to challenge News's one-rogue-reporter defence on three separate occasions, in 2007, 2009 and 2010, even though they had known it to be a lie. Indeed, the Met had done exactly the opposite of this, by rubbishing *The Guardian* and the *New York Times* investigations and making it much simpler for the *News of the World* to protest its innocence.

And, of course, this attitude had also spread to Assistant Commissioner John Yates, who had decided so precipitously in

2009 not to reopen the hacking investigation. The Home Affairs Committee readily agreed with Yates's own assessment that this had been a 'very poor' decision and a 'serious misjudgment', and suggested he should resign. But by the time their report was published on 20 July, he had already taken their advice, as had London's other top cop, the Met's Commissioner, Sir Paul Stephenson.

Yates was about to be suspended anyway for helping the daughter of the *News of the World*'s deputy editor, Neil Wallis (who had by the time been arrested by Operation Weeting), to find a job with the Met. Stephenson might well have clung on, despite his eighteen meetings with News International during his time in the job. But he now had to admit he had received regular PR advice from Wallis during his tenure, and had also accepted five weeks free accommodation, worth £12 000, at the luxury health resort, Champneys, which was owned by a family friend, but where Wallis happened to act as PR.

News of these latest embarrassments caused Chris Bryant to tweet to his 27 000 followers: 'I am firmly convinced now that the Metropolitan Police was corrupted to its core by NI [News International]. Stephenson and Yates have to go.'

But, as the world now discovered, it was not just London's top cops who were on close, first-name terms with the people who ran Rupert's British papers.

18
POWER GAMES

'I have never asked for anything from a Prime Minister.'

Rupert Murdoch

Two weeks after *The Guardian*'s Milly Dowler story began shaking the foundations of the Murdochs' British empire, David Cameron was forced to admit to the public that he and his ministers had enjoyed an extraordinary number of private meetings with News International and its executives. Over the next nine months, the full extent of these contacts between the Murdochs and the Tory party would be uncovered by the Leveson Inquiry, which showed that a succession of British governments had enjoyed warm and intimate relations with the nation's most powerful media group, even as they took vital decisions about media regulation that could add billions of dollars to the Murdoch fortune.

And, once again, it was Rupert's favourite, Rebekah Brooks, who was right at the centre of all the action. Back in June 2009, when she was still editor of *The Sun*, Rebekah had married a colourful old-Etonian racehorse trainer called Charlie Brooks at the magnificent Sarsden Estate near her Cotswold home. Several top Tory politicians, including the future PM, had come to the lavish reception and sipped champagne by the lake, as had Britain's Labour Prime Minister, Gordon Brown. And so, of course, had Rupert, who flew in from New York for the occasion.

The stellar guest list was testimony to the political power of Rupert Murdoch, but also to the pulling power of Brooks, who had an incredible knack of charming the men and women in her orbit. In the decade that New Labour ran Britain, the Murdoch editor had become extremely close to the nation's prime minister, Tony Blair, sharing intimate private dinners with him and occasionally turning up on his arm at parties. But she had also become best friends with Tony's wife, Cherie, who sought her advice on dealing with the tabloids. And despite their respective spouses being rivals, she had managed to get close to Gordon Brown's wife, Sarah, who had invited her to the PM's official country residence, Chequers, for a pyjama party in 2008, along with Elisabeth Murdoch and Wendi Deng.

By 2009, Brooks had worked her magic on David Cameron too. A few weeks after he became Tory leader in December 2005, she met him for dinner at Liz Murdoch's country home. A few months after that, she invited him and his wife, Samantha, to a lavish World Cup party hosted by David and Victoria Beckham at their mansion in Hertfordshire. In the meantime, she and Rupert twice had lunch with the would-be prime minister. And before long the two of them were best of friends, especially when she hooked up with Charlie, who had been to Eton with Cameron's elder brother and had known the family for 30 years. Charlie Brooks trained horses at Sarsden, five minutes away from Cameron's weekender in the Oxfordshire village of Dean, and the Tory leader rode out with him occasionally, and perhaps also with Rebekah, although she was known to be a nervous rider.

By this time, the Brookses and the Camerons were leading lights in the so-called 'Chipping Norton Set', a collection of rich, well-connected Londoners who popped in and out of each other's Cotswold country houses at weekends and ran into each other at Daylesford Farm, with its organic food shop, yoga rooms and fashionable restaurant. Also part of the club were Elisabeth Murdoch and Matthew Freud, who lived ten minutes down the road in Burford. And in August 2008, this little gang all ended up together on Rupert Murdoch's 56-metre yacht, *Rosehearty*, which was moored alongside Elisabeth and Matthew's oceangoing cruiser, the 55-metre *Elisabeth F*, just off the Aegean island of Santorini. The catch-up had been suggested by Matthew Freud, also an old friend of Cameron's, who flew the Tory leader and his wife out there on his private jet to meet the media tycoon for drinks and a chat, while Rupert was cruising the Greek islands.

Remarkably, the 81-year-old Murdoch would tell Lord Leveson in 2012 that he had no memory of this rendezvous with Britain's future PM. But perhaps that is because he and his family were entertaining the Tory hopeful so frequently around this time that it all became a bit of a blur. In the four years that Cameron led the Opposition, Rupert and James Murdoch and Rebekah Brooks met him no less than 30 times for dinner, drinks, breakfast, lunch or a chat. Naturally, the world knew nothing about these private trysts until the hacking scandal forced the information out into the open.

Most often, the assignations were between Cameron and Rebekah Brooks, who broke bread together nineteen times between January 2006 and May 2010, often at each other's homes and at weekends, with the occasional birthday or Christmas party thrown in. But the would-be PM sat down with James Murdoch almost as often, meeting the media scion a dozen times in very similar circumstances.

Not only was the Tory chief's contact with the Murdochs far more frequent than with any other British media proprietor, and with a far greater degree of intimacy, it added up to four or five times as many meetings as the Murdochs had enjoyed with all other British Tory leaders over the previous decade, which strongly suggested that the courtship was deliberate and considered on both sides.

Cameron had initially vowed to stay at arm's length from Rupert and the other media barons because he didn't want to get as close to them as Tony Blair had done. But he was soon forced to accept that he needed *The Sun*'s support to get into power and stay there, if only because it had so often proved disastrous to have the raucous tabloid offside. His predecessor, John Major, had discovered how hard life could be made by Rupert's favourite paper, whose editor Kelvin MacKenzie once famously told him, 'I've got a bucket of shit on my desk and I'm going to pour it all over you.'

Paddy Ashdown, the former Liberal Democrat leader, also knew how easily Murdoch's men could bring you down. In February 1992 (two months before the general election), *The Sun* had gone to town on an affair he had had with his secretary five years earlier, devoting nine full pages to the story, and coining the unforgettable headline, PADDY PANTSDOWN. This story had only found its way into the public domain via the theft of private papers from Ashdown's solicitor's office, which had been bought by the *News of the World*.

But it was Britain's Labour leaders who really knew how political careers could be destroyed by Rupert's redtop. In the April 1992 election, *The Sun*'s front page on polling day carried a picture of Neil Kinnock inside a light bulb, with the headline, IF KINNOCK WINS TODAY WILL THE LAST PERSON TO LEAVE BRITAIN PLEASE TURN OUT THE LIGHTS. After the Tories' narrow victory, against the predictions of the pollsters who forecast a Labour win, the paper's front page famously boasted, IT'S THE SUN WOT WON IT.

At the previous election in 1987, the Murdoch tabloid had reacted to a Kinnock lead in the opinion polls with another clever piece of propaganda, mocking up a front page of the Labour leader outside 10 Downing Street, just three days before the vote, with the headline, LABOUR WINS: SPECIAL NIGHTMARE ISSUE.

And four years before that, at the 1983 election, *The Sun* had dished out similar treatment to Michael Foot, with a picture of him hunched in his old duffle coat and the pointed question, DO YOU SERIOUSLY WANT THIS OLD MAN TO RUN BRITAIN? Calling him 'an amiable old buffer', 'a willing dupe' and 'a ventrilo-quist's dummy', it had warned that Foot's backers on the Left of the party were 'dedicated, ruthless men...who would return the nation to the days of feudalism'. During the campaign, *The Sun*'s picture desk allegedly gave orders to freelance photographers to take 'No pictures of Foot unless falling over, shot or talking to militants.'

Not surprisingly, the 'New Labour' leader, Tony Blair, was determined that his bid to run Britain would not end in the same way. As he put it to the *Daily Mirror* editor, Piers Morgan, 'It is better to be riding the tiger's back than let it rip your throat out.' So he had deliberately set out to win Murdoch's support. Blair first met Rupert in September 1994 at a private lunch in London, just months after becoming leader of the Opposition. A couple of lunches later, he flew to Australia in July 1995 for News Corp's annual get-together at Hayman Island, and convinced Rupert that he was the natural successor to Margaret Thatcher and that he could revitalise Britain. Plus, of course, that he was going to win.

After a series of private chats with Rupert's political enforcer, Irwin Stelzer, he duly won the media mogul's endorsement. The front page of *The Sun* on 18 March 1997, six weeks before the general election, carried a cute picture of a smiling Blair holding the newspaper, which already bore the headline, THE SUN BACKS BLAIR, showing that he had co-operated in the stunt. In the poll that followed, Blair was elected in a landslide. As it had done in every other vote since 1970, *The Sun* and its owner had backed the winner.

So what had the young Prime Minister promised in return for this support? In his memoirs, Blair jokingly compared the process of dealing with Murdoch to Faust's efforts to 'cut a really great deal with this bloke called Satan'. But the serious side to his discussions was that Labour had dropped its plan to introduce tough cross-media laws and tackle Murdoch's media power, which the party had pledged to do. The ex-editor of Rupert's *Sunday Times*, Andrew Neil, claims that Blair promised the media mogul an easy ride on this at a private dinner in 1994. The PM's former press secretary, Alastair Campbell, says Blair abandoned the party's commitment shortly after his famous trip to Hayman Island in 1995. But whenever, and however, the decision was reached, even Blair admits that he ducked the battle because it would have taken up too much time and resources and stood in the way of other reforms.

Blair also did his best to make the media mogul feel wanted and clearly listened to him. According to Lance Price, who was Number 10's deputy press secretary, Rupert was like 'a 24th member of the Cabinet', whose views always had to be considered when the government was making big decisions.

'Murdoch asks the price...There's always a price,' Labour's former deputy PM, John Prescott, told the Leveson Inquiry, before adding rhetorically, 'Why do they have these relationships? I mean, he's not interested in the dinners, is he? He just wants what he wants.' And there was never any doubt what this was, according to Tom Watson, who added, 'I have never met a minister who did not know the corporate aims of Rupert Murdoch.'

Certainly, Blair had plenty of opportunity to discover what they were. During his time as Britain's PM, he had 31 dinners, breakfasts, lunches, meetings and the occasional weekend with Rupert, and a further 30 meetings with Rebekah Brooks, including at least three dinners à deux. He also sent her birthday cards, invited her to stay at Chequers, and sent her his commiserations when the phone-hacking scandal forced her to resign, as, indeed, did David Cameron. Nor was his relationship with the Murdochs purely professional. After leaving office, Blair became godfather to one of Rupert's young daughters, Grace, and attended her baptism on the banks of the River Jordan; a fact that did not emerge till some years later.

Yet Murdoch swore to the Leveson Inquiry that no deals of any sort had emerged from all this chummery, claiming, 'I never asked Mr Blair for anything. Nor indeed did I receive any favours. If you want to check that, I think you should call him.'

Despite an admitted lack of subtlety and inability to hold his tongue—which Rupert also confessed to Leveson—the tycoon somehow negotiated ten years of Blair's government and three years of foreplay while Blair led the Opposition without asking for the smallest thing. Indeed, he asked Leveson to believe that he had not sought a favour from any prime minister: that he had met Britain's leaders regularly, written nice things to their wives, admired their children, popped in for tea, lunch, dinner or a chat at least a couple of times a year, and received their birthday greetings, yet had never done anything so base as to mention his commercial interests.

This was a truly remarkable statement to make, but since Murdoch denied lobbying Maggie Thatcher over *The Times* (and had concealed their private lunch at Chequers for 30 years), and since John Major and Gordon Brown both testified that he had asked things of them, his claim of clean hands was not entirely to be trusted. Indeed, his own right-hand man from the early 1990s, Gus Fischer, who set up the initial contacts with Blair, said he had 'never seen anyone more astute at manipulating politicians to his advantage then Rupert'.

And, whether he asked for them or not, Murdoch certainly got important concessions on media policy when it mattered. Lord Fowler, who steered the 2003 Communications Bill through the House of Lords for the Conservatives, claimed that Blair was responsible for the late amendment to this law, which effectively made it possible for Murdoch to bid for BSkyB. 'It had come straight from Number 10,' he reported.

It must be said in Blair's defence that the Labour PM was no pushover. His government set up the media regulator Ofcom, which the Murdochs hated, increased the BBC licence fee, which was anathema to them, and opposed the family's takeover of Manchester United Football Club. 'We decided more stuff against Murdoch interests than in favour of it,' he told Leveson. 'Did that mean they changed their support for me? No, it didn't.'

But whether David Cameron played his cards so well is less clear. And he certainly finished up as close to Brooks and the Murdochs as Blair had been.

Four months after meeting Rupert on his yacht at Santorini, the would-be PM was invited to a New Year's Eve party at the Brookses' farm. In May 2009, he had dinner with Rebekah and James at the mini-mogul's house in London. In June, he was high-fiving Matthew Freud at Rebekah's wedding in the gardens at Sarsden. And in September 2009, he was meeting Brooks again, and then having drinks with James at a swanky Mayfair club called George, at which point the youngest Murdoch gave him the good news that *The Sun* would be backing him in the next election, and that the endorsement would be announced shortly. Three weeks later, *The Sun* dumped Gordon Brown's government after twelve years of supporting the party, with the simple but effective headline LABOUR'S LOST IT.

By this time, David's relationship with Rebekah had reached the point where they were exchanging intimate and jokey texts on a regular basis, with Cameron signing them off LOL until the News boss told him this meant Laugh Out Loud. Two weeks after *The Sun* made its historic switch to the Tories, she wished him luck for his speech to his party conference in Manchester, texting him to say, 'I am so rooting for you tomorrow and not just as a personal friend but because professionally we're definitely in this together.' After suggesting they meet for 'a country supper soon', Brooks signed off simperingly, 'Speech of your life? Yes he Cam!'

No sooner had Cameron delivered his oration than she was sending him congratulations, gushing, 'Brilliant speech. I cried twice. Will love "working together".' This, remember, was from the editor of Britain's most powerful newspaper, who had just been promoted to run all of Rupert's national papers, and whose duty it was to stay a professional distance from politicians and keep them honest.

The morning after Cameron's rally cry, Rebekah's sign-off, YES HE CAM, became *The Sun*'s headline for its editorial, which told readers that the 'Tough-talking Tory leader' in his 'commanding and passionate speech' had 'swept aside any last doubts about his capacity to lead this nation'.

There then followed another flurry of contacts, with Rupert meeting Cameron for breakfast and the two Murdochs backing that up with a celebratory dinner at the Brookes' farm just before Christmas, at which Cameron and his wife were present, along with the future Chancellor of the Exchequer, George Osborne, and his wife, Frances.

Come election day on 6 May 2010, the Tory leader duly woke up to find his picture on *The Sun*'s front page, treated to look like Barack Obama's famous campaign poster, and head-lined OUR ONLY HOPE. With Murdoch's paper behind him, Cameron squeaked home by a whisker, and *The Sun* extended its record of backing every British election winner for the last 40 years.

And now the meetings came thicker and faster. After Cameron moved into 10 Downing Street, Rupert was one of the first to call. Aware of how bad this might look to the public if the cameras caught him visiting the Prime Minister he had just put into office, he was asked to enter round the back. During the months that followed, Rebekah was invited to Chequers three times, and James once, and there was another Christmas dinner for Cam and the gang at the Brookses' farm, followed by a Boxing Day party where the PM dropped in for a glass of mulled wine.

Nor was it now just Cameron, who had 26 meetings with Murdoch's editors or executives in his first fifteen months of office. During this same period, a government minister met, lunched, dined or partied with a senior Murdoch executive every week. And on top of that, there were undoubtedly thousands of phone calls, emails, text messages and cosy chats with the ministers' political advisers.

This avalanche of contacts between the Murdochs and the new Tory-led Coalition government gave News an excellent opportunity to gain support for its planned £8 billion takeover of Britain's most profitable media group, BSkyB, which was so close to James's heart, and which would—if all went well—help secure his future as his father's heir. And the Murdochs grasped this opportunity with both hands.

19
SKY'S THE LIMIT

'Great and congrats on Brussels. Just Ofcom to go!'

Jeremy Hunt text to James Murdoch

News Corp's bid for the 61 per cent of BSkyB that it did not already own was launched a month after the Tories got into power. Almost exactly one year later, on 30 June 2011, it was approved by Britain's Culture Secretary, Jeremy Hunt, subject to a few last formalities, which were never completed because Milly Dowler spoiled the party. During that intervening period, the Murdoch group lobbied tirelessly to get the deal approved, both in private meetings with David Cameron and George Osborne, but also via direct contact with the minister who was making the decision.

In the space of twelve months, News Corp's chief government lobbyist, Fred Michel, was in touch with Jeremy Hunt or his special adviser, Adam Smith, more than 1000 times, through emails, text messages and phone calls, at an average of about three contacts a day. In the same period, Hunt and Smith had little or no contact with the bid's opponents, who included the

Daily Mail group, the BBC, *The Guardian* and public pressure groups like Avaaz.

The Culture Secretary was required to reach his decision on BSkyB in a quasi-judicial fashion, which meant he was supposed to be impartial. The rules also required that he behave like a judge, which precluded him and his special adviser having frequent and intimate contact with one of the parties. Yet that's exactly what Hunt and Smith did with News and its senior executives. In January 2011, Michel texted the minister to say, 'Great to see you today. We should get little [names redacted] together in the future to socialise. Nearly born the same day at the same place! Warm regards, Fred.'

Hunt texted back, 'Good to see you too. Hope u understand why we have to have the long process. Let's meet up when things are resolved. J.'

Two months later, Michel texted the minister again to say, 'You were great at the Commons today. Hope all well. Warm regards, Fred.'

Hunt texted back, 'Merci. Large drink tonight.'

Five months later, after Hunt told the House of Commons he was approving the bid, Michel texted Hunt's adviser to say, 'Just showed to Rupert! Great statement by the way.' An hour later, he inquired, 'Think we are in a good place, no?' To which Smith fired back, 'Very, yes, Jeremy happy.'

Even allowing for a degree of exaggeration by the News lobbyist about the closeness of their relationship, this was not how a minister and his adviser were supposed to conduct themselves, especially when the takeover was so contentious and there were so many reasons why the Government should have been reluctant to wave it through.

The main objection to the Murdochs getting full control of BSkyB was that News was already too powerful. It was responsible for 40 per cent of Britain's Sunday newspaper circulation and 34 per cent of its national daily sales. It also owned the most powerful and aggressive tabloid in the country, which made a habit of bullying politicians. So it was hard to justify giving the Murdochs yet more muscle. Yet, there would have been even louder protests if people had read Rupert's evidence to a House of Lords select committee in 2007, when he had confessed that he wanted Sky to be more like his notoriously rabid US broadcaster, Fox News. The key reason he had not been able to make this happen, he complained, was that nobody at Sky ever listened to him. But they would be much more likely to do so if he owned 100 per cent of the British pay-TV network.

Taking full control of BSkyB had been on the News Corp agenda for years, but it had first become a real plan in August 2009, around the time that James and Rebekah had begun their meetings with Cameron and agreed to endorse him. By this stage, the Tory leader was already threatening to cut the BBC's budget and rein in the powers of Britain's TV regulator, Ofcom—which the Murdochs really hoped he would do—so it was likely he would be far more relaxed than Labour about BSkyB.

Jeremy Hunt was also known to be a friend. He had met James Murdoch a couple of times in Opposition, and had spent several days with News Corp executives in New York in 2009, before writing opinion pieces in favour of cutting the power of Ofcom. He had even boasted on his website that he was 'a cheerleader for Rupert Murdoch's contribution' to the media industry. As he happily admitted to Leveson, he was a fan of the BSkyB bid from the very beginning.

However, it was not initially Hunt's role to make the decision, because this was the preserve of the Secretary of State for Business, Vince Cable, a tough-talking Liberal Democrat. And Cable had told James Murdoch from the outset that he and his political advisers would not be meeting anyone from News while he considered the bid.

As the regulatory process got under way in late 2010, and it seemed likely that Cable would refer the bid to Ofcom, and thence perhaps to the Competition Commission, the Murdoch camp became worried by the minister's refusal to talk, so Michel decided to move things along by lobbying some of the Lib Dem MPs in Parliament. Bright and early on 27 October 2010 he went to the House of Commons to see Norman Lamb MP, who took notes of the meeting that he later supplied to Leveson. 'An extraordinary encounter,' Lamb wrote with alarm. 'FM is very charming... They are certain there are no grounds for referral. They realise the political pressures. He wants things to run smoothly. They have been supportive of the Coalition but if it goes the wrong way, he is worried about the implications. It was brazen. VC refers case to Ofcom—they turn nasty.'

Lamb told Leveson he could not recall the exact words used by Murdoch's man, but that he was left with 'a very clear understanding that...if things went the wrong way in terms of the actions that Vince Cable took...things could change, and I took that to mean very clearly that the positive coverage that...he said they had given might change.' Or to put it more bluntly, that the Murdoch press would turn against the Lib Dems and oppose their campaign for electoral reform.

Soon after this meeting, on 4 November, Cable did indeed refer the bid to Ofcom, on the grounds that it would reduce the plurality of voices in the British media. But with the deal now under threat, the BSkyB decision was dramatically snatched away from him. Just before Christmas 2010, the Business Secretary was caught in a sting by a couple of female journalists from the *Telegraph*, posing as his constituents, who coaxed him into criticising his Conservative coalition partners and musing about bringing down the government. Cable was forced into an apology when these rash remarks were published, but worse soon followed. He had also boasted unwisely that he had 'declared war on the Murdochs' and 'expected to win'. And when this comment was leaked to the BBC a few hours later, the Prime Minister immediately stripped the minister of responsibility for the bid on the grounds of bias, citing his 'totally unacceptable and inappropriate' comments. This, of course, made the takeover a great deal more likely to succeed.

Later, the *Telegraph* would hire an internationally renowned firm of investigators, Krolls, to trace the source of the leak that had so changed the BSkyB bid's prospects of success, and would be told there was a 'strong suspicion' that it had been orchestrated by two ex-employees of the *Telegraph* who had just joined News International. Remarkably, one of these, Will Lewis, had been best man at Rebekah Brooks's wedding. When asked point blank by the Leveson Inquiry whether he was responsible—yes or no—Lewis refused to say.

On the day that all this happened, Jeremy Hunt had agreed to chat to James Murdoch by phone at 4 p.m., which was 90 minutes after Cable's comments became public. After talking to him at the appointed time, the minister (who still did not have responsibility for the bid) texted the Chancellor, George Osborne, to say, 'Cld we chat about Murdoch Sky bid am seriously worried we are going to screw this up. Jeremy.' Moments later, he fired off another, telling him, 'Just been called by James M. His lawyers are meeting now and saying it calls into question legitimacy of whole process from. beginning "acute bias" etc.' Straight after that, Hunt rushed off an email to Andy Coulson, who was still the PM's Head of Communications at 10 Downing Street, saying, 'Could we chat about this? Am seriously worried Vince will do real damage to Coalition with his comments.' An hour later, Chancellor Osborne texted back to say that they had dealt with the crisis and to add, 'I hope you like our solution.'

This 'solution' to the problem (that James was upset) was to hand the BSkyB decision to Hunt, despite the fact that he was clearly just as biased as Vince Cable, but in the opposite direction. Earlier that day, before speaking to James on the phone, Hunt had sent Murdoch a cheery text message, congratulating him on getting European approval for the bid, saying, 'Great and congrats on Brussels. Just Ofcom to go!' A month earlier, on 19 November, he had tried to get the PM to intervene in the Murdochs' favour, firing off a memo to say that James was 'furious' about the referral to Ofcom, and advising the Prime Minister that it would be 'totally wrong to cave in' to the bid's opponents. Despite having no official role in the process, Hunt had tried to arrange a meeting to discuss the bid with Cameron, Osborne and Cable, but had been vetoed.

Hunt had been able to relay News Corp's fury to his bosses on that occasion, too, because he had just spoken to James Murdoch, despite being warned by his civil servants to have no contact. 'Jeremy tried to call you,' News's lobbyist, Fred Michel explained to his boss. 'He has received...legal advice not to meet us today as the current process is treated as a judicial one...Jeremy is very frustrated about it...but you could have a chat with him on his mobile which is...fine.'

James had replied, 'You must be f****** joking. I will text him and find a time.' And they had then talked on the phone instead, although why Hunt felt this was allowed when a face-to-face conversation was not is unclear.

Now that Hunt was officially dealing with the bid, contact with News Corp moved up another gear. In the next five weeks, James Murdoch met the minister twice and spoke to him once on the phone, although the Culture Secretary now had his officials listening in. He also met the Chancellor. And on 23 December, he and Rebekah Brooks had Christmas lunch with Cameron at the Brookses' farm, at which the subject of the BSkyB bid was raised (although Cameron did his best to deny this). Brooks also had a separate dinner with the Chancellor on 13 December and bent Osborne's ear about Ofcom's objections to the bid.

By early January, the Murdochs and the government were in possession of the Ofcom report, which recommended referring the bid to the Competition Commission because it would reduce media plurality. This clearly posed a serious threat to the £8 billion takeover, but Hunt had some helpful ideas. On 10 January, Michel emailed Murdoch to say the minister had asked them to 'find as many errors as we can in the Ofcom report' and to say that Hunt wanted *The Sun*'s gung-ho columnist, Richard Littlejohn, to provide 'some favourable op-ed coverage'.

Hunt's next suggestion, according to Michel, was that he could avoid referring the bid to the Competition Commission if News gave him strong 'Undertakings in Lieu' (UIL) to meet the plurality concerns, for example, by promising to hive off Sky News into a new company not fully controlled by the Murdochs. (News had suggested this.) The minister was confident this would do the trick, and was keen for it to succeed. On Sunday 23 January, following a lengthy phone call with Hunt's special adviser, Michel told Murdoch in an email:

> His [Hunt's] view is that once he announces publicly he has a strong UIL it is almost game over for the opposition...
>
> He says he understands fully our concerns/fears...
>
> He very specifically said he was keen to get to the same outcome and wants JRM to understand that he needs to build some political cover on the process...
>
> He said we would get there in the end and he shared our objectives.

The following day, on the eve of Hunt releasing the Ofcom report to Parliament, Michel sent another email to James, with a message in bold type, boasting that he had 'Managed to get some infos on the plans for tomorrow, although absolutely illegal.'

This cosy communiqué was sent on 24 January 2011 just as the *News of the World* hacking scandal reached a critical stage. Ten days earlier, the police and Crown Prosecution Service had reopened the original inquiry. Shortly after that, Andy Coulson had sniffed the wind and quit his job as the Prime Minister's head of communications. Two days later, Operation Weeting would be launched. It was also around this time that a vast quantity of emails and other records—including James's email from Colin Myler, perhaps—were deleted on the orders of a senior News International executive.

It was now a race against time to get the bid approved before the scandal went nuclear. With civil actions against News queuing up in the courts and scores of detectives raking through the material seized from Glenn Mulcaire, it was almost certain to blow sooner or later. So the question was would the government hold its nerve, or would it regard criminal activity by Murdoch journalists as a reason to refer the decision to an independent arbiter?

On 5 April 2011, the first hacking arrests were made, as Ian Edmondson and Neville Thurlbeck were taken in for questioning. Eight days later, Michel emailed his boss to say that Hunt had assured him the *News of the World*'s problems would not get in the way of the deal, which he said was already locked in.

> Catch up with JH…debriefed him on the NOW [*News of the World*] issues…There is no question that NOW will not play any part in his decision…He managed to avoid a massive backlash against the deal despite attempts by Prescott and other Labour figures. Given the current onslaught in the media…there will be a strategic decision to make for the government as to the day it will choose to clear the deal. We know it will clear it. We just need to push them strongly now to announce it as early as possible.

Around this time, Hunt received legal advice from his department that hacking by the *News of the World* might be a problem because it could reflect on the trustworthiness of News Corp's management, but he took the view that the companies were separate so he need do nothing. He later told Leveson that he had no idea the scandal was 'about to erupt'. But he could easily have discovered the gravity of the allegations by reading *The Guardian*, the *New York Times* or the Culture Committee's 2010 report. Given that his job as Culture Secretary included oversight of Britain's media, it was extraordinary that he could claim to be so ill-informed.

By now, opposition from pressure groups like Avaaz was mounting and News knew the bomb was ticking. On 12 May, Michel emailed Hunt's adviser to warn that if the bid was not approved by mid-June it would be 'catastrophic for many important reasons'. Hunt's office replied that it would be sorted by 24 June, six days after the News International summer party. But as the month drew to a close, it still didn't have the green light. On 27 June, Michel emailed Rebekah Brooks to say that Hunt was about to make an 'extremely helpful' statement to the House of Commons, which would emphasise that the *News of the World*'s hacking would not affect his decision. But the minister wanted some advice. As the lobbyist put it, 'JH is now starting to look into phone-hacking/practices more thoroughly...[and] has asked me to advise him privately in the coming weeks and guide his and No 10's positioning.' In other words, Hunt wanted News to tell the government how to play down the phone-hacking story. A more appropriate response from the minister in charge of Britain's media might have been to order a public inquiry into allegations of industrial-scale lawbreaking at the best-selling tabloid. But clearly this idea didn't even get onto his radar.

On 30 June, Hunt told Parliament that he intended to approve the bid, and that hacking at the *News of the World* was not relevant to the decision. Four days later, on Monday 4 July, Michel and Murdoch were intending to take Hunt and his adviser to Take That's sell-out concert in Manchester. But they never made it to the gig. Five hours before the band came on stage, the Milly Dowler story went up on *The Guardian* website.

Nine days later, News withdrew its offer for BSkyB and admitted the takeover was dead. By this time, Hunt had sent the proposal back to Ofcom, after which he was expected to refer it to the Competition Commission, as he should surely have done in the first place.

Had the hacking scandal not exploded when it did, there's no doubt that the Murdochs would have ended up with 100 per cent of BSkyB as planned. And it is hard to believe that their cosy relationship with Britain's politicians had not played a part in it so nearly succeeding. Lord Leveson concluded—somewhat bizarrely—that Hunt was scrupulous in sticking to the proper process, and always acted on advice. In other words, that the decision was above reproach. But others who read the emails and text messages might not agree.

The warmth and intimacy between the Murdochs and the Tories, and the bullying behaviour of *The Sun* over many years, may also have prevented the hacking scandal from being properly investigated. Tom Watson believes that the media group's closeness to Britain's leaders was one reason why repeated calls for a public inquiry into phone hacking went unheeded. 'In the end this scandal is about political failure,' he told the Leveson Inquiry. 'Successive prime ministers, from Margaret Thatcher to David Cameron, must share responsibility for allowing executives at News International and other media groups to believe they had become unaccountable.'

Certainly, the Murdochs' close links to the people who ran Britain made News more optimistic that they could get away with it all. 'I came to believe, along with other journalists, that the newspaper group were confident that they were indeed untouchable,' says Matt Driscoll, the *News of the World* reporter who won a bullying case against the paper, 'because they were sure they had government and police fighting their corner. Thus they felt they were almost beyond the reach of the law.' Or, as the paper's former features editor, Jules Stenson, put it: 'The humbling of Rupert Murdoch and his cohorts came about because of their arrogance. They really did think they ruled Britain, and, frankly, who could blame them when the prime minister was writing text messages to the chief executive that he thought were ending "Lots of Love".'

20
JUDGEMENT DAY

'News International and its parent News Corporation exhibited wilful blindness, for which the companies' directors—including Rupert Murdoch and James Murdoch—should ultimately be prepared to take responsibility.'

Culture, Media and Sport Committee report, May 2012

In February 2012, Charlotte Church settled her legal action against News Group Newspapers for £600 000 just four days before it was due to go to trial. She had wanted to take it all the way but looked at the forces ranged against her and decided it was a battle she could not win.

'I almost felt a responsibility as a citizen that I had to go through with it,' she said after dropping the case. 'But it was made impossible at the end in terms of the collateral damage and what they were going to put my mother and my family through. There was a horrifying moment when we realised their trial strategy: that they were going to go after the most vulnerable person—my mother. If we'd gone to trial, they were never going to make it about hacking. They were going to make it about everything else.'

In the previous days and weeks, News had also bought off the five other claimants chosen as test cases and avoided lurid details of its journalists' crimes emerging in London's High Court. In all, it had settled actions brought by 58 hacking victims and coughed up around £3 million in costs and damages. But even if the money was insignificant, the Murdoch group had paid a price because it had been forced to make damaging admissions, read grovelling apologies in open court, and allow the victims to say how much hacking had blighted their lives. The actor Jude Law gave a flavour of this in a victim statement, in which he complained, 'No aspect of my private life was safe from intrusion by News Group newspapers, including the lives of my children and the people who work for me. It was not just that my phone messages were listened to: News Group also paid people to watch me and my house for days at a time and to follow me and those close to me both in this country and abroad.'

But even more damaging than this public caning was Justice Vos's revelation that News had made 'an admission of sorts' that it had deliberately covered up evidence of its crimes. Quoting from the victims' statement of claim, Vos told the High Court that News had 'put out public statements that it knew to be false', 'deliberately deceived the police' and destroyed evidence of wrongdoing including 'a very substantial number of emails' and computers. News had not actually admitted to doing this, but had agreed to pay aggravated damages on the basis that the claims were true, and Justice Vos was in no doubt what this meant. 'They are to be treated as deliberate destroyers of evidence,' he said.

Two months later, Rupert was forced to admit to the Leveson Inquiry that News had in fact concealed the truth about phone hacking from the start. It was a surprise that he was at last being so blunt about it, but the twist was that it was still no *mea culpa* because he claimed that he was the biggest victim. Someone at News had made sure, he said, that the extent of hacking at the paper was kept secret from him and James. 'I think the senior executives and I were all misinformed and shielded from anything that was going on there,' Rupert told the inquiry. 'And I do blame one or two people for that, who perhaps I shouldn't name, because for all I know they may be arrested yet, but there's no question in my mind that maybe even the editor, but certainly beyond that, someone took charge of a cover-up, which we were victim to and I regret.'

Asked who had orchestrated this, Rupert replied in somewhat garbled prose, 'I think from within the *News of the World*, and there were one or two very strong characters there, who I think had been there many, many, many years and were friends with the journalists—or the person I'm thinking of was a friend of the journalists, drinking pal, and was a clever lawyer, and forbade them to go and see the evidence—or there had been statements reporting that this person forbade people to go and report to Mrs Brooks or to James.'

There was no question now that he was pointing the finger at Tom Crone and Colin Myler, and also no question that they were easy targets. They had led the cover-up by misleading the Culture Committee in 2009, and, in Myler's case, the Press Complaints Commission in 2007 and 2009 as well. And to judge by their admissions to Leveson, they had done this knowingly. But the key question was whether they had covered it all up *from* the Murdochs or *for* them.

Crone might have had some motive to conceal the extent of phone hacking on the paper because he had been the *News of the World*'s chief lawyer while it was in full swing, and either would or should have known that it was going on. But Myler had no reason to lie about it at all, except to protect the newspaper and his employers, because he had arrived well after the crimes had taken place. He had also sent the email to James in 2008 that would have told his boss all he needed to know, had James bothered to read it.

Crone immediately responded—without the protection of parliamentary privilege—that Murdoch's accusations were a 'shameful lie', adding: 'It is perhaps no coincidence that the two people he [Rupert Murdoch] has identified in relation to his cover-up allegations are the same two people who pointed out that his son's evidence to the Parliamentary Select Committee last year was inaccurate.'

As this spat went public in early May 2012, the Culture Committee was preparing to publish its verdict on whether James Murdoch and his executives had misled Parliament when they gave evidence about phone hacking in 2007, 2009 and 2011. The report was already three months past its due date because its members were deeply divided over how hard James should be whacked.

With five Conservative and five Labour MPs trying to reach agreement, it was not surprising that it was being fought over line by line. At one extreme, Labour firebrand Tom Watson had accused James of being a Mafia boss. At the other, the Tories' Therese Coffey had been about the only person in Britain to rush to Rebekah Brooks's defence when the hacking scandal broke. In the middle, the committee's Tory chairman, John Whittingdale, had begun the process as an out-and-out Murdoch supporter and liked to think the best of people. But the balance of power on the eleven-person panel was held by a Liberal Democrat, whose party had long disliked the way the Murdochs' British papers behaved. So a critical majority was almost guaranteed.

In the run-up to the decision, James wrote the committee a seven-page letter in the hope of moderating its findings.

Admitting that 'it would have been better if I had asked more questions, requested more documents and scrutinised them carefully', he nevertheless blamed his ignorance squarely on Crone and Myler, whom he accused of keeping him in the dark. And once again he affirmed his innocence by saying, 'I have not misled Parliament. I did not know about, nor did I try to hide wrongdoing. I do not believe the evidence before you supports any other conclusion.'

But whether the MPs accepted this or not, it was hard to see how their report could be anything but damaging to James's career prospects, in that it was almost certain to say that he either did know or should have done.

However, when the verdict finally arrived, its headline conclusion did not mention James at all. It was that Rupert should take the blame, and that he was 'not a fit person' to run a 'major international company'. This deliberately employed the language used by Ofcom, which was investigating whether the Murdochs and News Corp should be allowed to retain control of BSKyB and its British TV licence.

The immediate response from News was that the committee's damnation was 'unjustified and highly partisan'. But for once there was some element of truth to its complaints because the Tory members had not signed up to the one-line condemnation or to the harshest criticisms of James and Rupert.

Nevertheless, even though the MPs were divided on how far the Murdochs were to blame, they were unanimous on all the other important questions, such as whether Tom Crone, Colin Myler, Les Hinton and News International had misled Parliament. And to all these their answer was a resounding yes. After accusing the *News of the World*'s chief lawyer and editor of misleading the committee by 'answering questions falsely', not telling the truth, and giving 'demonstrably unreliable' evidence, the report concluded:

> Tom Crone and Colin Myler gave repeated assurances that there was no evidence that any further *News of the World* employee, beyond Clive Goodman, had been involved in phone-hacking. This was not true and, as further evidence disclosed to us by the newspaper's solicitors Farrer & Co now shows, they would have known this was untrue when they made those statements. Both Tom Crone and Colin Myler deliberately avoided disclosing crucial information to the Committee and, when asked to do, answered questions falsely.

The MPs were equally damning about Rupert's great friend, Les Hinton, who had begun the cover-up in 2007 by assuring MPs that hacking had not gone beyond Goodman, and had then sanctioned a massive £243 500 pay-off to the jailed reporter to keep him quiet.

Branding the pay-off as 'over-generous' and 'extraordinary' for someone who had been convicted of a crime, the MPs said it was 'impossible...not to question the company's motives'. It then got stuck into Hinton, who had approved the payments and refused to tell MPs that he had done so.

> When questioned...in 2009, he was startlingly vague and, inexcusably, sought to portray his role as a passive one, simply following the advice given to him by his subordinates. The evidence we took in 2011 suggests that he not only authorised the payments, but took the decision to make them in the first place...His 'selective amnesia' notwithstanding, he would have been perfectly well aware of what he had done. We consider, therefore, that Les Hinton misled the Committee.

Their next broadside was also unanimous in saying that Hinton had misled Parliament with the claim that hacking had not gone beyond Goodman. As they pointed out, Murdoch's man had told them this after receiving the letter in which Goodman accused several editors and senior journalists at the *News of the World* of knowing about phone hacking and of doing it themselves:

> Whether or not Les Hinton had seen this letter before his appearance in 2007, he certainly had by the time he did so on 15 September 2009 when he said: 'There was never firm evidence provided or suspicion provided that I am aware of that implicated anybody else other than Clive within the staff of the *News of the World*. It just did not happen.' This was not true...At no stage did Les Hinton seek to correct the record, even when invited by the Committee to do so. We consider, therefore, that Les Hinton was complicit in the cover-up at News International, which included making misleading statements and giving a misleading picture to this Committee.

The MPs then gave an explicit warning of what such a finding could mean. 'Witnesses found to have misled a select committee, to have wilfully suppressed the truth, to have provided false evidence and even to have prevaricated, have all been considered to be guilty of contempt of Parliament in the past,' they warned. 'This is no trivial matter.'

Moving on to the role of News International, the MPs were also unanimous in finding the company guilty of a whole range of offences, including covering up criminal activity, buying silence with huge pay-offs, exaggerating the extent of investigations, withholding vital information from the committee and not releasing their lawyers from professional privilege. Naturally, they also dismissed as 'false' News International's claim that phone hacking was the work of one rogue reporter, adding bluntly, 'This is beyond dispute.'

The MPs were also unanimous in their conclusion that the important documents provided to the committee—the Goodman letter, the 'For Neville' email, the Michael Silverleaf legal opinion, the Julian Pike file notes, the Tom Crone briefing and the original Mulcaire contract from 2005—had all come from sources other than News International, even though they had been in the company's possession all along.

The same was true of almost all the tips they had received, such as the fact that Goodman and Mulcaire had been bought off, that Taylor had been given £700 000 to stay silent, and that neither Harbottle & Lewis nor Burton Copeland had conducted proper investigations, despite News's claims that they had. News had neither volunteered this information nor been willing to say more when it was revealed.

And, finally, the MPs were unanimous in concluding that, 'The behaviour of News International and certain witnesses in this affair demonstrated contempt...[for Parliament] in the most blatant fashion.'

All in all, it could hardly have been more damning.

It was only when James and Rupert Murdoch were specifically placed on the charge sheet that the committee failed to reach agreement. But even its most swingeing condemnation of News and its directors was endorsed by seven of the ten MPs who voted. And this could also not have been stronger without actually using the 'L' word:

> Corporately, the *News of the World* and News International misled the Committee...by making statements they would have known were not fully truthful; and by failing to disclose documents which would have helped expose the truth. Their instinct throughout, until it was too late, was to cover up rather than seek out wrongdoing and discipline the perpetrators...In failing to investigate properly, and by ignoring evidence of widespread wrongdoing, News International and its parent

News Corporation exhibited wilful blindness, for which the companies' directors—including Rupert Murdoch and James Murdoch—should ultimately be prepared to take responsibility.

The report then moved onto a direct consideration of what the Murdochs had actually known. And here the committee finally split on party lines. The majority verdict was that it was 'simply astonishing' that Rupert and James had stuck to the one-rogue-reporter defence until December 2010, in the face of so much evidence that it was false.

The majority were also astonished by James's 'lack of curiosity' in failing to ask about the Gordon Taylor settlement in 2008 and his further 'astonishing lack of curiosity—wilful ignorance even' in failing to ask any relevant questions between the publication of *The Guardian*'s allegations about widespread hacking in July 2009 and disclosures in the Sienna Miller case in December 2010.

Finally, they concluded that James and Rupert had either known what had gone on in their newspapers or had deliberately turned a blind eye. And then came the headline verdict:

On the basis of the facts and evidence before the Committee, we conclude that, if at all relevant times Rupert Murdoch did not take steps to become fully informed about phone-hacking, he turned a blind eye and exhibited wilful blindness to what was going on in his companies and publications. This culture, we consider, permeated from the top throughout the organisation and speaks volumes about the lack of effective corporate governance at News Corporation and News International. We conclude, therefore, that Rupert Murdoch is not a fit person to exercise the stewardship of a major international company.

According to one of Rupert Murdoch's former advisers, who worked by his side for many years, this 'culture' that MPs referred to as permeating through News was one that 'encouraged naughtiness' among his employees. Rupert displayed scant respect for rules or traditions, he said, and the people who worked for him often followed his lead. Or, as another twenty-year veteran of the group explained: 'The culture was bullish. We had a false sense of arrogance about the world. Whatever shit you caused there was always someone who could come in and clean it up. Even if you were wrong you were going to be right. We had the best lawyers, the best accountants. Most of us were mongrels, hard core people who'd get out there and make it happen.'

You could see this self-confidence in *The Sun*'s treatment of Elton John in the 1980s or the *News of the World*'s savaging of Max Mosley in 2008, and in the subsequent refusal of the Murdoch group to accept criticism from the High Court or to discipline both of the editors involved. But you could trace it back much further than that. In April 1983, amid great fanfare, London's *Sunday Times* boasted that it was in possession of Adolf Hitler's secret diaries, which portrayed the Nazi dictator as less of a monster than history believed him to be. Rupert had bought them himself for US$400 000 from the German news magazine *Stern* after flying to Hamburg to inspect them. The manuscripts had been examined and authenticated by an eminent historian, Lord Dacre, who was a director of Times Newspapers, but no tests had been made of the ink, paper or handwriting, and there had been no detailed examination to ensure they weren't a forgery. As the presses began to roll, with Saturday's *The Times* trumpeting the diaries imminent arrival, Dacre suddenly changed his mind about their provenance. But despite these doubts about their authenticity, Murdoch still pressed ahead, with the immortal words, 'Fuck Dacre. Publish.' When the diaries were revealed, within days, to be a forgery, Rupert was unrepentant, telling his journalists it was no great matter. 'After all, we're in the entertainment business.'

The media mogul displayed a similar insouciance over *The Sun*'s famous GOTCHA headline that greeted the sinking of the Argentine flagship, *General Belgrano*, during the Falklands War. As it became clear that the ship had sunk and hundreds of sailors had drowned, Kelvin MacKenzie decided to tone it down out of respect for the dead. Murdoch alone expressed disappointment, saying he liked the headline and could see nothing wrong with it.

But more broadly, there was a fierce competitive ethos inside News—and particularly its British tabloids—that made Murdoch's journalists determined to get the story ahead of their rivals, at almost any cost. Visitors to the newsroom at Britain's top-selling tabloid were greeted by a notice telling them, 'You are now entering SUN country', and it really was a different land.

'I was in awe,' says one antipodean visitor from Murdoch's Australian papers. 'It was an amazing operation. They put out 33 editions a night. They were so powerful, so arrogant, and had so little self doubt; they felt they could do anything.' And they pretty much did. Everyone on *The Sun*'s news desk had the authority to spend £10 000 on a story without seeking management approval, and this money was routinely handed out to informants and others who could deliver a story. 'Paying policemen was just such standard practice for so long that no one could see it was wrong anymore,' says this former senior journalist.

This view is echoed by a senior lawyer in the hacking cases against News International, who has probably seen more evidence than anybody about the way the Murdoch tabloids behaved. 'Bribing people and paying for information was the way they did business. They didn't think about it. And that's the attitude they took when it was exposed. Nobody paid any attention because systematic illegality is what they did. Bribing of police officers was absolutely standard. They had lost the idea that there was anything untoward about it.'

Whether Rupert Murdoch knew that this was happening on a massive scale is not clear, but in March 2013 he was secretly taped by his own journalists at *The Sun* telling them that editors and reporters on the paper facing criminal charges had done nothing that wasn't common practice across Fleet Street. Significantly, Rupert readily admitted that his journalists has been making these payments and he made no attempt to deny knowing about it, or to claim he had only just discovered this. 'Payments for news tips from the cops', as he called it, had been going on 'for 100 years', he said. Murdoch also made clear that he didn't regard paying public officials to break the law as a serious offence, describing the huge police investigation as 'laughable', 'outrageous' and 'over next to nothing'. This, of course, was absolutely in conflict with everything he had said in public with his hand on his heart.

Whether or not Murdoch knew about these payments at the time they were being made, it is certain that the dark arts flourished in the organisation he commanded. And he must surely take some responsibility for this. 'The standards and culture of a journalistic institution are set from the top down, by its owner, publisher, and top editors,' the Watergate veteran Carl Bernstein commented when the Dowler story broke in 2011. 'Reporters and editors do not routinely break the law, bribe policemen, wiretap, and generally conduct themselves like thugs unless it is a matter of recognized and understood policy. Private detectives and phone hackers do not become the primary sources of a newspaper's information without the tacit knowledge and approval of the people at the top.'

Or as the *Sunday Times*'s former editor, Andrew Neil, opined, 'Rupert Murdoch, with his take-no-prisoners attitude to tabloid journalism, the ends will justify the means, do whatever it takes... That created the kind of newsroom climate in which hacking and other things were done with impunity on an industrial scale.'

However, it wasn't only in journalism that the Murdoch group was prepared to push the boundaries. Between 2009 and 2011, News Corp paid out almost US$655 million in damages to settle three separate legal actions over anti-competitive behaviour by one of its subsidiaries, News America Marketing, which was run by one of Rupert's capos, Paul Carlucci. One of the admissions in court was that News America had hacked into the password-protected computer system of a rival company, Floorgraphics, 'on at least eleven separate occasions' between 2003 and 2004, and stolen confidential information about its advertising and market-ing programs. Courts in Michigan and New Jersey also heard that Carlucci warned Floorgraphics' founder, George Rebh, at a meeting in a New York restaurant, 'If you ever get into any of our businesses, I will destroy you...I work for a man who wants it all, and doesn't understand anybody telling him he can't have it all.' He was referring, of course, to Rupert Murdoch.

The same Paul Carlucci admitted using Mafia references to motivate his sales force and showing them a tape of *The Untouch-ables*, although he denied the allegation that it was the scene in which Al Capone beats a man to death with a baseball bat. He also told his sales force that they had pushed another rival, Valassis, to 'the brink of utter desperation', and that Rupert Murdoch was urging them to finish it off: 'Now you have to really go after them.'

One year after the first lawsuit was filed, by which time the substance of the claim was clear, Carlucci was promoted by

Murdoch to be publisher of the *New York Post*, as well as chief executive of News America. And despite the damaging testimony that then came out against him, and the US$655 million in settlements between 2009 and 2011, Carlucci was never sacked or disciplined. Which suggested that such behaviour was either tolerated or condoned.

21
TRIALS AHEAD

'I am not guilty of these charges.'

Rebekah Brooks

By the time the House of Commons' damning report on the hacking scandal was published in May 2012, the Murdochs' reputation was probably damaged beyond repair. Their political power in Britain was gone. And James's career was, for the moment, in ruins. He had quit as chairman of News International at the end of February to ensure a guilty verdict from the House of Commons did not force him to resign, and five weeks later he had been bustled out of his job as executive chairman of BSkyB after being asked to step down by the board. Britain's most valuable media company could hardly have a leader who did not read his emails and had no idea what was going on under his nose.

By April 2012, the would-be heir was back in New York in a US$23 million house on the Upper East Side, acting as News Corp's chief operating officer. Naturally, this was presented as a promotion, even if many people felt he had cut and run.

But in one important way, father and son had got away scot-free. If anyone was going to be hauled before Parliament to be punished for the cover-up that had taken place, it would be Tom Crone, Les Hinton and Colin Myler. Not them. And if anyone was going to end up in jail it was going to be their journalists. And quite possibly, lots of them.

In late January 2012, four key members of *The Sun*'s editorial team were arrested by Operation Elveden on suspicion of bribing police and public officials, or authorising such payments. These were the first arrests outside the *News of the World*, and they were starting at the top of the tree: *The Sun*'s current executive editor Fergus Shanahan, crime editor Mike Sullivan, head of news Chris Pharo, and the former managing editor Graham Dudman.

Almost as significantly, all these senior people had been caught because News's Management and Standards Committee (MSC) had handed over evidence to the police.

Four weeks later, the officer in charge of Operations Weeting, Elveden and Tuleta, Deputy Assistant Commissioner Sue Akers, told the Leveson Inquiry how useful her new friends at News were being to the police investigations, and how much her team had already uncovered. Journalists on the Murdoch daily tabloid, said Akers, had paid money to police officers and 'a wide range of public officials' in the armed forces, health service, prison service and government bureaucracy, in fact in 'all areas of public life'.

There appeared to have been 'a culture at *The Sun* of illegal payments', she said, and systems had 'been created to facilitate those payments, whilst hiding the identity of the officials receiving the money'. Police had also found evidence that the authority for these payments had been made 'at a very senior level—or a senior level within the newspaper'.

According to the Deputy Assistant Commissioner, there was no great crusading journalism to justify this spending, which had seen one official receive £80 000 and a journalist draw £150 000 in cash to pay to informants. 'The vast majority of the disclosures that have been made have led to stories which I would describe as salacious gossip,' said Akers, 'rather than anything that could be remotely regarded as in the public interest, and they often involve a breach of trust by the public official and an invasion into the privacy of the subject of the newspaper article.'

As to where all this new evidence was coming from, *The Guardian*'s Nick Davies reported that detectives were being given access to 'A mass of internal paperwork—invoices, reporters' expense claims, accounts, bank records, phone records', which had been retrieved from News International's central computer servers. This huge cache of information, which was known as Data Pool 3, contained around 300 million emails sent and received over the years by staff at the *News of the World*, *The Sun*, *The Times* and *Sunday Times*, and had been reconstructed by computer experts, after being deliberately deleted from News International's IT system.

Exactly how this information had been rebirthed was not clear, but it was a stroke of ill fortune for the reporters and editors on *The Sun* that the company that managed News International's emails, Essential Computing in Bristol, was expert in data recovery. As its managing director, Keith Quinn, had once advised his clients, 'Whether an email is deleted inadvertently or intentionally, the good (or perhaps bad) news is that it can almost always be recovered.'

There were now six cops dragging this dark pool for leads, using search software to target words like 'bribe', 'copper' and 'official'. There were also 32 civilians trawling it for the MSC, which was employing around 100 computer experts and lawyers in all at massive expense. No one knew what was in the pool or what it would cough up, said Davies. They could only wait to see how bad it got.

But for staff at *The Sun* it was already quite bad enough. Less than a week after Akers gave evidence, there was a second wave of arrests. On 11 February, another five senior journalists and editors on the paper were turfed out of bed in another series of dawn raids, in which police arrived mob-handed and proceeded to turn over the houses while their startled occupants looked on.

It was worse than the Soviet Union, *The Sun*'s associate editor Trevor Kavanagh complained, with enthusiastic support from the paper's former head-kicking columnist, Richard Littlejohn, who likened it to East Germany and the Stasi. 'Squads of up to twenty police officers raid suburban houses at six o'clock in the morning,' he wrote in the *Daily Mail*. 'Dozens more detectives rip out car doors, tear up floorboards and search through underwear drawers and beneath mattresses, terrifying innocent women and children. Men are arrested just as they are about to take their families to the countryside on half-term holidays. Suspects are carted off to police stations where they are interrogated for hours.'

Having long been such avid cheerleaders for the police, the Murdoch law-and-order brigade suddenly found there were other things to say about the boys in blue.

This time around, it was *The Sun*'s deputy editor Geoff Webster and chief reporter John Kay, who were taken off for questioning, along with chief foreign correspondent Nick Parker, news editor John Sturgis, and the picture editor John Edwards, all of whom were still working on the paper. Also arrested were a Ministry of Defence official, a Surrey policeman and a member of the Armed

Forces. And once again, the MSC claimed credit for the arrests, with one anonymous source boasting to the media that it was their job to 'drain the swamp'.

Reporters at *The Sun* were furious at what they saw as a monumental betrayal, and claimed that the Murdochs were throwing them to the wolves to save themselves. 'What we've seen…since the hacking scandal exploded,' the head of the journalists union told CNN, 'is Rupert has put his own immediate family, his son, and those executives who are like children to him, foremost in everything that he's done…He's tried consistently to pin the blame on those lower down the tree within News International and to try and defend and sustain the reputation and the future of those right at the top.'

Whether or not this was true, the company was certainly at war with itself. One part of News was turning material over to the police and ensuring that journalists were arrested. Another was hiring lawyers to defend them against the charges. Morale had never been lower. With nine of *The Sun*'s most senior editors and reporters on bail, suspended from work, it was almost impossible to get the paper out, and there were fears that it would follow its sister paper, the *News of the World*, into history. No one was even trying to stop the police search teams from entering the newsroom at Wapping to hunt for evidence against people they had just arrested.

'People are as angry as hell,' said one journalist. 'The management has done nothing to protect us from this appalling invasion of our work,' said another.

As tempers rose, Rupert arrived in London to quell the growing rebellion and tour the newsroom with Lachlan, who had flown in from Sydney to be by his father's side. James was nowhere to be seen, despite still being executive chairman at this stage.

Perhaps his father had told him to stay away, or perhaps he had realised he was no longer welcome.

Rupert was soon assuring staff that they had his 'unwavering support' and that, having lived and breathed *The Sun* for 40 years, he would never close it down. He also had good news: a new *Sun on Sunday* would be launched immediately to replace the *News of the World*, and he would be staying in London to make it happen. The masthead had been reserved in 2011, before the old Sunday tabloid was laid to rest, suggesting that they had been contemplating closing the *Screws* before the crisis hit.

Even better news was that the eleven journalists who had been arrested would have their suspensions lifted immediately and could all return to work. The paper would need them if it was to produce another edition. But Rupert didn't present it in such pedestrian terms. 'We're doing everything we can to assist those who are arrested,' he said. 'Everyone is innocent until proven otherwise.'

Yet for all that, there was still no softening on the MSC. 'Illegal activities simply cannot and will not be tolerated at any of our publications,' Rupert told staff in an email. 'Our Board of Directors, our management team and I take these issues very seriously. Our independently chaired Management & Standards Committee, which operates outside of News International, has been instructed to cooperate with the police. We will turn over every piece of evidence we find, not just because we are obligated to but because it is the right thing to do.'

Rupert's royal visit squashed the uprising and lifted the mood. But it did not last long. Three weeks later, the paper's veteran chief reporter, John Kay, had to be talked down from the parapet of Blackfriars Bridge whence he was about to jump into the wintry waters of the Thames. The paper's defence editor, Virginia Wheeler, also felt the tide of despair wash over her and tried to slit her wrists. Both were checked into hospital on Rupert's orders; the company would foot the bill.

And thus the revolt began again. One anonymous News International executive told the media, 'People think that they've been thrown under a bus. They're beyond angry; there's an utter sense of betrayal.' Reserving his biggest barbs for Will Lewis and Simon Greenberg, who were leading the MSC, he warned, 'These former journalists are turning their own people over to police for "crimes" that newspapers have indulged in for centuries. I doubt whether Will Lewis and Greenberg will be able to show their face around News International. They have both shat all over their colleagues.'

Neville Thurlbeck also joined the chorus of outrage, using his new blog to publish the name of the street where Lewis lived. He was immediately arrested for intimidating a witness, but was later told he would not be charged.

Meanwhile, the police were making progress with the hacking investigation.

On 13 March 2012, a mob of police burst into the Brookses' Oxfordshire farmhouse in the early morning dark and arrested Rebekah and her husband Charlie, who was all set to go off to Cheltenham races for the first day of the festival meeting. It was usually the happiest day of his year, but there would be no racing for him: he would spend the day in custody instead. Once again, the style of the arrests appeared heavy-handed. 'Baby asleep. Eighteen of them. They came running up the stairs shouting their heads off,' Charlie later recounted. 'It felt like a very over-the-top operation. The nanny was totally traumatised.'

Two months later, on 15 May 2012, the couple answered bail at a South London police station, where Rebekah was charged with three counts of perverting the course of justice, for allegedly concealing evidence from police in the hacking and corruption investigations. Charlie was also charged, along with four others, including Rebekah's PA, chauffeur and security guard, plus News International's head of security, Mark Hanna. These were the first charges to be brought by Operation Weeting and it was fitting that it should be her, given that she had become the public face of the scandal. The charges alleged that Rebekah and others had conspired to remove seven boxes of documents from News International's archives between 6 and 9 of July 2011—at a time when she was pledging publicly to hunt down the culprits—and that she had concealed computers and other electronic equipment from police between 15 and 19 of July—around the time she was arrested on suspicion of phone hacking. Charlie's sole charge related to concealing documents, computers and other electronic equipment, which perhaps related to the laptop bag found in the Chelsea car park.

Prior to their rendezvous with detectives, the couple put out a statement saying, 'We deplore this weak and unjust decision.' Three hours later they fronted the cameras outside their solicitor's office, so Charlie could brand the investigation a witch hunt, and Rebekah could express her outrage. Looking drawn, blotchy and worn out, she said she had faith in the justice system but had to question whether the decision to prosecute had been made on the evidence. Claiming to be 'baffled' by the charges, she told the assembled media, 'I cannot express my anger enough that those closest to me have been dragged into this unfairly. As the details of the case emerge people will see today as an expensive sideshow, and a waste of public money.' Watching her rage on TV from his office at the House of Commons, her old foe Chris Bryant MP shook his head in amazement. 'I've never seen anything like it,' he said. 'It was like putting two fingers up to the court.'

Brooks's old paper, *The Sun*, would have loved this story, had it not been one of its own now threatened with the slammer, and its subs would have been sorely tempted to recycle the famous headline that greeted the sinking of the Argentine flagship, *General Belgrano*, all those years ago. Yes, it was 'Gotcha' all right: one of the elites the Murdoch papers so hated was being taken down. But the best-selling tabloid hardly bothered with the news, which it buried down the bottom of its website, beneath 50 other stories and pictures that its editor deemed more important.

Up in the Twittersphere, there was much more excitement, with comments of 'finally' and 'at last', and several quips about *The Sun*'s vigorous campaigns to toughen up jail time for criminals. There was also speculation about how long Brooks might serve, should a jury find her guilty. The maximum penalty for perverting the course of justice was life imprisonment, while the average was twelve months, but the popular novelist Jeffrey Archer had copped a hefty four-year sentence in 2001 for concealing a diary during his famous libel action against *The Star*, which had won him £500 000 damages. However, that had included time for perjury, of which the former Tory politician had also been convicted.

In Brooks's favour, were the verdict to go against her—and she was clearly confident it would not—was that she had just become the mother of a four-month-old baby, delivered by surrogate, which might serve to moderate any potential jail sentence.

A month later, Rupert's erstwhile favourite was greeted by a scrum of photographers and TV crews outside Southwark Crown Court, where she appeared briefly for a trial date to be set. Wearing a 'tight-fitting, pencil-slim black dress' and '4-inch Christian

Louboutin heels' she looked harassed as the snappers called out 'Rebekah, Rebekah' to make her look in their direction. In court, with Charlie and her four other co-defendants, she was ordered to return in September to enter a plea.

But before she could do that, she was hit with further charges, resulting from her arrest more than a year earlier. This time, it was with three counts of unlawfully intercepting communications, including the specific charge of conspiring to hack into Milly Dowler's voicemails, for which Andy Coulson, Glenn Mulcaire, Neville Thurlbeck, Stuart Kuttner and Greg Miskiw were also charged.

Two other senior *News of the World* journalists, Ian Edmondson and James Weatherup, brought the number up to eight, with all (except Mulcaire) charged with a catch-all conspiracy to hack into the voicemails of some 600 people between October 2000 and August 2006. There were a further seventeen specific charges of hacking into the voicemails of Sir Paul McCartney and Heather Mills, Angelina Jolie and Brad Pitt, Sienna Miller and Jude Law, John Prescott MP, Wayne Rooney, Sven-Göran Eriksson, and others.

Within an hour of the announcement, Brooks issued an impassioned statement: 'I am not guilty of these charges. I did not authorise, nor was I aware of, phone hacking under my editorship. I am distressed and angry that the CPS have reached this decision when they knew all the facts and were in a position to stop the case at this stage. The charge concerning Milly Dowler is particularly upsetting, not only as it is untrue but also because I have spent my journalistic career campaigning for victims of crime. I will vigorously defend these allegations.'

Andy Coulson said he was disappointed by the decision to

prosecute and would fight the allegations in court. Neville Thurlbeck said he was 'most surprised and disappointed', and sent a veiled warning to his former bosses, saying, 'I have always operated under the strict guidance and advice of News International's lawyers and under the instructions of the newspaper's editors, which will be abundantly clear when this matter comes to court.' He had previously predicted that there would be 'explosive revelations in court, should any trials take place' but had declined to turn Queen's Evidence.

Ian Edmondson told the media he had only learnt of the charges by watching the media conference on TV, and also hinted at interesting times ahead, warning, 'I have much to say on this subject and I now look forward to saying it. I will clear my name at trial when the truth finally emerges.' Edmondson had told the Leveson Inquiry a few months earlier that there was a 'culture of bullying' at the *News of the World*, that every part of the paper was 'dictated and controlled by the editor', and that, 'you don't do anything unless you are told to'.

Even though he had been asked not to talk about phone hacking, in case his answers should prejudice future trials, it gave a pointer to what he might say in the witness box.

'Does it amount to this,' Lord Leveson had asked him. 'You do as you're told, and sometimes you have to do things you are uncomfortable about doing?'

'Yes, absolutely,' Edmondson replied.

'And that's so even if you're the news editor?'

'Yes, absolutely,' he responded. 'It's not a democracy at a newspaper. Autocratic.'

These latest charges were an even bigger story than Brooks's original indictment, in that they were definitely the main game rather than the side show. Seven top journalists and a private investigator were to be tried for the crime that had closed the *News of the World* and caused widespread public revulsion. One of the accused had shared Christmas dinners and country suppers with the Prime Minister; another had been head of the PM's media operation at Number 10 Downing Street. And the paper where it had allegedly taken place was owned by the world's most powerful media baron. But you would have been hard pressed to spot the news in Rupert's favourite paper, *The Sun*, which led its website with the much more interesting GB TEEN's TROLL WEB TORMENT and CARLY RAE: SEX VIDEO IS NOT ME. True, the story of the charges could be found at the foot of the site, if you pushed past twenty pairs of breasts and a dozen Premier League footballers, and didn't get distracted by PIXIE GELDOF AND NICK GRIMSHAW GET THEIR BOOBS OUT IN IBIZA, but even then it was hard to find.

Nor was there a peep out of Rupert Murdoch himself. Even though he had been busy tweeting madly over the weekend to his 425 000 followers about US gun control, education reform, the American dream and the Tour de France, he had not a word to say about his favourite's fall.

Brooks and her seven co-defendants from the *News of the World* would go to trial in September 2013, and would have to suffer the humiliation of regular court appearances, whatever the ultimate result. And unless they all pleaded guilty to the charges—which seemed unlikely—their ordeal would ensure that the Murdoch tabloid's dirty deeds continued to be aired in the media until 2014 or beyond.

It was also just about certain that more charges would follow. The Metropolitan Police now had 96 detectives and support staff working on Operation Weeting, and another 70 on Operation Elveden, which was investigating corrupt payments to public officials. There were another nineteen on Operation Tuleta, investigating computer hacking. Having made a mess of it all the first time around, the police and the Crown Prosecution Service were making sure they did not fail again. The investigations were being run by a veteran of the Met's Internal Affairs branch, Sue Akers, who had provided the inspiration for Helen Mirren's DCI Tennyson in *Prime Suspect*. She soon announced that they had identified 1069 likely hacking victims and a further 3675 potential victims, many of whom had yet to be contacted. And she again confirmed how helpful the MSC was being. By October 2012, its information had led to half the 52 arrests made by Operation Elveden, and perhaps an even greater proportion of the journalists.

And these arrests were now producing a new crop of charges, including the first involving *The Sun*. In November 2012, Andy Coulson and Clive Goodman were charged with conspiracy to commit misconduct in public office by allegedly paying to obtain a copy of the Green Book, which listed the phone numbers of members of the Royal Household. That same day, Rebekah Brooks and John Kay were charged with conspiracy over payments amounting to £100 000 to a Ministry of Defence official, Bettina Jordan-Barber, who had allegedly supplied confidential information to *The Sun* over an eight-year period from 2004 to January 2012. What was remarkable about this, apart from it being the first charge to affect the daily tabloid, was that these offences had allegedly continued years after phone hacking had been exposed and well past the point at which Brooks and James Murdoch were vowing to clean it all up.

So where was Rupert while his former lieutenants were helping police with their inquiries? On the day of Rebekah's first court appearance in June, he was a thousand miles away from the action in more ways than one, sitting in a gondola in Venice, looking tanned, fit and well, in a smart blue shirt, white shorts and matching white hat. He was holidaying in the grand old city with Wendi and their two daughters, Grace and Chloe, and staying on his yacht, *Rosehearty*, on which he and Rebekah had entertained David Cameron, Britain's would-be Prime Minister, some four years earlier.

But if he appeared to have abandoned the woman he had once been so close to, and moved on to other things, he was still taking care of her. In December 2012, when News International's accounts were published, the true size of the company's pay-out to its former CEO was finally revealed. Rebekah had originally been thought to be receiving £1.7 million, which many felt was too much. The *Financial Times* later claimed it was £7 million, which most deemed outrageous. But now it was shown to be almost £11 million, which almost all thought incredible. This was five times as much as the Dowlers had received, and almost as much as had been paid to all the other people at the *News of the World* who had lost their jobs, put together. This extraordinarily generous handout included an office in Marylebone, plus staff, for two years, a company car and chauffeur, and 'all legal and other professional costs' to fight the three sets of criminal charges that Brooks now faced.

'Innocent journalists lost their jobs, victims had their lives turned over and the person at the top of the company has been handed one of the biggest settlements in UK corporate history,' was Tom Watson's appalled reaction.

Journalists at News International were even more shocked and angry, with one observing that they were 'fucking furious'.

PART IV

SPLIT, SURVIVAL, SUCCESSION

22
THE SPLIT

'Pure rubbish, pure and total rubbish.'

Rupert Murdoch

Back in July 2011, at the height of the crisis, Rupert was under attack from all sides, and not just from his traditional enemies. News Corp's shareholders were furious at the collapse of the BSkyB bid and a plunge in the share price that had wiped US$6 billion off the value of the company. Some stock market analysts were saying the old man had lost his knack and the business would be better off without him. Others were talking about a 'Murdoch discount' and claiming the share price would rocket if he retired. Still more were pointing to figures that showed the media group was the fourth worst-performing stock in Australia's ASX Top 50 over the previous decade.

And, of course, the media pundits were predicting that Rupert would be out within a year and that the Murdoch empire would collapse around him.

As all this noise reached a crescendo, several groups of share-holders and corporate governance advisers began calling on the

Murdochs to change the way News Corp was run. Some wanted Rupert to step down. Others wanted to strengthen the board so that the group no longer relied on the whim and wisdom of its charismatic founder. And all began sharpening their knives for the battle, which would come at News Corp's annual general meeting in October.

The case against the company's directors was compelling. They had failed to investigate claims made by *The Guardian* in July 2009 and the *New York Times* in September 2010 that the company's journalists were breaking the law on an industrial scale, and had ignored scathing criticism of News executives from the House of Commons. They had then failed to seize control of the situation in April 2011 when the first of the *News of the World*'s journalists were arrested. And after it had all blown up, they had failed to punish the two people who should really have carried the can for it all. In any other public company, Rupert and his youngest son could have been out on their ear, but News Corp's board had reacted by awarding them cash bonuses of US$12.5 million and US$6 million respectively. To his credit, James Murdoch had declined to take the money. But his father had felt no such qualms.

'This isn't just a dysfunctional board, it's a nonfunctional board,' railed Paul Hodgson of GovernanceMetrics International, which had given News Corp its lowest-possible F-grade since 2003, and had long rated the company 'worst in class'. The group's governance standards were so poor, he said, that they had virtually guaranteed 'a major scandal of this kind'.

The truth was that News Corp's board had always been a pushover, and this one was not the worst. In the early 1990s, it had been composed almost entirely of Murdoch family members, current and former executives, and suppliers to News Corp. And Rupert's most forceful and outspoken critic had been his then wife. One old stager, Keith MacDonald, had even confessed to *Business Review Weekly* in 1994 that he was past his 'use-by date' and made 'virtually no contribution' to proceedings. 'I am yesterday's man,' he admitted cheerfully, 'an interested passenger.' The 68-year-old MacDonald, who had been a director for seven years, said it was up to Rupert to decide how long he should stay, and had then continued to ride the gravy train for another four years.

Seven of the current board's fifteen directors also owed their livelihood to the emperor's patronage, and all could be relied upon to back the boss. Rupert, James and Lachlan were family, while Chase Carey, David DeVoe, Arthur Siskind and Joel Klein made up the cabal that ran the group. An eighth, Stanley Shuman, who could speak at meetings but not vote (as a director *emeritus*), ran the investment bank that had advised Murdoch for 40 years.

Among the so-called independents was Sir Rod Eddington, who had worked for News in the 1990s, running the ill-fated Ansett Airlines until its collapse, and had almost been picked to replace Lachlan as head of News Ltd in late 2000. As 'lead director', he was actually in charge of keeping his old boss in check, but insiders believed he was incapable of standing up to him. As one of them put it, 'If he was planning to do so, he would surely have done it by now.' Another leading independent, Andrew Knight, had also been with Rupert since the 1990s and had once been seen as his successor. Murdoch's long-time lieutenant in Australia, Ken Cowley, who was now resigning, had also been a board stalwart for many years.

As GovernanceMetrics pointed out, there was little or no chance that such a group would ever hold Rupert to account, which is why there was a chorus for change.

The leading US adviser on corporate governance, Institutional Shareholder Services, recommended that thirteen of the fifteen directors be removed. The leading British adviser, Pensions Investment Research Consultants Ltd, wanted to chop eleven, including all three Murdochs. The Australian Shareholders' Association suggested that five of them be dumped, so there was still someone left to run the company. And all agreed that the board could never be truly independent while the founder continued to act as chairman and chief executive.

But they might as well have been whistling in the wind because they could not get rid of anyone unless Rupert gave them the nod. His control of the company was absolute.

Despite the fact that 88 per cent of News Corp shares belonged to outsiders and only 12 per cent to the Murdochs, it was impossible to think of it as anything but a family affair because that's how Rupert had always treated the business he had created and that was how it had always been run. His dominance was possible because a gerrymander split the company's owners into A and B shareholders, with only the B shares carrying the right to vote in the company's affairs. The Murdochs owned almost 40 per cent of these B shares through the Murdoch Family Trust, while their ally, the Saudi prince, Alwaleed bin Talal, could throw in another 7 per cent if necessary. This essentially allowed Rupert to control who was appointed to the board and to run the company as he saw fit. It also disenfranchised 39 000 of the company's 40 000 shareholders—who had no vote at all because they held A shares—and a further 998 shareholders who could realistically only win if they voted with Rupert.

As a result, rebellions were unlikely to get far, however many shareholders rallied to the flag. The only way they could hope to succeed was by embarrassing Rupert into giving up his power. And Rupert didn't do embarrassment because he was incredibly thick-skinned.

Nevertheless, there was much excitement in advance of the October AGM, which was to take place on the sprawling Fox Studios lot in Los Angeles, in the Darryl F Zanuck Theater with its black-painted stage and bank upon bank of red velvet seats. Outside the studio entrance, shareholders were hailed by a mob of noisy protesters with placards, and a big media contingent primed for action. Tom Watson had made the trip from London to confront the tycoon and was bravely promising 'fresh revelations'. The veteran shareholder activist from Australia, Stephen Mayne, who had been to ten such meetings, was also there to cause trouble. And a posse of bankers, investment managers, trade unionists and church groups had come to join the throng.

One prominent newspaper—the *Los Angeles Times*—was forecasting that Rupert could be forced to step down as chief executive and hand over to Chase Carey. But it was a mystery where it got such an idea. The crowd was small and well-behaved, with no mobs, no shouting and no angry scenes. No more than 50 shareholders had bothered to turn up—or one for every US$800 million worth of shares—and they were outnumbered by black-suited security staff and News Corp executives with shiny jackets and expensive tans. Making up the numbers were about 35 journalists, who were not allowed to record or film the proceedings and were not permitted to speak, unless they had been smart enough to become shareholders in advance. Those who did ask questions were limited to two per person, with a maximum one minute apiece.

Most chief executives in situations like this at least feign interest in what their critics have to say, if only to calm things down.

But Rupert had never been one for pretence. Secure in the knowledge that he would not be outvoted, he made little attempt to show he cared. When the Church of England's Edward Mason got up to argue that News Corp needed an independent chairman, and complained of 'difficulty getting the company to listen', Rupert immediately interrupted him to chide, 'Your investments haven't been that great.' He was obviously back to his old self again: combative, brusque, carping and ever ready to score a cheap point.

Consequently, there was an air of futility to the proceedings, and to the official ballot, in which 92 million votes—representing one-in-four independent shareholders—called for Rupert to be sacked from the board. More than double that number voted to dump James, Lachlan and three other directors, with the youngest son topping the unpopularity poll on 232 million votes, which meant that two-thirds of the outside shareholders wanted him out. Yet at the end of the day, it all meant nothing. The Murdochs' 40 per cent block vote made Rupert and his extended family invulnerable to external attack.

However, Rupert was soon coming under pressure from inside the company, from his senior executives, Chase Carey, David DeVoe and John Nallen, and this he could not so easily dodge.

Newspapers everywhere were losing money or going out of business as readers and advertisers migrated to the internet. And News was no different, even if it was fighting the battle better than most. But the hacking scandal was now scaring off investors and damaging the rest of the company, which brought in around four-fifths of the profit. Rupert loved the papers, and especially the tabloids, which were in his blood. He loved the headlines, the gossip, the smell and feel of the papers, and all the memories they evoked. He had even confessed as much to the Leveson Inquiry, telling his lordship enthusiastically, 'I love newspapers.'

But did he not have a duty to his shareholders as well, he had been asked? 'They tell me so,' Rupert had replied. 'They'd like me to get rid of them all.' And sure enough, Chase Carey had been openly canvassing this option at investment conferences.

Rupert's problem was that, aside from Lachlan, the rest of the family didn't share his enthusiasm for the printed word, and nor did News Corp's senior US executives, who regarded the papers as an irrelevance at best. Within two years of Rupert insisting that they buy the *Wall Street Journal* for US$5.6 billion, his accountants had been forced to write off almost exactly half the purchase price. And in the meantime, his senior people were condemned to watch *The Times*, *The Australian* and the *New York Post* bleed around US$500 million a year between them.

Casting the papers adrift from the rest of the company had long been talked about by News Corp's top executives, but it had always been ruled out by Rupert for sentimental reasons: they had made his fortune; they were what he knew best; they were where his heart really lay. But the problems at *The Sun* and *News of the World* made it obvious that they took up a huge amount of management time and now delivered mainly grief in return.

In July 2011, Rupert had vehemently denied rumours that he was planning to split the company in two, telling the *Wall Street Journal* tersely that such talk was 'pure rubbish, pure and total rubbish' and instructing the reporter to 'give it the strongest possible denial'. But eleven months later, in June 2012, he lost the battle with Carey and DeVoe and was forced to accept they should cut the papers loose. And, once he had decided this, his conversion was absolute. Announcing that the media group would be divided into two separate companies with their own shareholders, he promised that everyone would be better off as a result. In an email to his 51 000 employees, he told them: 'Our publishing businesses are greatly undervalued by the sceptics. Through this transformation we will unleash their real potential, and be able to better articulate the true value they hold for shareholders. Our aim is to create the most ambitious, well-capitalised and highly motivated publishing company in the world.'

Certainly, the break-up made perfect sense to shareholders because it would stop Rupert pumping more money into the papers and would cut the film studios and cable TV networks off from further damaging publicity. It might even allow another tilt at BSkyB, although that would have to be a long way off.

But, as everyone also knew, it would make the newspapers more vulnerable and threaten their future because they would have to pay their own way in the world. And this would be even more of a problem after Rupert since no one else was likely to tolerate the losses. 'There's only one person in the world who would run *The Times*, the *New York Post* and *The Australian* at a massive loss and that's Rupert,' one of his editors predicted. 'If he died today do you think that News Corp would still own those papers in three years time? No way. The *Post* would be the first to go, because it loses a stack of money. But Rupert keeps it because if he wants to give Obama a whack he can ring Col Allan and get him to make up a front page.'

'He loves the *Post*. He loves the influence it brings,' agreed an ex-Murdoch executive. 'And he's not going to let Mort Zuckerman and the *Daily News* have a free run. In fact all the papers will stay open while he's in charge.'

But whether that turned out to be true or not, the world's investors didn't really care. News Corp's shares jumped 8 per cent when the carve up was announced, as a bevy of broking analysts decreed that it was a 'significant positive' for the group and commented that Rupert's love of buying newspapers had been the main thing that stopped people buying the stock. Four months later, when the annual general meeting came round again in October 2012, and the rebels regrouped for a second attack, the share price had risen further, and the US$40 billion media group had become a $US60 billion group. Which made it even more difficult to argue for change.

Running the show from a lectern on stage in the Darryl F Zanuck Theater yet again, the 81-year-old Rupert looked sharp and in control, and not like a man who was planning to leave. Nor were the independent directors ready to push him out. It was a bad omen, perhaps, that they had all chosen to wear pink ties. It was even worse when they giggled dutifully as Rupert made a nasty crack about the *New York Times*. That one moment spoke volumes about who was really in charge.

In the middle of the Fox Studios lot, surrounded by a hundred years of movie history, it was almost as if Rupert were shooting a scene from an old Hollywood film, where the king is approached by his loyal subjects who throw themselves at his feet, praise his wisdom and kindness, and beg to be heard; the king waves his hand, the courtiers laugh and the petitioner's claim is dismissed.

This time round, the outside shareholders were proposing to split the role of chair and chief executive, so Rupert could not hold both, and to end the dual-class share structure which gave the Murdochs their iron grip on the company. But even before their speeches began, Rupert announced that their motions had been defeated by 'more than a majority of the votes cast'. He also informed the rebels that their attempts to unseat directors and vote against the executive pay package had failed.

In many ways, the final tally was a great result for the critics. Two-thirds of the independent shareholders supported an end to the dual-class structure and two-thirds voted for him to step down as chairman. But once again, it meant nothing because the Murdoch block vote swept them away. And this time they had already been warned not to waste their breath. In the run-up to the meeting, Rupert had tweeted some free advice, telling his opponents, 'Shareholders with complaints should take profits and sell!'

None of the speakers was game to mention this until one brave soul inquired whether he had meant what he said. Without missing a beat, Murdoch replied that there were many media stocks on the market and if they didn't like News Corp they should go and buy another. 'When you buy the stock, you know what the company is,' the group's founder continued. 'If you don't like it, don't buy the stock.'

After that putdown, no one even bothered to raise the comment that Rupert had made a few days earlier in which he had referred to some of the *News of the World*'s victims as 'scumbags'. In response to headlines that Hugh Grant, Charlotte Church and a former police-woman, Jacqui Hames, had met Britain's PM at the Tory Party conference to discuss press reform, Murdoch had tweeted: 'Told UK's Cameron receiving scumbag celebrities pushing for even more privacy laws. Trust the toffs! Transparency under attack. Bad.'

Given that he had never owned up to his Christmas parties with Cameron, his secret lunch with Thatcher in 1981, and countless cosy chats with politicians all over the globe, it showed extraordinary nerve and lack of self-awareness for Murdoch to present himself as a defender of transparency. And it was even more outrageous that he dared abuse his paper's victims in this way. But the most humble day of his life was obviously long forgotten.

'By "scumbag celebs" do u mean the WPC u put under surveil-lance, the teen girl yr papers perved over, or the actor u hacked?' the former Liberal Democrat MP, Evan Harris, asked in response.

'Scumbags? And your journalists and executives are what?' another Twitter user inquired.

But Rupert was unrepentant. 'They don't get arrested for indecency on major LA highways! Or abandon love child's,' he replied ungrammatically, before being forced to acknowledge that Hugh Grant had in fact taken good care of his daughter.

Rupert's tweeting had been a source of wonder since discover-ing its delights in January 2012 while on holiday in the Caribbean. Within two days of his first emission, he had collected 40 000 followers and was already getting into trouble. Bored with the beach, he had decided it would be a good idea to tell those layabouts back in London to work harder. 'Maybe Brits have too many holidays for broke country,' he tweeted from his sun lounger.

Moments later, Wendi Deng, or in fact someone pretending to be her, tweeted urgently, 'RUPERT!! delete tweet!!' Which she soon followed with another, 'EVERY1 @rupertmurdoch was only having a joke pROMSIE!!!' Five hours later, Murdoch managed to sneak out again and give the world an update, telling his growing band of fans, 'I'm getting killed for fooling around here and friends frightened what I may really say!'

And indeed they had good reason to be nervous. When Katie Holmes announced she was filing for divorce from Tom Cruise, he tweeted, 'Watch Katie Holmes and Scientology story develop. Something creepy, maybe even evil, about these people.'

'What was wrong with the Iraq war?' he asked a little later.

'Why protect crooks and scumbags?' he inquired, re privacy laws.

And, 'No wonder rich layabouts contribute nothing when immigrants work harder better,' he offered. 'Honest Brits work and resent system.'

His family hated it and tried to get him to stop. But Rupert was enjoying himself, despite the torrent of abuse it provoked. Clearly, he had an immensely thick skin, and there was nothing he felt he could not say.

'Seems every competitor and enemy piling on with lies and libels,' he tweeted in March, after the BBC's *Panorama* ran a program accusing a News Corp company of pay-TV piracy. 'So bad, easy to hit back hard, which preparing,' he continued. Moments later, he fired óff another, summing up his perennially paranoid view of the world: 'Enemies many different agendas, but worst old toffs and right wingers who still want last century's status quo with their monopolies.'

Week in, week out, and often in bursts when he was bored at the airport or had nothing to do, Rupert would tell the world how to behave: what to do about Israel, gun laws, the US Presidency and how bad the old mother country had become. 'Britain more an entitlement state,' he tweeted, six months after his quip about holidays. 'Bigger than ever with growing debts. Is it too late to change culture and restore energy?'

'What happened to "land of hope and glory"?' he asked on another occasion. 'New poll today shows 48 percent of Brits would like to emigrate.'

If there was a thread running through it all it was that he had a right, nay a duty, to tell us these things. 'Where does he get that self-belief?' asked the respected British media strategist, Claire Enders. 'His psychological outlook is that he's entitled to tell us who to be; entitled to say his underlings have let him down; entitled to tell us we don't need public broadcasting. It's extraordinary. I don't know any other public figure who has that sense of entitlement.'

But Rupert was not just tweeting. He was busy being Rupert all over again. In December 2012 he managed to get rid of the editor of *The Times*, James Harding, despite the fact that the paper's guardian could only be dismissed with the approval of the national directors of Times Newspapers Holdings, and despite the fact that Murdoch was no longer an executive of the company or on its board. He and Harding had been at odds for several months, and the boss had ignored him on recent visits to Wapping. 'It has been made clear to me that News Corporation would like to appoint a new editor,' Harding told staff in his farewell speech. 'I have, therefore, agreed to stand down. I called Rupert this morning to offer my resignation and he accepted it.'

It was plain to journalists that the editor's crime had been to make *The Times* too robust in its coverage of phone hacking. He had accused News of succumbing to 'the most dangerous delusion of the powerful, namely that it could play by its own set of rules' and had reacted to Rupert's evidence to Leveson by charging that 'Instead of listening and responding to those asking legitimate questions, the company pursued its critics as enemies.'

This independent line had been a source of pride to *Times* journalists, who were happy to distance themselves from their tabloid cousins. And many were distressed that their boss was paying with his job. The paper's managing editor, Anne Spackman, and its associate editor, Martin Fletcher, soon headed for the exit too, telling friends that they were leaving because their boss had got the bullet.

But they weren't the only ones to jump ship. News International's chief executive, Tom Mockridge, had left ten days earlier after failing to land the top job in 'New News Corp', the newly created publishing arm of the group. Emailing staff to explain his decision, he dispensed with the flummery that normally fills such farewells and told them: 'To be direct, the reason I am leaving is that the new structure does not offer me a role I am comfortable with and, after 22 years with the company in five countries, I feel I have made enough of a contribution to make a personal choice to go.' After two decades with the Murdoch family, he was going back to his wife and two kids in Italy, declaring, 'This family is my future.' The former Sky Italia boss and adviser to Australian PM Paul Keating was tired of baby-sitting all *The Sun* journalists who had been arrested, and of spending his days with lawyers, which is what his job had become. He had also discovered that there was no longer any joy in working at Wapping, where morale was so low.

Mockridge was unlikely to get any postcards from his old boss, even though he was one of his most loyal and talented executives. 'Once you leave the company, you leave Rupert's direct line of sight,' another former top aide observed from experience. 'It's just how he is. He'd never call me and say, "Hi how you doing, let's have a drink". He'd never pick up the phone. You can't be good friends with Rupert. It's all about the business and family for him. There is nothing else.

'I think a telling moment was his wedding with Wendi,' the ex-lieutenant continued. 'It was actually a really beautiful occasion, on the yacht near the Statue of Liberty, but it was attended by family, News Corp executives and people like Jim Wolfensohn from the World Bank, who were ultimately related to the business.'

In line with this observation, Rupert's new best friend was the man who had beaten Mockridge in the race to run the newspaper and book business, the Australian journalist Robert Thomson, who was becoming almost as loved as Rebekah Brooks had been. Dry, funny and a good listener, he was extremely smart, spoke fluent Mandarin and had a Chinese wife, which at the time gave him plenty in common with Rupert. And he was undoubtedly a terrific journalist, who had edited *The Times* and *Wall Street Journal*. But those who knew him well said he could not stand up to his boss, and feared he would be out of his depth running a multinational media company in an industry facing huge strategic challenges. It was a sign, they said, that Rupert really wanted to run the news-papers himself. But there would be no surprise in that. Once again, it was business as usual.

23
LONG LIVE THE KING

'Things are different these days. We're all going to live to be 100;
120, I hope, but certainly 100. There's plenty of time.'

Rupert Murdoch

If Rupert had fallen under a bus in July 2011, it would have been Chase Carey who took over the running of the Murdoch empire. But two years on, he had not been mown down by a double-decker, the House of Murdoch hadn't fallen, and Rupert was still in charge of the company he created.

In October 2013, all being well, he would embark on his seventh decade as the head of the News group of companies, and in October 2023, if he had his way, he would cruise into his eighth. With a little bit of luck, he would still be going strong for his ninth in October 2033, when he would be only 102, or one year younger than his mother Dame Elisabeth was when she died in 2012. Which made you wonder why everyone remained so obsessed with who would succeed him.

The grand old lady had gone to her grave telling people she would never retire, predicting her son would do the same, and

Rupert had said as much on many occasions. Retirement was not on his radar and his leaving plan was to be carried out in a box.

'We're all going to live to be 100,' he once remarked, with tongue only half in cheek. 'One-hundred-and-twenty, I hope, but certainly 100. There's plenty of time.'

And sure enough, he was now behaving like he was at the dawn of his life: scrapping, sacking, tweeting, flying around the world and talking of his excitement about the future. The crisis had given him a new sense of energy and enthusiasm. Reports of his death had been greatly exaggerated.

'He's really invigorated. He's talking louder, he's hearing better,' one of his Australian editors observed on Murdoch's visit to Sydney in November 2011, just four months after his geriatric appearance before the House of Commons. 'He's sitting down with the editors for hours and pulling the papers apart; he's going through circulation figures and comparing them with the opposition. He's been seeing his advertising bosses, his editors, his managing directors. He's really on top of things.'

'Rupert is a very strong man,' his wife Wendi reported. 'He takes it, he takes the blame. He moves on. He's doing good.'

'He forgives himself immediately and utterly,' one of his former senior executives agreed. 'There's no self-doubt, flagellation or regret. He never dwells on his actions. He just charges forward.'

And reports of him doing this flooded in wherever he went. At the consumer electronics fair in Las Vegas in January 2012, he was in sparkling form, holding court with Elisabeth in a suite at the Bellagio, as Apple, Sony and AT&T filed in to show their wares. At dinner in February in New York he seemed to an Australian friend to have not a care in the world. And at the Allen & Company media conference in Sun Valley in July 2012, a year on from the crisis, his old sparring partner, John Malone, found him in cracking form as he, James and News Corp's CEO, Chase Carey, discussed the state of the world.

It was Rupert's refusal to abandon this hectic life that had been one of the main reasons for his divorce from Anna back in 1999. After more than 30 years of marriage he had promised he would slow down and pay her back for all the times he had been absent. But he had been unable to keep his pledge. He hated museums, theatres and art galleries—which his wife loved—and he couldn't bear the thought of not being at the centre of things.

'My work has been so much part of my life,' he had confessed. 'I cannot imagine spending half my life on the golf course...It is the saddest thing to see people who go out when they are at the top.' So he had changed partners, remade himself, and forged on, much as he was doing now. Indeed, far more than anyone had yet realised.

From the outside, his partnership with Anna had looked like the perfect marriage. She was his closest friend, his greatest supporter and his fiercest critic. Much as Wendi would later appear to be. She was also beautiful, poised, intelligent and the mother of the three children in whom they had invested so much hope. But, because she stood in the way of his desire and ambition, it had counted for nought.

And when it came to it, Rupert had discarded his faithful wife just as easily as the executives and editors he so often sacked. Only to Anna could it have been a surprise that he was so single-minded, selfish and egotistical. 'Rupert was extremely hard, ruthless, and determined that he was going to go through with this no matter what I wanted or what I was trying to do to save the marriage,' Anna confided to the *Australian Women's Weekly* in the only interview she gave after their divorce. 'Rupert's affair with Wendi Deng—it's not an original plot—was the end of the marriage. I thought we had a wonderful, happy marriage. Obviously we didn't.'

Asked whether his critics had perhaps been right about him all along, she agreed it was possible: 'I began to think the Rupert Murdoch that I loved died a long time ago.'

The woman he had left her for, Wendi Deng, was less than half his age. She had not been born when he and Anna got hitched in 1967, and was ten years younger than his eldest daughter Prue. But her key attraction, apart from youth and beauty, was that she was excited by his wealth, power and ambition in a way that Anna had long ceased to be, so she was more than happy for him to keep on keeping on.

Deng Wen Gi had been born in December 1968, in the industrial city of Xuzhou in north-eastern China, around the time that her future husband was buying the *News of the World*. Arriving as she did, just after the Red Guard rampage, in what was still a very Communist country, it was no surprise that her name was shorthand for Cultural Revolution, and that she had a pedigree to match. Her father was a Communist Party official who managed a machinery factory, and her family came from humble stock. 'I grew up in a very small town, very poor, we have no hot water,' she would later tell China's CCTV. 'My grandmother died in childbirth, my mother's aunty lived with us. She had little bound feet.'

Wendi's journey from these beginnings to a billionaire's wife was such an amazing story that some suggested she must be a Communist agent, on a mission to trap the West's most powerful media mogul; or the great tycoon must be marrying her for business reasons, to help him conquer the Chinese market. But his daughter

Prue summed it up more convincingly than the conspiracy theorists: her dad was just a dirty old man.

Rupert claimed that he and Wendi had first become involved in June 1998, a month after leaving Anna, while they were both in England. 'I was a recently separated, lonely man, and I said, "Let's go out to dinner one night", and I talked her into staying in London a couple of extra days—and that was the start of it.'

But this was not how others remembered it. His China boss, Bruce Dover, had introduced the couple a year earlier at a party to celebrate the Hong Kong handover in June 1997, when Wendi was still 28. And he recalled Rupert remarking afterwards that strong, intelligent, young women like her would be China's way forward. By coincidence, she had confided only weeks earlier to her colleagues at STAR TV, where she had been working for a year, that her perfect catch would be 'a richer, older man'.

By that stage, the brash young Chinese trainee was already famous at Murdoch's Asian pay-TV network for being 'fearless', 'refreshing' and 'full of charming natural confidence'. Within a week of starting there, she had latched onto everyone worth knowing. As an ex-colleague recounted to *The Monthly*'s Eric Ellis, 'She would waltz in to someone important's office, unannounced, and exclaim, "Hello, I'm Wendi, I'm the intern…um, who are you?" It was excruciating. It made some people uncomfortable, but she would get away with it; in fact, she perfected it.'

And she used the same magic charm on Rupert. In September 1997, three months after their first meeting, she accompanied him and Bruce Dover on a trip to Shanghai as their interpreter, and, when Dover was called off for a meeting, she grabbed her boss's arm and took him shopping. 'When he returned home some hours later, Murdoch was absolutely abuzz with excitement,' wrote Dover.

He had got himself a haircut for a dollar, and was 'radiating pleasure and excitement, completely taken by the city's energy and vitality—at least that's what I thought had inspired him.' The next morning, Bruce came down to the gym at 6 a.m. to find the pair of them laughing and chatting as they pumped away on a pair of exercise bicycles.

Dover and his fellow Australian ex-pat, Gary Davey, then STAR's chief executive, soon realised that the couple were continuing to talk because Rupert kept spouting 'Wendi-isms' and she kept parroting things that Rupert had said in business meetings. But neither twigged for a moment that the boss's marriage to Anna might be on the rocks, or that he would think of tearing it up for a woman who was 37 years his junior. It was all too silly. And Rupert wasn't like that.

But by early 1998, the signs were even stronger. When Murdoch paid his next visit to Hong Kong, he booked into a different hotel on the opposite side of town, and told his top executives he'd be taking the weekend off. As Dover soon discovered, he was also ordering flowers on his hotel account and booking a dinner cruise on the harbour, to which executives were not invited. A few weeks after that, in May, came the official news that Rupert and Anna had separated. They hadn't exchanged a word for months, one News insider revealed.

Asked by William Shawcross a year later about the breakdown of his marriage to Anna, Rupert said it had happened gradually. They had moved from New York to Los Angeles, so he was travelling constantly. And, as a result, he had become 'very obsessed with business and perhaps more than normally inconsiderate'.

'We drifted apart to the point where things became very unhappy,' he continued. 'You always feel very sad about these things, but you've got to get on with life.'

And with barely a backward glance he had. Seventeen days after the divorce was finalised, he and Wendi were married on his yacht *Morning Glory* as it cruised off Manhattan with the Statue of Liberty in the background, while the 'Voice of an Angel' and future *News of the World* hacking victim, Charlotte Church, sang *Pie Jesu* at Rupert's request.

Soon afterwards, he was being photographed by Annie Liebovitz, draped across a bed in New York's trendy Mercer Hotel, wearing black jeans, black skivvy and black shoes, and talking about his new protein shake breakfast which allowed him to power through the day. By this time, the 68-year-old billionaire was on a serious health kick, had bought a loft in SoHo, and had hired a personal trainer to torture him for an hour every morning, making him do curls and sit-ups, lift weights and ride an exercise bike. Before long, he was also dyeing his hair orange, in an even more desperate attempt to recapture his youth. And in true Murdoch style he was doing it himself, either to save money or because he was too embarrassed to ask his barber. To the amusement of his executives, and the shock of his two sons, he and Wendi were also often to be seen leaving News Corp's Manhattan offices holding hands.

But comical though it may have been, Wendi had clearly given Rupert a new lease of life, and some of his inner circle gave her the thumbs-up. She was easy to like. She lightened him up. She was much more normal than he was. And if she talked a mile a minute, just like a kid, and interrupted dinner party conversations with comments that had nothing to do with what people had been talking about, it was fine. Rupert humoured her.

'She's not a genius, she's a sweetheart, she's a party girl,' said one executive who appreciated her qualities. 'She loves it when everyone is having fun. She likes to facilitate that. It's what she does.'

But Rupert's mother was appalled, and told him so. 'I did tell him that I thought he was very wrong,' she admitted on her 100th birthday, a decade after his divorce from Anna. 'They'd had a most wonderful marriage, you know, for 32 years. These things happen, it's quite extraordinary.' Yet even Dame Elisabeth accepted that Wendi was looking after her son and making him happy, even if she was barely on speaking terms with this brash, young consort.

Back in the beginning, no one had known much about Wendi's background. Perhaps not even Rupert. But the truth came out some eighteen months after the wedding in a 4000-word article for the *Wall Street Journal*, which dug deep into his new wife's history to see where she had come from, and revealed that she had climbed over a few people in her ascent to the top. One of three kids, she had grown up in a three-room flat in the southern city of Guangzhou and done well enough at school to study medicine. She had also starred in the volleyball team. But after two years at university she had realised her lifelong ambition of escaping to America. And to get there she had taken advantage of a trusting, older man.

Wendi had been taking English lessons in Guangzhou from an American teacher, Joyce Cherry, whose husband Jake was building a freezer factory in the city. Then Joyce had gone back to the US to put their kids into school, leaving her husband behind, and the nineteen-year-old student had begun an affair with him. Jake, who was in his fifties, had been persuaded to sponsor Wendi for a US student visa, and had invited the girl to live with his family in Los Angeles, where she shared a bedroom with the Cherrys' five-year-old daughter. But this did not last long. Joyce soon discovered coquettish photos of Wendi taken by her husband back in China. Then the pair started staying out all night. There was a showdown; Wendi was kicked out, and Jake followed shortly after. They set up house together and married in 1990, only for Wendi to leave him after four months for a younger man. She divorced her American husband a few months after her Green Card came through, telling him he could only ever be a father figure to her. 'I loved that girl,' was Cherry's flat response almost a decade later.

Rupert and his PR machine were furious that the *Wall Street Journal* had invested so much time and space on this kiss-and-tell story. But they could hardly complain because the *News of the World* and *The Sun* made a living out of stories like this, which they covered in far more lurid fashion. Unlike his raucous tabloids, the *Wall Street Journal* had not focused on his organ size, need for Viagra or preferences in bed. Yet he was still horrified at what it had revealed, because so much of it was news to him. According to one of the *Wall Street Journal*'s reporting team, he didn't know the secrets of Wendi's previous life because she had never told him.

If the Cherrys' story was to be believed—and they were both on the record and Rupert didn't sue—Wendi was ambitious, manipulative and out for herself. And the obvious implication was that she was also taking Rupert for a ride. Soon she was being described in the media as a 'gold-digger' and worse.

The couple's first child, Grace, was born in November 2001; their second, Chloe, followed twenty months later in July 2003. And naturally the question then arose as to the daughters' place in the multi-billion-dollar dynasty. As part of the divorce settlement, Anna had insisted that the deed of the Murdoch Family Trust, which contained the bulk of the family's shareholding in News Corp, be amended to prevent any of Rupert's kids from his third marriage being given a share in the family fortune or any say in the empire's future. In 2003, she had assured the *Australian Women's Weekly* that Rupert's successor would never come from his new family. 'So it can't be Wendi Deng?' the interviewer, David Leser, had asked. 'Not at all,' Anna replied.

'And it can't be Wendi's children?'

'Not at all, not at all.'

But Rupert was never one to accept a deal like that as final because he had spent his whole life as a businessman negotiating and renegotiating agreements and removing apparently immovable obstacles. And this one was no different. He wanted Grace and Chloe to have an equal share. And so of course did Wendi.

He raised it with the older kids in 2004, when News Corp was shifting its domicile to the US and ownership of the group was being restructured, and was met with an outright veto. Without the consent of Prue, Elisabeth, Lachlan and James, he could go no further.

That Christmas, according to the Murdochs' then nanny, Ying-Shu Hsu, who doubled as a tutor for the two young girls, Wendi and Rupert spent an entire evening in a screaming match over this issue. 'They were fighting all night over the estate for the kids,' Hsu told the US website, *Gawker*, in 2011. In Hsu's account in 2012, some of which came second-hand from the six other staff employed by the Murdochs in New York, it was Wendi who did most of the screaming. 'She had a very bad temper and would get angry very easily,' said Hsu, who claimed that working for Deng was like being in a 'war zone'. Nor was it just the staff she shouted at. 'She also curses Rupert all the time,' said Hsu in an early warning that the marriage was neither as stable nor as happy as it seemed to outsiders. 'A lot of F-words. She's always yelling, crying. Murdoch is the calm type.' They frequently slept in other bedrooms, Hsu also claimed.

The issue of the younger kids' share in the estate bubbled along for the next eighteen months, with a number of discussions, but nothing settled. Then, in July 2006, Rupert went on the *Charlie Rose Show* on America's PBS network and announced that it had all been sorted.

Rose: Where does that stand today? Succession. Lachlan—

Murdoch: It's really up to them…If I go under a bus tomorrow, um, it'll be the four of them will have to decide which of the ones should lead them.

Rose: Your four children?

Murdoch: Yeah, well, and my, uhh, the two little girls are too young to consider this at the moment.

Rose: Now do you consider them? You've said they are all my children.

Murdoch: They'll all be treated equally—financially, absolutely.

Rose: You ran into some buzz saw within the family because of that decision?

Murdoch: No, just on a question of power. Would their trustees have votes and these things at the moment, you know? We've resolved everything very happily.

Rose: It's your personal business. So, if something happens to you, if you get run over by a bus when you leave this studio, the four kids have to decide who among them ought to be the heir apparent.

Murdoch: In terms of power, yes, in terms of leadership. They'll all get treated equally financially.

Despite what Rose was told, the question of the succession had not been settled, or not to Wendi's satisfaction, and there was an instant explosion. 'She was just furious. She really cracked the shits,' says one News Corp insider who was in the thick of it all. 'We thought the marriage might end that weekend. It was very ugly. But it was Rupert at his most human. There's really not much guile to him. He does an interview which he probably shouldn't have done, and then starts talking openly. Was this his way of talking to the missus? She didn't even know he'd decided.'

However, the older children stood firm in the face of it all, with Anna's enthusiastic support, and Rupert had to follow suit. In January 2007, he paid Lachlan, James, Elisabeth and Prudence US$100 million each in compensation for allowing Grace and Chloe to have equal shares in the family fortune. In October, he handed over another US$50 million apiece. But in doing so, he also confirmed that the two youngest children would have no say in the succession. And that's how it stands six years later and is likely to remain.

So it will be up to Rupert and the four older kids to decide who takes over when he is gone, whether that be in 2013, 2023 or 2033. This question will be formally decided by the Murdoch Family Trust, which controls 306 million voting shares in News Corp, or some 38.4 per cent of the total. (Another 10 million in the KR Murdoch 2004 Revocable Trust brings the family holding to 39.7 per cent.) This trust is in turn controlled by Rupert, who has four votes, and the four oldest children, Prue, Elisabeth, Lachlan and James, who have one vote apiece.

The mathematics of this are that Rupert currently has the power to name his successor because he only needs the vote of one of those four children to secure a 5:3 majority and dictate the trust's course of action. And with the possible exception of Prue, who won't be chosen, and Lachlan, who might turn him down, the children would almost certainly accept his offer of the job. But when Rupert dies, his votes will die with him, and the four children will then be in sole charge of their destiny.

And if Rupert were to let it get that far, that's when it could get interesting.

24
THE MURDOCH DYNASTY

*'Their sibling rivalry is no different from any other family, except the
numbers are bigger. And there's so much more at stake.'*

Ex-News Corp executive

When you see Rupert and his children side by side you can see
why the Murdoch family has a succession problem. None of the
potential heirs is in his class, and none would ever get to run
the show if their surname did not begin with M. No doubt this
pleases Rupert. But it also gives him a problem because he does
want to pass on the News Corp empire to his children, even if he is
never quite ready to do so. And the carnage at the *News of the World*
and *The Sun* has made it more difficult, if not impossible, because
it has weakened his grip on the business, thrust the issue into the
spotlight, and cruelled the chances of his chosen succcessor.

At the beginning of 2011, James Murdoch was formally
anointed Rupert's heir, and a succession plan was put in place.
With the BSkyB takeover safely locked away, the youngest son
would move to New York to learn the movie and cable TV business
from Chase Carey. And when the latter's contract expired in July

2014, he would take over as chief executive, with his father staying on as chairman to smooth the transition. Or that was the theory. But that is now not going to happen, or not straight away.

There had been problems in arriving at this solution, and it was not yet set in stone. The family was worried about James's arrogance and confrontational style, while his siblings were concerned that he and Rupert were always fighting. And there was no guarantee that Murdoch's top executives would be prepared to play along. You didn't have to dig very far to find that the younger son was unpopular at Wapping because he had no great love for journalism or newspapers, which was what News Corp had been built on, and his style was the antithesis of Rupert's, which is what everyone was used to. One top executive at News International claimed that James was 'overconfident' and 'not a good listener'. Others found his communication skills left much to be desired.

To journalists at News's London HQ, it was as if he was from another planet. One fellow editor reported the *News of the World*'s Colin Myler arriving at a party and saying, 'I just met with James for an hour and I've no idea what he was saying.'

News Corp's American bosses didn't much like him either. 'James is smart but not as smart as he thinks he is,' said one former top US executive, who then added more bluntly, 'He can be charming and personable if he wants to be, and he's reasonably witty, but he's entirely disingenuous. I would trust him with nothing.'

But these concerns were nothing compared to the doubts raised by the hacking scandal. It was James who had trusted Rebekah Brooks and let it all get so out of hand. It was James who had looked so naïve and charmless before the House of Commons, after which he had been savagely criticised by the Culture Committee, Leveson and Ofcom. And it was James who was to blame for the disasters that had befallen the company, or so Rupert, Elisabeth and News Corp's top executives believed.

In James's view, by contrast, it was largely his father's fault. Things had gone wrong at the British newspapers because of the casual way Rupert had always run them, with no proper processes or chain of command—or so James claimed—and it was he who had the company back on the straight and narrow by closing the *News of the World* against his father's wishes. More broadly, he told friends that he had been ordered to take charge of News International at very short notice and had not been allowed to refuse. He had then been forced to carry the can for crimes that he had nothing to do with and knew nothing about. He had simply been in the wrong place at the wrong time, the fall guy. Naturally he also maintained that he had been let down by his advisers, and by Rebekah Brooks in particular.

Surprisingly, some well-informed observers, including the seasoned Murdoch watcher, Claire Enders, accepted this. 'James didn't read his emails,' she said. 'He didn't read the *New York Times* piece. He didn't read *Private Eye*. He was the Prince, the Dauphin, the heir apparent. No one bothered him. 'And a top lawyer in the hacking cases agreed, saying, 'James thought of himself as far too big and important. He was running a multi-billion-pound business, and this was too small and trivial for him to bother with. He would just have told them to get on with it.'

But even if this defence was accepted, it did not necessarily improve James's chances of succeeding his father or replacing a world-class executive like Chase Carey, who was doing such an excellent job. Being 'wilfully blind' was no qualification for running a multi-billion-dollar media empire. Nor was a cold, stiff personality of much use in the movie business. 'James just isn't

Hollywood,' said one of his father's former American executives who knew him well. Nevertheless, James was not yet the write-off that many commentators believed him to be. America cared little about phone hacking or bribing British coppers, and he had not been charged with any crime, apart from strangling the English language. His friends insisted he was smart and determined, and would work his way back. And memories were already fading: at the 2012 annual general meeting only about one-third as many votes as in 2011 were cast against him, while his brother Lachlan was now more unpopular than he was with the group's shareholders.

Moreover, if Rupert stuck around for a few more years—and you could bet that he planned to—there would be ample time for James to repair his reputation. He was the only Murdoch child who had experience running a big media group, and he had added billions of dollars to the value of BSkyB; the family's Saudi friend, Prince Alwaleed bin Talal, was still backing him; and word was that Lachlan would vote for him in the Murdoch Family Trust. So, despite everything that had happened and the disgraces he had suffered, he was still very much in the box seat.

The big question was whether News Corp's powerful US executives could work with him, and what would happen if they refused. There had been plenty of hostility to James when he was running the British operations, with accusations that he was trying to establish a rival court, and Rupert's biographer Michael Wolff, who had more access to the inner workings of News Corp than most, was adamant that his move to the US would provoke the same sort of fight that had forced Lachlan out seven years earlier. And even if there was a touch of hyperbole in this prediction, Murdoch's youngest son was certain to face problems. 'There's no way that Chase will report to James,' one top News executive predicted bluntly. 'Take it from me.' He would also face trouble from Roger Ailes, the right-wing warrior who ran Fox News, which brought in so much of News Corp's profit. James was pro-Clinton, pro-Obama, anti-guns and worried about global warming, and stood for just about everything that Fox News despised. Would he really be able to run a group that relied so heavily on rabid right-wing politics to make its money? Would Ailes be able to stomach him getting the job? And would the board back the young Murdoch against such a powerful and valuable executive if it came to a fight?

Technically, James's succession was still on track. He had been promoted to chief operating officer of News Corp, or number three in the company, and had not been banished to the boondocks. But spies at the Murdochs' Sixth Avenue headquarters in New York reported he had little to do, except leap to attention when his dad walked past. And others observed that his job was a made-up affair that had been created especially for him. Moreover, with the criminal trials of Brooks, Andy Coulson and others due to start in London in September 2013, there was much that could still go wrong. If he could get through the next two years unscathed, and if Rupert remained in control, James might well succeed. But he had a fair way yet to go.

And that brought Lachlan back into the frame, however reluctant he was to play a part. He was the oldest and favourite son, and had been the chosen one until he quit in 2005. But he too had a testy relationship with his father. Before moving to New York in 2000 there had been one or two nasty arguments, and these had continued even after he returned to Australia. On a couple of occasions, father and son had been set to go to the company's annual News Awards together; the seating plans had been drawn up and a script written for Lachlan to deliver, whereupon Rupert and his entourage had flown in and Lachlan had withdrawn without notice. 'They've had another fight,' was the explanation given, as arrangements were hurriedly recast.

Generally, however, relations had improved since the reluctant heir had stepped back from his duties. He had made a point of accompanying his dad to the Allen & Company media conference in Sun Valley every year and had pretty much been on call since the hacking crisis erupted. In July 2011 he had flown to London to support his father, and seven months later he had been by his side when they toured *The Sun*. He and Sarah had also taken the kids on holiday with Rupert and Wendi that Christmas. And in November 2011, he had been in the thick of it when Rupert flew into Sydney to sack News's local boss, John Hartigan (once Lachlan's best friend) and replace him with Kim Williams (his new one). Harto and Lachlan had shared 6 a.m. power sessions in the gym and squired each other round town for years, but had fallen out and were no longer speaking. One suggestion was that Harto had taken Rupert's side against his son; another was that he had told Lachlan to vacate his office at News Ltd in 2005. But whatever had happened, it was further warning that it rarely paid to cross Rupert's kids.

As Hartigan left and Williams arrived, it was reported that Lachlan had turned down Rupert's request to come back and run the newspapers himself, or at least be chairman. But even if he could eventually be persuaded to change his mind on this, he was surely never going to run the show in the US. 'He has been sending signals that he doesn't want it,' said Malcolm Colless, an ex-director of News Ltd. 'If it was put on his plate he might take it, but I don't think that's going to happen. I can't imagine Rupert wanting to force it onto the American company against the wishes of the board and shareholders. Maybe he would have done years ago, but not now.'

Others were even more adamant that Lachlan would never agree to take up Rupert's mantle, despite his deep sense of duty to the family and desire to please his dad. He had been monstered by Ailes and Peter Chernin the last time he was in New York, and would not risk that again. He was also in love with Australia. 'I cannot imagine any circumstances in which he could take over,' was the verdict of one US executive who had lived through it all.

'Rupert has asked him three or four times to come back,' said another top News executive from Murdoch's inner cicrcle, 'and he's said "No" every time. He's made it very clear that he wants to stay in Australia.'

But there was also the question of whether Lachlan was capable of running one of the world's leading media groups and fighting the smartest beasts in the corporate jungle. 'Has he got the nous? I don't think so,' said one Sydney media executive who had recently worked with him. 'Is he intelligent enough? I don't think so. He's got the arrogance but not the intelligence.' Or, as another put it, 'Lachlan is not very bright but he thinks he knows a lot about the media. That's the dangerous thing. He doesn't understand the basics.'

In addition to his famous slip-ups with Super League and One. Tel, the favoured son had struggled since coming back to Sydney. After walking out of News Corp in 2005, he had set up in a converted warehouse in Surry Hills, with his own private company, Illyria. But eight years later he had lost a good chunk of the US$150 million inheritance that had come his way for letting Wendi's kids share the family fortune, and had narrowly escaped far worse. In 2008, he had famously made a $3.3 billion bid for Consolidated Media Holdings, owner of 50 per cent of Fox Sports and 25 per cent of Foxtel, only to discover his bankers would not fund the takeover. This had turned out to be a godsend because the shares then crashed from his $4.80 offer price to a low of $1.80.

'He is by some margin the least successful of the Murdoch children,' said one former News Ltd executive. 'Nothing he has done since he left has made a cracker.' And while this verdict was too harsh, since he had actually made money from his $220 million purchase of Australia's DMG radio group (owners of Nova FM), he had certainly suffered one huge and very public failure.

In October 2010, Lachlan and James Packer had snapped up 18 per cent of the country's third commercial TV network, Channel Ten, for $280 million. Nearly three years later, they had lost around four-fifths of their money, and the business was fighting for its life. Their first decision had been to dump Ten's experienced chief executive, Nick Falloon, who had run Channel Nine for Kerry Packer, but fallen out with James; their second had been to sack the man who replaced him, Grant Blackley, who had been at Ten for 25 years. After that, Lachlan had run the show himself for a year, talking about the mess his predecessors had left and promising revival. Instead, ratings slumped, revenue plunged, profits plummeted by 90 per cent, and the share price went into freefall.

Then a new managing director took a turn at the controls. James Warburton was Lachlan's personal choice and a bright young talent who had been destined for great things at Channel Seven. But he was an advertising salesman, whereas Ten really needed a programmer. With him at the wheel, ratings fell further, revenue slipped lower and the network began breaching its banking covenants,

despite the fact that more than 200 people had been made redund-
ant. So Warburton was sacked as well. By this time, Lachlan and
his board had also got rid of Ten's chief operating officer Kerry
Kingston, its chief financial officer John Kelly, its digital boss Nick
Spooner, its head of sport David White, its chief programmer
David Mott, and its head of news Jim Carroll. In fact, just about
everyone with TV experience or corporate memory.

By mid-2013 the shares had fallen below 30 cents (from Lachlan's
entry price of $1.45) and were still rated a 'Sell' by brokers covering
the stock, with a couple predicting the network would go bust.
Lachlan had also been forced to put in another $40 million-or-so,
with two capital raisings in six months, and had dropped some
of this money too, bringing his losses to more than $110 million.
Meanwhile, the network was coming fourth in the ratings, behind
the ABC, with an audience that was less than half the size of
its two commercial rivals.

Asked what Lachlan and his team were doing wrong, one
of the many executives he had sacked said, 'Everything. Everything they do is a disaster.'

Another suggested, 'Either they're completely inept and a bunch
of idiots—and I certainly wouldn't rule that out—or they're doing
it to drive the share price down so it's cheaper for News Ltd to
take it over. I tend to think that there's not enough money involved
to be bothered with doing that, so I think it's just incompetence.'

Murdoch and Packer had started the collapse by failing to renew
Ten's rights to the AFL, which had cost a fortune but had allowed
it to play in the big league. It had then invested in a series of duds
like *The Renovators*, produced by Liz Murdoch's Shine, which was
the flop of 2011, and *Everybody Dance Now*, hosted by Lachlan's
wife Sarah, which was the flop of 2012, lasting just nine days

before it was taken off. But perhaps the worst example was the new *Breakfast* show, costing around $8 million a year, which pulled in only 40 000 people a day, on average, or roughly one-tenth of its commercial rivals, in the short time it was on air.

The show's host—who was Lachlan's personal pick—was a large part of the problem. The Kiwi shock-jock Paul Henry had famously resigned from a similar program on TV-NZ after referring repeatedly on air to Delhi's Chief Minister, Sheila Dikshit, as 'dick shit' and 'dip shit', between bursts of high-pitched laughter. Shortly after this, Lachlan had rung to offer him a salary of NZ$1 million a year to export his sparkling wit to Sydney. One ex-Ten executive described it bluntly as, 'The worst on-air appointment I've seen in twenty years.'

Perhaps Lachlan had just been unlucky—like his brother James—to be in the wrong place at the wrong time, and to have bought a network that was destined to fail. But he had not earned many good reviews from the people who worked with him. One Channel Ten executive who got to know him well said, 'I don't dislike him, and he's certainly not unpleasant. He has a bit of the rock star about him, wandering round in jeans, black skivvy and boots, and he has a certain presence because of who he is, whose son he is.' But he then added, 'He is not very bright. He thinks he's pretty good because he's been around TV for so long, but his judgement is poor.'

Others described him as 'lazy' or 'not fully committed', and recalled that he was prone to cancel meetings, with excuses like 'Bono's in town, I've got to have dinner with him.'

Another colleague reported him to be 'thin-skinned', 'insecure' and worried about his public image. 'He can take offence at minor things, if he thinks someone has slighted him, or not treated him with enough respect. If a politician used to ring him every month and it went to every six months, it was noted.'

And politicians certainly did ring. They also cleared their diaries when he went down to Canberra. So perhaps that alone made him worth having in Australia, if only as the face of News Ltd. Certainly, Rupert was determined to have him back if he could, and it had to be said his skills were sharper in newspapers. He had always shared his father's love of the printed word and had spent five years running the Australian papers, plus another five at the *New York Post*. One ex-News Ltd executive recalled how he would stand in the printing plant at Chullora and wait for the presses to switch on. So he could breathe in the ink. 'He's very savvy in lots of ways; he understands tabloids, and he had the respect of some of the old newspapermen,' said one ex-News Ltd executive.

Others reckoned he'd happily come back if he could run the publishing business and stay in Australia, and the split in the company had made this possible. 'There's every chance that Lachlan will take over, especially now the newspaper assets have been hived off,' said another senior ex-News Ltd executive who knew him well. 'The problem has always been to find something he can run from here. With the papers and book publishing business he can do that. He's always wanted to be chairman of what used to be News Corp. He can live here, spend only one week a month outside Australia.'

Indeed, splitting off the newspapers appeared to have been engineered with Lachlan in mind. The local pay-TV assets had not been thrown into 21st Century Fox along with Fox News, Fox Studios, BSkyB and STAR, even though News had just spent $2 billion to raise its stake in Australia's Foxtel and Fox Sports, by buying the company Lachlan had failed to capture four years earlier (for

$1.3 billion more). 'The new structure is specifically designed to please Lachlan,' said Claire Enders. 'Eventually, he will be chairman of News Corp, and James will be chairman of 21st Century Fox.'

Sharing the birthright between the two boys seemed like an excellent idea. But how would their ambitious older sister Elisabeth like the solution, given that she had her own powerful claim to the Murdoch throne? Not long after launching Shine in 2001, her father had admitted he was keen to get her back, saying wistfully, 'She will probably sell it for a bloody fortune to someone, and then she will come knocking on the door, and she will be very welcome.' And he had proved to be right. But in the end her 'bloody fortune' had come from Rupert and his shareholders. In January 2011, as the phone-hacking scandal began bubbling up, Elisabeth had sold out to News Corp for US$675 million and pocketed US$214 million in cash.

The London *Evening Standard* had greeted the news with the front-page headline, MURDOCH'S DAUGHTER TO GET £370M FROM DADDY. And within weeks a salvo of public criticism had cannoned into legal action, in which a group of big US shareholders led by New York's Amalgamated Bank charged that it was a conflict of interest for Rupert to be paying his daughter such an enormous sum of money. 'In addition to larding the executive ranks of the company with his offspring, Murdoch constantly engages in transactions designed to benefit family members,' said the claim, which also cited the purchase of Rawkus from James way back in 1996, and accused Murdoch of treating News Corp like a 'wholly-owned family candy store'.

This damages action against Rupert, James, Lachlan and their fellow News Corp directors was eventually settled by the insurers in April 2013 for US$139 million, which was paid to the company, on the basis that its shareholders (including Rupert and Elisabeth) had all been damaged by the old man's favouritism. And this perhaps made her preferment a little bit harder. But Liz already faced plenty of obstacles, such as being a woman, which made it unlikely that Rupert or the Saudi prince would choose her ahead of Lachlan and James. She was also unlikely to be Roger Ailes's first pick, after his excoriation by her husband in 2010 when Freud had told the *New York Times*, 'I am by no means alone within the family or the company in being ashamed and sickened by Roger Ailes's horrendous and sustained disregard of the journalistic standards that News Corporation, its founder, and every other global media business aspires to.'

Liz had tried to dissociate herself from that comment, but as someone who raised funds for Obama, lionised Nelson Mandela and once volunteered for the Gay Men's Health Crisis, she could hardly pretend she was a fan of Fox News, which was too far off the dial even for Rupert. So she was likely to face even bigger problems than James in this respect. She would also have difficulty convincing the other senior US executives at News that she had the capacity or the experience to do the top job. And this was not helped by having given up day-to-day management of Shine not long after selling the company. Nevertheless, her father clearly wanted her in the business and would need to find her a role to ensure family harmony.

However, as always, Elisabeth was proving difficult. As part of the Shine deal, she had originally accepted a seat on the News Corp board, on which she was already a non-voting observer. But, shortly after the arrests of Brooks and Coulson in July 2011, she had changed her mind, and told the directors it would be better to have fewer Murdochs. Her lawyers and husband had clearly advised her to stay as far as possible from the mess. And since then, she had done her best to put even more distance between herself and her family, starting with a speech to the Edinburgh TV Festival in August 2012, in which she had given James and Rupert a very public smack.

Cheered as she took the stage, and cheered as she finished, Elisabeth told her audience wryly, 'You do love a Murdoch,' as she noted she was the third family member in two decades to be giving the keynote address. And love her they did. Despite all the dirt that had been dug up over the previous year about the *News of the World*, *The Sun*, and the Murdochs' dealings with Britain's politicians, she was received almost like royalty: the King is dead; long live the Queen.

It was hardly a tour de force: she was a bit wooden; the gestures too obvious; the pauses too long; like a twelve-year old practising for a debate. But her message that News Corp had lost its way, and that the hacking crisis would not have happened if the company had maintained stricter corporate governance, still made headlines around the world. This was what James also believed, but he would never have dared attack Rupert in public over the way he ran his fiefdom. You had to hand it to Elisabeth: she did not lack guts.

She moved on to talk about values and community, which was strange coming from a Murdoch, and said she loved the BBC because a strong public broadcaster was good for everyone, which was guaranteed to annoy her family, who were constantly attacking the corporation or its Australian equivalent. Then to cap it all, she lavished praise on the controversial English TV playwright Dennis Potter for his great story-telling ability. And this seemed particularly pointed given that he had famously christened the cancer that killed him 'Rupert', to celebrate his loathing of her father's British tabloids.

Finally, she laid into her brother James, who had told the same audience three years earlier that the BBC's licence fee should be cut because its ambition was 'chilling' and 'profit was the only reliable guarantor' of media independence.

'Profit without purpose,' retorted Liz, 'is a recipe for disaster. It is increasingly apparent that the absence of purpose, or of a moral language, within government, media or business, could become one of the most dangerous own goals for capitalism and for freedom. We have a responsibility to each other and not just to our bottom line. Profit must be our servant, not our master.'

Not surprisingly, in the weeks that followed, scores of people rang or wrote to congratulate her on her courageous moral stand. And not surprisingly, Rupert and James were not among the well-wishers. Indeed, she and her youngest brother had barely spoken in the thirteen months since she had pressed her father to make him step down. But what was surprising is that she seemed shocked that her dad also cut her dead. In a family where daily contact is the norm, she and Rupert did not speak a word for nine weeks. Finally, she was persuaded by his friend, Robert Thomson, to give him a call, whereupon father and daughter had dinner in New York and repaired the rift. But even then she was indignant at his lack of praise. 'I think he realized it was not a loving reaction,' she complained to the *New Yorker*, as if Rupert had an obligation to thank her for so publicly attacking him.

Exactly what this said about Elisabeth and her relationship with her father was hard to divine, but a few ideas suggested themselves: first was that she was still daddy's little girl after all these years and desperately needed his approval; second was that she was so self-focused and sure she was right that she felt any reasonable person, including her father, must agree with her; and third was that she probably had what it took to run the family's media business, where sentiment was a handicap and steel was essential.

A couple of months after the speech, Elisabeth returned to her theme of mistakes the family had made, by telling the *New Yorker* that she had tried to warn James and Rupert in 2010 not to bury the *News of the World*'s crimes. After some of Freud's clients had learned that their phones had been hacked by Murdoch journalists, she had supposedly advised her father not to pay hush money to the victims. 'Investigate and punish the miscreants,' she claimed to have urged him. 'Turn over e-mails and documents to the authorities; don't risk a cover-up.'

While this may well have been true, it was also self-serving and somewhat self-righteous. Back in August 2008, when David Cameron had flown to Santorini to seek support from the Murdoch papers in the upcoming election, it was Elisabeth's yacht, the *Elisabeth F*, they had dined on and Matthew's private jet that had flown him there. And just 36 hours before the hacking scandal erupted in July 2011, her old friend Rebekah Brooks had been whooping it up at Burford Priory at Liz's big summer bash. So she had not exactly been on another planet while all this was happening.

More to the point, the blame game would not endear her to Rupert, whose support she needed if she wanted him to anoint her, or to James, whose backing might be crucial after their father died. But there was clearly a long history to the sibling rivalry. A few years earlier, Rupert had mused that his daughter might sell Shine for lots of money and buy News Corp shares 'to give James trouble'.

And while she probably hadn't made enough to be a nuisance, it was revealing that Rupert thought she might want to try.

In initially agreeing to join the News Corp board, Elisabeth had assured the directors she had no interest in Rupert's job. And she repeated this after her Edinburgh speech, telling the BBC's Steve Hewlett that she had 'absolutely no ambition' to replace him. But a couple of months later, she deflected a similar question about succeeding her father by asking, 'In what? The company is changing its shape so much. I think no one person will succeed him.' So maybe she was falling in with a plan to share the spoils. The latest speculation was that the rivalry had become too much for the children and they did not want the winner to take all. So perhaps Elisabeth could run the creative side of News Corp and be its programming guru, James could run the cable-TV and movie business, and Lachlan could take over the newspapers and books. This was the family's (and perhaps Rupert's) ideal solution: there would be something for everyone. It would, of course, only be possible if James's rehabilitation succeeded and if Lachlan was prepared to run the papers. And James and Elisabeth would need to start talking to each other again if they were to run 21st Century Fox together.

Naturally, this convenient compromise would also depend on there not being a revolt by News Corp's shareholders, or directors. And this could hardly be guaranteed. While it was true that the board had never been a problem in the past, there was no saying what would happen once Rupert had gone. A common view among former News executives was that the edifice would crumble and the Murdoch family would lose control once the strongman departed. As in Yugoslavia after the death of Marshall Tito, there would be Balkanisation of the empire and internecine warfare. 'The company will be unbundled, no question,' Murdoch's former editor, Andrew Neil, predicted in 2007. 'My guess is [the break-up] will be messy because these things usually are.'

'I think he's going to lose his company. I can't see him hanging on,' another former top executive echoed five years later. 'I think John Malone [the US media baron who built Tele-Communications Inc (TCI)] will get it. He would break it up and keep the bits he wants.'

And plenty of others were ready to join this chorus. 'The board have let Rupert have control because he's a genius,' said Eric Beecher, former editor of Murdoch's *Melbourne Herald*, himself a media entrepreneur. 'But they won't let that continue after he's gone.'

'Once Rupert is gone, the board will do what's best for shareholders,' a more recent ex-Murdoch executive agreed, citing the 'genius' word again to justify its history of compliance. Others ventured that the hacking scandal had changed the landscape for good, and that the group's directors would henceforth hold sway. 'It's the end of the dynasty,' one of Rupert's most senior former executives pronounced privately in mid-2013, predicting that the Murdoch succession could not now take place.

If the House of Murdoch were indeed to fall, it was suggested it might happen like this: first, the 21st Century Fox board would choose Chase Carey as Rupert's successor because he was a better chief executive than any of Murdoch's children; second, Rupert would not risk a bloody fight to impose James, Lachlan or Elisabeth on the shareholders because it would wreck the company; and third, the Murdochs' dominance depended entirely on the dual-class share structure, and this could easily be scrapped.

However, there was one massive problem with this scenario, and that was Rupert: the man who had built the News empire and made it his life. It would be totally out of character for him or his family to surrender control, especially while the old man was still alive. And there was practically no way it could be wrested from the Murdochs without their consent. For 21st Century Fox or News Corp to scrap their dual-class structures (which had just survived the splitting of the company), it would need a 51 per cent majority of the B-class shares to vote in favour of elimination, which meant that almost everyone would have to gang up against Rupert and his children and cast votes against them. That sort of unanimous revolt was unprecedented in corporate history and almost impossible to conceive. Moreover, if Rupert did put a succession plan in place while he was still alive, it is hard to believe that the board would dare speak against him, let alone declare war. They had certainly shown no signs of such bravery to date.

After his death, of course, it might be a different story, especially if the children argued. Rupert knew very well what could happen when rich families fought. The *Wall Street Journal* had fallen into his lap in 2007 because of dissent among the Bancrofts. The *Chicago Sun Times* had come his way in 1984 when the Field family divided. And the *News of the World* had become part of his empire in 1969 because the Carr family had gone to war with one another. But even if James and Elisabeth were no longer talking, and even if Prue's support could not be taken for granted, the Murdochs were a close-knit family who had spent their lives in the line of duty, and they were unlikely to abandon the cause. What's more, splitting the empire had defused much of their rivalry. There was no longer a need to choose one person to replace Rupert, which all agreed was impossible. Nor was there a need to carve up the empire to get shot of the newspapers. And with the share price riding high, there was far less value for corporate raiders to unlock.

Best of all, from the point of view of peace and harmony, there was now far less danger of Wendi trying to deal her two young children, Chloe and Grace, back into the action. Anyone who had seen Rupert's feisty Chinese wife smack the House of Commons pie thrower would have marked her as a woman who was likely to demand equal rights for her children. And, even though the 2006 settlement had denied the girls a say in the Murdoch Family Trust, Rupert had mused that this might change when they were '25 or 30 or something'. But any chance of that occurring was dealt a huge blow in mid-2013 when Rupert suddenly announced that he was going to divorce Wendi after fourteen years of marriage on the grounds that their relationship had irretrievably broken down. Amid the shock and amazement that greeted his announcement, it emerged that the couple had been living separate lives for some time, and that Wendi's courageous pie-throwing defence had nearly not happened because she had only decided at the last minute to be in London to support Rupert. Even Wendi, it seemed, was blindsided and confused by his decision, which caught everyone off balance. 'We knew the rumours, and we could see they weren't a happy loving couple,' said one recently departed senior executive. 'But we were certainly surprised. I mean, why would he bother?'

Why indeed? At the age of 82, Rupert surely couldn't be planning to marry again? And however much they had grown apart, did he really need to cut Wendi loose? In the search for an explanation, all sorts of wild speculation was offered, and all of it denied: that Wendi had given him a black eye the day before the announcement; that she was having an affair with Tony Blair or Google's Eric Schmidt, or with MySpace's Chris de Wolfe. But a more prosaic reason was that he had simply had enough. According to one report, he had recently told his son Lachlan, who had never really fallen for Wendi's charms, that he realised their marriage had been 'a mistake'.

'I think Rupert got irritated and bored with her and just decided to get rid of her,' a senior ex-executive suggested. 'That's Rupert. That's the way he does things. Maybe he thinks it will improve his relationship with the older children.'

But perhaps it also had to do with his inheritance and the fact that he didn't want Wendi to be his widow. And, since he was splitting the company and reorganising his affairs, it made sense to split with her and reorganise his marriage too: to tidy things up for the future and ensure she could not reopen discussions about the succession. All such matters would now be capped off by a pre-nuptial agreement they had signed in 1999 and by two more financial settlements that had been made since the girls were born. The courts in York State, where the divorce would be heard, were famously reluctant to overturn such contracts. So the two young girls would hang on to their one-sixth shares in the Murdoch family fortune, but never get a vote, and Wendi would walk away with hundreds of millions of dollars. Almost certainly it would all be settled quietly and without a fight, despite the media's desire for a messy and scandalous public battle.

But this wasn't all that one could glean from Rupert's latest surprise. It was that you never really knew what he planned to do next. Perhaps his children had guessed how unhappy the marriage was, or how little he cared for it. Perhaps some in his inner circle had an inkling that it was past its use-by date. But aside from a couple of rumbles the previous year, there appeared to have been no warning that they might separate or that divorce was in the offing. It made one wonder how much anyone knew of what Rupert was really thinking.

Rupert's decision also left a clear impression that he was planning for the future and clearing the decks for another tilt at life, and that he reckoned he had a long time left. His executives said he was pulling back from TV and 21st Century Fox, even though he was the CEO, to concentrate on his new pared-down News Corp, with its logo crafted from his own and his father's handwriting. He professed to be excited about having a chance to do it again: to undo some of the mistakes he'd made and bring his beloved newspapers into the digital age. If there was anyone in the world who could do this successfully, it was the man who had built his global media empire on the strength of the printed word. A man who, after 60 years in the business, still spoke longingly of his days as a sub on the *Daily Express* in London, just after leaving Oxford, which he clearly regarded as among the best in his life. So, perhaps this, after all, would be Rupert's epitaph, 'The Man who Saved Newspapers'. But whatever happened, it seemed likely that his children and his directors could be waiting a fair time yet to settle the tricky question of who might follow him.

Of course, family businesses always face difficult succession problems, and it's not just the old saw about shirtsleeves to shirtsleeves in three generations. It's that the people who build empires tend to be driven, selfish and hard to please, which makes them reluctant to let go. And Rupert is almost the paradigm. He is desperate to keep it all in the family, but he can't bring himself to hand over power, even to them.

You can see why his older children, who are now in their forties and fifties, have resorted to family counselling. Elisabeth, Lachlan and James are all desperate to impress him, to live up to his expectations and to earn his respect. But despite their undoubted love and admiration, which he clearly returns, they sometimes resent him. He rarely praises them to their face, he competes with his sons, he abandoned the mother they loved, he has never been the sort of father that James and Lachlan now try so hard to be, and most of all, he still shows no signs of moving aside.

And in his eyes, perhaps, they have disappointed him too: Lachlan because he isn't smart enough, or tough enough to stand up to his American executives; James because he wasn't wise enough to avert the hacking crisis; and Liz because she is a woman, who refuses to accept her place. In mid-2013, long after his 82nd birthday, Rupert was still tweeting that he hoped to pass it all on to his children 'one day', but only 'if kids worthy'. As if after all this time they still hadn't passed his test.

It is hardly surprising that he is so often compared to King Lear, a proud old man who wants to divide his kingdom between his three daughters and pledges the largest share to the one who loves him most. Only King Rupert has neither vacated his throne nor given his power away. His version of the famous Shakespeare play is for him to be forever stuck in the first act, and he may never get beyond it.

Murdoch has said many times that he wants to be carried out of News Corp and will live to be 100 or more. And if he holds on to his sanity, he may well get his wish. In this, as in everything else, he tends to do just as he pleases. And no one has the nerve to challenge him. There is no doubt what song they will play at his funeral— if he ever dies—made famous by another old fella who could not retire. It may well be cheesy, but it hits the right note, and there are a few lines in particular that could serve as an epitaph. You should try reading them; *My Way* might almost have been written for him. Rupert Murdoch is certainly making it his anthem.

EPILOGUE
THE RECKONING

'I hope the police will consider charges against the body corporate and the directors of this thoroughly corrupt company.'

Chris Bryant MP

One consequence of the Great British hacking scandal, starring Rupert Murdoch's *News of the World*, and the Fantastic Fleet Street corruption scandal, featuring his favourite tabloid, *The Sun,* is that Britain will soon have its toughest and most restrictive press watchdog since the time when newspapers had to be licensed. And however this finally turns out—as a much-needed curb on the tabloids' excesses or a terrible blight on media freedom—the British public will know who they have to thank for it. To borrow an old phrase, IT'S THE SUN WOT WON IT, with more than a little help from the *News of the World.* But certainly Rupert Murdoch's papers will be responsible for this brave new media world. And it will doubtless be a part of Rupert's legacy.

Another consequence could be that an unprecedented number of Murdoch's reporters and editors will end up behind bars.

By mid-2013 there were more than 40 current or former Murdoch journalists potentially facing charges for hacking, corruption, perverting the course of justice or perjury, with roughly half of these from the *News of the World* and half from *The Sun*. Some twenty of these journalists had already been charged and would have to face trial, as would a further five security staff, PAs and drivers from News International who had worked for Rebekah Brooks. 'It was not just one rogue reporter. Not just one rogue newspaper. Not even one rogue department,' observed Chris Bryant MP, who was now Labour's shadow home affairs minister. 'I hope the police will consider charges against the body corporate and the directors of this thoroughly corrupt company.'

Working out the exact tally was a challenge because some people, like Brooks, Coulson and Stuart Kuttner, had been arrested for more than one offence, and the police never named names until charges were laid. But it appeared that the journalistic arrests split fairly evenly between Operations Weeting and Elveden, between hacking and corruption, and between those who had been charged and those who were awaiting their fate. However, there were also scores of public officials facing charges, and the numbers were growing all the time. In February 2013, six more journalists from the *News of the World* were arrested in a new wave of dawn raids by the Met's freshly minted Operation Pinetree. Once again, they were forced to watch as their homes were searched. Once again, the offices at Wapping were invaded. And once again, the journalists were taken off for questioning before being released on bail.

The Metropolitan Police soon announced that they had uncovered an entirely new hacking conspiracy at the old Murdoch paper, which appeared to involve at least another 800 victims. This time, the lead had come not from the Management & Standards

Committee but from a supergrass, arrested by Operation Weeting, who had decided to become a prosecution witness. Unconfirmed reports suggested that the police had also uncovered incriminating emails in a sock drawer during one of their much-criticised home invasions, which had apparently never made it onto News International's central computer system, so their searches had not been a waste of time.

This alleged new hacking ring—which did not involve Glenn Mulcaire—centred on the features and showbiz desks at the *News of the World*, which had competed fiercely for scoops against their rivals in news. Top of the arrest list was the ex-features editor Jules Stenson, the editor of *Fabulous* magazine Rachel Richardson, and the well-known showbiz reporter Rav Singh. The three others were former features journalists Matt Nixson, Polly Graham and Jane Atkinson. On past form, it would be anything up to a year before they would know if charges were to be laid.

Meanwhile, three big criminal trials involving more than a dozen Murdoch journalists and News International employees were set to kick off on 9 September 2013, with Rebekah Brooks, Andy Coulson, Ian Edmondson and Stuart Kuttner from the *News of the World* first in the dock at the Old Bailey on phone hacking charges brought by Operation Weeting. In this trial, which was expected to last until Christmas, Rebekah Brooks, Andy Coulson and Clive Goodman would also face corruption charges, while Brooks and her husband Charlie would face charges of perverting the course of justice, along with her former PA, Cheryl Carter, and the former head of security at News International, Mark Hanna. The following March, three others would go on trial at the Old Bailey for perverting the course of justice (assuming the hacking charges against Rebekah had not been thrown out of court in the meantime). And in between, *The Sun*'s John Kay, Geoff Webster, Fergus Shanahan and Duncan Larcombe would face trial at the Old Bailey in January 2014 for conspiracy to commit misconduct in public office, which carried a maximum sentence of life imprisonment. Several more journalists from *The Sun* would be tried at a later date.

An army of public officials, who had allegedly sold information to the Murdoch papers, was also set to march through the Old Bailey's courts. These included eleven current or former police officers, four soldiers, four prison officers, three health service workers, two Ministry of Defence officials and one Customs & Revenue officer, plus a raft of others who had not been identified. Six had already been convicted and sentenced (to between ten months and two years in jail), five had been cleared, another six had been charged, and a further 28 were awaiting a decision. In addition, there were 20 journalists, private investigators and public officials who had been arrested by Operation Tuleta, which was investigating computer hacking to obtain private information, all of whom were awaiting a decision as to whether they would be charged.

Finally, Andy Coulson would face trial in Glasgow for perjury, for allegedly lying on oath about phone hacking during the trial of a Scottish Labour MP, Tommy Sheridan, who had been targeted by the *News of the World*. This was probably the most serious charge of all.

All in all, the courts were going to be busy, quite possibly until 2015. And if the trials brought in guilty verdicts there was the chance that further action would be taken against News International or its directors.

'If the Elveden charges are eventually upheld, James and Rupert Murdoch will have been directors of UK companies that were engaged in serious and long-sustained wrongdoing,' Claire Enders wrote in a note to her high-paying media clients. 'Phone hacking was serious. But bribery of public officials is far worse.'

Significantly for News, some of the alleged offences had occurred after the implementation of the tough new *Bribery Act 2010*, which had come into force on 1 July 2011. At least two of the alleged offences also involved payment by cheque, and possibly a company cheque. This raised the possibility that News International could itself be charged with bribery, since companies could be prosecuted under the act if a senior person was involved, or if they had failed to take proper measures to prevent bribery from taking place.

This in turn could bring repercussions for James Murdoch, who might be deemed to be not a fit and proper person to hold a role at BSkyB, where he remained a non-executive director. James had already suffered severe criticism from the TV regulator, Ofcom, in September 2012, over his failure to uncover the hacking scandal at the *News of the World*, with the accusation that he 'repeatedly fell short of the conduct to be expected of him as a chief executive officer'. Further censure would clearly affect his chances of taking over the helm from his dad. It was possible that Ofcom could also deem 21st Century Fox unfit to hold the BSkyB licence because of its links to the Murdochs, which might force the sale of its BSkyB shares.

And, finally, there was a risk that the British prosecutions of *The Sun* and *News of the World* journalists for corruption would result in the US Department of Justice following up with action under the *Foreign Corrupt Practices Act*, which could lead to heavy fines and the possibility of further regulatory action. Indeed, there were unconfirmed rumours in mid-2013 that an expensive settlement was afoot.

In the meantime, Britain's civil courts were also busy, even though more than 200 hacking claims against News had already been settled and a similar number dealt with by the group's compensation scheme. One of the main firms of plaintiffs' solicitors, Collyer Bristow, was still getting a couple of new customers every week. Others were reportedly getting even more. 'It's still fairly early days,' said the firm's Steven Heffer, who reported that News was being obstructive. 'The public face is that they're decent guys, doing everything they can to help clear it up. That's not what we find on a day-to-day level. They try to fight everything to the last corner and beat you into submission whenever they can.'

In June 2013, these actions spread to the US for the first time, with a Hollywood stuntwoman, Eunice Huthart, alleging that the *News of the World* and *The Sun* had hacked into her voicemails and obtained private information about Brad Pitt and Angelina Jolie, which had then been published in the two newspapers. The damages claim, which was filed in Los Angeles, targeted the American company News Corp and claimed that Rupert Murdoch regularly called the editors of these papers and either 'knew or should have known that executives, employees and agents of *The Sun* and *News of the World* were engaged in widespread phone hacking'.

This avalanche of legal actions, and the work of the Management & Standards Committee, had cost News Corp US$347 million in fees and damages by the end of 2012, and perhaps another US$100 million by mid-2013. But this was by no means the full financial reckoning. The group had spent another US$150 million on shutting the *News of the World* and sacking staff, and had been forced to say goodbye to at least US$200 million in profit it would have earned had the paper stayed open. Adding on the

US$63 million termination fee for the BSkyB bid, the cash cost of the hacking scandal was already pushing close to US$900 million, with the likelihood of more to come. And if you counted the write-downs of News Corp's UK newspapers it would be even more. This, too, ignored the biggest cost of all, which was the failure to capture BSkyB, with its £1.4 billion-a-year profit, which would have diverted rivers of cash to News Corp and boosted the value of all its British businesses.

Yet this was all chump change compared to what had happened to the News Corp share price, which had rocketed up from US$14 in July 2011 to US$33 in mid-2013, and turned the group from a US$33 billion business into a US$80 billion business. Since the darkest days of the hacking scandal, the Murdochs had more than doubled their wealth from around US$4 billion to almost US$9 billion. And, strangely enough, much of this was due to the crisis, which had forced Rupert to split the papers from the rest of the group and set the share price free.

Flushed with this new wave of money, Rupert was looking to expand his empire once again. In October 2012, staff at the *Los Angeles Times* and *Chicago Tribune* expressed horror at rumours that News might buy them out of bankruptcy, which would give Rupert another 23 television stations and ten local papers as well as the two big-city mastheads, and put him in control of four of America's top ten newspaper titles. This acquisition was still on the menu in mid-2013, by which time Murdoch was lobbying in Washington to have the Federal Communications Commission change the rules to allow him to go ahead.

But just as it seemed that Rupert Murdoch had emerged unscathed from the whole sorry saga, something else happened. In July 2013, Britain's Channel 4 and the investigative website

ExaroNews published a secret recording made in March that year by Rupert's journalists at *The Sun*, in which he poured scorn on the police investigation, belittled the seriousness of bribing police and indicated it was at least possible he had known that his journalists were breaking the law—which News Corp instantly denied. The tape had Murdoch admitting it might have been a 'mistake' to set up the Management & Standards Committee and telling his staff that it was no longer co-operating so enthusiastically with the police. Finally, it revealed Rupert's promise to do his utmost to support journalists facing charges, even if they were convicted and sent to jail. 'I think it's just outrageous,' he told them. 'You're all innocent until proven guilty. What you're asking is what happens if some of you are proven guilty. What afterwards? I'm not allowed to promise you. I will promise you continued health support, but your jobs…I've got to be careful what comes out, but frankly, I won't say it, but just trust me. Okay?'

The Metropolitan Police promptly demanded a copy of these remarkable indiscretions and said they would seek a production order if the tape was not handed over. Simultaneously, the House of Commons Culture Committee announced it would question Rupert once again to see if he had misled Parliament. And so, with a happy ending looking a little less likely, the stage was set for yet another act in this extraordinary continuing drama, and the possibility that, after all Rupert had survived, it was his very own journalists who might bring him down.

ACKNOWLEDGEMENTS

Writing about Rupert Murdoch and his family is perhaps not a great career move, given that they have such power and patronage in the media in Australia, the UK, the US and the rest of the world. But it is this power that makes the Murdochs so fascinating. And I found it impossible to resist such a fabulous story.

This has not been the easiest book to write because Rupert Murdoch has done so much in his lifetime and he rarely sits still for a moment, even at 82. After delivering the 'finished' manuscript in May 2013, I found myself rewriting chapters on a weekly basis as more and more happened to take the story further: Rupert announcing his divorce from Wendi Deng; Rupert splitting News Corp into two and casting the newspapers adrift; and Rupert being secretly recorded by his own journalists at *The Sun*, hinting that he knew they had been paying police and public officials for years.

As I write this in mid-July 2013, Murdoch is about to reappear before the House of Commons Culture Committee in London and tell them how much he really knew about those illegal activities and to explain his claims that the police investigation was 'outrageous', 'a disgrace', and 'over next to nothing'. The Metropolitan Police have now obtained a copy of the tape and may also want to interview him.

Whatever comes of all this, the first *News of the World* hacking trial will be under way by the time this book hits the shelves. Soon afterwards, the corruption trials involving journalists from *The Sun* will begin. And it is conceivable that there will then be further enforcement action against News International in the UK and/or News Corp in the US.

But any book about Murdoch has to draw a line somewhere. And it also has to find a focus. This book aims to look at Rupert's life and family through the prism of the *News of the World* hacking scandal and the corruption scandal at *The Sun*, showing how he and his papers got into the mess, and trying to assess what impact it will all have on the vexed question of who will succeed him.

I've been helped in this by numerous public inquiries and court cases in the UK, which have forced most of the main players, including James and Rupert Murdoch, to answer questions about what happened at their British tabloids and why. These have included the Leveson Inquiry and the various investigations by the House of Commons Home Affairs Committee and the House of Commons Culture Committee, but there have also been legal actions by hacking victims and others who have dared to take the tabloids on. These have produced a mountain of first-hand testimony which hardly anyone has bothered to mine.

For some of the early story I have drawn on the work of previous biographers, authors, reporters and documentary makers, who have attempted to capture the essence of Murdoch and preserve it for posterity. I am particularly indebted to the celebrated Australian journalist, George Munster, who died shortly before his excellent work, *Rupert Murdoch: A Paper Prince*, was published in 1985; to William Shawcross, whose seminal biography, *Murdoch: the Making of a Media Empire*, was first published in 1992; to Michael Wolff, whose biography, *The Man Who Owns the News*, came out in 2008; to Julie Browning, Laurie Critchley and the team at the ABC who produced the documentary series, *Dynasties*, and the excellent book that accompanied it; to Andrew Neil, whose memoir *Full Disclosure* provided such an insight into working for Murdoch in Britain; and to Bruce Dover, whose book, *The Adventures of Rupert in China*, gave similar glimpses of working for the Murdochs in Asia. For the history of *The Sun*, I am especially grateful to Peter Chippindale and Chris Horrie whose hilarious but shocking account, *Stick it up Your Punter: The Rise & Fall of The Sun*, was an entertaining reference work.

I have endeavoured to credit all these (and other) published sources and have given links wherever possible. I have also read most of what has been written in the papers or online about the Murdochs in the last 25 years, and have tried to credit where it has been useful. My apologies for any I have missed and for any who feel their contribution deserves to be highlighted. Among those who have covered the hacking story in Britain, I should particularly thank Nick Davies, Amelia Hill and Lisa O'Carroll, of *The Guardian*; Martin Hickman of *The Independent*; and Peter Jukes, writing in the *Daily Beast*. I should also thank Professor Brian Cathcart of Hacked Off and Martin Moore of the Media Standards Trust. Among those who have covered the Murdochs for the

US media over the years, I am especially grateful to Ken Auletta, Sarah Ellison, Steve Fishman, and Judith Newman, and the publications they wrote for, *New York*, *New Yorker* and *Vanity Fair*. And in Australia, I would like to make particular mention of Rodney Lever, Alex Mitchell, Dimity Torbett and Pam Williams.

But I have also undertaken a huge amount of my own original research for this book. Over the course of the last two years, I have conducted fruitful interviews with at least 100 people and had less fruitful contacts with perhaps 200 more. In addition, my excellent researcher, Alice Brennan, has talked to scores more people in the US, where she is based. Not surprisingly, most of these have chosen to help anonymously. But whether they have agreed to be named or not, I would like to thank them all for taking the time to talk to me or Alice and share their stories and opinions thrown into the mix.

The conclusions I have come to at the end of this process are mine alone, as are any mistakes I may have made (which I would be happy to correct if readers point them out). I hope, as always, that I have done the job fairly and without animus. I should say that I worked for News Ltd in Australia as a contributor to Sydney's *Sunday Telegraph* for a couple of years and enjoyed the experience so much that I came within a whisker of joining the Murdoch organisation fulltime. Despite its excesses in Britain, News Corp has produced and still produces some excellent journalism and employs excellent journalists.

As to the other people who have made this book a reality, I would like to single out Richard Walsh, whose idea it was in the first place. He has also been a constant source of advice and reassurance along the way and has made it a far better book than it would otherwise have been. Next time, if there is one, I'll try not to ring him in a panic on Christmas Day. My researcher Alice Brennan has also been a delight. Through sheer persistence she has managed to persuade some of the most unlikely people to talk. As usual, my editor, Rebecca Kaiser, has been brilliant and calm in the face of the continual changes, updates and rewrites that have been needed to cope with this ever changing story. Thanks also to Richard Potter, whose legal advice I value greatly, and to all the team at my publishers, Allen & Unwin, and especially Sue Hines.

Finally, as always, I'd like to thank my wife Lisa, who endured my Murdoch obsession for the many months it took me to research and write this book and who offered me unfailing love and support. It's hard yakka being a writer. But it's even worse being married to one. Thanks also to all my children for putting up with a distracted and eternally busy father. Unlike Rupert, I promise I won't still be working this hard when I'm 82.

NOTES

References are given where quotes or an account are taken from published sources.

PROLOGUE   EVER SO HUMBLE

Page 1: 'I'd just like to say one sentence…', House of Commons Culture, Media & Sport Committee, Rupert Murdoch, Minutes of Evidence, London, 19 July 2011, http://www.parliament.uk/documents/commons-committees/culture-media-sport/Uncorrected_transcript_19_July_phone_hacking.pdf

Page 2: '…his US$40 billion empire', The value of News Corp obviously depends on its current share price. It has varied between US$33 billion at the depths of the hacking crisis in July 2011 and US$80 billion in May 2013. This figure is calculated on its average value in the second half of 2011.

CHAPTER 1   PAPER PRINCE

Page 8: '…a shy man with a stammer'. Geoffrey Serle wrote of Sir Keith Murdoch in the *Australian Dictionary of Biography* that, 'He was afflicted with a humiliating stammer which made school a torture; his speech would collapse under stress; he sometimes could not even buy a railway ticket without scribbling a note. Extreme shyness, difficulty in making friends and possibly unusually determined ambition were the consequences.' *Australian Dictionary of Biography*, Vol 10, Melbourne University Press, Melbourne, 1986, http://adb.anu.edu.au/biography/murdoch-sir-keith-arthur-7693

Page 8: 'a gift for financial wizardry' and 'boyish piratical tendencies', John Hetherington, *Australians: Nine Profiles*, F.W. Cheshire, Melbourne, 1960, pp 81–103.

Page 10: 'Never do anything with your hands', Patrick John Murdoch, S*idelights on the Shorter Catechism,* Presbyterian Church of Victoria, Melbourne, 1908, http://trove.nla.gov.au/work/11998699?q&sort=holdings+desc&_=1354178064920&versionld+22074917

Page 10: '...he was a chronic and hopeless gambler', Julie Browning and Laurie Critchley, *Dynasties*, ABC Books, Sydney, 2002, pp 174–5.

Page 11: '...Keith Murdoch spotted a picture of her in one of his magazines, Desmond Zwar, *In Search of Keith Murdoch*, Macmillan, Melbourne, 1980, p 76.

Page 11: 'The newly wedded couple bought one of the best mansions in Toorak, Heathfield...' Pictures of Heathfield (which was demolished in 1958) can be found at http://trove.nla.gov.au/picture/result?q=HEATHFIELD+TOORAK&l-availability=y. Also at http://home.vicnet.net.au/~malvern/whos_who.htm The house was sold to the Murdochs by William Baillieu and was previously known as Wombalano. It was built in 1884 for John Bruce, father of the Australian Prime Minister, Stanley Bruce.

Page 11: 'Like a scene from an opera pageant', *The Argus*, 9 July 1934, p 4, http://trove.nla.gov.au/ndp/del/article/10975211

Page 13: 'Rupert was "naughty, daring, a terrific tease", Browning and Critchley, *op cit.*

Page 13: '...an unforgettable spectacle—a sort of mediaeval cavalcade', John Monks, *Elisabeth Murdoch: Two Lives*, Pan Macmillan, Sydney, 1994, p 144.

Page 13: 'Sir Keith complained to a family friend that he was a "disobedient, wild sullen boy"', Neil Chenoweth, *Virtual Murdoch*, Random House, Sydney, 2001, p 12.

Page 14: 'But she also avowed that her own parents had been "very fond of each other"', *Elders, with Andrew Denton*, ABC TV, Sydney, 23 June 2008, http://www.abc.net.au/tv/elders/transcripts/s2721490.htm

Page 14: '...even though her father had once threatened to cut her mother into pieces', Monks, *op cit*, cited in David Leser, 'The Modest Matriarch', *Australian Women's Weekly*, Sydney, June 2003, http://davidleser.com/slippages/uploads/download/file/df-9-168-58.pdf

Page 14: 'I was looked on as rather a disciplinarian', 'Driving Dame Elisabeth', *Australian Story*, ABC TV, Sydney, March 1999.

Page 14: 'She was an okay mother', Michael Wolff, *The Man who Owns the News*, Random House, New York, 2008.

Page 15: 'I was very young, rather determined, and perhaps I wasn't always very wise', *Six Australians: Profiles of Power*, ABC TV, Sydney, 1966.

Page 15: 'I think perhaps there was a slight feeling of resentment that he'd been sent away', *ibid.*

Page 15: 'He regarded young Rupert as the nastiest of the rich boys he taught', James Darling to author, 1993.

Page 16: 'What is vile they offer to gloating eyes, what is vindictive they applaud', Shawcross, William, *Rupert Murdoch, the Making of a Media Empire*, Simon & Schuster, New York, 1992.

Page 16: '...known by his mates as "Bullo"', Original interview with anonymous schoolmate by Australian journalist, Dimity Torbett, cited in Chenoweth, *op cit*, p 13.

Page 16: 'He was called "the brat"', Rodney Lever, 'How Rupert Murdoch took over the News', *Independent Australia.net*, 8 September 2012. http://www.independentaustralia.net/2012/australian-identity/australian-history/how-rupert-murdoch-took-over-the-news/

Page 17: '...it was like having a private plane or a Rolls-Royce', Michael Weigall, interviewed by Dimity Torbett, quoted in Chenoweth, *op cit*, p 14.

Page 18: 'Back in Australian, the good knight's passing was met with gushing tributes', especially in Sir Keith's *Courier-Mail*, http://trove.nla.gov.au/ndp/del/article/50523057

Page 18: 'I desire that my said son Rupert Murdoch should have a great opportunity', George Munster, *Rupert Murdoch, A Paper Prince*, Viking, Melbourne, 1985, p 28.

Page 20: 'It was very hard to know what to do, because he wanted to keep certain properties', Wolff, *op cit*, p 70.

Page 20: 'I was so young and so new to the business', *Boyer Lectures*, ABC Radio National, Sydney, 2008, http://www.abc.net.au/rn/boyerlectures/stories/2008/2397940.htm

Page 20: '...with curly hair that had still only receded as far as Julius Caesar's', Keith Bashford, 'How to get ahead in publishing', *Salon.com*, 12 October 1999, https://www.salon.com/1999/10/12/murdoch/

Page 21: 'All boundless energy, sleeves rolled up', Browning and Critchley, *op cit*, p 189.

Page 24: 'He stood apart from the stiff-necked and conservative end of town', Alex Mitchell, 'Fatal obsessions, Murdoch's early years', *Overland Literary Journal*, 208, Melbourne, Spring 2012, http://overland.org.au/previous-issues/issue-208/feature-alex-mitchell/

Page 25: 'Sir Frank's sons, Kerry and Clyde, promptly reacted by seizing the Anglican Press', Paul Barry, *The Rise and Rise of Kerry Packer Uncut*, Bantam, Sydney, 1993, pp 125–30.

CHAPTER 2   RULE BRITANNIA

Page 27: 'I am constantly amazed at the ease with which I entered British newspapers', Peter Chippindale and Chris Horrie, *Stick it Up Your Punter, The Rise and Fall of The Sun*, Heinemann, London, 1990.

Page 27: 'The only honest answer to that is', BBC TV, London, 1968, http://www.youtube.com/watch?v=TgaEOslC1IA

Page 29: 'Thank God you've come.' The story of the meeting at Sir William Carr's flat is from Chippindale and Horrie, *op cit*. There are other notable accounts in George Munster's *Rupert Murdoch, A Paper Prince*, Viking, Melbourne, 1985; Thomas Kiernan's *Citizen Murdoch*, Dodd, Mead, New York, 1986; William Shawcross's *Rupert Murdoch, Simon & Schuster, New York, 1992*, and contemporary BBC and ABC TV reports, which have interviews with Murdoch and Maxwell.

Page 29: 'After taking him to lunch in Mayfair, she reported that he had little small talk...', Adam Curtis, *Rupert Murdoch, A Portrait of Satan*, BBC.co.uk, London, 30 January 2011, http://www.bbc.co.uk/blogs/adamcurtis/2011/01/rupert_murdoch_-_a_portrait_of.html

Page 30: '...beaming from ear to ear', Alex Mitchell,'Fatal obsessions, Murdoch's early years', *Overland Literary Journal*, 208, Melbourne, Spring 2012.

Page 31: 'I'm now going to fucking tell you', Munster, *op cit*.

Page 32: 'When he bought the *News of the World* it nearly killed me,' *Dynasties*, 'The Murdochs', ABC TV, Sydney, 17 July 2002

Page 33: 'Certainly it's going to sell newspapers', *Panorama*, BBC TV, London, 1969. In Adam Curtis blog at, http://www.bbc.co.uk/programmes/p00dr94w

Page 34: 'When a newspaper resorts to sex and sensationalism it's a surefire circulation builder', *Panorama*, BBC TV, *ibid*

Page 35: 'What has happened on my paper', Chippindale and Horrie, *op cit*, p 36.

Page 36: 'Goody after goody after goody', 'Murdoch's Scandal', *Frontline*, WGBH, Boston, http://www.pbs.org/wgbh/pages/*Frontline*/murdochs-scandal/

Page 36: '...full of bright young readers and semi-naked girls', Chippindale and Horrie, *op cit*, p 33.

Page 37: 'Great Britain will accept you if you're willing to join and play by the rules', William H. Meyers, 'Murdoch's Global Power Play', *New York Times*, New York, 12 June 1988, http://www.nytimes.com/1988/06/12/magazine/murdoch-s-global-power-play.html?pagewanted=all&src=pm

Page 37: 'Just as we were being invited round to places we'd catch Lord Lambton in bed or something ...', Alexander Cockburn, *Village Voice*, 1976. Quoted in Adam Curtis, *A Portrait of Satan*, http://www.bbc.co.uk/blogs/adamcurtis/2011/01/rupert_murdoch_-_a_portrait_of.html

Page 37: 'Part of the Australian character is wanting to take on the world', Meyers, *op cit*.

Page 38: 'Ferocious swarms of man-killing bees'. The best account of the *Express*'s style is in, 'What's black and white and red all over?' *Texas Monthly*, November 1976; see also, 'Wild in the streets', *San Antonio Express-News*, 4 November 2010; David Shaw, 'Meet the Press King', *Los Angeles Times News Service*, 20 June 1983.

Page 39: 'With few other opportunities on offer...' Details of US newspaper deals and prices from, 'Publisher Murdoch's U.S. Track Record, A PEJ Backgrounder', *Journalism.org*, Pew Research Center. http://www.journalism.org/node/6757. Also from, 'News America Publishing Inc. History', *Funding Universe*, http://www.fundinguniverse.com/company-histories/news-america-publishing-inc-history/

Page 40: 'Find a good murder', Rodney Lever, 'A Good Murder', *Independent Australia.net*, 3 September 2012, http://www.independentaustralia.net/2012/australian-identity/australian-history/a-good-murder/

Page 41: 'LYRIC MAY YIELD SON OF SAM CLUE', Jonathan Mahler, 'What Rupert Wrought', *New York*, New York, 11 April 2005, http://nymag.com/nymetro/news/people/features/11673/

Page 42: 'I will not have our children walking down on their way to school'. This quote comes from, 'Who's Afraid of Rupert Murdoch?' *Frontline*, WGBH, Boston, 1995, http://www.pbs.org/wgbh/pages/frontline/programs/transcripts/1404.html. A similar story is told in, Thomas Kiernan, *Citizen Murdoch*, Dodd, Mead & Company, Inc., New York, 1986, p 224.

Page 42: 'From what I've seen of Murdoch's papers in this country', 'Mike Royko 1932–1997 Newspaper Legend Mike Royko Dies, Pulitzer Prize-winning Columnist Was The Voice Of Chicago For More Than 30 Years', *Chicago Tribune*, 30 April 1997. See also Roger Ebert, 'The Dirty Digger', *Roger Ebert's Journal*, http://www.rogerebert.com/rogers-journal/the-dirty-digger

CHAPTER 3   PLAYING POLITICS

Page 43: 'He said, "Congressman, this is Rupert"', *Frontline*, WGBH, Boston, 2012.

Page 44: 'In the twenty-day-long Democratic primary campaign…the *Post* gave Koch four favourable front-page stories', George Munster , *Rupert Murdoch, A Paper Prince*, Viking, Melbourne, 1985, pp 171–4.

Page 44: 'I think he loves the idea that presidents and prime ministers pick up the phone…', *Frontline*, 1995, *op cit*.

Page 45: 'Rupert is a power junkie…', Munster, *op cit*.

Page 45: 'Politicians live by fragile reputations…', Munster, *op cit*.

Page 45: 'Following a face-to-face meeting', Wayne Barrett, 'Rudy's Cozy Murdoch Ties', *Daily Beast*, New York, 21 July 2011, http://www.thedailybeast.com/articles/2011/07/21/rupert-murdoch-scandal-rudy-giuliani-s-ties-to-newscorp.html

Page 46: 'I put him there and I'll put him out', Geoffrey Serle , *Australian Dictionary of Biography*, Vol 10, Melbourne University Press, Melbourne, 1986, http://adb.anu.edu.au/biography/murdoch-sir-keith.arthur-7693

Page 46: '…a second-hand society, a reflection of another hemisphere', from Rupert Murdoch's Australia Day speech, 1972, quoted in Simon Regan, *Rupert Murdoch: a business biography*, Angus & Robertson, Sydney, 1976, pp 98–100. A good account of the campaign can be found in Munster, *op cit*, pp 99–103.

Page 47: '…"ferocious", "unfair" and "undoubtedly in breach of journalistic ethics"', Max Suich, *Frontline*, 1995, *op cit*.

Page 47: '..."blind, biased, tunnel-visioned, ad hoc, logically confused and relentless"', Munster, *op cit*, p 110.

Page 48: '...*The Australian*'s coverage was overwhelmingly favourable to Gough's rival', Munster, *op cit*, p 111.

Page 48: 'Journalists...were given specific instructions,' *ibid*.

Page 48: 'You saw the people on the street, all carrying their red flags, rent-a-picket stuff', 'Who's Afraid of Rupert Murdoch?' *Panorama*, BBC TV, London, 1981.

Page 49: 'Maggie knew how important *The Sun*'s support could be and went out of her way to flatter the editor, Larry Lamb', Peter Chippindale and Chris Horrie, *Stick it Up Your Punter, The Rise and Fall of The Sun*, Heinemann, London, 1990, p 56.

Page 50: 'Are you still pushing that bloody woman?' James Thomas , *Popular Newspapers, the Labour Party and British Politics*, Routledge, Abingdon, 2005, p 77.

Page 50: 'Why are you so opposed to Rupert? He is going to get us in', Norman Fowler, 'In the post-Murdoch era, we must reform media ownership', *The Guardian*, London, 11 May 2102, http://www.guardian.co.uk/commentisfree/2012/may/11/post-murdoch-reform-media-ownership

Page 50: 'We depend on him to fight for us. *The Sun* is marvellous', Sarah Curtis, ed., *The Journals of Woodrow Wyatt: Vol 1*, Macmillan, London, 1998, p 316.

Page 51: 'He has on the whole, a pleasing character and has luck on his side', letter from Sir Denis Hamilton, chairman of Times Newspaper Holdings Ltd, to the directors, Thomson British Holdings, 16 January 1981, Exhibit KRM5 to witness statement of Keith Rupert Murdoch, 12 April 2012, Leveson Inquiry, http://www.levesoninquiry.org.uk/wp-content/uploads/2012/04/Exhibit-KRM–5.pdf.   There is a list of all the relevant Times documents supplied to Leveson at http://www.levesoninquiry.org.uk/wp-content/uploads/2012/04/Index-to-KRM-Exhibits.pdf

Page 52: '...would not be allowed to buy another successful daily newspaper', Jonathan Aitken MP, *Hansard*, House of Commons, London, 27 January 1981, Exhibit KRM12, Leveson Inquiry, *op cit*, http://www.levesoninquiry.org.uk/wp-content/uploads/2012/04/Exhibit-KRM-12.pdf

Page 53: 'The purpose of this meeting...Mrs Thatcher listened with interest, but "did no more than wish him well"', Exhibit KRM14, Leveson Inquiry, *op cit*, http://www.levesoninquiry.org.uk/wp-content/uploads/2012/04/Exhibit-KRM-14.pdf.

Page 53: 'The official history of *The Times* asserted baldly that Rupert and Maggie "had no communication whatsoever" during the bid. The source of this claim, which was clearly false, was Rupert Murdoch himself'. See Graham Stewart, *The History of The Times: The Murdoch Years, Volume 7*, p 29 and footnote 75, which gives the source as an interview with Rupert Murdoch in 2003.

Page 54: 'I reminded Rupert during the evening how at his request and at my instigation she (Mrs Thatcher) had stopped *The Times* acquisition', Wyatt, *op cit*.

Page 54: 'I had all the rules bent for him over *The Times* and *Sunday Times*', Wyatt, *op cit*, *Vol 3*, London, 2000.

Page 54: 'These reveal that Biffen was initially minded to refer the bid to the commission', Exhibit KRM10, Leveson Inquiry, *op cit*, http://www.levesoninquiry. org.uk/wp-content/uploads/2012/04/Exhibit-KRM-10.pdf

Page 54: 'And the Cabinet minutes tend to confirm this verdict', Exhibit KRM16, Leveson Inquiry, *op cit*, http://www.levesoninquiry.org.uk/wp-content/ uploads/2012/04/Exhibit-KRM-16.pdf

Page 55: 'Six "national directors" of Times Newspapers Holdings were therefore required to "agree"', Exhibit KRM6, Leveson Inquiry, *op cit*, http://www. levesoninquiry.org.uk/wp-content/uploads/2012/04/Exhibit-KRM-6.pdf

Page 55: 'Would you play any part in determining', *Panorama*, BBC TV, London, 1981, *op cit*.

Page 55: 'The plain fact', *Hansard*, House of Commons, 27 January 1981, KRM12, *op cit*.

Page 56: 'I give instructions to my editors all round the world', Harold Evans, *Good Times, Bad Times*, Coronet Books, London, 1983, pp 489–90.

Page 57: 'This great distinguished man', Harold Evans, Transcript of Evidence, Leveson Inquiry, 17 May 2012, p 16, http://www.levesoninquiry.org.uk/wp-content/ uploads/2012/05/Transcript-of-Afternoon-Hearing–17–May–20124.pdf

Page 58: 'We employed 300 people to print the paper; we only needed 80', *Frontline*, 1995, *op cit*.

Page 58: 'He made it clear to me one night in late 1985', Andrew Neil, Witness Statement, Leveson Inquiry, 9 July 2012, http://www.levesoninquiry.org.uk/ wp-content/uploads/2012/07/Witness-statement-of-Andrew-Neil.pdf

Page 62: 'You could say that was a mistake', David Mellor, Transcript of Evidence, Leveson Inquiry, 26 June 2012, p 23, http://www.levesoninquiry.org.uk/ wp-content/uploads/2012/06/Transcript-of-Afternoon-Hearing–26-June–2012. pdf

Page 62: 'There was one person that I had to go and see...and that was Rupert Murdoch', *ibid*, p 28.

Page 62: 'The most incredible aspect I have seen in my lifetime', *Frontline*, 2012, *op cit*.

Page 63: 'I think the important thing is that there be plenty of newspapers', *Panorama*, BBC TV, 1969, *op cit*.

CHAPTER 4 THE SUN KING

Page 65: '*The Sun* King is everywhere, even when he is nowhere', Andrew Neil, *Full Disclosure*, Macmillan, London, 1996, p 160.

Page 65: 'I love them, I enjoy them', *Panorama*, BBC TV, London, 1981.

Page 67: 'For the next three months the book scored not a single mention…', Jonathon Gatehouse, *Macleans*, Toronto, 18 July 2011, http://www2.macleans.ca/2011/07/18/murdochs-day-of-reckoning/. Also foreword to paperback edition, Michael Wolff, *The Man who Owns the News*, Broadway, New York, 2010.

Page 68: 'All life revolves around *The Sun* King', Andrew Neil , *op cit*, p 160.

Page 68: 'Rupert seemed to be everywhere and nowhere', Rodney Lever, 'Rupert Murdoch's crazy house', *Independent Australia.net*, 15 September 2012, http://www.independentaustralia.net/2012/politics/rupert-murdochs-crazy-house/

Page 69: 'He would bark down the phone', Peter Chippindale and Chris Horrie, *Stick it Up Your Punter: The Rise and Fall of The Sun*, Heinemann, London, 1990, p 31.

Page 69: 'Murdoch without a telephone was like an alcoholic without a drink', Bruce Dover , Rup*ert's Adventures in China*, Viking, Melbourne, 2008, p 127.

Page 70: 'Rebekah Brooks…was also in constant phone contact', Rebekah Brooks, Transcript of Evidence, Leveson Inquiry, morning, 17 May 2012, p 19, http://www.levesoninquiry.org.uk/wp-content/uploads/2012/05/Transcript-of-Morning-Hearing–11-May–2012.pdf

Page 71: 'He knew what he was looking for', said Deamer', *Panorama*, 1981, *op cit*.

Page 71: 'Oh, he's a tremendous sacker', *ibid*.

Page 75: 'By mid–2012, these TV and movie businesses made up around three-quarters of News Corp's now US\$60 billion market capitalisation', News Corp Annual Report 2012, p16. The share price in mid–2012 was around US\$25; hence the group was worth US\$20 billion more than a year earlier.

Page 76: 'Most boards meet to make decisions', Andrew Neil, 'Murdoch and Me', *Vanity Fair*, New York, December 1996, http://www.vanityfair.com/business/features/1996/12/rupert-murdoch-199612

CHAPTER 5   LACHLAN

Page 81: 'Lachlan will take over', Mathew Horsman, *Sky High, The Inside Story of BSkyB*, Orion Business Books, London, 1997, p 189.

Page 82: 'She branded him a dirty old man when he married Wendi Deng', *Dynasties*, 'The Murdochs', ABC TV, Sydney, 17 July 2002

Page 83: 'I thought she was a very pretty girl', Andrea Chambers, 'Now There's a New Murdoch in the World of Publishing—Rupert's Novelist Wife, Anna', *People*, New York, 28 October 1985, http://www.people.com/people/archive/article/0,,20092042,00.html

Page 84: 'Personal modesty is becoming', *Dynasties*, 'The Murdochs', ABC TV, *op cit*.

Page 84: '…until their father appeared on the cover of *Time* in 1977 as a monster King Kong', *Time*, New York, 17 January 1977, , http://www.coverbrowser.com/covers/time/57#i2815

Page 84: 'Liz, James and I would come up for breakfast before we had to get the bus to school', Julie Browning and Laurie Critchley, *Dynasties*, ABC Books, Sydney 2002, pp 197–8.

Page 85: '...to challenge the old world order on behalf of the people', Elisabeth Murdoch, James Mactaggart Lecture, Edinburgh, 23 August 2012, http://www.edinburghguide.com/video/11381-videotranscriptelisabethmurdochsmactaggartlecture

Page 85: 'My father would come home', Browning and Critchley, *op cit*, p 196.

Page 86: 'Is Daddy going deaf?' *Sunday Express*, London, 7 July 1985, quoted in William Shawcross, *Rupert Murdoch, the Making of a Media Empire*, Simon & Schuster, New York, 1992, p 220.

Page 86: 'It was always part of my universe,' Marianne Macdonald, 'Elisabeth Murdoch—Rupert's screen test', *The Observer*, London, 27 September 1998.

Page 86: 'I don't know of any son of any prominent media family', *Dynasties*, ABC TV, *op cit*.

Page 87: 'Lachlan, he has great leadership abilities', James Harding, 'Rupert Murdoch: Media King warms to his subjects', *Financial Times*, 11 June 2002.

Page 87: 'We're not losers at all', Macdonald, *op cit*.

Page 87: 'Tore it up, crushed it into a ball', Steve Fishman, 'The Boy Who Wouldn't Be King', *New York*, New York, 11 September 2005, http://nymag.com/nymetro/news/media/features/14302/

Page 88: 'In her novel *Family Business*', Anna Murdoch, *Family Business*, William Morrow & Co, New York, 1988.

Page 88: 'I'd like none of them to [succeed]', David Leser, 'Anna and her Kingdom', *Australian Women's Weekly*, Sydney, August 2001, http://davidleser.com/slippages/uploads/download/file/df–9–167–57.pdf

Page 91: 'News Corporation business is my life', *Dynasties*, ABC TV, *op cit*.

Page 95: 'Peter Chernin would not let him get involved in Hollywood', Sarah Ellison, 'The Rules of Succession', *Vanity Fair*, New York, December 2011, http://www.vanityfair.com/society/features/2011/12/murdoch-kids-201112. This article and several others are available as an e-book: Michael Wolff; Bryan Burrough; James Wolcott; Graydon Carter; Sarah Ellison, *RUPERT MURDOCH, The Master Mogul of Fleet Street: 24 Tales from the Pages of Vanity Fair* (Kindle Locations 5291–5292). *Vanity Fair*, Kindle Edition.

Page 96: 'Do the show. Don't listen to Lachlan', Steve Fishman, *op cit*.

CHAPTER 6   ELISABETH

Page 100: '...a runny-nosed kid with knee socks and a pom-pom, who was "completely uncool"', Judith Newman, 'Scions in Love, New Britain's ultimate power couple', *Vanity Fair*, New York, August 2001, http://www.vanityfair.com/politics/features/2001/08/murdoch–200108

Page 100: '...completely turned herself around', Marianne Macdonald, 'Elisabeth Murdoch—Rupert's screen test', *The Observer*, London, 27 September 1998.

Page 106: 'You don't need a fucking MBA', Q&A with Steve Hewlett, Edinburgh TV Festival, 24 August 2012; 'Elisabeth Murdoch discusses succession', *Variety*, New York, 24 August 2012, http://variety.com/2012/tv/news/elisabeth-murdoch-discusses-succession–1118058257/

Page 108: 'Dad, you are so pissed at me now', Sarah Ellison, 'The Rules of Succession', *Vanity Fair*, New York, December 2011.

Page 109: '...skin-tight Agnes B leather pants', Newman, *op cit*.

Page 110: 'I'll never leave the family business', Janine Gibson and Matt Wells, *The Guardian*, London, 8 May 2000, http://www.guardian.co.uk/media/2000/may/08/newscorporation.broadcasting

Page 110: 'She is very ambitious, very ambitious', David Leser, '*The Modest Matriarch*', *Australian Women's Weekly*, June 2003, http://davidleser.com/slippages/uploads/download/file/df–9–168–58.pdf

Page 111: 'I called Dad because I was so excited about it', this version from Ken Auletta, 'The Heiress, The rise of Elisabeth Murdoch', *New Yorker*, New York, 10 December 2012, http://www.newyorker.com/reporting/2012/12/10/121210fa_fact_auletta

Page 111: 'She wants to be sure she has been successful in her own right', David D Kirkpatrick, 'Murdoch Gets a Jewel. Who'll Get His Crown?' *New York Times*, New York, 28 December 2003, http://www.nytimes.com/2003/12/28/business/murdoch-gets-a-jewel-who-ll-get-his-crown.html?pagewanted=all&src=pm

Page 112: 'Originally an Elizabethan house'. See history in Walter F Godfrey, Burford Priory, 1939, Oxford Historical Society, *Oxoniensia*, February 1939, http://oxoniensia.org/volumes/1939/godfrey.pdf

Page 112: '...the world's most powerful blonde', *Sydney Morning Herald*, 9 October 2006, 'Blonde power: the top 10', http://www.smh.com.au/news/people/blonde-power-the-top–10/2006/10/09/1160246054492.html

Page 112: 'If the media is the new royalty', 'London's 1000 Most Influential People, 2007', *Evening Standard*, London, 9 October 2007, http://www.standard.co.uk/news/social-london–6636437.html

CHAPTER 7　JAMES

Page 116: '...which counts the celebrated Winkelvoss twins amont its members'. The Winkelvoss twins were made famous by the film *Social Network*, which told the story of Facebook and its founder, Mark Zuckerburg. Tyler and Cameron Winkelvoss sued Zuckerburg for failing to give them a share of the social networking business, started at Harvard, which they claimed was based on their original idea. They won US$65 million in an out-of-court settlement. http://online.wsj.com/article/SB1000087239639044443350457765175066207097 4.html?KEYWORDS=Winklevoss

Page 117: 'I wanted to break out on my own', Brett Thomas, '*Sunday Profile, James Who?*' *Sun Herald*, Sydney, 5 May 1996.

Page 117: '...a funky Tribeca loft situated between a porn shop and a falafel joint', Andrew Essex, 'A Grass-Roots Murdoch', *New Yorker*, New York, 16 September 1996, http://www.newyorker.com/archive/1996/09/16/1996_09_16_044_TNY_CARDS_000375860

Page 117: 'When tackled by a journalist about nepotism...he snapped back', *ibid*.

Page 119: '...a nice-enough young man but naïve and full of himself', David Higgins, 'A Long Way to the Bottom', *Good Weekend, Sydney Morning Herald*, Sydney, 9 November 2005, http://www.smh.com.au/articles/2005/11/09/1131407684176.html

Page 122: '...a change-the-world kind of product', Ken Auletta, 'The Last Sure Thing', *New Yorker*, New York, 19 November 1998, http://www.newyorker.com/archive/1998/11/09/1998_11_09_040_TNY_LIBRY_000016764

Page122: 'They were planning to go public that summer', *ibid*.

Page 123: 'Within a year none of these investments would be worth a fraction of the value paid for them', Bruce Dover, *Rupert's Adventures in China*, Viking, Melbourne, 2008, p 188.

Page 123: 'Think about China', Michelle Levander, 'Making of a Mogul', *Time Asia*, Hong Kong, 17 December 2001, http://www.time.com/time/magazine/article/0,9171,187658,00.html

Page 125: '...a political old monk in Gucci shoes', William Shawcross, 'Murdoch's New Life', *Vanity Fair*, New York, October 1999, in Sarah Ellison, *RUPERT MURDOCH, The Master Mogul of Fleet Street, 24 Tales from the Pages of Vanity Fair* (Kindle Locations 5291-5292*), Vanity Fair*, Kindle Edition.

Page 125: '...which he characterised as "dangerous" and "an apocalyptic cult"', Evelyn Iritani, 'News Corp. Heir Woos China With Show of Support', *Los Angeles Times*, Los Angeles, 23 March 2001, http://articles.latimes.com/2001/mar/23/business/fi–41576

Page 126: '...a "historic agreement" and a "milestone"', Dover *op cit*, p 210.

Page 126: '...hit a brick wall', *ibid*, p 271.

Page 128: 'I know everybody in the business', David D Kirkpatrick, 'Murdoch Gets a Jewel. Who'll Get His Crown?'*New York Times*, New York, 28 December 2003, http://www.nytimes.com/2003/12/28/business/murdoch-gets-a-jewel-who-ll-get-his-crown.html?pagewanted=all&src=pm

Page 128: 'His American wife...insisted he was romantic, who loved seersucker suits, panama hats and mint juleps', Wendy Goldman Rohm , *The Murdoch Mission, The digital transformation of a media empire*, John Wiley & Sons, New York, 2001.

Page 130: '...James delivered a scathing attack on the BBC at the annual Edinburgh TV Festival', James Murdoch, 'The Absence of Trust', James MacTaggart Lecture, Edinburgh, 28 August 2009, http://www.geitf.co.uk/sites/default/files/geitf/GEITF_MacTaggart_2009_James_Murdoch.pdf

Page 131: 'James's response was to storm into the paper's offices late at night', Simon Kelner, 'The day James and Rebekah revealed the arrogant Murdoch way of business', *The Guardian*, London, 24 April 2012, http://www.guardian.co.uk/commentisfree/2012/apr/24/james-murdoch-rebekah-brooks-simon-kelner-independen

Page 132: '...*The Guardian* newspaper revealed that in 2002 the *News of the World*', Nick Davies and Amelia Hill, 'Missing Milly Dowler's voicemail was hacked by *News of the World*', *The Guardian*, London, 5 July 2011 (first published on the paper's website at 16.29, 4 July), http://www.guardian.co.uk/uk/2011/jul/04/milly-dowler-voicemail-hacked-news-of-world

Page 135: '..."deliberate obfuscation, "collective amnesia" and attempting "to conceal the truth', James Robinson, '*News of the World* phone-hacking scandal: the verdicts', *The Guardian*, London, 24 February 2010, http://www.guardian.co.uk/media/2010/feb/24/phone-hacking-scandal-mps-verdicts

CHAPTER 8   TABLOID TALES

Page 139: 'This is what we do', *The Telegraph*, London, 6 September 2002, http://www.telegraph.co.uk/news/uknews/1406429/Pottergate-we-publish-the-secret-tapes.html

Page 139: 'Ethics?', Peter Chippindale and Chris Horrie, *Stick It Up Your Punter, The Rise and Fall of the Sun*, Heinemann, London, 1990, p 350.

Page 140: 'GEORGE IN NEW SEX SHAME', Neville Thurlbeck, 'George's Sex Shame, EXCLUSIVE: Caught "cruising" in woods', *News of the World*, London, 23 July 2006.

Page 141: 'RANDY ANDY's TEENY WEENY TARTAN HANKY SPANKY', Neville Thurlbeck, *News of the World*, London, 9 July 2006.

Page 141: '...EXCLUSIVE on the star of *The Trip*', Amanda Evans, Georgina Dickinson, 'The shocking hidden world of Alan Partridge star. EXCLUSIVE', *News of the World*, London, 11 June 2006.

Page 142: ' 'Russell B-randy 3am he beds Kimberley 12pm he smooches Sadie', *News of the World*, London, 2 July 2006.

Page 142: 'FLIRTY HARRY TRIED TO DO DIRTY WITH ME', *News of the World*, London, 2 July 2006.

Page 143: 'It was just water off a duck's back', Jacques Peretti, 'The Mogul who Screwed the News', Channel 4, London, 27 July 2011.

Page 143: 'I was utterly terrified', Witness statement of Anne Diamond, 11 November 2011, Leveson Inquiry, http://www.levesoninquiry.org.uk/wp-content/uploads/2011/11/Witness-Statement-of-Anne-Diamond1.pdf

Page 143: '...Britain's Press Council later ruled *The Sun*'s article to be, "an irresponsible and grievous intrusion into privacy"', *ibid.*

Page 143: 'His ex-butler, Philip Townsend, told Channel 4', Peretti, *op cit.*

Page 144: 'Having asked that one question of Murdoch', Diamond, *op cit.*

Page 144: 'Even when you see someone's life has been stomped on', BBC TV, 1989, Adam Curtis, *op cit*, http://www.bbc.co.uk/programmes/p00dr991.

Page 145: 'We have pictures of him', *Frontline*, op cit, 2012.

Page 145: '…most entertaining and caustic on the subject of other people's losses, lapses and screw-ups', Michael Wolff, *The Man who Owns the News*, Random House, New York, 2008, p 19.

Page 145: 'It was utterly horrifying at times', Witness statement of Charlotte Maria Church, 10 November 2011, Leveson Inquiry, http://www.levesoninquiry.org.uk/wp-content/uploads/2011/11/Witness-Statement-of-Charlotte-Church.pdf

Page 146: 'CHURCH's 3 IN-A-BED COCAINE SHOCK', *News of the World*, London, 11 December 2005.

Page 146: 'The *News of the World* wanted an exclusive story of her breakdown', Church, Leveson Inquiry, *op cit.*

Page 146: 'Singer Charlotte Church's distraught mum', 'How Charlotte saved my life. SUICIDE BID, SECRET SELF-HARM and KINKY SEX—Star's mum tells all', *News of the World*, London, 18 December 2005.

Page 146: 'This sequence of events drove my mother to additional self-harming', Church, Leveson Inquiry, *op cit.*

Page 147: 'He's afraid of the unions, afraid of the Russians, hates the queers', Chippindale and Horrie, *op cit*, p 148.

Page 147: 'ELTON IN VICE BOYS SCANDAL', Chippindale and Horrie, *op cit*, Chapter 14: 'Elton John Ate my Brother'.

Page 147: 'Yet MacKenzie went ahead and ran it anyway,' Kelvin MacKenzie told the Leveson Inquiry's seminar on press standards on 13 October 2011: 'Basically my view was that if it sounded right it was probably right and therefore we should lob it in', http://www.guardian.co.uk/media/2011/oct/13/kelvin-mackenzie-leveson-inquiry

Page 149: 'A dozen years later, Murdoch's biographer, William Shawcross, challenged Murdoch about this sort of journalism in an interview for *Vanity Fair*', William Shawcross, *Vanity Fair*, *op cit*, October 1999.

Page 150: 'The tale of Mosley's NAZI DEATH CAMP ORGIES', *Max Mosley v News Group Newspapers*, Approved Judgement, Justice Eady, High Court of Justice, Queen's Bench Division, London, 24 July 2008, http://news.bbc.co.uk/2/shared/bsp/hi/pdfs/24_07_08mosleyvnewsgroup.pdf

Page 151: 'It was like "coming home and finding your front door open and everything in your house removed by thieves"', House of Commons Culture Committee, *Press standards, privacy and libel, Second Report of Session 2009–10, Volume II, Oral and written evidence*, Ev 56, Max Mosley, q127, 10 March 2009, http://www.publications.parliament.uk/pa/cm200910/cmselect/cmcumeds/362/362ii.pdf

Page 153: 'The *News of the World*'s claim that he was a Nazi sympathiser had been repeated in a second series of articles', Eady Judgement, *op cit*.

Page 154: 'In particular, the judge suggested'. In his evidence to the Leveson Inquiry in April 2012, Rupert Murdoch was asked whether he had read a letter that Max Moseley wrote to him after the court case in March 2011. He said he had been 'out of town' when it was sent and that it had been dealt with by News International's CEO at the time (Rebekah Brooks). It had been brought to his attention, Murdoch said, the day before giving evidence. He was then asked if he was aware that Justice Eady had accused his journalists at the *News of the World* of blackmail. He replied: 'I am now.' Finally, he was asked: 'Have you read Mr Justice Eady's judgement?' Murdoch replied: 'No.' Leveson Inquiry, Minutes of Oral Evidence, 26 April 2012, pp 48–9, http://www.levesoninquiry.org.uk/wp-content/uploads/2012/04/Transcript-of-Morning-Hearing-26-April-2012.pdf

Page 156: 'On one memorable occasion', Hayley Barlow, 'Betrayed by a belligerent old man on the brink', *The Independent*, London, 27 April 2012, http://www.independent.co.uk/voices/commentators/hayley-barlow-betrayed-by-a-belligerent-old-man-on-the-brink-7682541.html

CHAPTER 9   RUPERT'S REDTOP QUEEN

Page 159: 'She was like the Queen Bee and we were the workers', McMullan to author.

Page 160: 'Dig out a copy of the *Warrington Guardian*', *Warrington Guardian*, 15 April 1965, p 2.

Page 160: '...and when the local paper announced her engagement in 1996 to a TV soapie star, Ross Kemp, he admitted he'd never even met his daughter's beau'. John Wade told the paper he was surprised to hear Rebekah was engaged, had no idea the pair were dating and had never met her fiancee.

Page 161: 'It was obvious she was going to get places in life', Edward Stourton, 'Profile: Rebekah Brooks, ex-News International chief', BBC.co.uk, 24 July 2012, http://www.bbc.co.uk/news/uk-politics-13117456.

Page 163: 'She was very tactile', Suzanna Andrews, 'Untangling Rebekah Brooks', *Vanity Fair*, New York, February 2012, http://www.vanityfair.com/business/2012/02/rebekah-brooks-201202

Page 164: 'There are 110,000 child sex offenders in Britain', 'NAMED, SHAMED', *News of the World*, London, 23 July 2000.

Page 164: 'Four families in the town were forced to flee'; also 'In south London, another man sought police protection' letterboxes', 'Police condemn vigilante violence', BBC.co.uk, 4 August 2000. Other violent incidents, 'Mob mistakes man for sex abuser', BBC.co.uk, 25 July 2000; 'Vigilante attack on innocent man', BBC.co.uk, 25 July 2000; Rebecca Allison, 'Doctor driven out of home by vigilantes', *The Guardian*, London, 30 August 2000, http://news.bbc.co.uk/2/hi/uk_news/865633.stm

Page 165: 'Our job now is to force the government to act', '"Sarah's Law" backing demanded', BBC.co.uk, 4 August 2000, http://news.bbc.co.uk/2/hi/uk_news/866397.stm

Page 165: 'Four days after the name and shame campaign was called off', Nigel Bunyan, 'Persecuted paedophile "kills himself"', *The Telegraph*, London, 9 August 2000, http://philia.ws/pvap/uknamene.htm

Page 166: 'I asked to see how they screened Boy Scouts leaders', Paul McMullan to author.

Page 166: 'We pay big money for sizzling shots of showbiz love-cheats', *News of the World*, London, 24 October 2004, quoted in Peter Jukes , *The Fall of the House of Murdoch*, Unbound, London, 2012, p 55.

Page 167: 'We bought up Princess Di's security team', Paul McMullan to author.

Page 168: 'The culture did change when I first joined', Sharon Marshall, Transcript of Evidence, Leveson Inquiry, 20 December 2011, p 43, http://www.levesoninquiry.org.uk/wp-content/uploads/2011/12/Transcript-of-Morning-Hearing-20-December-2011.pdf

Page 168: 'Hacks are pushed by deadlines, pushed to fill the paper', Sharon Marshall, *Tabloid Girl*, Sphere, London, 2010.

Page 168: 'There was massive pressure from the top to break stories', Witness statement of Matt Driscoll, Leveson Inquiry, 12 November 2011, http://www.levesoninquiry.org.uk/wp-content/uploads/2011/12/Witness-Statement-of-Matthew-Driscoll.pdf

Page 169: 'Everything emanates from the editor', Ian Edmondson, Transcript of Evidence, Leveson Inquiry, 9 February 2012, p 73, http://www.levesoninquiry.org.uk/wp-content/uploads/2012/02/Transcript-of-Morning-Hearing-9-February-2012.pdf

Page 169: '... Peter Chippindale and Chris Horrie's seminal book, *Stick it up Your Punter*', Peter Chippindale and Chris Horrie, , *Stick it up Your Punter, The Rise and Fall of The Sun*, Heinemann, London, 1990.

Page 170: 'Amazed, angry and incredulous, he had phoned Neville Thurlbeck the next day to see whether she was serious', 'Pottergate: we publish the secret tapes', *The Telegraph*, London, 6 September 2002, http://www.telegraph.co.uk/news/uknews/1406429/Pottergate-we-publish-the-secret-tapes.html

Page 170: 'That is just ridiculous', Ciar Byrne, 'Former NoW journalist reignites Harry Potter row', *The Guardian*, London, 28 August 2002, http://www.guardian.co.uk/media/2002/aug/28/newsoftheworld.september112001

Page 170: 'Complete drivel', *ibid*.

Page 170: 'If he doesn't get into that river', Don Van Natta Jr., Jo Becker and Graham Bowley, 'Tabloid Hack Attack on Royals, and Beyond', *New York Times*, New York, 1 September 2010, http://www.nytimes.com/2010/09/05/magazine/05hacking-t.html?pagewanted=all&_r=0

Page 171: 'You can't get through the day on a tabloid newspaper if you don't lie, if you don't deceive', 'I made up stories for *News of the World*—Graham Johnson', BBC TV, 12 May 2012, http://www.bbc.co.uk/news/world-us-canada–18044696

Page 171: 'Almost all stories that you worked on involved the use of private detectives', Cass Jones, 'Former *News of the World* reporter claims journalists made up stories', *The Guardian*, London, 12 May 2012, http://www.guardian.co.uk/media/2012/may/12/news-of-the-world-made-up-stories

Page 171: 'Fleet Street's roaring trade in confidential information was first exposed in March 2003', See Tom Watson, and Martin Hickman, *Dial M for Murdoch*, Allen Lane, London, 2012, Chapter 3; also *What Price Privacy?* Information Commissioner's Office, London, May 2006, Chapter 5, http://www.ico.org.uk/~/media/documents/library/corporate/research_and_reports/what_price_privacy.ashx

Page 172: '...the stories he chased were typical tabloid fare', Nick Davies, 'Operation Motorman: the full story revealed', *The Guardian*, London, 31 August 2009, http://www.guardian.co.uk/media/2009/aug/31/press-privacy-information-commmissioner.

Page 173: '...Greg Miskiw, still managed to be one of Whittamore's best customers', Minutes of Evidence, Nick Davies, House of Commons Culture Committee, 14 July 2009, Q1212, http://www.publications.parliament.uk/pa/cm200910/cmselect/cmcumeds/362/9071401.htm. See also Q1679–81 Adam Price MP questions to Andy Coulson, 21 July 2009, http://www.publications.parliament.uk/pa/cm200910/cmselect/cmcumeds/362/9072101.htm

Page 174: 'Asked by Chris Bryant MP whether the *News of the World* had ever paid private detectives', House of Commons Culture Committee, Minutes of Evidence, 11 March 2003, Q466–469. http://www.publications.parliament.uk/pa/cm200203/cmselect/cmcumeds/458/3031115.htm. Watch it here: http://www.youtube.com/watch?v=v1AJjnl2y8U.

Page 175: 'I'D LOVE A GOOD LONG F***', First witness statement of Chris Bryant MP (and exhibits), Leveson Inquiry: *Culture, Practices and Ethics of the Press*, 2 May 2012. http://www.levesoninquiry.org.uk/wp-content/uploads/2012/07/Witness-Statement-by-Chris-Bryant-MP.pdf.

CHAPTER 10   GOTCHA

Page 177: 'They are confident they have Clive and GM bang to rights on the palace intercepts', Tom Crone email to Andy Coulson, 15 September 2006, 'Phone hacking: *News of the World* lawyer's email to editor—full text', *The Guardian*, London, 27 February 2012, http://www.guardian.co.uk/media/2012/feb/27/phone-hacking-news-world-email

Page 177: '...*The Sun*day tabloid published a short story in its *Blackadder* column about the heir to the British throne', Clive Goodman, *Blackadder*, *News of the World*, London, 6 November 2005, p 32, http://s.telegraph.co.uk/graphics/viewer.html?doc=215871-princewilliam

Page 178: "CHELSY TEARS A STRIP OFF HARRY', Clive Goodman and Neville Thurlbeck, *News of the World*, London, 9 April 2006.

Page 178: 'The main concern of Operation Caryatid was that members of the Royal Family might be at risk'. The best account of the police hacking investigation is in the Leveson Report, *An Inquiry into the Culture, Practices and Ethics of the Press*, The Right Honourable Lord Justice Leveson, London, November 2012, Volume I, Chapter 4, http://www.official-documents.gov.uk/document/hc1213/hc07/0780/0780_iv.pdf; Greater detail of the investigation can be found in written and oral evidence given to the inquiry by DI Mark Maberly, http://www.levesoninquiry.org.uk/wp-content/uploads/2012/02/Witness-Statement-of-DI-Mark-Maberly.pdf; DCS Keith Surtees, particularly in the decision logs of Operation Caryatid, which is Exhibit KS1 to his second written statement, http://www.levesoninquiry.org.uk/wp-content/uploads/2012/11/Exhibit-KS1-to-second-ws-of-Keith-Surtees.pdf; and in the summary given by Surtees to DAC John Yates in July 2009, which is Exhibit JY3A to the written statement of John Yates, http://www.levesoninquiry.org.uk/wp-content/uploads/2012/03/Exhibit-JMY3A–14.pdf. DAC John Yates's appearances before the House of Commons Culture Committee are also useful, as is DCS Philip Williams's evidence to Leveson.

Page 181: 'It, I think, had gone, quite frankly', DCS Keith Surtees, Transcript of Evidence, Leveson Inquiry, 29 February 2012, p 48, http://www.levesoninquiry.org.uk/wp-content/uploads/2012/02/Transcript-of-Afternoon-Hearing-29-February-2012.pdf

Page 181: '...promising him £7000 for information on a former professional footballer, Gordon Taylor.' The contract was with 'Paul Williams', an alias Mulcaire used. It said, *inter alia*, 'The *News of the World* agrees to pay a minimum sum of £7000 on publication of the story based on information provided by Mr Williams. The figure will be renegotiable on the basis of prominence given to the story.' House of Commons Culture Committee, *Press standards, privacy and libel*, London, 9 February 2010, p 97, http://www.publications.parliament.uk/pa/cm200910/cmselect/cmcumeds/362/362i.pdf

Page 184: '...News had hired a firm of criminal lawyers, Burton Copeland, to "help" the police with their inquiries.' Burton Copeland was a specialist in defending people accused of white-collar crime. 'For those who find themselves in the sights of the Serious Fraud Office...Burton Copeland is, more often than not, the first port of call,' said the UK's *Law Gazette*, noting that the firm had acted for the defence in most of the famous UK fraud trials. Helping police with their inquiries was not what the firm was paid to do, http://www.lawgazette.co.uk/news/the-trial-century-maxwell-case-lessons-be-learned-usa

Page 185: 'There was also no phone map, no floor plan, and no call data.' DCS Philip Williams and Assistant Commissioner John Yates both gave evidence about this to the House of Commons Culture Committee in September 2009. Yates told MPs: 'We clearly set out to the solicitors acting for the *News of the World*, and this was in September 2006, a range of issues that we wanted them to disclose to us, and we finished the letter by saying, "The investigation is attempting to identify all persons that may be involved, including fellow conspirators". One of the bullet points we looked for was: "Who does Mr Mulcaire work for? Has he completed work for other editors and journalists at the *News of the World*? Can we have a copy of any other records for work completed by Mulcaire for these editors and journalists, including the subjects on which you might have provided information?'" Q1890, Minutes of Evidence, House of Commons Culture Committee, 2 September 2009, http://www.publications.parliament.uk/pa/cm200910/cmselect/cmcumeds/362/9090214.htm

Williams read out a reply from the *News of the World* claiming: 'No documents exist recording any work completed by Mr Mulcaire, monitoring of Mr Mulcaire's return of work, reporting structure of any persons for whom Mr Mulcaire may have provided information. There is no floor plan. The telephone system installed at News Group Newspapers does not provide an itemised breakdown in respect of any particular extension number.' He then told MPs, 'What I would say is that they answered our questions by and large by saying, "We do not have it". Q1939, *op cit.*

Page 186: 'Headed, "Strictly private and confidential", it warned', Tom Crone email to Andy Coulson, 15 September 2006, 'Phone hacking: *News of the World* lawyer's email to editor—full text', *The Guardian*, London, 27 February 2012. The email was read to the Leveson Inquiry by Robert Jay QC.

Page 189: 'In his sentencing remarks, Justice Gross also flagged this point by noting that Mulcaire, "*had not dealt with Goodman but with others at News International*"', Leveson Report, Volume IV, Chapter 4, p308, http://www.official-documents.gov.uk/document/hc1213/hc07/0780/0780_iv.pdf.

Page 189: 'Crone later admitted', Tom Crone, Transcript of Evidence, Leveson Inquiry, 13 December 2011, p 95, , http://www.levesoninquiry.org.uk/wp-content/uploads/2011/12/Transcript-of-Afternoon-Hearing-13-December-20111.pdf

Page 190: 'But these weren't the only reasons to stop.' Early on in the investigation, the police were advised by the Crown Prosecution Service (wrongly) that Goodman could only be charged under the *Regulation of Investigatory Powers Act 2000* if he had listened to the message before its owner did. This was on the 'unopened letter' principle, that it is not an offence to read someone's private mail unless you slit open the envelope. This may have made it appear even more difficult to extend the investigation to hundreds of victims.

Page 190: 'As SO13's commander, Assistant Commissioner Peter Clarke, explained', House of Commons Home Affairs Committee, *Unauthorised Tapping Into or Hacking of Mobile Communications*, Oral Evidence, Peter Clarke, 12 July 2011, http://www.publications.parliament.uk/pa/cm201012/cmselect/cmhaff/uc907-v/uc90701.htm

CHAPTER 11 ONE ROGUE REPORTER

Page 193: 'Other members of staff were carrying out the same illegal procedures', Clive Goodman letter to Daniel Cloke, Head of Human Resources at News International, copied to Les Hinton, 2 March 2007. The letter was supplied to the Culture Committee by News International's lawyers, Harbottle & Lewis. James Robinson, 'Clive Goodman's letter to News International', *The Guardian*, London, 16 August 2010, http://www.guardian.co.uk/media/interactive/2011/aug/16/clive-goodman-letter-phone-hacking

Page 194: 'Tom Crone and the editor promised', *ibid.*

Page 194: 'The actions leading to this criminal charge were carried out with the full knowledge and support of xxxx', *ibid.* Names were removed to ensure criminal trials were not prejudiced.

Page 195: 'Even so, Abrahamson still had some concerns', Second Witness statement of Lawrence Abrahamson, Leveson Inquiry, 8 December 2011, http://www.levesoninquiry.org.uk/wp-content/uploads/2011/12/Second-Witness-Statement-of-Lawrence-Abramson.pdf

Page 195: 'A number of the emails suggested that *News of the World* journalists had been breaking the law'. The BBC's Robert Peston reported in July 2011 that: 'In one of the dynamite e-mails, Clive Goodman—the paper's disgraced former royal editor—was requesting cash from the newspaper's editor, Andy Coulson, to buy a confidential directory of the Royal Family's landline telephone numbers, and all the phone numbers—including mobiles—of the household staff'. It seems likely, but is not proven, that this was one of the batch that Harbottles examined, http://lawyerwatch.wordpress.com/2011/07/12/hackgate-ii-the-fight-back/

Page 196: 'As Chapman later admitted, the pay-off was made purely for "reputational" reasons', Jonathan Chapman, Transcript of Evidence, Leveson Inquiry, 14 December 2011, morning, p 41, http://www.levesoninquiry.org.uk/wp-content/uploads/2011/12/Transcript-of-Morning-Hearing-14-December-2011.pdf

Page 196: 'Illegal tapping by a private investigator...is not part of our culture anywhere in the world', Chris Tryhorn, 'Murdoch defends NoW journalists', *The Guardian*, London, 7 February 2007, http://www.guardian.co.uk/media/2007/feb/07/newsoftheworld.pressandpublishing

Page 197: 'I believe he was the only person, but that investigation, under the new editor, continues', Les Hinton, Minutes of Evidence, House of Commons Culture Committee, London, 6 March 2007, q95 http://www.publications.parliament.uk/pa/cm200607/cmselect/cmcumeds/375/375.pdf

Page 198: '...bombs under the newsroom floor', Colin Myler, Transcript of Evidence, Leveson Inquiry, 15 December 2011, p 10, http://www.levesoninquiry.org.uk/wp-content/uploads/2011/12/Transcript-of-Morning-Hearing-15-December-2011.pdf

Page 198: 'And nine years earlier he had provoked a huge row by publishing peephole pictures of Princess Di in a London gym', Nick Cohen, 'Sex, Di and the Mirror Man: Nick Cohen investigates the way press violation of privacy became front-page news', *The Independent*, London, 14 November 1993, http://www.independent.co.uk/news/uk/sex-di-and-the-mirror-man-nick-cohen-investigates-the-way-press-violation-of-privacy-became-frontpage-news–1504201.html

Page 199: '...an exceptional and unhappy event in the 163-year history of the *News of the World*', *PCC Report on Subterfuge and Newsgathering*, Press Complaints Commission, 18 May 2007, http://www.pcc.org.uk/assets/218/PCC_subterfuge_report.pdf

CHAPTER 12   BUYING SILENCE

Page 201: 'Our position is very perilous.', Tom Crone memo to Colin Myler and Farrer & Co, News International's lawyers, for use in meeting with James Murdoch to discuss Gordon Taylor hacking claim, 24 May 2008. House of Commons Culture Committee, *News International and Phone-hacking*, Vol I, May 2012, p 47. Full text is at committee's 'Attachments', JCP1, 2, 3, http://www.publications.parliament.uk/pa/cm201012/cmselect/cmcumeds/903/903we64.htm

Page 202: 'He is very single-minded and a very clear thinker', Sophie Barker, 'Murdoch's Heir Apparent?', *Intelligent Life*, Spring 2009, http://moreintelligentlife.com/story/invisible-mogul

Page 204: 'This is the transcript for Neville.' The full email has never been published. Its significance is that it was sent by a reporter at the *News of the World* to Mulcaire, and is supposedly on its way to another reporter at the *News of the World*, Neville Thurlbeck. It also contains the transcripts of intercepted voicemails on Gordon Taylor's and Joanne Armstrong's mobile phones. It shows that journalists at the *News of the World* other than Clive Goodman were involved in hacking phones with Glenn Mulcaire. It therefore nullifies the 'one rogue reporter' defence that News International continued to use for the next three years, until April 2011.

Page 205: 'This so-called "For Neville" email had been sent to Mulcaire by a second *News of the World* reporter, Ross Hindley.' Hindley was also known as Ross Hall. He was the nephew of a former *News of the World* editor, Phil Hall.

Page 205: 'Amongst the prosecution paperwork...was a contract dated 4th February', Tom Crone memo to Colin Myler and Farrer & Co, *op cit.*

Page 207: 'Spoke to James Murdoch', Attachments, *op cit*, JCP5–7.

Page 207: '... the legal opinion from Michael Silverleaf QC brought even more devastating news', *ibid* JCP 20–26.

Page 208: 'Taylor now wanted "seven figures not to open his mouth" ', *ibid*, JCP 11.

Page 208: 'Pike again took notes as Lewis laid out his demands', Written evidence submitted to the Culture Committee by Linklaters LLP, on behalf of the Management and Standards Committee, 12 December 2011, http://www.publications.parliament.uk/pa/cm201012/cmselect/cmcumeds/903/903we87.htm

Page 209: '…Myler forwarded it all to James Murdoch', *ibid.*

Page 209: 'No worries. I'm in during the afternoon', *ibid.*

CHAPTER 13   LIES, LIES, LIES

Page 213: 'All of these irresponsible and unsubstantiated allegations', News International statement in response to allegations in *The Guardian* that there were thousands of hacking victims and that the company had paid £1 million to keep victims quiet, http://www.newscorp.com/news/bunews_40.html

Page 213: '*The Guardian* newspaper dropped a bomb…', Nick Davies, 'Trail of hacking and deceit under nose of Tory PR chief', *The Guardian*, London, 9 July 2009, http://www.guardian.co.uk/media/2009/jul/08/murdoch-newspapers-phone-hacking

Page 214: 'By then, News had also issued a statement,' 'News International denies reporters hacked into phones: full statement', News International, *op cit*

Page 216: 'That it wasn't true, that there was no other evidence', James Murdoch, Transcript of Evidence, Leveson Inquiry, 24 April 2012, p 16.

Page 216: 'If that had happened I would know about it', Vidya Root and Robert Hutton, 'Murdoch Newspapers to Be Probed Over Hacking Claims', Bloomberg, 9 July 2009, http://www.bloomberg.com/apps/news?pid=newsarchive&sid=a1_Ce1OkPe8A

Page 216: 'And his response was soon delighting and shocking his critics on You Tube', Stuart Varney, Fox Business, 9 July 2009, http://www.youtube.com/watch?v=_0nN_snrOtk

Page 217: 'No additional evidence has come to light', 'New Phone Hack Inquiry Ruled Out', BBC TV News, 9 July 2009, http://news.bbc.co.uk/2/hi/8143120.stm

Page 218: 'There was no evidence to expand the investigation', Exhibit JMY3A–3 to Witness statement of John Michael Yates, Leveson Inquiry, http://www.levesoninquiry.org.uk/wp-content/uploads/2012/03/Exhibit-JMY3A–3.pdf. See also: Leveson Report, Vol I, Ch 4, pp 357–70; and John Yates, Transcript of Evidence, Leveson Inquiry, 1 March 2012, pp 70–1.

Page 219: 'Had there been evidence of tampering in the other cases', Andy Hayman, '*News of the World* investigation was no half-hearted affair', *The Times*, London, 11 July 2009.

Page 219: 'A week later, when DCS Williams and DS Surtees dug the files out of archives', Operation Caryatid—Briefing for ACSO John Yates', Exhibit JMY3A–14 to Witness Statement of John Yates, Leveson Inquiry, http://www.levesoninquiry.org.uk/wp-content/uploads/2012/03/Exhibit-JMY3A–14.pdf

Page 220: 'In the case of Assistant Commissioner John Yates', Yates oral evidence, *op cit*; also Neil Wallis, Transcript of Evidence, Leveson Inquiry, 12 December 2011, and both men's written statements to the inquiry, http://www.levesoninquiry.org.uk/wp-content/uploads/2011/12/Transcript-of-Afternoon-Hearing- 12-December-20111.pdf

Page 221: 'But it's obvious that his refusal to reopen the investigation, was "pretty crap" and "a poor decision"', Robert Mendick, Alasdair Palmer and Patrick Hennessy, 'John Yates: I failed victims of *News of the World* phone hacking', *The Telegraph*, London, 9 July 2011, http://www.telegraph.co.uk/news/uknews/phone-hacking/8628052/John-Yates-I-failed-victims-of-News-of-the-World-phone-hacking.html

Page 222: 'The Met's Commissioner, Sir Paul Stephenson, paid a visit to the newspaper's editor', 'Phone hacking: Met police put pressure on *Guardian* over coverage', *The Guardian*, London, 15 July 2011, http://www.guardian.co.uk/media/2011/jul/15/phone-hacking-met-police-guardian

Page 222: 'But Coulson, Crone and Myler nevertheless repeated the Murdoch mantra that Clive Goodman had acted alone'. The same litany of denials was offered up to the Press Complaints Commission, which was assured by Colin Myler that *The Guardian*'s allegations were, 'not just unsubstantiated and irresponsible, they were wholly false'. The PCC duly brought out a new report in November 2009 that not only swallowed News's version of events for a second time, but also took a swipe at *The Guardian*, saying: 'The PCC has seen no new evidence to suggest that the practice of phone-message tapping was undertaken by others beyond Goodman and Mulcaire, or evidence that the *News of the World* knew about Goodman and Mulcaire's activities ...' Indeed, having reviewed the matter, the Commission could not help but conclude that *The Guardian*'s stories did not live up to the dramatic billing they were initially given, http://www.pcc.org.uk/news/?article=NjAyOA

Page 223: 'I'm absolutely sure that Clive Goodman's case was a very unfortunate, rogue case', Andy Coulson, Minutes of Evidence, House of Commons Culture Committee, 21 July 2009, q1670, http://www.publications.parliament.uk/pa/cm200910/cmselect/cmcumeds/362/9072121.htm

Page 223: 'At no stage did any evidence arise that the problem of accessing by our reporters', Tom Crone, Minutes of Oral Evidence, House of Commons Culture Committee, 21 July 2009, q1339, http://www.publications.parliament.uk/pa/cm200809/cmselect/cmcumeds/uc275-xiii/uc27502.htm

Page 223: '...no evidence of anything going beyond', *ibid*, 1396.

Page 223: '...seized every available document', *ibid*, q1339.

Page 223: '...brought in Burton Copeland, an independent firm of solicitors to carry out an investigation', Andy Coulson, *op cit*, q1719, http://www.publications.parliament.uk/pa/cm200910/cmselect/cmcumeds/362/9072123.htm

Page 223: '...to go over everything and find out what had gone on', Crone, *op cit*, q1395.

Page 224: 'To give whatever facility the police required', *ibid*, q1384.

Page 224: 'This, of course, was totally untrue, as Burton Copeland would eventually admit', Written evidence submitted by BCL Burton Copeland to House of Commons Culture Committee, 30 August 2011, stated *inter alia*, 'BCL was not instructed to carry out an investigation into "phone hacking" at the *News* *of the World'*, http://www.publications.parliament.uk/pa/cm201012/cmselect/cmcumeds/903/903we46.htm

Page 224: 'Was the size of that payment greater in order that the proceedings should be kept secret?', Crone/Myler, *op cit*, q1333.

Page 224: 'I am not aware of any payment that has been made', *ibid*, q1411.

Page 225: '...Goodman and Mulcaire had both received settlements', Letter from Rebekah Brooks, CEO of News International, to John Whittingdale MP, Chairman of House of Commons Culture Committee, 4 November 2009, http://www.parliament.uk/documents/commons-committees/culture-media-sport/Rebekah_Brooks_to_Chairman_4_Nov_2009.pdf

Page 225: 'I am not going to discuss the terms of the agreement', Les Hinton, Examination of Witness, 15 September 2009, q2197, http://www.publications.parliament.uk/pa/cm200910/cmselect/cmcumeds/362/9091506.htm

Page 226: 'First of all, did you in any way pay for any of the legal fees for Clive Goodman or Glenn Mulcaire?', Les Hinton, *op cit*, q2117, http://www.publications.parliament.uk/pa/cm200910/cmselect/cmcumeds/362/9091502.htm

Page 227: 'And, while the MPs did ask Rebekah Brooks to appear, she simply refused'. MPs also tried to interview Ross Hindley, sender of the 'For Neville' email, but were told by Crone that he was backpacking around the world. Back in 2005, he had been just 16 and had been working on the paper for a month, the lawyer assured them, and he was really a messenger being trained as a reporter. This was nonsense. Ross Hall, as he was more often known, was 28 years old, and by 2005 had been contributing to the News of the World for years. He was arrested on 2 September 2011, but has since been told no charges will be brought.

Page 227: 'But she did have time to write a letter to the committee claiming', 'Rebekah Brooks's 2009 letter to John Whittingdale: *"The Guardian* has misled the British public"', *The Guardian*, London, 6 July 2011, http://www.guardian.co.uk/media/interactive/2011/jul/06/rebekah-brooks-email

Page 228: 'All I know is that when the [Culture, Media and Sport Committee] got onto all the hacking stuff', See Tom Watson and Martin Hickman, *Dial M for Murdoch*, Allen Lane, London, 2012, p 94. Thurlbeck claimed that this conversation was off-the-record, Andrew Pugh, 'Thurlbeck says Watson quoted off-the-record comments', *UK Press Gazette*, 20 April 2012, http://www.pressgazette.co.uk/node/49159

Page 228: 'The objective was to find as much embarrassing sleaze on', Neville Thurlbeck, 'Review: *Dial M for Murdoch* by Tom Watson and Martin Hickman', *New Statesman*, London, 3 May 2012, http://www.newstatesman.com/politics/uk-politics/2012/05/review-dial-m-murdoch-tom-watson-and-martin-hickman

Page 228: 'Mazher Mahmood, who was better known as the *News of the World*'s Fake Sheikh', Martin Hickman, 'Email trail: How Tom Watson was stalked', *The Independent*, London, 22 May 2012, http://www.independent.co.uk/news/media/press/email-trail-how-tom-watson-was-stalked-7771341.html

Page 229: 'Initially hired by Thurlbeck, he had subsequently been used by 27 named reporters', Witness Statement of Derek Frank Webb, Leveson Inquiry, http://www.levesoninquiry.org.uk/wp-content/uploads/2011/12/Witness-Statement-of-Derek-Webb.pdf; also Derek Webb, Transcript of Evidence, 15 December 2011, http://www.levesoninquiry.org.uk/wp-content/uploads/2011/12/Transcript-of-Afternoon-Hearing–15-December–20111.pdf

Page 230: 'She didn't like you at all', Watson and Hickman, *op cit*, p 281. Repeated in Witness Statement of Tom Watson MP, Leveson Inquiry, May 2012, http://www.levesoninquiry.org.uk/wp-content/uploads/2012/05/Witness-Statement-of-Tom-Watson-MP.pdf

Page 230: 'Rebekah will never forgive you for what you did to her Tony', Watson, Leveson, *ibid*

Page 230: '...the tabloid had branded him "poisonous", a "hatchet man", and a liar', *ibid*, pp 8–12. See also Watson, Leveson, *op cit*.

Page 231: 'Amazingly, Blair's senior adviser also found himself under attack', *ibid*, p 95.

CHAPTER 14   KEEPING IT BURIED

Page 233: 'We have repeatedly encountered an unwillingness to provide the detailed information', House of Commons Culture Committee, *Press standards, privacy and libel, Second Report of Session 2009–10,* 9 February 2010, para 495.

Page 233: 'Evidence we have seen', *ibid*, para 63.

Page 233: '...struck by the collective amnesia afflicting witnesses from the *News of the World*', *ibid*, para 442.

Page 234: 'The victims here are YOU, the public', quoted in, House of Commons Culture Committee, *News International and Phone-hacking, Eleventh Report of Session 2010–12,* 12 May 2012, para 24, http://www.publications.parliament.uk/pa/cm201012/cmselect/cmcumeds/903/903i.pdf

Page 235: 'FREDDIE STARR ATE MY HAMSTER'. The infamous headline was on *The Sun*'s front page March 1986. The story was a total fabrication, concocted by PR guru Max Clifford, who told Starr it would be good for his image.

Page 235: 'The so-called secret settlement wasn't secret for more than, I think, a day', Rod Tiffen, 'UK phone hacking victims' lawyer Charlotte Harris in Conversation: full transcript', *The Conversation*, Melbourne, 22 November 2012, http://theconversation.com/uk-phone-hacking-victims-lawyer-charlotte-harris-in-conversation-full-transcript-10880

Page 237: 'James would later be forced to admit that he knew about the Clifford settlement "in very general terms"', James Murdoch, Minutes of Oral Evidence, House of Commons Culture Committee, 11 November 2011, q1702, http://www.publications.parliament.uk/pa/cm201012/cmselect/cmcumeds/uc903-vi/uc90301.htm

Page 238: 'In September 2010, they published the results in a 5000-word investiga-tion', Don Van Natta Jr, Jo Becker and Graham Bowley, 'Tabloid Hack Attack on Royals, and Beyond', *New York Times*, New York, 1 September 2010.

Page 239: 'The paper was paying Glenn Mulcaire £2000 a week', Nick Davies, 'Phone hacking was rife at *News of the World*, claims new witness', *The Guardian*, London, 8 September 2010, http://www.guardian.co.uk/media/2010/sep/08/phone-hacking-news-of-the-world-witness

Page 240: 'We reject absolutely any suggestion or assertion', Culture Committee, *News International and Phone-hacking, op cit*, para 25.

Page 240: 'They've had six years to look at it', Eric Campbell, "Allo, 'Allo, 'Allo', *Foreign Correspondent*, ABC TV, 2 November 2010, http://www.abc.net.au/foreign/content/2010/s3055224.htm

Page 241: 'There was an incident more than five years ago', Stephen Mayne, '2010 News Corp AGM transcript', *Mayne Report*, 16 October 2010, http://www.maynereport.com/articles/2010/10/16–0311–8905.html

Page 243: 'If the deletion need to wait till tomorrow that is fine', Brian Cathcart, 'After the "for Neville" email they decided to wipe the database', 24 February 2012, http://hackinginquiry.org/comment/after-the-%E2%80%98for-neville%E2%80%99-email-they-decided-to-wipe-the-database/

Page 244: 'We will vigorously pursue the truth, and we will not tolerate wrong-doing', Rupert Murdoch, 'Rupert Murdoch's inaugural Margaret Thatcher lecture', *The Guardian*, London, 21 October 2010, http://www.guardian.co.uk/media/2010/oct/21/rupert-murdoch-inaugural-margaret-thatcher-lecture

Page 244: 'In mid-December, this damning new evidence was presented to the public', Nick Davies, 'Phone hacking approved by top *News of the World* executive—new files', *The Guardian*, London, 15 December 2010, http://www.guardian.co.uk/media/2010/dec/15/phone-hacking-sienna-miller-evidence

Page 245: 'I was absolutely clear in my mind at the beginning of that meeting', Keir Starmer QC, Transcript of Evidence, 4 April 2012, afternoon, p 53.

Page 245: '...Rupert Murdoch himself apologised "unreservedly" and promised to pay compensation', Robert Peston, '*News of the World* apologises for phone hacking scandal', BBC.co.uk, 8 April 2011, http://www.bbc.co.uk/news/uk-13014161. Despite the apology on 8 April and the promise to come clean, News still did not co-operate with police. When James Weatherup was arrested at home in an early morning raid, on 14 April, the *News of the World* quickly bagged up everything on his desk and gave it to Burton Copeland, who refused to hand it to the police. A furious Sue Akers threatened to charge the law firm's principal, Ian Burton, with obstruction of justice unless they handed it over.

Page 246: 'According to *Business Week*, who reconstructed the meeting in February 2012, Rebekah and Rupert took their places as hosts at each end of the table', Greg Farrell, 'Dinner at Rupert's', *Business Week*, 9 February 2012, http://www.businessweek.com/magazine/dinner-at-ruperts-02092012.html

CHAPTER 15 FAMILY FEUDS

Page 249: 'Rebekah has fucked the company', John Bingham, 'Phone Hacking: Rupert Murdoch's daughter in "furious" attack on Rebekah Brooks', *The Telegraph*, London, 15 July 2011. The quote has been denied by Elisabeth Murdoch; the reporter, John Bingham has told the author, 'She would say that, wouldn't she?' and says he stands by his story, http://www.telegraph.co.uk/news/uknews/phone-hacking/8639163/Phone-Hacking-Rupert-Murdochs-daughter-in-furious-attack-on-Rebekah-Brooks.html

Page 249: 'The report by Nick Davies and Amelia Hill that went up on *The Guardian*'s website', Nick Davies and Amelia Hill, 'Missing Milly Dowler's voicemail was hacked by *News of the World*', *The Guardian*, London, 5 July 2011 (but published on the paper's website at 16.29 on 4 July), http://www.guardian.co.uk/uk/2011/jul/04/milly-dowler-voicemail-hacked-news-of-world

Page 250: 'I had got through to her personal voice message. I jumped out of my seat and screamed', Witness Statement of Sally and Bob Dowler, Leveson Inquiry, 3 November 2011, http://www.levesoninquiry.org.uk/wp-content/uploads/2011/11/Witness-Statement-of-Sally-Bob-Dowler.pdf

Page 251: 'We're going to make it personal to you. We won't forget', Tom Watson and Martin Hickman, *Dial M for Murdoch*, Allen Lane, London, 2012, p 194.

Page 251: 'My heart goes out to the Dowler family', Martin Hickman & Cahal Milmo, 'MPs to grill officers who led bungled investigation', *The Independent*, London, 6 July 2011, http://www.highbeam.com/publications/the-independent-london-england-p6001/jul-6-2011

Page 252: 'It would in fact turn out The Guardian was wrong'. In May 2012, Det. Chief Inspector John MacDonald told the Leveson Inquiry that the truth about the deletion of Milly Dowler's phone messages would never be known. He said it was possible that two of the messages had been manually deleted, but the 'false-hope moment' was likely to have occurred after an automatic purge of messages by the phone company. 'Milly Dowler's phone messages a mystery, police say', BBC.co.uk, 9 May 2012, http://www.bbc.co.uk/news/uk-18002180

Page 253: 'To get the agency to give them more details', David Leigh, 'Phone hacking: *News of the World* journalists lied to Milly Dowler police', *The Guardian*, London, 23 January 2012, http://www.guardian.co.uk/media/2012/jan/23/phone-hacking-news-world-milly-dowler

Page 253: 'MESSAGES ON MOBILE PROBED', Steve Stecklow and Jeanne Whalen, 'Tabloid's Pursuit of Missing Girl Led to Its Own Demise', *Online Wall Street Journal*, 20 August 2011, http://online.wsj.com/article/SB100014240531119 03596904576516314142801424.html

Page 254: 'She also made it clear she had "spoken to Rupert Murdoch"', 'News International's Rebekah Brooks "won't resign"', Robert Peston, BBC.co.uk, http://www.bbc.co.uk/news/business-14026369

NOTES

Page 254: 'I hope that you all realise it is inconceivable that I knew or worse, sanctioned these appalling allegations', 'Milly Dowler hacking: Rebekah Brooks statement in full', BBC.co.uk, 5 July 2011, http://www.bbc.co.uk/news/uk-14033887

Page 254: 'Graham Foulkes…was horrified when he heard the news', '7/7 victim "filled with horror" at phone hacking', *Today*, BBC Radio 4, 6 July 2011, http://news.bbc.co.uk/today/hi/today/newsid_9531000/9531534.stm

Page 255: 'Rose Gentle…told the BBC she was, "Totally disgusted"', Karolina Tagaris, 'UK soldiers targeted in Murdoch phone-hacking scandal-media', Reuters, 6 July 2011, http://www.reuters.com/article/2011/07/07/newscorp-hacking-idUSLDE76600520110707

Page 255: 'Chaired by a distinguished senior judge, Lord Justice Brian Leveson, with powers to compel witnesses to appear'. Leveson's terms of reference were to inquire into relations between the press and politicians, and the press and police; to inquire into any failure of the regulatory system and any failure to deal with media misconduct; also to make recommendations in these areas, in particular by recommending a new regulatory system to prevent media misconduct. The inquiry was also tasked with examining criminal and improper conduct at News International and other newspaper organisations and its investigation by police and/or politicians. This second part of the inquiry will not begin until all criminal cases have been dealt with, which may not be till 2015 or even later. The full terms are at http://www.levesoninquiry.org.uk/about/terms-of-reference/

Page 256: 'That afternoon, Brooks called staff to the middle of the newsroom and broke the news', Jules Stenson, 'There Is Life After The *News of the World*', *The Huffington Post*, 8 July 2012, http://www.huffingtonpost.co.uk/jules-stenson/news-of-the-world-closure-life-afterwards_b_1654016.html

Page 256: 'James then sent a much lengthier email to employees, explaining why the decision was inevitable', Joel Gunter, '*News of the World* closure: statement in full', journalism.co.uk, 7 July 2011, http://www.journalism.co.uk/news/news-of-the-world-closure-statement-in-full/s2/a545051/

Page 256: 'The next day, Brooks braved staff again in a town hall meeting', Audio Of Brooks Meeting NOTW Staff, Sky News, 9 July 2011, http://news.sky.com/story/867777/audio-of-brooks-meeting-notw-staff

Page 257: '…I am satisfied that Rebekah, her leadership of this business and her standard of ethics and her standard of conduct throughout her career are, are very good', 'James Murdoch backs Rebekah Brooks', Channel 4 News, 7 July 2011, http://www.youtube.com/watch?v=LAVd9RySOrI

Page 257: 'Or as one communications analyst transcribed it—suggesting that his hesitations signalled doubt', Max Atkinson, 'James Murdoch backs Rebekah Brooks, but not without pausing every 2 seconds', Max Atkinson's Blog, 7 July 2011, http://maxatkinson.blogspot.fr/2011/07/james-murdoch-backs-rebekah-brooks-but.html

Page 258: 'We've already apologised', Rupert Murdoch interviewed on the run in Sun Valley, 9 July 2011, http://www.youtube.com/watch?v=vuSxMiH3-Z0

Page 258: 'Quite simply we lost our way', Cherry Wilson, *'News of the World's* last edition reads "Thank you & goodbye"', *The Guardian*, London, 9 July 2011, http://www.guardian.co.uk/media/2011/jul/09/news-of-the-world-thank-you-and-goodbye

Page 258: 'Asked by a reporter, "What's your first priority?"' Luckily, the reporters heard the reply. In this TV news clip it's inaudible, 'Murdoch says chief Rebekah Brooks is his first priority', BBC TV News, 10 July 2011, http://www.bbc.co.uk/news/uk–14100053

Page 259: '...up there with the most hurtful moments in this whole sordid ordeal', @Hayley_Barlow tweet, as Rupert Murdoch gave evidence to Leveson Inquiry, 26 April 2012.

Page 259: 'Not long afterwards, the *Telegraph* was reporting...that Elisabeth had told friends that Rebekah had "fucked the company"', John Bingham, the *Telegraph*, *op cit*, 15 July 2011.

Page 259: '...his hand was forced by Prince Alwaleed bin Talal, a Saudi billionaire supporter of the Murdochs', 'Interview: Saudi Prince Al-Waleed bin Talal Alsaud', *Newsnight*, BBC TV, 15 July 2011, http://www.bbc.co.uk/news/business–14171053

Page 260: 'With rumours raging that James was for the chop', Bruce Orwall, 'In Interview, Murdoch Defends News Corp', *Wall Street Journal*, 14 July 2011, http://online.wsj.com/article/SB10001424052702304521304576446261304709284.html

Page 261: '...it was clear that the crucial £8 billion BSkyB deal could no longer go ahead', 'News Corp withdraws bid for BSkyB', BBC.co.uk, 13 July 2011, http://www.bbc.co.uk/news/business-14142307

Page 261: '...Rupert's ex-wife Anna flew in from New York to be with her youngest son and make sure his father stood by him', Sarah Ellison, 'The Rules of Succession', *Vanity Fair*, New York, December 2011.

Page 261: 'A year earlier, Rupert and his four grown-up children had resorted to family counselling', Ellison, *ibid*; also Ken Auletta, 'The Heiress, The rise of Elisabeth Murdoch', *New Yorker*, New York, 10 December 2012.

Page 262: *'The News of the World* was in the business of holding others to account', 'See Rupert Murdoch's "We Are Sorry" Newspaper Ad', *Ad Age*, London, 15 July 2011, http://adage.com/article/media/rupert-murdoch-s-newspaper-ad/228753/

Page 263: 'The MSC would take charge of dealing with the Metropolitan Police'. The committee's constitution and tasks are set out in the News Corp website: 'Terms of reference of Management and Standards Committee', News Corp, New York, http://www.newscorp.com/corp_gov/MSC_terms.html

CHAPTER 16   BETRAYED

Page 265: 'People I trusted...have let me down', Minutes of Evidence, House of Commons Culture Committee, London, 19 July 2011, http://www.parliament.

uk/documents/commons-committees/culture-media-sport/Uncorrected_
transcript_19_July_phone_hacking.pdf

Page 266: '...a spokesman told the media that the computer belonged to Charlie and had "nothing to do with Rebekah or the case", Amelia Hill, 'Police examine bag found in bin near Rebekah Brooks's home', *The Guardian*, London, 18 July 2011, http://www.guardian.co.uk/media/2011/jul/18/mystery-bag-bin-rebekah-brooks

Page 266: 'There is going to be no killer blow', Patrick Wintour, 'Tom Watson: tireless campaigner gears up for Murdoch showdown', *The Guardian*, London, 17 July 2011, http://www.guardian.co.uk/politics/2011/jul/17/tom-watson-rupert-murdoch

Page 267: 'It was very, very, very, very intense', Sarah Ellison, 'The Rules of Succession', *Vanity Fair*, New York, December 2011.

Page 268: 'Mr Murdoch, do you accept that ultimately you are responsible for this whole fiasco?', Culture Commitee, *op cit*, 19 July 2011.

Page 270: 'Bumbling into a parliamentary hearing', Conrad Black, 'The Real Rupert Murdoch', The Huffington Post, New York, 21 October 2011, http://www.huffingtonpost.com/conrad-black/rupert-murdoch-news-corp-_b_1017372.html

Page 271: 'So if you were not lying then, somebody lied to you. Who was it?" Watson asked', Culture Commitee, *op cit*, 19 July 2011.

Page 271: 'Again I think the very fact that the provision', *ibid*.

Page 272: 'I have no knowledge and there is no evidence', *ibid*.

Page 273: 'In fact, we did inform him of the "For Neville" email, which had been produced to us by Gordon Taylor's lawyers', Emma Bazillian, 'Is This the End for James Murdoch? Former staffers say he read incriminating email', *Ad Week*, New York, 21 July 2011, http://www.adweek.com/news/press/end-james-murdoch–133589

Page 273: 'NBC News gave it two-and-a-half minutes, while the network's top-rating *Today* program devoted almost seven', *Today*, NBC, 20 July 2011.

Page 274: 'It's an amazing PR move. They couldn't have asked for better', 'Gabriel Sherman on *Today*: Wendi the 'smackdown Sister''', *New York*, http://nymag.com/daily/intelligencer/2011/07/gabriel_sherman_on_today_wendi.html

CHAPTER 17 UNDER ATTACK

Page 275: 'You must be the first mafia boss in history who didn't know he was running a criminal enterprise', James Murdoch, Minutes of Oral Evidence, House of Commons Culture Committee, 10 November 2011, http://www.parliament.uk/documents/commons-committees/culture-media-sport/Uncorrected_transcript_CMSC_10_November_11_James_Murdoch.pdf

Page 275: 'Martin Bashir predicted that Rupert would be gone in eighteen months', and 'Michael Wolff was even quicker to write him off', *Today*, NBC, 20 July 2011.

Page 276: 'Now Macdonald told the Home Affairs Committee that it was "blindingly obvious" to him', Lord Macdonald of River Glaven, QC, Minutes of Oral Evidence, House of Commons, Home Affairs Committee, London, 19 July 2011, http://www.publications.parliament.uk/pa/cm201012/cmselect/cmhaff/uc907-vii/uc90701.htm

Page 277: '...James and Rupert were assuring the Culture Committee that Harbottle & Lewis had conducted a thorough investigation in 2007', Minutes of Evidence, House of Commons Culture Committee, London, 19 July 2011, http://www.parliament.uk/documents/commons-committees/culture-media-sport/Uncorrected_transcript_19_July_phone_hacking.pdf

Page 277: 'Given limited exemption from professional privilege, the lawyers then proceeded to demolish a key part of their client's defence', 'Response from Harbottle & Lewis LLP to the Culture Media and Sport Committee and the Home Affairs Committee', 8 August 2011, http://www.parliament.uk/documents/commons-committees/culture-media-and-sport/ph20.2.pdf

Page 278: 'This is one of the largest cover-ups I have seen in my lifetime', Nick Davies, 'Phone hacking: *News of the World* reporter's letter reveals cover-up', *The Guardian*, London, 16 August 2011, http://www.guardian.co.uk/media/2011/aug/16/phone-hacking-now-reporter-letter

Page 278: 'It was clear evidence that phone-hacking was taking place beyond Clive Goodman', Tom Crone, Minutes of Oral Evidence, House of Commons, Culture Media and Sport Committee, London, 6 September 2011, http://www.publications.parliament.uk/pa/cm201012/cmselect/cmcumeds/uc903-iii/uc90301.htm

Page 278: 'Crone had been News International's lawyer...despite his threat in July to speak out "if they completely screw me over"', Oliver Wright and Nigel Morris, 'Revealed: Cameron's 26 meetings in 15 months with Murdoch chiefs', *The Independent*, London, 16 July 2011, http://www.independent.co.uk/news/uk/politics/revealed-camerons–26-meetings-in–15-months-with-murdoch-chiefs–2314550.html

Page 278: 'Pike told MPs he had advised News in 2008 that, "three journalists other than Goodman were involved in phone hacking"', Julian Pike, Minutes of Oral Evidence, Culture Committee, 19 October 2011, http://www.publications.parliament.uk/pa/cm201012/cmselect/cmcumeds/uc903-iv/uc90301.htm

Page 279: 'Unluckily for James, Pike also agreed to give the committee three documents that could throw light on what James should have known.' The documents were supplied to the Culture Committee on 31 October 2011 in a letter from Farrer & Co to the committee chairman, John Whittingdale MP, which can be viewed at, http://www.publications.parliament.uk/pa/cm201012/cmselect/cmcumeds/uc903-iv/uc90301.htm

Page 280: '"I want to be very clear," he told the committee, "no documents were shown to me at that meeting or given to me at that meeting, or prior"', James Murdoch, Culture Committee, *op cit*, 10 November 2011.

Page 282: 'On 12 December 2011, the London law firm, Linklaters...gave MPs a copy of the email that Colin Myler had sent to James on 7 June 2008.' Copies of all the documents can be found at http://www.parliament.uk/documents/ commons-committees/culture-media-sport/PH%2050%20Letter_from_Link laters_to_Chairman_12_Dec_2011.pdf. Two further emails were supplied by the law firm on 20 December, and can be seen at, http://www.parliament.uk/ documents/commons-committees/culture-media-sport/PH51_Linklaters_LLP_ to_Chairman_20_December_2011.pdf

Page 283: '...the MSC confirmed that the email had been deleted from James Murdoch's inbox "by an IT worker" on 15 Jan 2011', letter from Linklaters to committee, 25 January 2012, http://www.parliament.uk/documents/commons- committees/culture-media-sport/PH_55_Linklaters_to_Chair_25_Jan_2012.pdf

Page 284: 'At what stage did it become clear to you that the line that we were being given was not the truth?', Julian Pike, Oral Evidence, Culture Committee, *op cit.*

Page 284: 'You, as the representative of a very senior firm of solicitors', Julian Pike, Oral Evidence, Culture Committee, *op cit.*

Page 285: 'Or as Rupert had so eloquently put it in his Thatcher lecture, that they had "zero tolerance of wrongdoing"', 'Rupert Murdoch's inaugural Margaret Thatcher lecture', *The Guardian*, London, 21 October 2010, http://www.guardian. co.uk/media/2010/oct/21/rupert-murdoch-inaugural-margaret-thatcher-lecture

Page 286: '...Assistant Commissioner Peter Clarke...accused News of trying to hinder the police investigation', Peter Clarke, Oral Evidence, Home Affairs Committee, 12 July 2011, http://www.publications.parliament.uk/pa/cm201012/ cmselect/cmhaff/uc907-v/uc90701.htm

Page 286: 'It is almost impossible to escape the conclusion', *Unauthorised tapping into or hacking of mobile communications. Thirteenth Report of Session 2010–12*, House of Commons Home Affairs Committee, http://www.parliament.uk/documents/ commons-committees/home-affairs/unauthorised_tapping_or_hacking_mobile_ communications_report.pdf

Page 286: '...Assistant Commissioner Andy Hayman, ex-head of Special Opera- tions, had met senior *News of the World* journalists and executives several times in 2006', Andy Hayman, Oral Evidence, Home Affairs Committee, 12 July 2011, http://www.publications.parliament.uk/pa/cm201012/cmselect/cmhaff/uc907- v/uc90701.htm

Page 288: 'We do not expressly accuse Mr Hayman of lying to us in his evidence', *Unauthorised tapping into or hacking of mobile communications*, Home Affairs Committee, *op cit.*

Page 289: 'The Home Affairs Committee readily agreed with Yates's own assess- ment', John Yates, Oral Evidence, Home Affairs Committee, 12 July 2011, http://www.publications.parliament.uk/pa/cm201012/cmselect/cmhaff/uc907- v/uc90701.htm

Page 289: 'But he now had to admit he had received regular PR advice from Wallis during his tenure, and had also accepted five weeks free accommodation, worth £12 000', Sir Paul Stephenson, Oral Evidence, Home Affairs Committee, 19 July 2011, http://www.parliament.uk/documents/commons-committees/home-affairs/HAC-transcript-phonehacking–110719.pdf

CHAPTER 18 POWER GAMES

Page 291: 'I have never asked for anything from a Prime Minister', Rupert Murdoch, Transcript of Evidence, Leveson Inquiry, 25 April 2012, morning, p 15. http://www.levesoninquiry.org.uk/wp-content/uploads/2012/04/Transcript-of-Morning-Hearing–25-April–2012.pdf

Page 291: '...David Cameron was forced to admit to the public that he and his ministers had enjoyed an extraordinary number of private meetings with News International', Oliver Wright and Nigel Morris, *The Independent*, London, *op cit*, 16 July 2011, http://www.independent.co.uk/news/uk/politics/revealed-camerons–26-meetings-in–15-months-with-murdoch-chiefs–2314550.html

Page 293: 'Remarkably, the 81-year-old Murdoch would tell Lord Leveson in 2012 that he had no memory of this rendezvous with Britain's future PM.' In his witness statement, Murdoch said he had no memory of it at all. In his oral evidence, having consulted his wife and daughter, he said, 'It's coming back to me vaguely'. Transcript of Evidence, Leveson Inquiry, 25 April 2012, afternoon, p 10, http://www.levesoninquiry.org.uk/wp-content/uploads/2012/04/Transcript-of-Afternoon-Hearing–25-April–2012.pdf

Page 293: 'In the four years that Cameron led the Opposition, Rupert and James Murdoch and Rebekah Brooks met him no less than 30 times.' In July 2011, Cameron provided a list of his meetings with Britain's press proprietors. The Murdochs, Brooks and Cameron then all listed their meetings for the Leveson Inquiry, as did Gordon Brown. Working out the exact number of contacts is something of a challenge, but the individual lists can be found at the Leveson website. Rupert has two lists, KRM27 (for Prime Ministers) and KRM29 (for Opposition leaders), each of which run to three pages. James's list of meetings with PMs is JRM9, and with Opposition leaders, JRM10. Rebekah Brooks has one list of meetings, RMB1, with PMs, Opposition leaders, Cabinet ministers, political advisers and senior police officers. It runs to fourteen pages. All can be found via the main 'Evidence' page at the Leveson website and clicking on the name of the person, http://www.levesoninquiry.org.uk/evidence/

Page 294: 'I have a bucket of shit on my desk and I'm going to pour it all over you.' Kelvin MacKenzie bragged about this famous story at the Leveson Inquiry, Transcript of Evidence, 9 January 2012, morning, p 37, http://www.levesoninquiry.org.uk/wp-content/uploads/2012/01/Transcript-of-Morning-Hearing–9-January–2012.pdf. Sir John Major told Leveson he had read reports of the conversation 'with wonder and surprise', and claimed it was a myth.

Page 294: '...*The Sun* had gone to town on an affair he had with his secretary', 'IT's PADDY PANTSDOWN', *The Sun*, 6 February 1992, p 1, http://sunheadlines. blogspot.fr/2008/12/classics-its-paddy-pantsdown.html

Page 295: 'IF KINNOCK WINS TODAY WILL THE LAST PERSON TO LEAVE BRITAIN PLEASE TURN OUT THE LIGHTS', *The Sun*, 9 April 1992, p 1, http://www.bl.uk/learning/histcitizen/fpage/elections/election.html

Page 295: 'IT'S *THE SUN* WOT WON IT!' *The Sun*, 11 April 1992, p 1, http:// en.wikipedia.org/wiki/It%27s_The_Sun_Wot_Won_It

Page 295: 'LABOUR WINS: SPECIAL NIGHTMARE ISSUE', *The Sun*, 8 June 1987, p 1, Peter Chippindale and Chris Horrie, *Stick It Up your Punter, The Rise and Fall of The Sun*, Heinemann, London, p 221.

Page 295: '...at the 1983 election, *The Sun* had dished out similar treatment to Michael Foot', *ibid*, p 140.

Page 295: 'It is better to be riding the tiger's back than let it rip your throat out', Piers Morgan, *The Insider: The Private Diaries of a Scandalous Decade*, Ebury Press, London, 2005, p 140.

Page 296: 'The front page of *The Sun* on 18 March 1997, six weeks before the general election, carried a cute picture of a smiling Blair holding the newspaper', *The Sun*, 18 March 1997, p 1, http://www.channel4.com/news/articles/politics/ domestic_politics/the+sun+drops+support+for+labour/3365897.html

Page 296: '...cut a really great deal with this bloke called Satan', Tony Blair, *A Journey*, Hutchinson, London, 2010, p 97.

Page 296: '...claims that Blair promised the media mogul an easy ride on this at a private dinner in 1994'. In his book *Full Disclosure*, Neil claimed that in September 1994 Blair had dinner with Murdoch's right-hand man in London, Gus Fischer, who was lobbying Labour on cross-media ownership, and made it clear that New Labour would not tighten the rules if he got into power. Andrew Neil , *Full Disclosure*, Macmillan, London, 1996.

More recently, Neil told the Leveson Inquiry, 'New Labour was prepared to pay a high price, in terms of access and influence, for the support of the Murdoch papers. There was no deal, as such. Nothing as unsophisticated as Mr Murdoch saying to Mr Blair: "We will back you in return for the following..." But there was, in my view, undoubtedly an understanding...New Labour in power did nothing to undermine or threaten Mr Murdoch's British media interests, despite a deep desire among many in the Labour party, especially (but not exclusively) on the Left, to "cut him down to size". Demands for a privacy law (which Mr Murdoch abhors) were kicked into the long grass. Control of 37 per cent of national newspaper circulation was tolerated (indeed supported now most of the 37 per cent was rooting for Labour). BSkyB was allowed to grow unhindered and light-touch media regulation became the consensus of the day'. Andrew Ferguson Neil, Written Statement, 8 May 2012, http://www.levesoninquiry.org.uk/wp-content/uploads/2012/07/ Witness-statement-of-Andrew-Neil.pdf

Page 296: '...even Blair admits that he ducked the battle'. Blair was asked by Leveson's counsel, Robert Jay QC, about the 1994 dinner:

Jay: You apparently indicated that media ownership rules would not be onerous under Labour. Is it possible that you said that?

Blair: I think "not onerous" is not the way I would have put it. I can't specifically remember what was said, but it's perfectly possible, if that issue came up, I would have said, "That's not an issue we're going to be taking on".

Blair also told Leveson: 'Our position was, as I say, I mean, I decided I was not going to take this issue on...It's not that, as it were, I was afraid of taking them on, in that sense, but I knew that if I did, you have to be very, very clear about this, and that was the debate I had with Alastair and others within government all the way through. If you take this on, do not think for a single moment you are not in a long, protracted battle that will shove everything else to one side whilst it's going on'.

Leveson, Transcript of Evidence, 28 May 2012, morning, p 41–46, http://www.levesoninquiry.org.uk/wp-content/uploads/2012/05/Transcript-of-Morning-Hearing–28-May–2012.pdf

Page 297: 'Murdoch asks the price...There's always a price', Lord Prescott, Transcript of Evidence, Leveson Inquiry, 27 February 2012, p 85, p 90, http://www.levesoninquiry.org.uk/wp-content/uploads/2012/02/lev270212pm.pdf

Page 297: 'I have never met a minister who did not know the corporate aims of Rupert Murdoch', Tom Watson MP, Written Statement to Leveson Inquiry, http://www.levesoninquiry.org.uk/wp-content/uploads/2012/05/Witness-Statement-of-Tom-Watson-MP.pdf

Page 297: 'During his time as Britain's PM, he had 31 dinners, breakfasts, lunches, meetings and the occasional weekend with Rupert', Leveson Exhibits, KRM27, KRM29, JRM9, JRM10, RMB1, http://www.levesoninquiry.org.uk/evidence/

Page 297: 'I've never asked Mr Blair for anything', Transcript of Evidence, Leveson Inquiry, 25 April 2012, morning, p 70, http://www.levesoninquiry.org.uk/wp-content/uploads/2012/04/Transcript-of-Morning-Hearing–25-April–2012.pdf

Page 298: 'Gus Fischer...claimed he had, "never seen anyone more astute at manipulating politicians to his advantage then Rupert"', Neil, *op cit*, p 171.

Page 298: 'It had come straight from Number 10', Lord Fowler, *Frontline*, Murdoch's Scandal, WGBH, Boston, 27 March 2012, http://www.pbs.org/wgbh/pages/*Frontline*/murdochs-scandal/

Page 298: 'We decided more stuff against the Murdoch interests than in favour of it', Blair, Leveson, *op cit*, p 32.

Page 299: '...*The Sun* dumped Gordon Brown's government after twelve years supporting the party, with the simple but effective headline, LABOUR's LOST IT', Nick Robinson, '"Labour's lost it," says *The Sun*', BBC.co.uk, 29 September 2009, http://www.bbc.co.uk/blogs/nickrobinson/2009/09/labours_lost_it.html

Page 299: 'I am so rooting for you tomorrow and not just as a personal friend but because professionally we're definitely in this together', phone text provided to Leveson Inquiry, 8 June 2012, http://www.levesoninquiry.org.uk/wp-content/uploads/2012/06/Copy-of-R-Brooks-text-message-to-D-Cameron–7.10.09.pdf. See also, 'The embarrassing text that reveals the cosy relationship between Prime Minister David Cameron and Rebekah Brooks', *Daily Mail*, 14 June 2012, http://www.dailymail.co.uk/news/article–2159231/Rebekah-Brooks-David-Cameron-text-reveals-cosy-relationship-two.html#ixzz2TRu0xiZg

Page 300: '...Rebekah's sign-off, YES HE CAM, became *The Sun*'s headline for its editorial', 'YES HE CAM', *The Sun*, 9 October 2009, http://www.thesun.co.uk/sol/homepage/news/sun_says/2676620/The-Sun-Says.html

Page 300: 'Come election day on 6 May 2010, the Tory leader duly woke up to find his picture on *The Sun*'s front page', 'Can Britain take five more years of hard Labour?' *The Sun*, 6 May 2010. thttp://www.thesun.co.uk/sol/homepage/news/sun_says/2961073/The-Sun-Says-David-Cameron-is-our-only-hope.html

Page 300: 'And now the meetings came thicker and faster', Leveson Exhibits, KRM27, KRM29, JRM9, JRM10, RMB1.

CHAPTER 19   SKY'S THE LIMIT

Page 303: 'In the space of twelve months, News Corp's chief government lobbyist, Fred Michel, was in touch with Jeremy Hunt'. Most of these are in the 163-page Leveson Exhibit KRM18, which is attached to the statement of Keith Rupert Murdoch, http://www.levesoninquiry.org.uk/wp-content/uploads/2012/04/Exhibit-KRM–18.pdf. Others are attached to Fred Michel's statement as Exhibit FM1, http://www.levesoninquiry.org.uk/wp-content/uploads/2012/04/Exhibit-FM–1.pdf

Page 305: 'It was responsible for 40 per cent of Britain's Sunday newspaper circulation and 34 per cent of its national daily sales', based on Audit Bureau of Circulation figures for first six months of 2010.

Page 305: '...if people had read Rupert's evidence to a House of Lords select committee in 2007, when he had told a delegation visiting New York that he wanted Sky to be more like Fox News', *The Ownership of the News*, House of Lords Select Committee on Communications, Volume I, Report, 27 June 2008, p 119, http://www.publications.parliament.uk/pa/ld200708/ldselect/ldcomuni/122/122i.pdf

Page 305: 'He had even boasted on his website that he was "a cheerleader for Rupert Murdoch's contribution" to the media industry', 'Jeremy Hunt was following the example set by his boss', *The Telegraph*, 24 April 2012, http://www.telegraph.co.uk/comment/telegraph-view/9223499/Jeremy-Hunt-was-following-the-example-set-by-his-boss.html

Page 306: 'An extraordinary encounter', transcript of written note of telephone conversation between Norman Lamb and Mr Fred Michel on Wed 27 October, provided to the Leveson Inquiry by Rt. Hon. Norman Lamb MP, http://www.

levesoninquiry.org.uk/wp-content/uploads/2012/06/Exhibit-to-Witness-Statement-of-Norman-Lamb-MP-Part–2.pdf

Page 306: 'Lamb told Leveson he could not recall the exact words used by Murdoch's man, but that he was left with, "a very clear understanding"', Norman Lamb, Transcript of Evidence, Leveson Inquiry, 26 June 2012, p 8, http://www.levesoninquiry.org.uk/wp-content/uploads/2012/06/Transcript-of-Afternoon-Hearing–26-June–2012.pdf

Page 307: '…the business secretary was caught in a sting by a couple of female journalists from the *Telegraph*, posing as his constituents', Holly Watt, Robert Winnett and Heidi Blake, 'Vince Cable: "I could bring down the Government if I'm pushed"', the *Telegraph*, 20 December 2010, http://www.telegraph.co.uk/news/politics/liberaldemocrats/8215462/Vince-Cable-I-could-bring-down-the-Government-if-Im-pushed.html

Page 307: 'And when this comment was leaked to the BBC', Robert Peston, 'What Vince Cable said about Rupert Murdoch and BSkyB', BBC.co.uk, 21 December 2010, http://www.bbc.co.uk/blogs/thereporters/robertpeston/2010/12/what_vince_cable_said_about_ru.html

Page 307: 'Later, the *Telegraph* would hire an internationally renowned firm of investigators', Josh Halliday, 'News Corp boss "linked" to leak of Vince Cable's Rupert Murdoch comments', *The Guardian*, London, 22 July 2011, http://www.guardian.co.uk/media/2011/jul/22/willlewis-telegraphmediagroup

Page 307: 'When asked point blank by the Leveson Inquiry whether he was responsible—yes or no—Lewis refused to say', Will Lewis, Transcript of Evidence, Leveson Inquiry, 10 January 2012, pp 63–4, http://www.levesoninquiry.org.uk/wp-content/uploads/2012/01/Transcript-of-Afternoon-Hearing–10-January–2012.pdf

Page 307: '…the minister texted the Chancellor, George Osborne, to say, "Cld we chat about Murdoch Sky bid am seriously worried we are going to screw this up. Jeremy', Paul Owen, 'The day Jeremy Hunt was given responsibility for BSkyB bid—timeline', *The Guardian*, London, 31 May 2012, http://www.guardian.co.uk/politics/2012/may/31/timeline-jeremy-hunt-bskyb-bid

Page 308: 'A month earlier, on 19 November, Hunt had tried to get the PM to intervene in the Murdochs' favour, firing off a memo to Cameron to say that James was "furious"', John Plunkett and Lisa O'Carroll, '"Congrats on Brussels!" Texts reveal Hunt's close alliance with Murdoch', *The Guardian*, London, 31 May 2012, http://www.guardian.co.uk/politics/2012/may/31/texts-hunt-murdoch

Page 309: 'James had replied, "You must be f****** joking. I will text him and find a time." And they had then talked on the phone instead.' The exchanges between Hunt, Michel and Murdoch are all dealt with in James Murdoch's oral evidence to the Leveson Inqury, 25 April 2012, afternoon, p 11, http://www.levesoninquiry.org.uk/wp-content/uploads/2012/04/Transcript-of-Afternoon-Hearing–24-April–2012.pdf

Page 309: 'Now that Hunt was officially dealing with the bid, contact with News Corp moved up another gear'. A list of News's meetings with politicians re the BSkyB bid is in Exhibit KRM19, attached to Rupert Murdoch's written statement, http://www.levesoninquiry.org.uk/wp-content/uploads/2012/04/Exhibit-KRM-19.pdf

Page 309: 'On 10 January, Michel emailed James to say the minister had asked them to, "find as many errors as we can in the Ofcom report".' All Michel's emails can be found in the two files (full details above) given to Leveson: KRM18, http://www.levesoninquiry.org.uk/wp-content/uploads/2012/04/Exhibit-KRM-18.pdf and FM1, http://www.levesoninquiry.org.uk/wp-content/uploads/2012/04/Exhibit-FM-1.pdf

Page 311: 'He would later tell Leveson that he had no idea the scandal was "about to erupt"', Jeremy Hunt, Transcript of Evidence, Leveson Inquiry, 31 May 2012, morning, p 103, http://www.levesoninquiry.org.uk/wp-content/uploads/2012/05/Transcript-of-Morning-Hearing-31-May-2012.pdf

Page 313: 'Lord Leveson concluded—somewhat bizarrely—that Hunt was scrupulous in sticking to the proper process', Dominic Gover, 'Leveson Report: No Evidence of Government and Murdoch Plot over BSkyB Bid', *International Business Times*, 29 November 2012, http://www.ibtimes.co.uk/articles/409833/20121129/leveson-murdoch-sky-hunt-deal.htm

Page 313: 'In the end this scandal is about political failure', Witness Statement of Tom Watson MP, Leveson Inquiry, May 2012, http://www.levesoninquiry.org.uk/wp-content/uploads/2012/05/Witness-Statement-of-Tom-Watson-MP.pdf

Page 313: '...I came to believe, along with other journalists, that the newspaper group were confident that they were indeed untouchable', Matt Driscoll, Written Statement to Leveson Inquiry, http://www.levesoninquiry.org.uk/wp-content/uploads/2011/12/Witness-Statement-of-Matthew-Driscoll.pdf

Page 313: 'The humbling of Rupert Murdoch and his cohorts came about because of their arrogance', Jules Stenson, 'There Is Life After The *News of the World*', *The Huffington Post*, 8 July 2012, http://www.huffingtonpost.co.uk/jules-stenson/news-of-the-world-closure-life-afterwards_b_1654016.html

CHAPTER 20   JUDGEMENT DAY

Page 315: 'News International and its parent News Corporation exhibited wilful blindness', House of Commons Culture Committee, *News International and Phone-hacking*, Vol I, May 2012, para 275, http://www.publications.parliament.uk/pa/cm201012/cmselect/cmcumeds/903/903i.pdf

Page 315: 'I almost felt a responsibility as a citizen that I had to go through with it', James Cusick, 'Charlotte Church: "Why did I settle the case? Because I found out their tactics. They were going to go after my mother again"', *The Independent*, London, 28 February 2012, http://www.independent.co.uk/news/uk/crime/charlotte-church-why-did-i-settle-the-case-because-i-found-out-their-tactics-they-were-going-to-go-after-my-mother-again-7447280.html

Page 316: 'The actor Jude Law, gave a flavour of this in a statement to the court', Amelia Hill, 'Jude Law: no aspect of my private life was safe from *News of the World*', *The Guardian*, London, 19 January 2012, http://www.guardian.co.uk/media/2012/jan/19/jude-law-news-of-the-world

Page 316: 'But even more damaging than this public caning was Justice Vos's revelation', Amelia Hill, 'Judge orders search of *News of the World* computers', *The Guardian*, London, 19 January 2012, http://www.guardian.co.uk/media/2012/jan/19/judge-orders-search-news-world-computers

Page 317: 'I think the senior executives and I were all misinformed', Rupert Murdoch, Transcript of Evidence, Leveson Inquiry, 26 April 2012, morning, p 24, http://www.levesoninquiry.org.uk/wp-content/uploads/2012/04/Transcript-of-Morning-Hearing–26-April–2012.pdf

Page 318: 'Crone immediately responded—without the protection of parliamentary privilege', Emily Allen, 'This "shameful lie": *News of the World* lawyer hits back in fury after Rupert Murdoch accuses "journalists' drinking pal" of covering up hacking scandal', *Daily Mail*, 26 April 2012, http://www.dailymail.co.uk/news/article–2135453/Its-shameful-lie-News-World-lawyer-hits-fury-Rupert-Murdoch-accuses-journalists-drinking-pal-covering-hacking-scandal.html

Page 318: 'The report was already three months past its due date'. Helpfully, the report tracks all the amendments proposed and the way the committee divided.

Page 318: 'In the run up to the decision, James wrote the committee a seven-page letter', 'James Murdoch: "I could have asked more questions"', *UK Press Gazette*, 14 March 2012, http://www.pressgazette.co.uk/node/48943

Page 319: '…Rupert should take the blame, and that he was "not a fit person" to run a "major international company"', *News International and Phone-hacking, op cit*, para 229.

Page 319: The immediate response from News was that the committee's damnation was 'unjustified and highly partisan', Peter Wilson, 'House of Commons media committee rejects attack on Murdoch as "not fit"', *The Australian*, 2 May 2012, http://www.theaustralian.com.au/business/in-depth/house-of-commons-media-committee-rejects-attack-on-murdoch-as-not-fit/story-fn9eci82–1226344354942

Page 320: 'Tom Crone and Colin Myler gave repeated assurances', *News International and Phone-hacking, op cit*, para 130.

Page 320: 'When questioned…in 2009, he was startlingly vague', *ibid*, para 84.

Page 321: 'Whether or not Les Hinton had seen this letter before his appearance in 2007', *ibid*, para 85.

Page 321: 'Witnesses found to have misled a select committee', *ibid*, para 10.

Page 321: 'This is beyond dispute', *ibid*, para 15.

Page 322: 'The behaviour of News International and certain witnesses in this affair demonstrated contempt', *ibid*, para 279.

Page 322: 'Corporately, the *News of the World* and News International misled the Committee', *ibid*, para 274.

Page 323: 'The majority verdict was that it was "simply astonishing"', *ibid*, para 163.

Page 323: 'The majority were also astonished by James's "lack of curiosity"', *ibid*, paras 177, 160.

Page 323: 'On the basis of the facts and evidence before the Committee', *ibid*, para 229.

Page 324: 'Fuck Dacre. Publish', Robert Harris, *Selling Hitler*, Penguin Books, Melbourne, 1987.

Page 325: 'After all, we're in the entertainment business', Harold Evans, *Good Times, Bad Times*, Coronet, London, 1983, p 492.

Page 325: 'The media mogul displayed a similar insouciance over *The Sun*'s famous GOTCHA headline', Chippindale and Horrie, *op cit*, p 119. See *The Sun* front page at Sun Headlines blog, http://sunheadlines.blogspot.fr/2008/11/classics-gotcha.html

Page 326: 'The standards and culture of a journalistic institution are set from the top down, by its owner, publisher, and top editors', Carl Bernstein, 'Murdoch's Watergate?', *Daily Beast*, New York, 9 July 2011, http://www.thedailybeast.com/newsweek/2011/07/10/murdoch-s-watergate.html

Page 327: 'Between 2009 and 2011, News Corp paid out almost US$655 million in damages'. A fair amount has been written in the American press about this. News America Marketing was sued successfully by Floorgraphics, Valassis and Insignia Systems, and settled several cases for a total of US$655 million. One of the best summaries is by David Carr, 'News Corp.'s Soft Power in the U.S.', *New York Times*, New York, 7 August 2011, http://www.nytimes.com/2011/08/08/business/media/news-corps-legal-trail-in-the-us.html?pagewanted=all&_r=0. There is also good coverage in Consumer Goods & Retail Litigation Blog, such as, 'News America CEO Admits Making Mafia References—Valassis v. News America Trial', http://cpg-retail-litigation.kotchen.com/2009/06/news-america-ceo-admits-making-mafia.html. There are also public trial transcripts, statements of claim etc, too numerous to list.

Page 327: '...Carlucci was promoted by Murdoch to be publisher of the *New York Post*, as well as chief executive of News America', Jim Edwards, 'Look Which News Corp. Exec Got His Wings Clipped When "The Daily" Closed', *Business Insider*, 9 December 2012, http://www.businessinsider.com/look-which-news-corp-exec-got-his-wings-clipped-when-the-daily-closed–2012–12

Page 327: 'Rupert Murdoch, with his take-no-prisoners attitude to tabloid journalism, the ends will justify the means, do whatever it takes', Nicholas Wapshott, 'Rupert Murdoch Bares Media's Reach to Leveson Inquiry on Phone Hacking', *Daily Beast*, New York, 28 April 2012, http://www.thedailybeast.com/articles/2012/04/28/rupert-murdoch-bares-media-s-reach-to-leveson-inquiry-on-phone-hacking.html

CHAPTER 21   TRIALS AHEAD

Page 329: 'I am not guilty of these charges', Rebekah Brooks re conspiring to hack into Milly Dowler's voicemails, 'Phone hacking: Rebekah Brooks and Andy Coulson face charges', BBC.co.uk, 24 July 2012, http://www.bbc.co.uk/news/uk–18961228

Page 330: 'In late January 2012, four key members of *The Sun*'s editorial team were arrested by Operation Elveden', David Barrett, Robert Mendick and Patrick Sawyer, 'Phone hacking: four Sun journalists arrested', the *Telegraph*, London, 28 January 2012, http://www.telegraph.co.uk/news/uknews/phone-hacking/9046405/Phone-hacking-four-Sun-journalists-arrested.html

Page 330: 'Four weeks later, the officer in charge of Operations Weeting, Elveden and Tuleta', DAC Sue Akers, Transcript of Evidence, 28 February 2012, pp 47–51, http://www.levesoninquiry.org.uk/wp-content/uploads/2012/02/lev270212am.pdf

Page 331: '...*The Guardian*'s Nick Davies reported that detectives were being given access to, "A mass of internal paperwork"', Nick Davies, 'Mysteries of Data Pool 3 give Rupert Murdoch a whole new headache', *The Guardian*, London, 29 January 2012, http://www.guardian.co.uk/media/2012/jan/29/data-pool-3-sun-arrests-murdoch

Page 331: 'Whether an email is deleted inadvertently', Keith Quinn, 'Email etiquette–so you think you have deleted it', Mesmo Blog, 31 October 2011, http://www.mesmo.co.uk/blog/2011/10/email-etiquette-so-you-think-you-have-deleted-it-guest-post-by-keith-quinn-essential-computing/

Page 332: 'On 11 February, another five senior journalists and editors on the paper were turfed out of bed', Robert Verkaik, 'What next for *The Sun*? Rupert Murdoch to fly to London after five more senior journalists are held in investigation into corrupt payments to police officers', *Daily Mail*, London, 12 February 2012, http://www.dailymail.co.uk/news/article-2099947/Rupert-Murdoch-fly-London–5-Sun-journalists-held.html

Page 332: 'It was worse than the Soviet Union', Trevor Kavanagh, 'Witch-hunt has put us behind ex-Soviet states on Press freedom', *The Sun*, 13 February 2012, http://www.thesun.co.uk/sol/homepage/news/4124870/The-Suns-Trevor-Kavanagh-Witch-hunt-puts-us-behind-ex-Soviet-states-on-Press-freedom.html

Page 332: 'Squads of up to twenty police officers', Richard Littlejohn, 'Scotland Yard Stasi and this sinister assault on a free Press', *Daily Mail*, London, 15 February 2012, http://www.dailymail.co.uk/debate/article–2100664/Scotland-Yard-Stasi-sinister-assault-free-Press.html

Page 333: 'What we've seen...since the hacking scandal exploded', Michelle Stanistreet, General Secretary, National Union of Journalists, *Quest Means Business*, CNN, 17 February 2012, http://transcripts.cnn.com/TRANSCRIPTS/1202/17/qmb.01.html

NOTES

Page 334: 'Rupert was soon assuring staff that they had his "unwavering support"', Katie Hodge, Ben Kendall, Leanne Rinne, '*The Sun* on Sunday to launch soon, says Rupert Murdoch', *The Independent*, London, 17 February 2012, http://www.independent.co.uk/news/media/press/the-sun-on-sunday-to-launch-soon-says-rupert-murdoch–7046068.html

Page 334: 'Illegal activities simply cannot and will not be tolerated at any of our publications', Josh Halliday, Lisa O'Carroll and Ben Dowell, 'Rupert Murdoch: *Sun on Sunday* to launch "very soon"', *The Guardian*, London, 17 February 2012, http://www.guardian.co.uk/media/2012/feb/17/rupert-murdoch-sun-on-sunday

Page 334: 'Three weeks later, the paper's veteran chief reporter', Tom Harper and Simon Freeman, 'Two Murdoch reporters feared to be in suicide bids', *Evening Standard*, London, 6 March 2012, http://www.standard.co.uk/news/uk/two-murdoch-reporters-feared-to-be-in-suicide-bids–7541864.html

Page 335: 'People think that they've been thrown under a bus', Dominic Ponsford, '*Standard* reports two suicide bids at News International', *UK Press Gazette*, 7 March 2012, http://www.pressgazette.co.uk/editor/2012/03/07/standard-reports-two-suicide-bids-at-news-international

Page 335: 'Baby asleep. Eighteen of them', Giles Hattersley, 'Charlie Brooks: Founder member of the Chipping Norton Upset', behind paywall at *Sunday Times*, 9 September 2012, http://www.thesundaytimes.co.uk/sto/newsreview/features/article1121381.ece. Roy Greenslade, 'Rebekah Brooks's husband: "people don't know the true story yet"', *The Guardian*, London, 9 September 2012, http://www.guardian.co.uk/media/greenslade/2012/sep/09/newsinternational-sundaytimes

Page 335: 'Two months later, on 15 May 2012, the couple answered bail at a South London police station', 'Phone-hacking police charge Rebekah Brooks', BBC.co.uk, 15 May 2012, http://www.bbc.co.uk/news/uk–18062485

Page 336: 'I cannot express my anger enough that those closest to me have been dragged into this unfairly', 'Rebekah Brooks anger over charges in phone-hacking probe', BBC.co.uk, 15 May 2012, http://www.bbc.co.uk/news/uk–18075775

Page 338: 'This time, it was with three counts of unlawfully intercepting communications', Martin Hickman, 'Rebekah Brooks and Andy Coulson "conspired to hack" Milly Dowler and 600 others', *The Independent*, London, 24 July 2012, http://www.independent.co.uk/news/uk/crime/rebekah-brooks-and-andy-coulson-conspired-to-hack-milly-dowler-and–600-others–7966265.html

Page 338: 'I am not guilty of these charges', BBC.co.uk, *op cit*, 24 July 2012.

Page 338: 'Andy Coulson said he was disappointed by the decision', 'PM's former spin man Andy Coulson says he will fight phone hacking allegations', *Evening Standard*, 24 July 2012, http://www.standard.co.uk/news/crime/pms-former-spin-man-andy-coulson-says-he-will-fight-phone-hacking-allegations–7972835.html

Page 339: 'Neville Thurlbeck said he was "most surprised and disappointed"', Neville Thurlbeck, blog, 24 July 2012, http://www.nevillethurlbeck.com/2012_07_01_archive.html

451

Page 339: 'I have much to say on this subject', BBC.co.uk, *op cit*, 24 July 2012.

Page 339: 'Edmondson had told the Leveson Inquiry a month earlier', Ian Edmondson, Transcript of Evidence, Leveson Inquiry, 9 February 2012, p 73, http://www.levesoninquiry.org.uk/wp-content/uploads/2012/02/Transcript-of-Morning-Hearing–9-February–2012.pdf

Page 341: 'She soon announced that they had identified 1069 likely hacking victims and a further 3675 potential victims', Deputy Assistant Commissioner Sue Akers, Oral evidence, Home Affairs Committee, 4 September 2012, http://www.publications.parliament.uk/pa/cm201213/cmselect/cmhaff/562/562i.pdf

Page 341: 'In November 2012, Andy Coulson and Clive Goodman were charged with conspiracy to commit misconduct in public office', William Dodd and Dominic Rushe, 'Rebekah Brooks and Andy Coulson to face fresh charges', *The Guardian*, London, 20 November 2012, http://www.guardian.co.uk/media/2012/nov/20/rebekah-brooks-andy-coulson-face-charges

Page 341: 'On the day of Rebekah's first court appearance', Matt Blake, 'Two worlds apart: Rebekah Brooks told she may face separate charges over phone hacking as old boss Rupert Murdoch suns himself abroad', *Daily Mail*, London, 22 June 2012, http://www.dailymail.co.uk/news/article–2163110/Rebekah-Brooks-told-face-charges-relating-phone-hacking-appears-crown-court.html

Page 342: 'But now it was shown to be almost £11 million', Michael Seamark, 'Rebekah Brooks was given £11m pay-off from News Corp after phone-hacking scandal, official documents reveal', *Daily Mail*, 12 December 2012, http://www.dailymail.co.uk/news/article–2247012/Rebekah-Brooks-given–11m-pay-News-Corp-phone-hacking-scandal-official-documents-reveal.html. 'Former NOTW editor Rebekah Brooks gets £11million handshake', *Metro*, London, 12 December 2012, http://metro.co.uk/2012/12/12/former-notw-editor-rebekah-brooks-gets–11million-handshake–3314506

CHAPTER 22   THE SPLIT

Page 345: 'Pure rubbish, pure and total', Bruce Orwall, 'In Interview, Murdoch Defends News Corp', *Wall Street Journal*, New York, 14 July 2011, http://online.wsj.com/article/SB10001424052702304521304576446261304709284.html

Page 346: '...News Corp's board had reacted by awarding them cash bonuses of US$12.5 million and US$6 million respectively', News Corp, *Definitive Proxy Statement*, DEFA14A, Securities & Exchange Commission, Washington, 2 September 2011, P43, http://investor.newscorp.com/secfiling.cfm?filing ID=1193125–11–240041

Page 346: 'This isn't just a dysfunctional board, it's a nonfunctional board', Rachel Beck, 'News Corp. board is far from independent', Associated Press, New York, 20 July 2011, http://www.startribune.com/printarticle/?id=125920568

Page 347: 'One old stager, Keith MacDonald, had even confessed', Ali Cromie, 'The Murdoch Succession', *Business Review Weekly*, 16 October 1994.

Page 347: 'Seven of the current board's fifteen directors also owed their livelihood to the emperor's patronage', News Corp, *op cit*, September 2011.

Page 348: 'The leading US adviser on corporate governance, Institutional Shareholder Services, recommended', Constantine Von Hoffman, 'Dump Murdoch Board Lapdogs, Proxy Firms Urge. Now They Notice?' *Money Watch*, CBS News, http://www.cbsnews.com/8301–505123_162–49641647/dump-murdoch-board-lapdogs-proxy-firms-urge-now-they-notice/

Page 348: 'The leading British adviser...wanted to chop eleven', Jill Treanor, 'Hermes calls on shareholders to protest at News Corp AGM', *The Guardian*, London, 14 October 2011, http://www.guardian.co.uk/business/blog/2011/oct/14/hermes-shareholders-protest-news-corp-agm

Page 348: 'The Murdochs owned almost 40 per cent of these B shares', News Corp, *op cit*, September 2011, p26.

Page 349: 'The veteran shareholder activist from Australia, Stephen Mayne, 'News Corp AGM: no doddery old men, or foam pies', *Crikey*, 24 October 2011, http://www.crikey.com.au/2011/10/24/news-corp-agm-no-doddery-old-men-or-foam-pies/

Page 349: 'One prominent newspaper—the *Los Angeles Times*—was forecasting that Rupert could be forced to step down as chief executive', Meg James and Joe Flint, 'A titan challenged', *Los Angeles Times*, 21 October 2011, http://articles.latimes.com/2011/oct/21/business/la-fi-rupert-murdoch–20111021

Page 350: 'Your investments haven't been that great', Amy Chozick and Brooks Barnes, 'At Annual Meeting, Murdoch Spars With Investors', *New York Times*, New York, 21 October 2011, http://www.nytimes.com/2011/10/22/business/murdoch-spars-with-investors-at-annual-meeting.html?_r=0

Page 350: 'More than double that number voted to dump James, Lachlan and three other directors', News Corp, *Current Report, Form 8-K*, SEC Filing, 21 October 2011, http://www.sec.gov/Archives/edgar/data/1308161/000119312511278761/d246192d8k.htm. Also Stephen Mayne, 'Record protests as News Corp shareholders get rankings dead right', *Crikey*, 25 October 2011, http://www.crikey.com.au/2011/10/25/record-protests-as-news-corp-shareholders-get-rankings-dead-right/

Page 350: '...damaging the rest of the company, which brought in around four-fifths of the profit', News Corp Annual Report 2012, http://www.newscorp.com/investor/annual_reports.html

Page 350: 'He loved the headlines, the gossip', Rupert Murdoch, Transcript of Evidence, 25 April 2012 morning, p 60, http://www.levesoninquiry.org.uk/wp-content/uploads/2012/04/Transcript-of-Morning-Hearing–25-April–2012.pdf

Page 352: 'In an email to his 51 000 employees', John Jannarone, 'News split: print losses not tolerated anywhere, says Murdoch', *Wall Street Journal*, New York, 28 June 2012, http://online.wsj.com/article/SB10001424052702303561504577494314282011658.html

Page 353: '...the US$40 billion media group had become a $US60 billion group', based on a share price of US$25 in October 2012.

Page 354: 'Two-thirds of the Independent shareholders supported an end to the dual-class structure', News Corp, *Current Report, Form 8-K*, SEC Filing, 16 October 2012, http://investor.newscorp.com/secfiling.cfm?filingID=1193125–12–424724

Page 354: 'Shareholders with complaints should take profits and sell!' Rupert Murdoch @rupertmurdoch, 11 October 2012.

Page 354: 'Told UK's Cameron receiving scumbag celebrities pushing for even more privacy laws', Rupert Murdoch @rupertmurdoch, 13 October 2012, https://twitter.com/rupertmurdoch/status/257215490462732289

Page 355: 'RUPERT!! delete tweet!!', Mimi Turner, *Hollywood Reporter*, 3 January 2012, http://www.hollywoodreporter.com/news/wendi-murdoch-fake-twitter-rupert-murdoch–277554

Page 357: 'It has been made clear to me that News Corporation would like to appoint a new editor', Andrew Pugh, 'Times editor James Harding resigns: "News Corp would like to appoint a new editor of *The Times*"', *UK Press Gazette*, 12 December 2012, http://www.pressgazette.co.uk/james-harding-quits-times-editor

Page 357: 'Instead of listening and responding to those asking legitimate questions', Jason Deans, 'James Harding to be next BBC News chief', *The Guardian*, London, 15 April 2013, http://www.guardian.co.uk/media/2013/apr/15/james-harding-next-bbc-news-chief

Page 358: 'To be direct, the reason I am leaving', 'Tom Mockridge's resignation email to News International staff', *The Guardian*, London, 3 December 2012, http://www.guardian.co.uk/media/2012/dec/03/tom-mockridge-resignation-email-news-international

Page 358: '...Rupert's new best friend was the man who had beaten Mockridge', John Jannarone and Martin Peers, 'Journal's Top Editor to Run Spin-Off', *Wall Street Journal*, 12 December 2012, http://online.wsj.com/article/SB10001424127887323751104578152940437699734.html

CHAPTER 23   LONG LIVE THE KING

Page 361: 'Things are different these days', Rupert Murdoch, *Dynasties*, 'The Murdochs', ABC TV, Sydney, 17 July 2002.

Page 361: 'If Rupert had fallen under a bus in 2011', Yinka Adegoke, 'Rupert Murdoch endorses Carey as next in line', Reuters, 10 August 2011, http://www.reuters.com/article/2011/08/10/us-newscorp-idUSTRE77967X20110810

Page 362: '...Rupert had said as much on many occasions. Retirement was not on his radar', Cromie, *op cit*, 1994.

Page 362: 'Rupert is a very strong man', Patricia Danaher, 'The Saturday Interview: Wendi Murdoch', *The Guardian*, London, 12 November 2011, http://www.guardian.co.uk/theguardian/2011/nov/12/wendi-deng-murdoch-interview

Page 363: 'My work has been so much part of my life', James Harding, 'Rupert Murdoch', *Financial Times*, 11 June 2002.

Page 363: 'Rupert was extremely hard, ruthless, and determined', David Leser, 'Anna and her Kingdom', *Australian Women's Weekly*, Sydney, August 2001.

Page 364: 'My grandmother died in childbirth', *Charlie Rose*, PBS, New York, 25 August 2011, http://www.charlierose.com/view/interview/11862

Page 365: 'But his daughter Prue summed it up most succinctly: her dad was just a dirty old man', *Dynasties*, 'The Murdochs', ABC TV, Sydney, 17 July 2002.

Page 365: 'I was a recently separated, lonely man', William Shawcross, 'Murdoch's New Life', *Vanity Fair*, New York, October 1999.

Page 365: 'By that stage, the brash young Chinese trainee was already famous at Murdoch's Asian pay-TV network', Eric Ellis, 'Wendi Deng Murdoch', *The Monthly*, June 2007, http://www.themonthly.com.au/issue/2007/june/1311127304/eric-ellis/wendi-deng-murdoch

Page 365: 'When he returned home some hours later, Murdoch was absolutely abuzz with excitement,' Bruce Dover, *Rupert's Adventures in China*, Melbourne, 2008, pp 130–40.

Page 366: '...he had become "very obsessed with business and perhaps more than normally inconsiderate"', Shawcross, *Vanity Fair, op cit.*

Page 368: 'But Rupert's mother was appalled, and told him so', Heather Ewart, 'Dame Elisabeth Murdoch approaches her century', *7.30 Report*, ABC TV, 4 February 2009, http://www.abc.net.au/7.30/content/2008/s2482546.htm

Page 368: 'But the truth came out some eighteen months after the wedding ', John Lippman, Leslie Chang & Robert Frank, 'Rupert Murdoch's Wife Wendi Wields Influence at News Corp', *Wall Street Journal*, 1 December 2000, http://online.wsj.com/article/SB973040597961471219.html

Page 370: 'So it can't be Wendi Deng?", Leser, *op cit*, 2001.

Page 370: 'They were fighting all night over the estate for the kids', John Cook, '"It Was Like a War Zone": A Former Nanny for Rupert Murdoch and Wendi Deng Speaks Out', *Gawker*, 18 July 2012, http://gawker.com/5926705/it-was-like-a-war-zone-a-former-nanny-for-rupert-murdoch-and-wendi-deng-speaks-out. In a statement released through a publicist, the Murdochs declined to address any of Hsu's specific claims: 'Ms. Hsu is a disgruntled former employee...A state court dismissed her claims, ruling that they were "inadmissible" and "unpersuasive". Having failed in court, she has apparently turned to the media with unfounded and untrue accusations. We will not dignify them with comment.'

Page 371: '...Rupert went on the *Charlie Rose* show on America's PBS network and announced that it had all been sorted', *Charlie Rose*, PBS, 20 July 2006, http://www.charlierose.com/view/interview/308

Page 372: 'The question will be formally decided by the Murdoch Family Trust, which controls 306 million voting shares', News Corp, *Definitive Proxy Statement,*

DEFA14A, Securities & Exchange Commission, Washington, 30 April 2012, p 16, http://investor.newscorp.com/secfiling.cfm?filingID=1193125–12–510887

CHAPTER 24   THE MURDOCH DYNASTY

Page 373: 'Their sibling rivalry is no different from any other family', ex-News executive to author.

Page 373: 'At the beginning of 2011, James was formally anointed Rupert's heir', 'News Corporation Names James Murdoch Deputy Chief Operating Officer and Chairman and CEO, International', News Corp media release, 30 March 2011, http://www.newscorp.com/news/news_481.html

Page 374: 'One fellow editor reported the *News of the World*'s Colin Myler arriving at a party', Steve Fishman, 'The Tabloid Turncoat', *New York*, 22 April 2012, http://nymag.com/news/features/colin-myler–2012–4/

Page 376: 'There had been plenty of hostility to James', 'James Murdoch: the rise and fall of a News Corp scion', *The Guardian*, London, 4 April 2012, http://www.guardian.co.uk/commentisfree/cifamerica/2012/apr/04/james-murdoch-news-corp-scion

Page 379: 'In 2008, he had famously made a $3.3 billion bid for Consolidated Media Holdings', 'Lachlan Murdoch's CMH deal falls over', *Sydney Morning Herald*, Sydney, 7 April 2008, http://news.smh.com.au/business/lachlan-murdochs-cmh-deal-falls-over–20080407–24ap.html

Page 381: 'By mid-2013 the shares had fallen below 30'. In May 2013, Ten was rated a SELL by all eight brokers contributing to the Invest Smart website, http://au.investsmart.com.au/shares/broker_consensus.asp?SecurityID=TEN&ExchangeID=ASX&Recommendation=SHOWALL

Page 382: 'But perhaps the worst example was the new *Breakfast* show', 'Henry's Aussie Breakfast canned', Stuff.co.nz, 12 November 2012, http://www.stuff.co.nz/entertainment/tv/7938110/Henrys-Aussie-Breakfast-canned

Page 382: 'The show's host—who was Lachlan's personal pick—was a large part of the problem.' Judge for yourself: watch Paul Henry's 'Dick Shit' joke at, http://www.youtube.com/watch?v=Aq5dUyiRKuA

Page 384: 'She will probably sell it for a bloody fortune to someone', David D Kirkpatrick, 'Murdoch Gets a Jewel. Who'll Get His Crown?' *New York Times*, New York, 28 December 2003, http://www.nytimes.com/2003/12/28/business/murdoch-gets-a-jewel-who-ll-get-his-crown.html?pagewanted=all&src=pm

Page 384: 'The London *Evening Standard* greeted the news with the front-page headline, MURDOCH's DAUGHTER TO GET £370M FROM DADDY', Ken Auletta, 'The Heiress', *New Yorker*, New York, 10 December 2012, http://www.newyorker.com/reporting/2012/12/10/121210fa_fact_auletta

Page 384: 'In addition to larding the executive ranks', *News Corporation Shareholder Derivative Litigation, Case No. 6285-VCN*, Delaware, 13 May 2011, http://

newsandinsight.thomsonreuters.com/uploadedFiles/Reuters_Content/2011/07_-_
July/News%20Corp%20Page%20Complaint.pdf

Page 384: 'This damages action against Rupert, James, Lachlan and their fellow
News Corp directors, was eventually settled by the insurers', 'Amalgamated Bank
Achieves Settlement of Derivative Suit with News Corporation', Amalgamated
Bank media release, 22 April 2013, http://www.amalgamatedbank.com/home/
fiFiles/static/documents/Amalg-NewsCorpFINAL.pdf

Page 385: 'I am by no means alone within the family or the company in being
ashamed', David Carr and Tim Arango, 'A Fox Chief at the Pinnacle of Media
and Politics', *New York Times*, New York, 9 January 2010, http://www.nytimes.
com/2010/01/10/business/media/10ailes.html?pagewanted=all&_r=0

Page 386: '...starting with a speech to the Edinburgh TV Festival in August 2012,
in which she gave James and Rupert a very public smack', Elisabeth Murdoch, James
MacTaggart Lecture, Edinburgh, 23 August 2012, http://www.edinburghguide.
com/video/11381-videotranscriptelisabethmurdochsmactaggartlecture

Page 387: 'Finally, she laid into her brother James, who had told the same audience
three years earlier that the BBC's licence fee should be cut', James Murdoch, 'The
Absence of Trust', James MacTaggart Lecture, Edinburgh, 28 August 2009. http://
www.geitf.co.uk/sites/default/files/geitf/GEITF_MacTaggart_2009_James_
Murdoch.pdf

Page 387: 'I think he realized it was not a loving reaction', Auletta, *op cit*.

Page 388: 'A few years earlier Rupert had mused that his daughter might sell Shine
for lots of money', Wolff, *The Man who Owns the News*, *op cit*, p 356

Page 389: '...telling the BBC's Steve Hewlett that she had "absolutely no ambition"
to replace him', *Variety*, New York, 24 August 2012, http://variety.com/2012/tv/
news/elisabeth-murdoch-discusses-succession–1118058257/.

Page 389: 'In what? The company is changing its shape so much. I think no one
person will succeed him', Elisabeth Murdoch to Ken Auletta, *New Yorker*, *op cit*, 2012.

Page 392: 'Rupert had mused that this might change when they were "25 or 30 or
something"', Wolff, *op cit*, pp 354–5.

Page 395: '*My Way* might almost have been written for him'. The lyrics for
My Way were written by Paul Anka, but the song was most famously performed
by Frank Sinatra.

EPILOGUE   THE RECKONING

Page 397: 'I hope the police will consider charges against the body corporate and the
directors of this thoroughly corrupt company', James Cusick, Ian Burrell and Martin
Hickman, 'Fresh hacking headache for Rupert Murdoch: six arrested in new line
of inquiry', *The Independent*, London, 13 February 2013, http://www.independent.
co.uk/news/uk/crime/fresh-hacking-headache-for-rupert-murdoch-six-arrested-in-
new-line-of-inquiry–8494020.html

Page 397: 'One consequence of the Great British hacking scandal'. In November 2012, Lord Leveson's inquiry recommended a new regulatory system, backed by law, that would allow the press to police itself, but would also create an independent body to ensure it did the job properly. His new Press Complaints Commission (PCC) would have the power to investigate abuses, and not just to act on complaints; the power to levy £1 million fines; the right to direct newspapers to print apologies and to say where they should be run. Most importantly, it would no longer be captive to the industry, because it would be forced to appoint an independent chair and an independent board, with a majority of non-industry members, and no serving newspaper editors. In other words, it would represent the society that Britain's media was supposed to serve.

Crucially for the hacking victims, this new PCC would also establish a cheap, quick arbitration service for people to get redress without going through the courts, and it would encourage newspapers to take part in this by exposing them to the risk of exemplary damages if they failed to sign up.

Above this new PCC there would sit a new regulatory body which would make sure that the voluntary system was set up along these lines and did what it was supposed to do. This new regulator would report to Parliament once a year and have the power to withdraw its approval if the voluntary body did not come up to scratch. Although what might happen after that was anybody's guess.

After much debate and brinkmanship, and a vigorous effort by Prime Minister David Cameron to avoid putting any of this into law, Lord Leveson's design was essentially adopted by Britain's three main political parties in March 2013, and it was agreed to set it up by Royal Charter, which could only be repealed with a two-thirds majority of both Houses of Parliament. But while Leveson's supporters celebrated the victory and his detractors wailed about an assault on press freedom that would give succour to dictators everywhere, there was one small problem that went largely unnoticed. And this was that Fleet Street's proprietors were not prepared to play. All except the *Financial Times*, *The Guardian* and the *Independent* were determined to boycott the new system, with *The Sun* and the *Daily Mail* leading the strike.

The press proprietors then put forward a weaker system, but with no sign of either side giving ground, it looked like there might be a long stand-off. As this book went to press, no agreement had been reached. For further reading, see:

Leveson Report, *Recommendations for a Self-Regulatory Body*, Volume IV, part K, Chapter 9, November 2012, http://www.official-documents.gov.uk/document/hc1213/hc07/0780/0780_i.pdf; *Draft Royal Charter on Self-Regulation of the Press, 18 March 2013*, https://www.gov.uk/government/uploads/system/uploads/attachment_data/file/142808/18_March_2013_v6_Draft_Royal_Charter.pdf; 'Q&A: Press regulation, BBC.co.uk, 25 April 2013, http://www.bbc.co.uk/news/uk-21797513

Page 398: 'By mid-2013 there were more than 40 current or former Murdoch journalists potentially facing charges'. Figures from Crown Prosecution Service,

Metropolitan Police, news reports of arrests, and BBC, http://www.bbc.co.uk/news/uk-politics–17014930

Page 398: 'The Metropolitan Police soon announced that they had uncovered an entirely new hacking conspiracy', Cusick, Burrell and Hickman, *op cit*, 13 February 2013.

Page 400: 'Finally, Andy Coulson would also face trial in Glasgow for perjury', 'Andy Coulson charged in Tommy Sheridan trial perjury inquiry', BBC.co.uk, 30 May 2012, http://www.bbc.co.uk/news/uk-scotland-glasgow-west–18262740

Page 400: 'If the Elveden charges are eventually upheld', Claire Enders, unpublished note to clients, http://www.endersanalysis.com/

Page 401: 'James had already suffered severe criticism from the TV regulator', *Decision Under Section 3(3) of the Broadcasting Act 1990 and Section 3(3) of the Broadcasting Act 1996: Licences held by British Sky Broadcasting Limited*, Ofcom, 20 September 2012, http://stakeholders.ofcom.org.uk/binaries/broadcast/tv-ops/fit-proper/bskyb-final.pdf

Page 402: 'The avalanche of legal actions'. Author's calculations from News Corp SEC filings and News International accounts filed in London.

Page 402: 'The group had spent another US$150 million'. *The Sun on Sunday* started off selling better than the paper it replaced, but brought in less money. At 50 pence a copy it was only half the price; it also attracted fewer ads; and by the end of its first year it had shed 40 per cent of its sales, slipping back to 1.9 million copies a week, against the *News of the World*'s 2.6 million.

Page 403: 'Flushed with this new wave of money', 'Rupert was back building his empire again', Joe Strupp, '*Chicago Tribune*, L.A. Times Veterans Fear Possible Murdoch Takeover', *Media Matters*, 25 October 2012, http://mediamatters.org/blog/2012/10/25/chicago-tribune-la-times-veterans-fear-possible/190927

INDEX

police protection 60, 219
protests 57–60, 219
Warburton, James 380–1
Warrington Guardian 160, 161
Watson, Tom 133, 227–31, 237, 251,
    266, 270–1, 272, 278–9, 281, 285,
    297, 313, 318, 342, 349
wealth 73
Weatherup, James 245, 265, 338
Webb, Derek 229–30, 237
WebMD 75, 123
Webster, Geoff 332, 400
Weinstein, Harvey 112
Weir, Louise 161
Wells, Holly 254
Wheeler, Virginia 334, 399
White, David 381
Whitlam, Gough 46–7, 62
Whitlam, Margaret 46
Whittamore, Steve 171–4, 205, 235,
    240
Whittingdale, John 197, 318
Wiley, Peter 70

Williams, Detective Chief
    Superintendent Philip 217–19
Williams, Kim 378
Wilson, Harold 49
Wogan, Terry 144
Wolfensohn, Jim 358
Wolff, Michael 14, 66–7, 145, 275,
    376
    The Man Who Owns the News 66–7
Worcester College, Oxford University
    16–17
Wyatt, Woodrow 53–4

Yahoo 121, 122
Yang, Jerry 121
Yates, Assistant Commissioner John
    217–18, 219, 220–1, 222, 241, 245,
    288–9
Yelland, David 68
YouTube 216–17

Zeta-Jones, Catherine 203
Zuckerman, Mort 352